RE-FORMING THE BODY

Theory, Culture & Society

Theory, Culture & Society caters for the resurgence of interest in culture within contemporary social science and the humanities. Building on the heritage of classical social theory, the book series examines ways in which this tradition has been reshaped by a new generation of theorists. It will also publish theoretically informed analyses of everyday life, popular culture, and new intellectual movements.

EDITOR: Mike Featherstone, *Nottingham Trent University*

SERIES EDITORIAL BOARD
Roy Boyne, *University of Durham*
Mike Hepworth, *University of Aberdeen*
Scott Lash, *Lancaster University*
Roland Robertson, *University of Pittsburgh*
Bryan S. Turner, *Deakin University*

THE TCS CENTRE
The Theory, Culture & Society book series, the journals *Theory, Culture & Society* and *Body & Society*, and related conference, seminar and post-graduate programmes operate from the TCS Centre at Nottingham Trent University. For further details of the TCS Centre's activities please contact:

Centre Administrator
The TCS Centre, Room 175
Faculty of Humanities
Nottingham Trent University
Clifton Land, Nottingham, NG11 8NS, UK e-mail: tcs@ntu.ac.uk

Recent volumes include:
Spatial Formations
Nigel Thrift

The Body and Society
Explorations in Social Theory
Second edition
Bryan S. Turner

The Social Construction of Nature
Klaus Eder

Deleuze and Guattari
An Introduction to the Politics of Desire
Philip Goodchild

Pierre Bourdieu and Cultural Theory
Critical Investigations
Bridget Fowler

RE-FORMING THE BODY

Religion, Community and Modernity

PHILIP A. MELLOR and CHRIS SHILLING

SAGE Publications
London • Thousand Oaks • New Delhi

First published in 1997

Published in association with *Theory, Culture & Society*,
Nottingham Trent University

 SAGE Publications Ltd
6 Bonhill Street
London EC2A 4PU

SAGE Publications Inc
2455 Teller Road
Thousand Oaks, California 91320

SAGE Publications India Pvt Ltd
32, M-Block Market
Greater Kailash – I
New Delhi 110 048

British Library Cataloguing in Publication data

A catalogue record for this book is available
from the British Library.

ISBN 0 8039 7722 0
ISBN 0 8039 7723 9 (pbk)

Library of Congress catalog record available

Typeset by Mayhew Typesetting, Rhayader, Powys
Printed in Great Britain by Biddles Ltd, Guildford, Surrey

CONTENTS

ACKNOWLEDGEMENTS

This study results from a collaborative research project, which began in 1992, based on our joint work on the shifting relationships and interactions between forms of embodiment, modes of sociality and the location and scope of the sacred. We would like to thank a number of colleagues for their comments on the ideas contained within this book, or in various sections of the manuscript itself. We have benefited from the help and encouragement of Graham Allan, Jim Beckford, Ian Burkitt, Eric Dunning, Michael Erben, Pasi Falk, Michel Gardaz, Jim Ginther, Adrian Hastings, Ingrid Lawrie, Don Levine, Stephen Mennell, Frank Reynolds, John Solomos, Bryan S. Turner, and R. Stephen Warner. Keith Tester provided us with advice and support when it was needed most, while the editorial guidance we received from Sage Publications was of great value: Stephen Barr encouraged us to pursue this project, while Chris Rojek and Robert Rojek provided us with the support needed to complete it. Various components of our argument have been presented in seminars during visits to the Institute for the Advanced Study of Religion, University of Chicago; the Department of Sociology at the University of Helsinki; and the Department of Sociology, University College Dublin. These visits would not have been possible without financial support from the J. William Fulbright Commission and the University of Leeds, the British Council and the University of Portsmouth, and the University of Helsinki. We gratefully acknowledge their assistance. Finally, and on a more personal note, we owe a considerable debt of thanks for the support and tolerance provided by Debbie, Melody, and Francesca. This book is dedicated to all three of them.

1

INTRODUCTION

The aim of this book is to provide a theoretical analysis of successive 're-formations of the body', and their relationships with various forms of cultural and religious life, in order to cast a fresh light upon the emergence, development and transformation of the modern Western world. While the conditions of modernity and postmodernity have come under intensive scrutiny in recent years (e.g. Lyotard, 1984; Harvey, 1990; Jameson, 1991; Touraine, 1995), relatively little attention has been devoted to the *corporeal constituents* of these conditions. In seeking to rectify this situation, which acts as an impediment to a satisfactory sociological understanding of modernity, our study can be introduced through Emile Durkheim's (1961 [1912]) contention that the creation, and evolution, of different forms of human community are intimately related to the immanence of powerful passions and emotions of a collective, sacred character.

Bodily experiences of what Durkheim refers to as 'collective effer-vescence' are sociologically significant as they have the potential to transform people's experience of their fleshy selves and the world around them. The somatic experience of the sacred, 'something added to and above the real', arises out of these transformations, and expresses a corporeal solidarity between people which can bind them into particular sectional groups, or into the social collectivity as a whole (Collins, 1988: 110; Durkheim, 1961 [1912]: 422ff.). It was Durkheim's view, in fact, that the very *possibility of society* is contingent upon individuals being incorporated into this corporeal experience of solidarity (Richman, 1995: 72). If this incorporation did not take place, if the beliefs, traditions and aspirations of the group were no longer felt by the individual, then 'society would die' along with the sacred (Durkheim, 1961 [1912]: 347).

Durkheim's writings have been interpreted in a wide variety of ways, yet sociologists have often been influenced by what Donald Levine (1995: 46) has called Talcott Parsons's 'strikingly partial' reading of Durkheim. In a similar vein, Bryan Turner (1991: 48) has noted the influence of Parsons's (1968 [1937]) reading of Durkheim's sociology as 'the heir of social contract theories' concerned with solving the 'Hobbesian problem of order'. In consequence, many sociologists have tended to focus on the, admittedly important, rationalist dimensions of Durkheim's thought, while being far less attentive to those other aspects of his work which reflect a concern with forms of embodiment and the transformative capacities of effervescent forms of sociality (Richman, 1995: 60).[1]

In contrast to this, however, Collins (1988, 1975), Lindholm (1990) and Turner (1991: 46) have suggested that Durkheim's work can be read as a direct, corporeally oriented challenge to such a cognitive and rationalist emphasis. Furthermore, Célestin Bouglé's (1926) recognition that for Durkheim society was a 'fiery furnace', as much as an ordered realm of 'social facts', has been developed by sociologists such as Stjepan Meštrović. As Meštrović (1991: 104) highlights, Durkheim and Mauss (1975 [1902]) emphasised the *irrational* bodily bases of human sociality. This is not to say that Durkheim did not place enormous importance on the rational dimensions of human experience. Nevertheless, it is clear that for Durkheim the rational demands of society are intimately related to the irrational and sacred 'fires' of effervescent sociality. Nisbet (1993 [1966]: 91) emphasises this in his comment that Durkheim rejected as 'untenable and meretricious' any attempt to see *contract* as either historically or logically primordial, since it only gives rise to 'transient relations and passing associations'. The pre-contractual, 'irrational', foundations of contract, in contrast, rest in the effervescence which allows certain forms of bodily experience and knowing to become possible, and certain types of relationship to be sanctified as normal (Nisbet, 1993 [1966]: 245; Durkheim, 1961 [1912]: 9).

In the following chapters we seek to build on, and develop in a distinctive direction, Durkheim's interest in these relationships between forms of embodiment, forms of sociality and forms of knowing in three major ways. First, we recognise the importance of Durkheim's (1973 [1914]) insistence on the *homo duplex* character of humans (which, in accounting for both the rational and the irrational components of human experience, provides sociologists with a reminder of the sensual, emotive sides of humans which provide a potentially unstable basis for modern contractual relationships), yet challenge the dualism and relatively static view of human embodiment contained in this view. The notion of *homo duplex* allows us, as Meštrović (1993: 100) has argued, to question the widespread assumption which has been expressed from Descartes, Kant and Hume, to Parsons, Giddens and Habermas, that the rationalist Enlightenment project has achieved control over the extra-rational senses and sensualities of humans. What this approach to the extra-rational dimensions of humans does not allow us to do, however, is to examine how these senses and sensualities are themselves differently structured by social forces over time. This is a major focus of our study.

Second, in tracing the relationship between forms of embodiment and forms of sociality, we pursue and develop the emphasis Durkheim placed on the importance of *religion* to the development and maintenance of human societies. Despite the fact that sociology has been, from its origins, centrally concerned with religion, this concern has nevertheless been increasingly marginalised within the discipline (Beckford, 1989). In contrast to this tendency, we build upon Durkheim's view of religion as *le clef de voûte*, the keystone of society (Pickering, 1984: 516), in the sense that somatic experiences of the sacred both symbolise and participate in the broader patterns of feelings, passions, aspirations and beliefs which characterise particular forms of social life. Consequently, we place hegemonically dominant religious forms of Western sociality at the very centre of our study, and view the forming and re-forming of Christianity as exerting an important influence on, and sharing an affinity with, other factors that have been central to the development of the modern world (Weber, 1991 [1904–5]). In broad terms, we take the view that the ideal typical study of medieval Catholic and early modern Protestant forms of sociality provides us with a highly illuminating *theoretical lens* through which to examine the development of the Western world (Thompson, 1990). In contrast to the consensus within much sociology we then go on to suggest that the collective and individual, beneficent and virulent, sensual experience of the sacred remains central to the 'binding' and 'unbinding' of social relationships within modernity (Turner, 1991: 8). By neglecting issues surrounding this experience of lived bodily relationships – and by focusing instead on the more conventional themes of culture, economics or social mobility – the discipline has frequently failed to investigate those experiences of collective effervescence that may appear insignificant to some but which are, in fact, integral to the maintenance and erosion of that contractarian mentality which permeates modern institutions.

Third, we are also concerned with how the relationships between forms of embodiment and forms of sociality are *restructured over time*. It is often said that Durkheim's general theory of society and religion cannot deal with such changes very comfortably (Alexander, 1988), partly because he sometimes works with a rather reified notion of 'society' (Pickering, 1984). Nevertheless, Durkheim's assertion that in modern societies religion would transform itself rather than disappear signals his concern with changes as well as continuities (Durkheim, 1961 [1912]: 430). The experiences of anomie, egoism and altruism, for example, could be forces for change as well as stasis by arousing in people dispositions to act which could challenge, as well as consolidate, the status quo. This feature of Durkheim's work can be highlighted in his study of suicide (Durkheim, 1951 [1897]). In this study, Durkheim suggested that Protestantism manifested, and encouraged, a significantly different experience of human community to that characteristic of Catholicism, and in so doing encouraged patterns of individual reflection, critical scrutiny, and perceptions of self and world which stimulated social change and which were influential for the emergence of modern societies (see also Gellner, 1992). The rise of the Protestant 'spirit of free enquiry' was not simply a matter of transpersonal *conceptions* of reality being replaced by a multiplicity of individually constructed beliefs, then, but a change in the *embodied process* of reality construction.

We have introduced our study by locating it within Durkheim's, often neglected, vision of the interrelationships of human sociality, the sacred and embodied patterns of reality construction. It should already be clear, though, that this is not a Durkheimian study in any straightforward sense. Our analysis of the consequences of collective effervescence, for example, is

concerned with both socially beneficent *and* violent and virulent manifestations of this phenomenon which, while by no means irrelevant to
Durkheim's work (Fields, 1995; Pickering, 1984: 369–399), are more commonly associated with other social theorists.[2] Furthermore, as well as being
attentive to such conflicts, we are also concerned with what happens when
the collective experience of powerful emotions breaks down to become
manifest in more individualised forms; a phenomenon far removed from
the transcendent humanism of Durkheim's 'cult of man' (Pickering, 1984:
483).

    In what follows, then, we also draw upon a range of disciplines, theor-
etical perspectives and empirical studies in order to develop our own
account of those 're-formations of the body' we consider to be central to
understanding the emergence and development of the modern Western
world. Subsequent chapters examine historically contrasting modes of
bodily-being-in-the-world, and their religious and cultural contexts, each of
which predisposes people towards particular types of *community* or *association* (Nisbet, 1993 [1966]), and contains within itself different *civilising
potentialities* (Elias, 1978 [1939], 1982 [1939]).[3] These modes of embodiment
and forms of sociality overlap: there is no neat cut-off point at which one
can be entirely separated from another, and they recur in different forms
through time. Nevertheless, that change does take place is undeniable, and
it is one of the central arguments of this book that unless we investigate the
forms of embodiment which underpin thought, belief and human interaction, we shall fail to understand the chief characteristics of how modern
persons come to act upon the world around them.

    After explaining in more detail what we mean by the term 'forms of
embodiment', this introductory chapter focuses on how it is we can talk
about changes, or *re-formations*, of these bodily forms. We then introduce
our examination of forms of sociality by looking at how these relationships
are restructured as people pursue different goals and ambitions over time.
The chapter concludes with a summary of the main themes which permeate
this book through a discussion of the impact that forms of embodiment
and forms of sociality have on what we refer to as the *carnal* and *cognitive*
ways in which people come to know themselves and the world in which
they live.

Forms of embodiment

Our use of the term 're-forming the body' reflects our concern with underlying 'forms of embodiment', which incorporate those general 'habits'
(Veblen (1967 [1899]; Meštrović, 1993: 14), 'techniques of the body' (Mauss,
1973 [1934]) and types of *habitus* (Bourdieu, 1984; Elias, 1978 [1939], 1982
[1939]) which tend to be characteristic of bodies within particular eras and
cultures. Forms of embodiment point us to the stubborn enfleshment of
humans; they cannot be dissolved into thought, nor can they be reduced to

a Foucauldian notion of 'discourse'. These bodily forms do not refer simply
to each and every body in a particular context, as individual bodies are
affected by their upbringing and continued existence in locations 'shot
through' with status-based, gendered, 'racial' and other social factors. What
we mean by 'forms of embodiment', in contrast, is more akin to Marx's
concept of 'modes of production', signifying those underlying structures
which provide the parameters for particular societies, though without
holding that bodily forms determine social epochs 'in the last instance'
(Bottomore, 1985: 335). This can be clarified further by a brief account of
historically and culturally diverse forms of sensory organisation (one
integral dimension of a bodily form), before introducing those wider re-
formations of the body which constitute the central subject matter of this
book.

The sensory body

Social studies of the body have grown at a time when our skin, blood and
bones have been investigated, interrogated and invaded as never before, yet
much contemporary research remains essentially an examination of
representations and images of human physicality. While analyses of the
discursive or textual construction of bodies tell us much about how the
body is *seen* and portrayed, they usually fail to account for what it is about
the body that allows it to be depicted and constructed in certain ways, or
why the body has become such a popular object of representation (Shilling,
1993a). Such analyses tell us little about the body's implication in human
agency, or the productive capabilities of the body, and even less about the
history of the body, or the phenomenology of how people experience the
'lived body' (Turner, 1992a). By not doing this, they rule out of court
Durkheim's concern with those social representations which bridge both a
mind/body division (by acting on people's senses), and an individual/society
division (by acting similarly on people who share a particular form of
embodiment). In seeking to move beyond a concern with representations
and images, it is useful to approach the body not simply as an *object* of
sociological investigation, but as an inherently sociological and historical
phenomenon (Featherstone and Burrows, 1995). Recent writings on the
sensory body, which can be seen as building on Simmel's (1971 [1903])
concern with the reaction of the sensual human body to the metropolis,
provide one means of clarifying what we mean by this.
   It may appear a statement of the obvious to say that people's knowledge
of themselves, others, and the world around them are, in every human
society, shaped by their senses. Nevertheless, the implications of this statement are frequently overlooked in those sociological discussions of culture,
belief and ideology dominated by the Enlightenment belief that the mind
has become more important than the flesh. Humans are not disembodied
rationalist beings. They do not have unmediated access to knowledge, but
acquire information *through* their bodies. As Constance Classen (1993)

notes, seeing, hearing, touching, smelling and tasting are activities which, quite literally, 'make sense' of the world in a *variety* of ways.

Some of this sensory variety is reflected in the different bodily forms we examine in this book, but it is an issue which is easily forgotten in the contemporary West. Here, the importance of images tends to both reflect and encourage a prioritisation of the visual sense which then becomes conflated with thought, while political and economic leaders often operate with the assumption that different cultures share their way of making sense of the world. This assumption is incorrect (Lakoff, 1991). Throughout the world there have been cultures which apprehend meaning primarily through their ears, noses, or through touch, and for whom the visual dimensions of life are relatively undeveloped. Consequently, Westerners seeking to 'observe' the 'world-*view*' of such cultures are highly likely to misapprehend them, however worthy their intentions may be (Howes, 1991). Furthermore, the history of the West itself includes periods where smell, gesture and appearance played a very different role in human contact than is the case today, and where the limits of sight were drawn much tighter (Elias, 1978 [1939]; Laqueur, 1992 [1990]; Schiebinger, 1987).

In the twentieth century, though, Western bodies tend to prioritise the visual sense. Jenks, for example, highlights the modern world's tendency to conflate 'seeing' with 'knowing' (such as when we ask 'do you see?' when we mean 'do you understand?') (Jenks, 1995: 3; Dundes, 1980). According to Meštrović (1993: 103), this was anticipated by Schopenhauer's argument that the senses of smell and hearing are significantly 'premodern', while the 'triumph of the visual can be interpreted as the triumph of the Enlightenment process overall'. A similar point is made by Classen, who notes that in the West 'to see' often means 'to reason' (Classen, 1993: 30). This conflation of seeing with reasoning and knowing provides us with a clue as to why Western philosophy in particular, and the social sciences in general, have often provided us with an inadequate analysis of the relationship between embodiment and culture. It is worth considering part of this Western tradition, as it enables us to grasp the assumptions that underpin conventional ways of understanding the validation and production of knowledge.

René Descartes provided a highly influential conceptualisation of the mind/body/senses relationship. His *Cogito ergo sum* ('I think, therefore I am') was linked at one level to a complete devaluation of all the body's senses. As Descartes once said, 'I shall consider myself as having no hands, no eyes, no flesh, no blood, nor any senses' (Descartes, 1973: 101; Synnott, 1991: 70). Such an approach says much about Western philosophy's inability to deal comprehensively or consistently with the human body (see Synnott, 1991: 70). Indeed, Descartes's distrust of the senses was paralleled by contradictory recognition of their importance, and an ultimate acceptance of the eye which helped promote among other philosophers and thinkers a more general 'I'll believe it when I see it' mentality (Slater, 1995: 221). In a similar vein, John Locke devalued the senses other than sight, and his *Essay on Human Understanding* expressed an emphasis on the visual basis of mental understanding (Classen, 1993: 27; see also Jenks, 1995.3, Rorty, 1980).

These examples indicate how *sight* became a 'highway' for the transport of knowledge between the *'outside' world* and the *'inside' mind* in Western philosophy (Jenks, 1995). There have, of course, been exceptions to this philosophical prioritisation of minds over bodies. David Hume, for example, rejected the certainties of Cartesianism, suggested that the 'light of reason' was *only* to be tolerated on a full stomach (Synnott, 1991: 71), and stands at the centre of a minority tradition in Western thought which suggested that the 'human passions' formed the basis of reason and thought (Lindholm, 1990). Nevertheless, the emphasis on mind and sight has been an extremely influential aspect of the conceptualisation of the links between culture and bodily forms in the West.

Changes in the modern body's relation to knowledge have been addressed by a variety of writers. Classen's (1993) valuable discussion of the increasing importance of the eye in the West, for example, traces the declining importance of smell since the Middle Ages (see also Corbin, 1986).[4] Classen understands herself to be an 'anthropologist of the senses' and her work represents a valuable contribution to our understanding of the body. However, she is much less interested in the social and cultural changes which have promoted other developments in the (re-formed) body. The focus of Marshall McLuhan's (1962) studies of the different 'ratio of the senses' apparent in various cultures is also selective. McLuhan contrasts the importance of hearing and touching in premodern cultures with the visual emphasis of modernity. In doing this, though, he reduces these transformations to technological developments in communications media (Howes, 1991: 170). This reflects a determinist view of embodiment as *constructed* rather than as simultaneously forming a basis for social changes. As Howes (1991: 172–173) points out, McLuhan's work also tends to ignore a variety of other dimensions of sensory experience.

The emerging sub-discipline of the 'sociology/anthropology of the senses', some of whose products we mentioned above, is concerned predominantly with the patterning of sense experience across various cultures. It also investigates the influence of such variations on social organisation, concepts of self and cosmos, and the regulation of emotions and other cultural expressions (Howes, 1991: 3). These issues are extremely important and serve as a useful antidote to the disembodied concerns of much philosophy. However, the idea of variable 'sense ratios' may in itself neglect expressions of the body's techniques and the embodied habitus as a *whole*. Furthermore, the sense of fragmentation and artificiality which tends to characterise certain areas of late modern life has led to a resurgence of sensuality which cannot be understood adequately simply by referring to the dominance of the eye. Nevertheless, this focus on the senses highlights a crucial part of the link between re-formations of the body and cultural change.

Re-forming the body

The term 'forms of embodiment' encapsulates the patterns of organisation and significance attached to human senses and sensualities, as well as to those related techniques of the body and types of habitus prevalent in particular societies. It also provides a basis on which to map out changes within societies over time. This is not to overemphasise the distinctions between different eras or cultures: continuities can be noted with regard to the various dimensions of embodiment which cycle in and out of the social habitus throughout time, though in different forms. It is our suggestion, nevertheless, that there are certain key changes in Western forms of embodiment which provide us with new insights into the development and particular character of the modern world. These re-formations may be gradual, and have an impact which is dependent on people's precise social locations (Roper, 1994), but this does not reduce their general importance. The three major re-formations we focus on in this book are associated with the emergence of what we can refer to in ideal type terms as the 'medieval body', the 'Protestant modern body', and what we call the 'baroque modern body'.

Sociology's concern with changes in Western forms of embodiment has been partial and limited. Contemporary discussions of 'cyberbodies', for example, point to important reconfigurations of the boundaries between people and machines and the possibilities of new disembodied subjectivities (Featherstone and Burrows, 1995; Haraway, 1994 [1985]), but shed little light upon the world in which most people live, and sometimes make few real attempts to put these changes in broader historical and sociological perspective. In this respect, Max Weber's (1991 [1904–5]) examination of the impact of Protestantism upon the emergence of modern societies, despite being of limited value with regard to the contemporary transformations of these societies, retains its relevance for understanding the development of modernity. In this book we seek to extend and develop some of his insights with regard to what we understand as the creation of the early modern Protestant body. We also look at other re-formations, however, which are in many ways just as important, but which tend to have been overlooked by sociologists. This comment is particularly applicable to the Catholic re-formation of medieval bodies and the Counter-Reformation attempt to restructure Protestant bodies; issues which have been ignored by sociologists keener to focus on the legacy of Puritanism for the modern world (Lehmann and Roth, 1990).

The first re-formation we consider in this book is the Catholic re-formation of the medieval body, whereby the Church engaged in a highly sensuous way with the volatile bodies of medieval Europe. Life could all too often be 'nasty brutish and short' and centred around a struggle for survival in the medieval era. However, as people sought to utilise any available resources which might help them explain or cope with the challenges facing them, knowledge was frequently gained through a sensory immersion in the natural and supernatural world of demons, spirits and angels (Kay and Rubin, 1994; Thomas, 1973 [1971]). Uncertainty in these relatively 'uncivilised' times was rife, then, but substantial portions of human life were (for better or worse) filled with meaning, with good and evil, and with the future prospect of heaven and hell (Ariès, 1974; Delumeau, 1990). It was in this context that the Church worked on, and sought to restructure, an organisation and appreciation of the senses which was quite different from that of later societies. The 'odour of sanctity' and the 'stench of sin', for example, were not merely linguistic metaphors, but reflected experiences which were *sensed*. The bodies of the holy were understood to emit a sweet odour, while 'great sinners could be recognised by their stench' (Classen, 1993: 21).

The processes which contributed to the volatile and frequently superstitious character of medieval bodies were, however, gradually eroded. Contributory factors included the need to engage in status competition; the teachings of Renaissance scientists and humanists; the global discoveries of travellers and explorers; and the capacity of state formation processes to establish increasingly effective monopolies of violence within a territory (Elias, 1982 [1939]; Manchester, 1992). These processes were highly uneven, multifaceted and stretched over a number of centuries. Nevertheless, no analysis of their effects would be complete without paying attention to the highly influential role that Protestantism played in re-forming medieval bodies and in distancing people from a sensuous engagement with the sacred. The Protestant attempt to promote disciplined bodies may for decades have been observed more in the breaking than in the making (Roper, 1994), and its success varied across Europe (Scribner et al., 1994), but this does not diminish the importance of the gradual internalisation of new codes of behaviour and new orientations to the body that did take place.

Both Durkheim's (1951 [1897]) and Weber's (1991 [1904–5]) studies of Protestantism have been criticised on the basis that they make generalisations about an inherently diverse form of religion. Protestantism is often understood to be so diverse that any attempt at generalisation will be, at best, misleading and, at worst, simply inaccurate (Pickering, 1984: 436–437). Such criticisms are, however, both highly partial and sociologically misplaced. The diversity of Protestantism is undeniable, but it is important to focus on the limited *nature* of this diversity and the general *conditions* which underpinned it and made it possible. It is our suggestion, then, that an attention to forms of embodiment enables us to account for Protestantism's diversity, while also allowing us to deal with this religious form at a general level. It is Protestantism's re-formation of the body which is the basis for the diverse expressions of its fundamentally cognitive account of human experience and religious meaning, and for the institutional fragmentation and entropy with which Durkheim (1951 [1897]) associated it.

The Protestant re-formation of the body, especially in its Lutheran and Calvinist forms, accelerated processes which did much to disinvest the human flesh of superstition and sacred significance, and emphasise instead the *mind's* ability (in this case, to receive the Word of God).[5] According to William Manchester (1992), Luther conceived the doctrine 'by faith alone' while he was sitting on the privy, moving his bowels, in a Wittenberg monastery tower. This evacuation of the body and focus on the mind may, perhaps, be as good a place as any to chart the birth of modernity. Early modern, Protestant bodies became oriented more towards words and symbols than to the wider sensory potentialities of bodies. The eye and ear were valued *insofar* as they had the potential to provide unsullied access to the word of God, but touch and smell were centrally implicated in the body's 'sinfulness' (Michalski, 1993). This, then, marks a significant stage in the Western tendency to equate the eye with the mind and to 'forget' that sight is itself a sense. More generally, emotions became things to be moderated and controlled and it was the 'spirit', separated from the impurities of the sensuous body, which sought contact with God.

For the Protestant body, the earth became a place more fully open to human design, rational knowledge and intervention (Berger, 1990 [1967]). These effects constitute part of the rationalising, secularising and civilising tendencies of Protestantism which have been seen as preparing the ground not only for the early modern body but for the modern project in general (Weber, 1991 [1904–5]; Gellner, 1992; Turner, 1991). This project had at its centre an attempt to subject the world to human control, and this required the obliteration of all that could *not* be controlled. As Mikhail Bakhtin (1984 [1965]) has suggested, this incorporated an attempt to eradicate all that was *grotesque* about the body. Grotesque bodies resist easy classification, and refuse to be individualised or separated from their natural environment. Their existence is dangerous for the modern project as it makes a mockery of any strict hierarchies, controls, or disembodied reason which seek universal recognition (Touraine, 1995).

The clearest manifestation of grotesque bodies may have been found in late medieval carnival (Bakhtin, 1984 [1965]), but their chief characteristics represent something much more enduring in the history of human embodiment.[6] The grotesque body's playfulness and spontaneity echoed the Dionysian sense of abandon and sensuality found in the ancient world (Nietzsche, 1993 [1871]), while their fluidity and resistance to normalisation continued to constitute a 'fearful Other' in Renaissance and Enlightenment visions of an ordered, controllable world (Elias, 1978 [1939]). The significance of grotesque bodies was not simply that they represented the threat of the 'uncivilised' Other in Western society (an Other which manifested itself variously in the form of race, the female sex, and the dangerous classes), but that even white, male elites could only become and remain civilised while they suppressed the grotesque passions and bad manners lurking inside themselves (Pateman, 1988). The Durkheimian notion of *homo duplex* may not be a wholly defensible ontology of the human body, but these developments illustrate how people could come to *experience* their 'lived bodies' in this dualistic manner: as divided into two irreconcilable halves.

The early modern suppression of the uncontrollable, of the grotesque, contained within it a defence against all that was considered irrational and excessive. It also sought to limit human contact to rational encounters with rational objects, and exhibited a fear of sensual encounters with the sacred that might lead to an 'uncontrollable' effervescence. While the battle against the grotesque started well before the Protestant Reformation, and employed its most powerful weapons well after it, it was strongly influenced by the Puritans. All that was grotesque about women's bodies, for example, was to be placed under the control of the male head of the household, while the Puritan battle against the uncontrollable was nowhere clearer than in its sobriety towards death. As Jean Baudrillard (1993a: 146) argues, 'Our death was really born in the sixteenth century. It has lost its scythe and its clock, it has lost the Apocalyptic Horseman and the grotesque and macabre plays of the Middle Ages.'

In certain respects, many contemporary modern bodies continue to share a strong affinity with Protestant bodies and develop in a cultural context which is not so far removed from these conditions as we might like to think. They can also find themselves coping with these conditions of control, order and careful presentation of self via the adoption of a 'disciplined habitus'. This steers an 'inner directed' pathway through the seemingly infinite options provided by the cultural sphere, and is characterised by a certain Puritan discipline and the adoption of a contract mentality (Reisman, 1950). An important part of our argument, however, is that the corporeal effects of the Protestant Reformation proved not only to be a *source* of modernity (through its association with that physicality required for the rationalising tendencies of a disenchanted world), but were also modernity's partial and limited *defence* against the magic, superstition and sensuality of the Middle Ages (see Turner, 1991 on this; Weber, 1948 [1919]; 1991 [1904–5]). This was a defence which was tested to its limit by the Counter-Reformation crusade against the Puritan habitus.

In contemporary Western societies, however, the continuing development of Protestant aspects of embodiment are increasingly matched by an altogether different expression of human corporeality. This third major re-formation of the body can be associated with the emergence of a 'baroque modern' form of embodiment: a form marked by a sensualisation of experience, partly analogous to that evident in Counter-Reformation baroque cultures, which develops hand in hand with an extension of certain aspects of the Protestant modern body.

This baroque modern form of embodiment is, in fact, thoroughly 'Janus-faced'. On the one hand, Giddens's (1991, 1992) discussions of 'pure relationships', the pervasiveness of chronic reflexivity, and the growing number of experts, counsellors and advisers ready to proffer guidance for all aspects of life (also discussed by Rueschemeyer, 1986 and Gellner, 1993), point to the extension of the cognitive, reflexive and contractarian characteristics of the Protestant modern body. This is also evident in Baumgartner's (1988) analysis of the moral order of suburbs, and the development of the 'cognitive elites' of Herrnstein and Murray's (1994) infamous analysis. On the other hand, however, a new sensuality is also more evident. Attention to this development is apparent in Harvie Ferguson's (1992) discussion of a 'recovered sensuousness', Lash and Urry's (1994) analysis of the emergence of 'aesthetic reflexivity', the notion of the reappearance of the baroque in the work of Buci-Glucksmann (1994), Turner (1991, 1994) and van Reijen (1992), and Maffesoli's account of the spread of a Dionysian, irrational and emotional resacralisation of contemporary bodies. Meštrović (1993: 100) suggests that the outcome of this Janus-faced form of embodiment 'yields an ideal-type civilised human who is simultaneously more polished and potentially more savage compared to our ancestors', yet this sensuality takes various forms and need not necessarily manifest itself in aggression.

Linking the two aspects of the Janus-faced character of baroque modern bodies are those conservative cultural laments for the decline of Protestant contractarian values (Bellah et al., 1985, 1992; Etzioni, 1993), the work ethic (Lasch, 1991 [1979]), the position of the father within the family (Blankenhorn, 1995), and rationality in the face of a resurgence of hedonism (Bloom, 1988). These two dimensions can also be linked internally within people, in that a growing sense of uncertainty and fragmentation can play upon the emotions and lead to a resurgence of 'irrational' sensuality. This stems from confronting a world which promises to increase control at a macro-level, but only by removing the means for that control from more and more individuals. In the simulational world examined by Baudrillard, for example, even death and childbirth (processes already managed by machines and professional procedures: Martin, 1989 [1987]; Mellor and Shilling, 1993) threaten to be absorbed into the 'simulacra' which stand above and beyond people as *the* 'social fact' of the twenty-first century (Baudrillard, 1993a). It is in this context that baroque modern bodies search for phenomena which can be reconsecrated as a sign that humanity still exists in a world which appears to many theorists as increasingly inhuman (Lyotard, 1991).

Baroque modern bodies are not simply *post* modern bodies then, but can more accurately be seen as possessing qualities which share affinities with past, present and future. Nor do they represent a simple continuation of Norbert Elias's (1978 [1939], 1982 [1939]) relatively civilised bodies which inhabited the first part of the twentieth century. What they do suggest, however, is that we need to reassess the validity of those traditional/post-traditional oppositions around which sociology has constructed its subject matter (Levine, 1985). As far as this study is concerned, this makes it particularly important that we reassess the relationships between bodies, modern and premodern forms of sociality, and the changing character and location of the sacred.

In summarising this introduction to how we view changes in the empbodied habitus over time, it would be wrong to think that rationalistic re-formations of the body have been able to eradicate the extra-cognitive dimensions of human being (dimensions which have actually undergone a renaissance with the baroque modern body). Indeed, it is possible to trace both Apollonian dimensions of control and Dionysian tendencies toward transcendence *throughout* those epochs and events which have caught the attention of such thinkers as Schopenhauer, Nietzsche, Weber, Freud and Elias. The passionate 'superman' Nietzsche wrote about, for example, lurked beneath the taming and softening effects of Western civilisation (Nietzsche, 1993 [1871]). Weber continued to see the influence of Dionysus in the restricted spheres of eroticism and charisma within rationalised society, and provided an account of the irrational basis of rationality and the irrational foundations of modern society (Weber, 1948 [1919]; Lindholm, 1990; Turner, 1991). Furthermore, both Freud (psychologically) and Elias (sociologically) analysed the turbulent inner life which was a necessary cost of civilising processes, and which could sometimes break through the controlled 'presentation of self' that Goffman (1969) suggests is common to modern westerners (Freud, 1961 [1930]; Elias, 1978 [1939]). In short, re-formations of the body are not unidimensional in their conse-quences, and continue to be 'shot through' with features often associated with previous epochs.

Forms of sociality

Forms of embodiment do not exist on their own, but are forged within the shifting patterns of interdependence people enter into during their daily lives. Indeed, the sociological analysis of sociality has long assumed that different patterns of human interaction and particular types of bodily habitus are interdependent. In mapping out these changes, Ferdinand Tönnies's models of *Gemeinschaft* and *Gesellschaft* have been of enduring influence.

The work of Tönnies (1957 [1887]) reflects a deep concern with the relations between forms of sociality and bodily orientation. Developing the previous insights of Fustel de Coulanges, H.J.S. Maine and Otto von Gierke, Tönnies explained the transition from medieval to modern as one from the corporate and communal to the individualistic and the rational; from social organisation on the basis of status to that based on contract; and from the sacred-communal to the secular-associational (Nisbet, 1993 [1966]: 73). He considered this move from *Gemeinschaft* to *Gesellschaft* type societies as the outcome of two forms of embodied will (Levine, 1985: 203). For him, *Gemeinschaft* 'community' was based on the expression of instinct, habit and spontaneity (*Wesenwille*). *Gesellschaft* 'society', on the other hand, was a contractually based arrangement dependent on a more deliberative, calculating and rational type of will (*Kurwille*). These 'wills' were located within forms of embodiment which enjoyed very different relationships with their surrounding environments. While *Wesenwille* was immersed within its social and natural surroundings, *Kurwille* was distanced, separated and individualised from them. For Tönnies, in *Gemeinschaft* human beings 'remain essentially united in spite of all separating factors, whereas in *Gesellschaft* they are essentially separated in spite of all uniting factors' (Tönnies, 1957 [1887]: 64).

Tönnies uses *Gemeinschaft* and *Gesellschaft* as ideal type distinctions, and is able to see characteristics of each in both modern and premodern contexts. Nevertheless his conceptualisation of the broad shift from sacred-communal to secular-associational patterns of social life was accepted by Durkheim (Meštrović, 1991: 190), and by Weber (Nisbet, 1993 [1966]: 80). These theorists make it clear that the development, parameters and bodily effects of community or associational contexts are vital to sociological understanding. In other words, neither communities nor embodied individuals can be examined in isolation from each other.

The persistence of the sacred

The subtleties of these analyses have, however, often been overlooked. Tönnies's models of *Gemeinschaft* and *Gesellschaft* societies, together with Durkheim's models of organic and mechanical solidarity and Weber's use of the community/association distinction, have been 'hardened up' by sociologists such as Giddens (1990, 1991) into a thoroughly dichotomised view of modern/premodern characteristics. Concerned principally with emphasising the distinctiveness of modern societies, Giddens defines the premodern West as all that modernity is not, failing to see how the medieval era contains elements which reappear in modern societies, and incorporating within his work a dualistic view of the body that swings from being a biological constraint to being almost infinitely malleable (Shilling, 1993a: 201–202; Shilling and Mellor, 1996).[7] Such a tendency has been depicted as philosophically dubious (Cascardi, 1992), as ideological (Touraine, 1995), as reflecting an inadequate account of human agency (Archer, 1988), and as empirically unsustainable (Levine, 1985). It also recalls the extreme views of the Middle Ages found in the work of Enlightenment thinkers such as Voltaire, Gibbon and Condorcet (Nisbet, 1993 [1966]: 55) and continues a sociological tendency to view Catholicism, when it is mentioned at all, as one component of a premodern, static era, ignoring its inherently dynamic character (Bossy, 1985; Levine, 1985).

Gemeinschaft and *Gesellschaft* were, for Tönnies, ideal types, overlapping and coexisting; while Weber's work suggested that goal-oriented associative relationships frequently gave rise to emotional bonds which surpassed the conscious objectives of such forms of sociality (Weber, 1947: 137). In *The Division of Labour* (1984 [1893]), Durkheim was eventually led to argue that there was no once and for all shift from mechanical to organic solidarity, since the latter is, in fact, inherently dependent upon the former (Nisbet, 1993 [1966]); a view developed in Collins's (1988) analysis of the contemporary coexistence of these forms of sociality. With regard to contractarian relationships, for example, Durkheim suggested that they were, in their own terms, untenable, unless underpinned by more enduring and authoritative social bonds (Nisbet, 1993 [1966]: 91). Durkheim's rejection of a strict dichotomisation of these societal forms, pointing towards the 'non-rational foundations of rationality', is rooted in his concern with the sacred; a phenomenon which provides the magnetism or 'attraction' for social relationships (Collins, 1988: 109; Tacussel, 1984). If 'religion has given birth to all that is essential in society' because the 'idea of society is the soul of religion' (Durkheim, 1961 [1912]: 419), then for Durkheim the sacred cannot disappear *entirely* from modern society. This view is to some extent reinforced by Georg Simmel (1950) in his writings on sociality, where he notes the persistence of forms of sociality where there is a feeling for, and satisfaction in, unions with others whereby the solitariness of the individual is dissolved into a sense of transcendent, collective order.

Forms of sociality, then, consist of patterns of interdependent individuals 'held together' partly as a result of their creation and experience of the sacred. In this respect, Georges Bataille (1986 [1957], 1992 [1973]) has developed Durkheim's concern with the persistence of the sacred, by exploring how shifting relationships between sacred and profane are closely related to transformations in how humans experience their relationships with social and natural environments, with the apprehension of knowledge and meaning, and with the passions and sensations of bodies. For Bataille (1992 [1973]: 36), the sacred is inherently ambiguous. Following Durkheim he understands it to be a source of attraction possessing an incomparable value, and which is rooted in an embodied, 'animal sense' of transcendent meaning immanent within human communities and their natural environments. He also suggests that the sacred is dangerous, however, as it constantly threatens the profane world of human projects, designs and goals. René Girard (1977 [1972]) carries this emphasis upon the simultaneously integrating and inherently violent nature of the sacred even further, by arguing that sacrifices serve to restore harmony to communities and reinforce the social fabric (Kearney, 1995). 'Good' and 'evil' variants of the sacred are also examined in the work of Robert Hertz (1960).

These authors argue that the sacred may persist in a variety of societal contexts, yet we also want to emphasise that in certain eras and cultures the sacred or profane spheres of life can expand or contract in relation to each other (Luckmann, 1967; Girard, 1977 [1972]; Tiryakian, 1974, 1988). As such, we now provide a brief introduction to how these patterns of expansion and contraction are intimately related to changing modes of sociality in this study.

Re-forming sociality

We have already introduced the three major bodily re-formations which are at the heart of this book, yet it is important to emphasise that these changes are tied up with particular re-formations of human sociality which can, in turn, be illuminated with regard to changing relationships with the sacred. We conceive of these diverging patterns of sociality as 'ideal types'; they cannot be 'hardened up' into absolute contrasts within the real world. Nevertheless, it is our view that there are identifiable, analytically distinct, patterns of sociality which can be associated with the re-formations of the body we explore in this book.

First, it is our suggestion that the medieval body was re-formed in the context of a collective effervescence of social relationships that can be typified as *sacred eating communities*. Pasi Falk (1994) has defined an 'eating community' as a 'two-way order' shaped (or 'eaten into') by individuals during their daily lives, but which simultaneously 'ate into' and 'filled up' the identities of these people. In the medieval era, the immanence of the sacred within bodies, community and nature made this two-way eating process an inherently religious phenomenon; an activity filled with effervescence. The Eucharist, for example, involved the incorporation of God *as food* into the body of the individual, and thereby incorporated the individual into the Body of Christ (the Church). The Church's thoroughgoing engagement with the body was also reflected in a participation in certain forms of violence (Brown, 1975; Duby, 1977; Asad, 1983), and a syncretistic incorporation of magic and superstition into Catholic beliefs and practices (Thomas, 1973 [1971]; Duffy, 1992). The marked pluralism of the Middle Ages, often underestimated by sociologists and historians alike (Cameron, 1991), was therefore to some extent 'contained' within the corporeal unity promoted by Catholicism.

Second, and in contrast, the Protestant re-formation of the body took place alongside the promotion of *profane associations*. Protestantism can be associated more with *Gesellschaft* than *Gemeinschaft* patterns of sociality, in that the Protestant Reformers promoted 'associations of faith' based on the shared commitment to particular *beliefs* based on an engagement with the Bible, rather than communities of bodily interaction bound together through ritual eating. This promotion of associational rather than communal patterns of meeting is related to the disenchantment of bodies, sociality and nature which follows from the removal of the sacred 'from all immediate reality' (Levine, 1971: 139), to become something more akin to what Kant (1951 [1790]) calls the *sublime*. As Eisenstadt (1969: 307) notes, Protestantism continued to emphasise the importance of the sacred but rendered it radically transcendent, so that the 'here and now' becomes thoroughly profane, facilitating both a social activism and a highly reflexive pattern of reformulating and redefining Christian tradition.

This prioritisation of the cognitive dimensions of Christianity in contrast to Catholicism's ritual engagement with corporeality encouraged both greater reflexivity and the development of individualism among men and women (Lerner, 1993). In Tönnies's (1957 [1887]: 64) terms, the individuals who participated in these Protestant associations were 'essentially separated in spite of all uniting factors'. This link between associational forms of sociality and the Protestant re-formation of the body also makes sense of those Protestant forms of living which appear to place great emphasis upon 'community'. Pickering (1984: 436–437), for example, criticises the treatment of Protestant individualism by both Durkheim and Weber on the basis that Calvinists are strongly community-oriented. But while this Calvinist emphasis on community is very real, it is also deeply ambivalent because community is not sacred but is based on *profane* human interactions. As such, this worldly association can have no ultimate morality or authenticity in comparison with the *individual's* relation with the Word of God (Peacock and Tyson, 1989: 4).

We have already noted, however, that for both Durkheim (1984 [1893]) and Weber (1947) associational patterns of sociality were frequently dependent upon, or gave rise to, patterns of sociality which are more 'mechanical', 'communal', or reflective of *Gemeinschaft* characteristics. In other words, we can draw attention to 'distinct' patterns of sociality, but they are inevitably, to a certain degree, 'overlapping'. Just as it would be wrong to think that rationalistic re-formations of the body have been able to eradicate the extra-cognitive dimensions of human being, the same can be said about the thoroughly embodied phenomenon of effervescent sociality. Collective effervescence could not be eliminated by Protestantism; it was merely 'sublimated' to cognitive projects and objectives, and became manifest in a series of 'fearful others' which continued to challenge the Protestant experience of the world. As Lyndal Roper (1994) demonstrates, the establishment of Discipline Ordinances was an important element of the Protestant Reformers' institutionalisation of discipline, yet these were frequently violated, and they coexisted with a literature of excess. Furthermore, just as the sensual dimensions of human experience have undergone a renaissance with the emergence of the baroque modern body, so too have effervescent forms of sociality expressing an immanence of the sacred.

This is clear in Chapter 6 when we discuss those patterns of sociality characteristic of the baroque modern habitus. These discussions highlight the fact that forms of both embodiment and sociality can be increasingly characterised as 'overlapping'. The baroque modern re-formation of the body takes place within what we refer to as both *banal associations* and *sensual solidarities*. Banal associations are developments of the Protestant modern body in the sense that they continue to be structured by rationality and cognitive apprehension, but have become dislocated from the sacred referent (the 'sublime') of Protestantism. Consequently, reciprocity and contracts replace standards of ultimate truth and morality, and there is nothing which cannot be subjected to critical scrutiny, nothing which cannot be explored or reconstructed, and nothing which remains 'out of bounds' because of its other-worldly status. Sensual solidarities, on the other hand, mark the resurgence of the 'shadow kingdom' of effervescence, and of the sacred as a sensually experienced phenomenon. This means that the experience of transcendence again becomes immanent within bodies, sociality and nature. Thus, contemporary Western societies are characterised by a pluralism to some extent (and only to *some* extent) analogous to that of the medieval era. In this respect, Maffesoli (1996: 42) has talked of the emergence of 'a religious syncretism with as yet unknown results'. However, there is no syncretistic integration of diversity into one embodied community analogous to that attempted by medieval Catholicism. Indeed, the effervescence produced by sensual solidarities is not necessarily supportive of those contracts which characterise modern banal associations. As Durkheim (1984 [1893]: 302) argued, 'The contract is only a truce, and a fairly precarious one at that.'

Bodies in time

So far, we have introduced some of our ideas concerning the *distinct* and *overlapping* relationships between forms of embodiment and forms of sociality. The tension between these two emphases is, as we have noted, apparent in the work of both Durkheim and Weber. This tension also serves to introduce some of the methodological assumptions underpinning our analysis, and our particular ontology of the body. We talk of 're-forming' rather than 'transforming' the body because of the long-term processes that ensure a 'stubbornness' of human bodies which both allows for, but also limits, the possibilities of change. The following section addresses 'what it is' about bodies that allows them to be re-formed (a question sociologists have generally tackled with regard to social relationships but have failed to deal with in relation to embodiment). The 'stubbornness' of bodies can be considered with regard to our own reading of what Fernand Braudel (1972) has called the *longue durée* of human evolution, before we go on to address what he terms the intermediate or conjunctural time represented by the establishment of a *habitus*, and the *micro-time* of individual bodily interactions.[8]

The longue durée

The human body's *longue durée* refers to those slow-moving biological, geographic, climactic and social processes involved in human evolution, and is the overall context for human embodiment which allows for both stability and change.[9] Modern and traditional societies are often portrayed as if they were separated by a series of breaks, discontinuities and opposites, yet this tends to overlook the simple but important fact that a *single* human species has populated these periods. This 'stubbornness' of human bodies is not, of course, complete. The death of one generation helps the next accomplish social change, while the emergence of radically different cultures is made possible by the relative 'openness' and malleability of the human form (Honneth and Joas, 1988). Furthermore, the sizes, health and capacities of bodies have historically undergone changes with profound implications for social relations and institutions (Turner, 1982, 1984). Nevertheless, the development of social formations is characterised by bodily *continuities* as well as differences. Bodies are re-formed, rather than made anew, from an evolutionary inheritance which has provided humans with species-specific capacities. These ensure the 'unfinishedness' of human embodiment which does not act as the opposite of culture, but which necessitates culture (Futuyama, 1986; Hirst and Woolley, 1982; Jones, 1994; Midgley, 1979).[10]

Examined from the *longue durée*, biological and cultural processes cannot be easily separated when we examine the body's capacities, senses and ways of knowing the world (Benton, 1991; Hirst and Woolley, 1982). For example, the body may have provided prehistoric people with the ability to use tools, but deploying this ability led to outcomes which would ordinarily be described as both 'social' and 'biological'. Tool use developed certain muscles at the expense of others but also helped facilitate increasingly complex socio-economic relations which may themselves have stimulated the evolution of a larger brain (Le Gros Clark, 1970, 1978; Livingstone, 1969; Washburn, 1960). These 'socio-natural' processes, as Ian Burkitt (forthcoming) refers to them, took place over hundreds of thousands of years. Nevertheless, modern and medieval cultures presuppose them, while the re-formations of the body (and, indeed, of sociality) we focus on in this book could not have taken place without them. Nowhere is this clearer than in Elias's (1991) exploration of 'symbol emancipation'; a concept which highlights an important link in the relationship between human embodiment and cultural knowledge.

Symbol emancipation results from evolutionary processes which provided humans with the physical means of communicating, thinking and orienting themselves to reality via symbols. So, symbols consist partly of tangible sound patterns of human communication (made possible by the formation of the vocal apparatus) which can be spoken, heard, thought with, and written down. Symbol emancipation provided humans with a unique ability to learn and synthesise symbols, to develop these into a language marked by reflexivity, variability and precision, and to transmit accumulated knowledge between generations (Elias, 1991: 31–32, 43, 131). This use of symbols, however, remains dependent on individuals learning language, and the contingencies associated with other practical tasks (Elias, 1991: 116; Kilminster, 1994). Furthermore, the space between the *potential* and *actuality* of language allows symbols to relate to the senses in a variety of ways. They can be seen as the most important pathway to knowledge, for example, or can be treated as subordinate to the information provided by the senses. Humans may have species-specific capacities, then, but these can be patterned and organised in a variety of ways between different generations and cultural contexts. Such patterning processes can be addressed with reference to the concept 'habitus'.

The habitus

'Habitus', a concept which dates back to Aristotle and Saint Thomas Aquinas and has been developed in the more recent work of Elias and

Bourdieu, refers to those pre-cognitive, embodied dispositions which promote particular forms of human orientation to the world, organise each generation's senses and sensualities into particular hierarchies, and predispose people towards specific ways of knowing and acting. The term implies that human bodies are permeated by, and contain within them, their own historical experience of social relations. This 'incorporation of the past' into the 'living body of the present' through the habitus, which Braudel (1972) calls 'intermediate' or 'conjunctural' time, is a phenomenon which can be examined initially through Marcel Mauss's (1973 [1934]) writings on 'techniques of the body' (techniques which form some of the constituent parts of a habitus).

Techniques of the body refer to how people learn to relate to and deploy their bodies in social life. This often takes place at a pre-cognitive level, but involves practice and accomplishment, and serves to mould the body in ways which make it fit for certain activities and unfit for others. The acquisition of body techniques, then, involves the acquisition of a particular bodily history. These techniques affect the very fundamentals of social and individual life: they are implicated in how people learn to walk, talk, look and think, and differ both historically and cross-culturally (Hunter and Saunders, 1995).

Norbert Elias also examines how body techniques change, with the 'advance' of manners and etiquette through time, but is additionally concerned with the permeability of the habitus at a somewhat broader level of analysis (Elias, 1987, 1991). Indeed, one of the major components of Elias's work is a focus on how the formation of an individual habitus involves the *internalisation* of large scale and world-transforming social processes. In this respect, the embodied habitus represents the highly permeable, but by no means completely reflected, 'flipside' of 'structural' forces.

Elias suggests that the habitus tends to change historically in a direction that heightens the reflexive monitoring of physical actions, and increases levels of self-control (Elias, 1983). Nevertheless, these shifts from 'external expression' to 'internal experience' (Falk, 1994) are neither automatic nor universal occurrences, as internalisation is dependent on the environments in which people live (Elias and Scotson, 1994 [1965]). Self-constraint, for example, is facilitated by monopolies of violence and increases in social interdependence; factors which raise the costs associated with ill-considered, 'illegitimate' outbursts. It is these developments which impact on the permeable body by providing incentives for people to plan ahead, take into account the views and interests of others, and engage in 'impression management' (Elias, 1978 [1939], 1982 [1939], 1983; see also Goffman, 1969).

Pierre Bourdieu's writings complement Elias's work by concentrating on the habitus as a bodily mechanism which is shaped by the quantities and qualities of particular resources that make up people's backgrounds. Forged by the totality of conditions which surround socialisation, the habitus manifests itself in an individual's *taste* (conscious preferences for food, art, sport, work, etc.). For Bourdieu, the habitus produces disposi-tions which 'function at every moment as a matrix of perceptions, appreci-ations and actions, and makes possible the achievement of infinitely diversified tasks' (Bourdieu, 1977: 72, 95; 1984: xi; see also Bourdieu and Wacquant, 1992). While by no means identical, both Bourdieu's and Elias's uses of 'habitus', then, presuppose the *longue durée* of human evolution, yet are concerned with signalling what it is about the body's character that allows it to be integrally and generationally involved in the development of human culture.

While it is appropriate to associate the habitus with stability rather than change, it is also important to supplement this with an awareness of the possibilities for change inherent within patterns of human interaction. The approaches of Mauss and Bourdieu, for example, examine how the habitus is inscribed by cultural traditions, but are less concerned with how social interaction reacts back on and leads to the development of *new* orien-tations to the body. This is an important gap, since culturally creative actions and interactions (those which cannot be reduced to extant traditions) can have an important impact on how bodies sense and work on the world around them. The bodily dimension of Braudel's third time-scale, concerned with 'individual-time' events, directs our attention to that flux and change that appears to mark daily life (Braudel, 1972: 21; 1984 [1979]: 622).

Daily time

Nick Crossley (1994, 1995) has suggested that Maurice Merleau-Ponty's work addresses the question of how culturally acquired techniques are transformed, through bodily performances, into effective actions. Merleau-Ponty highlights the importance of individual-time by insisting that our view of life is dependent on how we operationalise our 'bodily being in the world' (Merleau-Ponty, 1962). Nevertheless, as Crossley suggests, it is Erving Goffman who addresses in most *sociological* detail and sophisti-cation the place of the body in daily life.

Instead of dwelling on the cultural traditions which forge a habitus or body technique, Goffman's analysis of the 'interaction order' develops a battery of concepts sensitising us to how bodies are creatively deployed in social interaction (e.g. Goffman, 1963, 1983). The flow of daily life is marked by numerous interactions with others in which the body is managed in particular ways, seeks to give off various impressions, and must sometimes 'repair' moments of embarrassment (Goffman, 1961; Burns, 1992: 180–182). Much of our day-to-day activity may be taken for granted and managed by the pre-cognitive skills involved in what Giddens (1984) refers to as 'practical consciousness', but Goffman highlights the bodily intelligence and creativity which marks such activity. 'Supportive' or 'remedial interchanges', for example, highlight the work done in initiating and sustaining relationships (Goffman, 1971), while the activities of 'passing' or 'make work' remind us of what is involved if we are to be accepted as full members of society, or as competent employees (Goffman, 1969, 1971). Body management is, in other words, an integral part of civilised society (Elias, 1978 [1939]).[11]

The interpersonal interactions discussed by Goffman are particularly important in those modern contexts where people understand themselves to be related to each other on a profane, associational basis, and where highly reflexive and individual patterns of body management take precedence over collective forms. However, the modern body's repression or attempted elimination of sensual forms of knowing is incomplete, and, as Maffesoli's (1996) analysis of the 'warmth' generated by 'neo-tribes' suggests, modern forms of association may not be as 'profane' as they sometimes imagine themselves to be.

Re-formations of the body and re-formations of patterns of human sociality are, then, linked. These links are facilitated by the evolutionary 'unfinishedness' of bodies at birth (Benton, 1991; Futuyama, 1986), have to be reproduced within each new generation (Bourdieu, 1984; Elias, 1982 [1939]), and both shape and are shaped by the rhythms and events of daily life on both interpersonal (Goffman, 1969) and inter-group levels (Maffesoli, 1996). These factors are crucial to our understanding of what it is about bodies that allows them to be re-formed through history. Their ability to alter how people 'sense' their environment provides us with a crucial insight into the changing relationships which have existed between embodied identities and cultural knowledge.

Forms of knowing

We have introduced what we understand by 'forms of embodiment' and 'forms of sociality', and have focused on some of the methodological concerns underpinning this study through our discussion of bodies in time. We can now concentrate on some of the general themes that run through our account of those re-formations of embodiment which can, we believe, cast a fresh light upon the emergence, development and transformation of the modern Western world. These themes are related to the contrast between *carnal* and *cognitive* 'forms of knowing', which we now consider. Following this, we introduce the themes of self-referentiality, nostalgia and doubt as manifestations of the tendency towards 'losing touch' with the embodied basis of knowledge which characterises modern forms of bodily being in the world. This 'loss of touch' has been integral to the establishment of the rationalist Enlightenment project that treats people as undifferentiated minds. It is also what now threatens the maintenance of the modern contractarian mentality that seeks to bind people together on the basis of their mindfulness. As Durkheim (1984 [1893]: 316) suggested, while modern life seeks to colonise embodied human relationships by contracts, it is wrong to think that 'all social relationships can be reduced to contract, all the more so because a contract assumes the existence of something other than itself'. Once contracts are no longer supported by a positive collective effervescence, and are observed 'only by force or the fear of force, contractual solidarity would be in an extremely parlous state' (Durkheim, 1984 [1893]: 317). As the Los Angeles riots of the early 1990s suggested, and as the war in the former Yugoslavia blatantly revealed, a 'wholly external order would ill conceal a state of contestation too general to be contained indefinitely' (ibid.).

Carnal knowing and cognitive apprehension

We use the terms 'carnal knowing' and 'cognitive apprehension' to indicate the relative importance of knowledge gained through the body, or through the mind, in relation to the forms of embodiment and sociality addressed in this book. They represent, in other words, ideal typical accounts of the different embodied bases of knowledge and meaning construction.[12] They also touch upon relationships between the body and knowledge which engage with Elias's (1978 [1939], 1982 [1939]) theory of 'civilising processes'.[13]

Carnal knowing is a term used by the feminist historian Margaret Miles to indicate the inextricable links between thinking, sensing and understanding perceived to exist by medieval persons (Miles, 1992: 9). This could involve workaday contact with the elements which involves a 'reciprocal jostling with the world' (Scarry, 1994: 51), or a more spectacular effervescent contact with the sacred. Either way, knowledge, experience and understanding in the medieval era were often *corporeal* products; that is, they belonged to people who experienced their minds and bodies as inextricably related. Bodily experiences did not have to be considered cognitively, and then conceptualised and evaluated by the mind before they could be made sense of (though, as Lerner's [1993] discussions of Biblical interpretation suggest, this more cognitive form of knowing was by no means unheard of). Knowledge was gained instead from a *thinking body* in which sensuous understanding involved *all* of the body's senses, and from the intricate links which existed between the fleshy, physical body and the mind. As Elias notes, it would have appeared nonsensical in these premodern times to have suggested that the body was separate from, or wholly subordinate to, the mind. Instead, medieval bodies provided a comparatively immediate vent for fears and desires, and tended to be much more volatile than their modern counterparts (Elias, 1983; cf. Goffman, 1969; Hochschild, 1983).

Elias's analysis of the progressive 'civilisation' of Western bodies is highly relevant to our examination of the Protestant re-formation of the body and promotion of associational patterns of sociality. The Protestant Reformation encouraged people to experience their minds as separate from, and superior to, their limited and limiting bodies, and to reorder the importance they attached to their senses. In this context, carnal knowing gradually faded in importance, but was by no means wholly replaced by what we refer to as *cognitive apprehension*. Knowledge became an increasingly mental phenomenon in which the mind, experienced as divorced from the prejudices of the body's passions and senses, provided valid knowledge. These developments accompanied the Protestant attempt to remove effervescent contact with the sacred and make it *sublime*; something which could only be encountered indirectly through an inspired reading of the Word of God. It is not that the sensuous, fleshy body disappears from knowledge construction entirely, of course, but that the information provided by its feelings and emotions is apprehended as knowledge only *after* it has been filtered through the concepts and categories employed by the mind. Thus, 'civilising processes' and 'cognitive apprehension' are closely tied to each other; an association which helps explain why *mental reflection* has become more important than physical prowess to many modern persons.[14]

Recent developments in Western societies, however, take the early modern bodies of Protestantism and the relatively civilised bodies of the early twentieth century analysed by Elias in significantly new directions. These contain the potential not only to establish, but to *undermine* civilised bodies. The baroque modern habitus has provided us with the potential to exert an unprecedented degree of control over our physicality, but has also thrown into radical doubt our knowledge of what bodies are and how we should control them. Arthur Frank has suggested that these developments (which he refers to as 'embodied paranoia') could presage a re-formation 'that will eventually be as monumental as that from medieval violent bodies to courtly bodies' (Frank, 1995: 187). The emerging shape of this re-formation is already evident in the increasing role *carnal* fears play in the lives of many modern persons, as well as in the re-emergence of forms of sociality based on sensuous rather than cognitive criteria. In other words, the reappearance of carnal forms of knowing also marks a challenge to Elias's 'civilising processes' at the level of the individual (Mennell, 1990).

Central to much modern experience has been a literal loss of 'sense-contact' with knowledge. A fundamental anthropological condition of humanity, embodiment, has been forgotten in the pursuit of thoroughly cognitive projects, utopias and fantasies. This is why the question 'Can thought go on without a body?' is a question about inhumanity (Lyotard, 1991). From a purely cognitive point of view, we may 'know' more than our forebears did, but our sensory bodies frequently have very little contact with this knowledge. What we learn through our bodies is no longer validated in the way it used to be, and this is why 'experience' is popularised as individual, unique. It is also why a general sense of fragmentation and flux is characteristic of the modern condition (Berman, 1982). This loss of sense-contact can be explored further with reference to the themes of self-referentiality, nostalgia and doubt, which also touch upon what Georges Bataille and Georg Simmel highlight as two of the cultural 'tragedies' of modern life.

Self-referentiality

Bataille (1986 [1957], 1992 [1973]) points to the first of these 'tragedies' in his analysis of how modern culture has prompted a human retreat from the sacred and an accompanying inability to step beyond the limiting, profane world of objects. For Bataille (1992 [1973]: 93), this profane world is associated with 'a neutral image of life', wherein the sacred is no longer immanent, resulting in an estrangement (alienation) of individuals from community, and of minds from bodies. This is not to say, however, that modern societies have simply been 'secularised', if by this term is meant a general disappearance of the sacred rather than its relocation (Hammond, 1985). We have already endorsed Durkheim's view that the very possibility of society is contingent upon the incorporation of individuals into this corporeal solidarity of the sacred (Durkheim, 1961 [1912]: 347). It is what Eisenstadt (1969: 306) calls Protestantism's combination of (profane) 'this worldliness' and (sacred) 'transcendentalism' which provides the embodied basis for modernity's retreat from the sacred, and the promotion of distinctively modern forms of knowing.

As the sacred becomes removed 'from all immediate reality' (Levine, 1971: 139), becoming *sublime* (Kant, 1951 [1790]), there are tendencies towards the erosion of the social conditions supportive of morally motivated action, the weakening of borders between past and present, and the stimulation of the sensory conditions that promote the experiences of artificiality, fragmentation and isolation commonly associated with modern life (Bauman, 1993, 1995). As Charles Lindholm (1990) suggests, once culture becomes self-referential, once it concerns itself with the human world of things as outlined by Bataille, it erodes any sense of a *telos* (an ultimately meaningful human purpose). By cutting the ties which bound together the natural and supernatural worlds, Protestantism did much to promote this process of self-referentiality. Furthermore, as the economies which built on the 'Protestant spirit' produced a profane consumer culture, they also stimulated conditions conducive to the appearance of the 'one dimensional Man' analysed by Herbert Marcuse (1972 [1964]). In this context, the extension of the profane not only begins to marginalise the sacred, but stimulates the emergence of the *banal* (a culture which is self-referential and stimulates a sense of the blasé). Cultural artefacts, images and fashions become increasingly rationalised and can circulate at a quantity and with a quality which leaves people with a sense of fatigue, boredom and dissatisfaction (Campbell, 1987), and a feeling (a 'sensory intimation') that their lives are bereft of purpose (Marcuse, 1972 [1964]). The problem with this is that ways of living together positively, rather than just existing together indifferently, lose their attraction for those modern people who are no longer concerned with ordering and directing their behaviour in relation to the needs of others, but in response to their *own* emotions (Campbell, 1987; Tester, 1997).

Nostalgia

The extension of the profane to the point of becoming banal is also evident in the *nostalgia* increasingly evident within Western societies. Turner (1987: 149) reminds us that the literal meaning of nostalgia is homesickness. The bodily referents of homesickness include melancholy and despair, and involve a quite literal 'not feeling at home' in the body and its bodily routines (Turner, 1987; Featherstone, 1995a). The stifling and highly rationalised environments in which modern bodies developed helped stimulate this sense of alienation from the body: the feeling that the body was a case in which the real self was contained. They have also contributed to a nostalgia for the forms of freedom, immediacy and spontaneity which could sometimes characterise the medieval era (Elias, 1978 [1939]). This nostalgia is particularly evident in baroque modern bodies marked by a resurgence of sensual knowing.

Some of the chief characteristics of baroque modern bodies are reflected in those contemporary theories of postmodernity which claim to have charted the 'death' of the body and its replacement by technology (Baudrillard, 1983; Kroker et al., 1989). These writings provide us with a sense of the fracture, instability and fluidity of modern life. The postmodern concern with images and representations itself reflects what Jenks (1995:7) has called 'a serious commitment to surface', whose corresponding commitment to the visual has obliterated any sense of the body's ontological depth. In this context, it is no wonder that modern life may contain a certain nostalgia for the spontaneity and emotional passions often associated with medieval bodies. A desire for unmediated experiences and feelings, for a body which provides a sense of home, is understandable in a culture whose internal referentiality has made it banal. Modern bodies may conduct 'whispered conversations' with their dead, for example, but we should not be surprised if baroque modern bodies [re]turn to seances or other magical forms of communication, or display an increasing concern with other-worldly or extra-terrestrial phenomena (Kane, 1996; Richardson et al., 1991).

Ultimately, perhaps, people find cultures which have become banal unbearable and seek instead opportunities to reconsecrate the profane. The renewed interest in fate, destiny, the stars, magic, tarot, nature, cults and games of chance appear to reflect this (Adorno, 1994; Maffesoli, 1996: 39). It may also provide a motivation for the invention of traditions and national identities (Hobsbawm and Ranger, 1983), and is one specific manifestation of Robertson's argument about meaning and activity. As he suggests, 'all social groups (particularly in the modern era. . .) encounter, in diachronically patterned forms, the situational problem of rendering meaningful and redirecting their societally structured forms of socio-economic routine' (Robertson, 1992: 43). When this problem is ignored, when the very possibility of society becomes questionable, people seek new forms of sociality which may involve 'keeping warm together' (Maffesoli, 1996), but which can just as easily incorporate envy, hate, and the pursuit of identity through 'burning others together' (Theweleit, 1987 [1977], 1989 [1978]).

Doubt

This concern with the difficulties in rendering modern life meaningful can be pursued with reference to Georg Simmel's writings on culture, individuality and the metropolis. In these writings, Simmel points to a second cultural 'tragedy' of modern life: the sense of personal incompleteness which tends to arise as humans find themselves immersed in a culture which can never be wholly assimilated (Simmel, 1968). Simmel's suggestion is complemented by Elias's comments on the pervasiveness of doubt at the heart of the modern experience of the world. In examining the relation between the body, communication and representation, Elias views symbol emancipation as a 'one off' phenomenon. However, his comments on the paradox of modern knowing point to further shifts in the body's relation to knowledge. In knowing more about the world around us, there comes a time when people also learn that things are not always what they appear to be, that knowledge is finite and frequently associated with doubt:

> characteristic of the post-Cartesian period is the simultaneity of an accelerating process of knowledge growth and of a steady, perhaps even a growing uncertainty about the relationship between knowledge and that which it claims to represent, the unknown world. An unparalleled expansion of knowledge which presents itself as realistic with a built in animus against fantasy knowledge goes hand in hand with a continuous doubt as to the existence of anything independently of the knower. (Elias, 1991: 15)

This paradox of knowledge can be clarified by considering Baudrillard's writings on the autonomisation of signs, and Giddens's discussions of 'ontological security'. For Baudrillard (1993a) history has been characterised by an 'emptying out' of community from successive modes of representation. The world as represented loses its human referent; a loss which can be traced in part to Protestant and Catholic re-formations of the body. While premodern rituals exhausted the meaning of words by the use of rituals which tied people's sensory and sensual bodies together through an engagement with the sacred, Protestantism removed the meaning of words from their human speakers and writers and plunged individuals into an *isolated* relation with knowledge.

Just as important to this process was the Catholic Counter-Reformation's approach not just to words (which became more important with the increased stress accorded to correct dogma) but to symbolisation *in general*. As Baudrillard argues, the extensive use of stucco (fine, moulding plaster) during the Counter-Reformation allowed the world to be represented according to human design. That which was natural was *made* artificial, into a sign which could be juxtaposed with, compared with and contrasted to, any other sign. Thus begins the ability to 'counterfeit' the world, a degree of control which allows the world to be seen increasingly through signs; signs which interrupt the relation between communal ritual and knowing because they are *always there* for the individual; signs which begin to erode the sacred–profane distinction because they provide the means to replicate and move what is 'set apart' from everyday life into the mundane world.

Anthony Giddens's (1990, 1991) discussions of 'ontological security' also touch upon this 'paradox of knowledge', though in a manner which is less sensitive to historical changes. For Giddens, 'ontological security' refers to persons having a sense of order and continuity in relation to the events in which they participate, and the experiences they have, in their day-to-day lives (see also Mellor, 1993b). Drawing upon Garfinkel (1963) and Heritage (1984), though there are also observable continuities with the work of Gehlen (1956, 1957), Giddens (1991: 36) argues that ontological security has a cognitive anchor in the 'practical consciousness' of the meaningful-ness of day-to-day actions. Using Kierkegaard's (1944) concept of 'dread', he further suggests that there is the constant danger of this practical consciousness being overwhelmed by anxieties concerning the ultimate meaningfulness and reality of life, and that these must therefore be 'bracketed out' of everyday existence (Giddens, 1991: 37–38).

Much of Giddens's analysis of these tendencies towards 'radical doubt', which he sees as being particularly strong in modern societies due to the pervasiveness and depth of 'chronic reflexivity' (1990, 1991), is consistent with the earlier work of Peter Berger, though Berger places greater emphasis upon the importance of the sacred for containing such tendencies toward meaninglessness (1990 [1967]: 45). Both, however, tend to portray the construction of meaning and tendencies towards doubt in essentially *cognitive* terms (and this is despite Berger's debt to philosophical anthropology's emphasis on the bodily 'unfinishedness' of human beings). Our attention to re-formations of the body, and their relationships with changing patterns of sociality, different forms of knowing, and various relationships with the sacred, seeks to place these concerns in a broader context.

Giddens's (1990, 1991) and Berger's (1990 [1967]) emphases upon the cognitive basis of both meaningfulness and radical doubt is illuminating mainly with regard to modern contexts shaped by the Protestant re-formation of the body, and explains very little about contexts shaped by carnal knowing of the medieval body and the reappearance of sensual forms of knowing and sacred solidarities in the baroque modern habitus. The tendency towards doubt, which is 'the worm in the apple of modernity' (Elias, 1991: 15), is intimately related to a form of embodiment promoting cognitive apprehension. Similarly, the sense of personal incompleteness which may arise as humans find themselves immersed in a culture which can never be wholly assimilated (Simmel, 1971 [1908c]), is dependent upon a loss of sense-contact with the embodied grounds of knowledge, as is the autonomisation and proliferation of representation addressed by Baudrillard (1993a, 1993b). The processes examined by these authors can, however, only be understood adequately by appreciating their contingency upon forms of embodiment which vary historically.

Chapter outlines

Chapter 2, 'Re-formed Bodies', launches the substantive component of our study by focusing on three forms of embodiment especially important to the development of Western culture. This analysis of medieval, Protestant modern and baroque modern bodies is by necessity selective, and possesses an 'ideal type' flavour (we concentrate on those features of social habitus most important to each social epoch). Nevertheless, the scope of discussion ranges far and wide. We touch upon the lives of holy anorexics, and explore the various dimensions of carnal knowledge. The chapter progresses by examining the rise of textuality as a phenomenon which appropriates human experience, yet is insufficient in relation to this experience.

Exploring these forms of embodiment raises the question of how they arose, and Chapter 3, 'Volatile Bodies, Sacred Communities', starts to answer this by examining how the Catholic Church sought to harness to its own agenda pre-existing carnal ways of sensing the world. The impact of Catholicism is frequently overlooked in social theory, a neglect that is without justification. Indeed, medieval Catholicism was associated with a re-formation of the body which was, in its own way, just as significant as that stimulated by Protestantism. By seeking to harness the sensual volatility and pagan superstitions of medieval bodies to religious commitments, and to stimulate effervescent encounters with the sacred, Catholicism encouraged a limited increase in mutual identification and a partial growth in those webs of interdependency which bound together people in situations of co-presence. This re-formation of the body was constrained by the pursuance of the Crusades and other military conflicts but that does not diminish its importance.

Catholicism provides us with the first re-formation of medieval bodies (which remained volatile in an environment hostile to the careful regulation of human affects) but Chapter 4, 'Sinful Bodies, Profane Associations', examines how Protestantism *re-formed* this re-formation. It explores central aspects of the Protestant Reformations (in the plural), looking at how they encouraged people to adopt new approaches to their bodies, and to experience as 'abstract' their relationship to society and to God (Cascardi, 1992: 174). By highlighting the different human capacities and capabilities drawn on by Protestantism and Catholicism, we look at how the Protestant reconstruction of Catholic communities undermined the role and centrality of the Church as an institution (McGrath, 1993: 104), and stimulated a social and religious individualism that corroded traditional relationships and frowned on effervescent, potentially uncontrollable, contacts with the sacred (Dumont, 1982; Turner, 1991: 155–156). While medieval Catholicism can be referred to as a sacred 'eating community' (Falk, 1994), Protestantism was more a series of 'profane associations'. In conceiving of the sacred as radically transcendent, as 'sublime', Protestantism encouraged patterns of sociality based on individual commitment and contract, rather than the sacred bonds of effervescent sociality.

These events mark a significant stage in the Western tendency to equate the eye with the mind and to 'forget' that sight is itself a sense. More generally, emotions became things to be moderated and controlled and it was the 'spirit', separated from the impurities of the sensuous body, which sought contact with God. These effects did not disappear after the sixteenth century, and Chapter 5, 'Janus-faced Modernity', examines how these processes formed an important part of the basis on which modern culture was built. Here, we examine how the corporeal and social effects of Protestantism shaped the emergence of modern societies, exploring how the Reformers' focus on cognitive modes of apprehending self and society became incorporated into the agendas of subsequent social movements and institutions. We also consider the Catholic Counter-Reformation and the promotion of a 'baroque' culture which recognised not only the dangers of the senses but their importance. The Counter-Reformation sought to combine control of the discursive symbolisation of religion with the manipulation of the masses through the senses and represents a trend opposed to the dominance of cognition which endured into the modern period.

Chapter 6, 'Ambivalent Bodies', deals with the further development of Protestant and counter-Protestant forms of embodiment in the 'baroque modern' habitus. We endorse the views of Bauman, Giddens and Beck that modernity has not so much 'ended', as that certain aspects of modernity have developed at the expense of others. Contrary to Giddens, however, we see in advanced modern societies not merely the extension of chronic modern reflexivity, but also the reappearance of sensual forms of knowing and sociality. We explore how the decline of Protestant influence has created an increasing amount of space for many elements of modern culture to collapse under the weight of their own contradictions. The rise of identity politics, for example, is just one indication that all-inclusive social contracts may no longer be viable. More generally, Scott Lash and John Urry (1994: 53) suggest that social contracts do not sit easily with the contemporary rise of what they refer to as *allegoric sensibilities*; dispositions which express an awareness of complexity, are 'heterotopian', and reflect the transience and fragmentation of much contemporary life (Taylor, 1989). In this context, the ideal of society may indeed begin to disappear from people's *minds* (Durkheim, 1961 [1912]: 347), only to reappear in very different, sensual forms through their *bodies*.

Chapter 7 offers some concluding comments, focusing on these tensions between minds and bodies in the heavily 'frontiered' environments of late modern societies. We note a widening gulf between contractarian and effervescent forms of social life, and the tendencies towards the consolidation of these conflictual differences which mark many modern cities and states. We also suggest that sacred intimations of the body's continuing resilience in the face of attempts at cognitive control are increasingly likely to manifest themselves in conflictual, dangerous and morally disturbing ways.

Notes

1. Even sociologists attentive to these different dimensions of Durkheim's thought have often tended to prioritise his rationalism. W.S.F. Pickering (1984: 397), for example, notes that Durkheim's concern with the irrational is evident in his understanding that human actions spring not only from beliefs but from *desires* too. He also, nevertheless, argues that Durkheim's very attempt to explain the irrational signals the underlying rationalism which informs his work, manifest in the emphasis Durkheim's sociology of religion places on the *cognitive* dimensions of human experience (Pickering, 1984: 397, 516). This emphasis on cognition has, indeed, been particularly evident in the sociology of religion, where the corporate and corporeal dimensions of human experience have been neglected due to an assumption that religious beliefs and practices are ultimately directed towards what Bryan Turner (1991: 228) has called 'the existential problems of humanity'. The study of religion, in other words, has tended to have an intellectualist bias which reduces its object to a framework addressing specific *mental* problems rather than the needs of embodied persons in their totality (Featherstone, 1991: 118; Bell, 1980: 333). This tendency is also mirrored in many approaches toward the study of culture. In his assessment of the status of culture as a sociological concept, for example, Neil Smelser's (1992) analysis looks over the past century and demonstrates how culture tends to be associated with *values*, *beliefs*, *norms* and *attitudes*. Unfortunately, the 'postmodern turn' in cultural studies has done little to change this inclination toward a fundamentally disembodied focus as it has merely increased the importance attached to language and other signs as *autonomous* structures and systems of meaning.

2. Durkheim was not inattentive to the social conflicts that often arose as a result of effervescent forms of sociality, as is evident in his discussions of the Crusades, the French Revolution, and the 1870 Franco-Prussian War (Pickering, 1984: 391). Nevertheless, his contemporary Le Bon paid more explicit attention to the conflicts between different social groupings, as have subsequent social theorists such as Georges Bataille (1986 [1957], 1992 [1973]), René Girard (1977 [1972]) and Stjepan Meštrović (1991, 1993).

3. The implications of bringing both the body and religion 'back in' as necessary referents of patterns of human sociality becomes clearer if we consider the 'gap' which exists in Margaret Archer's (1988) analysis of culture and agency. Archer distinguishes between the 'cultural system' (that which is held to be valid knowledge at a given time) and 'socio-cultural interaction' (the influence that people exert on each other). Her concern is with how complementary or contradictory relations between different parts of the cultural system (which includes religious propositions) map onto orderly or conflictual relations between people at the socio-cultural level (which includes religious experience) to produce stability or change. Agents and culture are analytically distinct and cannot be reduced one to the other; this is what enables culture to form a *context for* social interaction and to be *reproduced* or *changed by* this interaction. As Roland Robertson (1992: 111) summarises, Archer's primary concern is to 'distinguish culture as an objective, ideational phenomenon – possessing considerable autonomy in terms of its own inner "logic" (but not necessarily consistency) – from agents

who, in specific circumstances, seek to comprehend, invoke, manipulate and act in reference to systems of ideas'.

Archer's analysis provides us with an extremely useful way of examining cultural change or stasis, but what Robertson (1992: 111) refers to as the 'rationalist' bias of her theory results in a neglect of the bodily bases of human knowledge. We may know what cultural ideas are available to actors, and we may investigate how these ideas form a context for, shape, and are elaborated on during, social interaction. We learn little, however, about the bodily bases which shape how people use, discard or build on these knowledges.

4. Classen (1993) has suggested that Protestantism contributed to the declining significance of smell in Western cultures, discrediting miraculous proofs of holiness such as the odour of sanctity, and prohibiting the use of incense in Protestant churches. Even perfumes became associated with a dangerous sensuality which had to be resisted, as discussed in the Puritan Philip Stubbes's *The Anatomy of Abuses* (1972: 28).

5. Such developments were going on before the Reformation, of course. Weber refers, for example, to the Cistercians as 'proto-Protestants' due to their distrust of sensuality and their extreme asceticism. His notion of 'worldly asceticism' remains significant because it explains how the body-denying asceticism of some Catholic monastics spread through Protestantism into Western cultures at large. Whereas such monastics had comprised a relatively small, specialised component of the pluralism of medieval Catholicism, the word-oriented, ascetic emphasis of the Protestant Reformers claimed universal significance.

6. We are deliberately taking as literal Bakhtin's emphasis on the grotesque as a cultural constant which can be used to symbolise the process of becoming human.

7. For example, Giddens (1990, 1991) contrasts the pervasive reflexivity, dynamism and future-orientedness of modernity with the limited reflexivity, lack of dynamism and past-orientedness of premodernity.

8. Given that the concerns of this book focus on re-formations of the body over *time*, we could describe our study as a historical sociology of the body. In this respect, it is important to stress that we are not in the business of employing historical records of bodily dimensions such as height (now used as an indicator of health), nor are we concerned with tracing in great detail the events and people responsible for establishing new ways of 'seeing' and investigating the body. Such studies exist and have been conducted with skill and rigour elsewhere (e.g. Floud et al., 1990; Sawday, 1995). In contrast to these types of studies, we trace the *broad contours* of those socially dominant forms of habitus which have influenced Western development. This approach is not empiricist history. It is, however, a sociological approach which has produced extremely powerful analyses. Norbert Elias (1978 [1939], 1982 [1939]) and Bryan Turner (1984, 1991, 1992a), for example, have pioneered this approach to the body in quite different ways, and we intend to complement their analyses by examining those 'critical cases' of human embodiment associated with the emergence of modernity.

9. While evolutionary biologists examine how these processes have altered the body's senses, brain and physiological capacities through the ages (Futuyama, 1986), philosophical anthropologists show us that bodies *still* remain 'unfinished' at birth and in need of 'completion' through investments of work and meaning (Berger, 1990 [1967]; Honneth and Joas, 1988). Evolution has left humans with a 'poverty of instincts' compared with (other) animals. This makes our bodies and our world relatively 'open', and means that we need to saturate ourselves and our environment with knowledge, meaning and shape (Berger, 1990 [1967]).

10. Postmodern critics may point to the liberating and differentiating potentialities of 'cyberspace', and dream of leaving their bodies behind in the scapes and corridors of virtual reality, but we continue to share much in the way of legs, arms and senses with our medieval ancestors and are likely to do so for some time. Far from being irrelevant to the concerns of sociology, the generationally specific ways in which these continuities are organised into a particular habitus has major implications for the structure of social formations.

11. Goffman richly illustrates the complex patterns of interaction that underpin individual-time (Burns, 1992), and there is little doubt that the consequences of even simple bodily actions have become increasingly significant. Nuclear weapons, for example, could massively influence

the *longue durée* of human evolution, yet their activation ultimately requires little more than the pressing of a button or turning of a key. Furthermore, advances in transplant surgery, genetic engineering and genetic mapping (e.g. the Human Genome project) are already reducing the limits of human inheritance (Jones, 1994; Kelly, 1994). People's capacity for transforming or destroying their environment has, in short, never been greater.

While portraying a world *apparently* full of creativity, however, Goffman's analysis of 'shared vocabularies of body idiom' suggests that people are ultimately 'tied into' a set system of classifying actions and appearances. There are times when people undoubtedly share systems of classification (Goffman, 1963: 33–35; see also Sennett, 1992 [1974]; Tseelon, 1995), but Goffman's analysis of body language tells us nothing about how these vocabularies were initially constructed (a major criticism of Goffman is his neglect of the white, middle-class motivations of his subjects), or what power individuals have to change them (Gouldner, 1970; Shilling, 1993a: 82–88). These problems are confirmed in Goffman's analysis of stigma. Here, an individual's virtual identity (how they see themselves) tends toward their actual social identity (how others see them); an assertion vigorously contested in studies of ageing and self-identity, and youth culture (Goffman, 1968: 12; Burns, 1992: 217; cf. Featherstone and Hepworth, 1991; Hall and Jefferson, 1976).

12. We examine the various dimensions of cognitive apprehension and carnal knowing in our next chapter, but it is important to say something about the conceptual status of these terms. First, carnal knowing and cognitive apprehension are used to denote broad tendencies rather than universal states. Sensuous knowledge has not disappeared entirely from modern society (indeed, it is undergoing a resurgence), and there were individuals and social spaces in medieval societies that prioritised the mind as a vehicle of learning. Second, these concepts make no value judgements about the desirability of one form of knowing over the other. In opposition to the major intellectual thrust of the Enlightenment, it is important to recognise the *decivilising*, as well as the civilising, effects of the modern priority accorded to the mind and to the totalising moral systems associated with reason (Bauman, 1993; Elias, 1978 [1939], 1982 [1939]). Nevertheless, despite these qualifications, 'carnal knowing' and 'cognitive apprehension' refer for us to real historical developments. As forms of embodiment have altered, the modes by which knowledge is acquired have changed over time.

13. 'Civilisation' is a concept generally employed in evaluative contexts as a way of ranking hierarchically the moral, economic and political progress of peoples. Instead of referring predominantly to the merits of different cultures, however, Elias analyses civilisation as a set of processes which encompass the degree of internal pacification in a society; the refinement of customs; the amount of self-restraint and reflexivity involved in relationships, and the experiences of growing up in a society (Kuzmics, 1988).

14. Three major processes link together civilisation with the development of embodied persons in Elias's writings. *Rationalisation* refers to the ability of people to exert self control over their bodies by preventing emotional impulses from being translated immediately into physical action. *Individualisation* is concerned with how an increasing capacity for affect control and reflection leads people to experience themselves as detached from other people and from their own bodies. Finally, *socialisation* refers to the progressive separation of the body from nature, and its promotion as a bearer of value and codes of communication in social and economic market places.

2

RE-FORMED BODIES

In our introduction we suggested that understanding the particular character of the modern world requires an appreciation of both what sets apart contemporary forms of embodiment from their predecessors, and how they 'overlap' with previous forms. In this chapter, we focus on the chief features of the baroque modern, Protestant modern and medieval bodies that help illuminate this particular character, and which therefore lie at the heart of this book. Comparing and contrasting bodies associated with such different sociological contexts presents us with considerable problems of evidence. Nevertheless, excellent work already exists on the dominant sources of identity people have drawn on through different eras (e.g. Taylor, 1989), the sensory pathways they have used to gain knowledge about their environments (e.g. Corbin, 1986), and the different ways in which they have represented and oriented their bodily selves to their world (e.g. Delumeau, 1990).

Such research enables us to construct broad, summary pictures of particular forms of embodiment, and we are concerned here with what these bodily forms have incorporated within, and excluded from, themselves. In tracing the main contours of these baroque modern, Protestant modern, and medieval physicalities we are clearly pursuing a limited, 'ideal type' analysis. Each of the bodily forms we describe has been differentiated according to gender, status and other variables; it has coexisted with less influential counterparts; and it has existed in a state of relative flux, rather than stasis. While seeking to convey a sense of the variety and dynamism within these general forms of embodiment, however, we concentrate on the *distinctions between them* as having the potential to tell us most about the modern experience of the world. By focusing on these contrasting bodily forms in this chapter, we prepare the ground for our subsequent analysis of those forms of sociality and their changing relationships with the sacred which are implicated in their re-formation.

Medieval bodies

We have already noted the sociological tendency to underestimate the dynamism of premodern bodies (Levine, 1985), and drawn attention to the volatility of medieval embodiment (Classen, 1993; Kay and Rubin, 1994; Delumeau, 1990; Thomas, 1973 [1971]). This form of embodiment is worth examining further for two major reasons: first, it provided the context out of which early modern forms of embodiment emerged; and second, understanding this context illuminates those contemporary changes in Western societies which reflect forms of knowing and life not as far removed from medieval forms as people often imagine them to be (Sennett, 1994; Maffesoli, 1996).[1] Initially, however, we intend to concentrate on *differences* between medieval and modern bodies.

Norbert Elias has suggested that medieval persons possessed instinctual and emotional responses to experiences and events which tended to be more impulsive, volatile and unpredictable than those of their modern counterparts (Elias, 1978 [1939], 1982 [1939]). This has to be set against an awareness of the relative *stillness* of day-to-day medieval life, much of the time, in contrast to the noise and bustle of modernity (Huizinga, 1995 [1954]: 10), but the overall context was marked by an evident volatility. The medieval habitus was, after all, formed in an environment where violence and disease could easily lead to the loss of food, shelter and even life, where the struggle for survival loomed large in people's actions and interactions, and where magic and superstition were aids to knowledge (Delumeau, 1990; Manchester, 1992; Mennell, 1985).

Body regimes

These conditions did little to promote the view that ordinary people were in charge of their own lives, and were hardly conducive to the general prioritisation of cognitive reflexivity, to the Enlightenment rule of the mind over the flesh, or to the carefully considered adoption of habits designed to cultivate the 'body beautiful'. In short, these circumstances did not encourage those forms of embodied identity-construction which came to characterise modernity. Outside of the relatively controlled environments provided by court societies, such approaches to the body were usually extremely rare (Duby, 1977; Elias, 1983). Nevertheless, this does not mean that structured approaches to the body were lacking in the medieval era. Indeed, the volatility of the medieval era could coexist quite happily with a tendency for the flesh to become a site for the pursuance of what can be referred to as religious 'body regimes'. Body regimes can be defined as aggressive, if structured, flights into physicality which sought to harness the emotional and physical extremes characteristic of the medieval era to religious goals.

Body regimes were associated with the Catholic Church and pursued by a minority of the population. These included monks, religious ascetics, and holy women whose uncompromising treatment of their flesh made them into corporeal receivers and carriers of religious meaning (Bynum, 1987; Brown, 1988; Miles, 1992). Their adoption by religious specialists does not make body regimes unimportant, as they represented the development and restructuring of *already existing*, highly popular ways of implicating the body in magical and superstitious activities. As Keith Thomas (1973 [1971]: 27–58) argues, people frequently sought meaning and material benefit through bodily immersion in supernatural activities. Many of these activities were drawn on and developed subsequently within a religious context by the medieval Church; a situation which changed their significance as a result of their removal from local contexts, and their relocation within a sacred cosmology (Thomas, 1973 [1971]: 761).

Medieval body regimes were the development of a long history of Christian preoccupation with the body. As Peter Brown (1988) points out, physicality was central to ancient religiosity as early Christians 'seized upon' the body as a symbol of Christ's victory over death and the old and corrupt human order. While regimes of caring for the self existed in the pre-Christian world (Foucault, 1988 [1984]: 41), early Christianity developed these by encouraging people to transform their fallen, sinful flesh. Christians viewed the body as an integral whole, but the Fall had produced a tension between passion and spirit that needed overcoming (Bottomley, 1979: 30, 57–58; Richardson, 1988).[2] The body could not be ignored or disciplined out of existence then, yet Christianity also implied that the individual could never be contained entirely by the flesh and was obliged to reach beyond the constraints of existing corporeality.

This approach towards the body persisted and expanded in the Middle Ages when the flesh continued to be at the heart of rituals designed to transform an irreligious habitus, and bring outsiders into the Catholic community (Cameron, 1991: McGrath, 1993). Baptism involved not just a lengthy preparation of the body, but the stripping of clothing to a state of nakedness and, after baptism, the donning of a white linen garment. As Margaret Miles points out, the key to Christian victory resided in fasting, sexual abstinence, vigils, prayers and exorcisms that 'effectively deconstruct the person's physical and social habits and make possible the reconstruction of a new orientation. Just as the unbaptised were seen as the property of the Devil, bearing evil in their bodies, so the baptised became, body and soul, flesh of Christ's flesh and bone of his bone' (Miles, 1992: 37). Far from being caught up in a human culture of ideas and objects, medieval bodies maintained a sensual relationship with the sacred.

As Michel Foucault has made clear in his studies of the history of sexuality, medieval religiosity was focused to a significant extent on the body as sinful flesh (Foucault, 1981 [1976]). Nevertheless, this did not occasion a cognitive distancing or flight *away* from the body, but brought about a flight *into* physicality no less intense or passionate than its counterpart: the maximum enjoyment of pleasures (Bynum, 1987; Mellor, 1991). Remedial action to be taken against sins could include such apparently extreme behaviours as self-flagellation and walking around with pins stuck in the flesh which were constantly agitated by clothes. Comparing these behaviours with the norms of contemporary culture, Piero Camporesi (1988: 43) has argued that 'No one, in these days of mass beauty culture and sublimated corporeality, would be prepared voluntarily to transform his or her body into a gruesome dummy of dead and larval matter.' In medieval Europe, though, devout penitents 'burned . . . with a desire to annihilate their physical selves in the most repugnant manner possible'.

Having emphasised their distinctiveness, it is also necessary to note how medieval regimes bear a striking resemblance to the form, if not the content, of contemporary body orientations in their *preoccupation* with the body. They also echo their successors in enabling certain individuals to reconstruct their self-identities. As Caroline Walker Bynum (1987) has shown, fasting, religious charity work, and the experience of bodily states of 'ecstasy', allowed a number of women to escape the roles of food preparer and nurturer, and bypass certain forms of clerical control. These identities were often surrounded with dangers; male priests could judge religious ecstasies to be inauthentic or even demonic. Nevertheless, these women drew on particular religious traditions, and integrated them into personal biographical narratives which provided status in the form of religious 'careers' and challenged extant male hierarchies (Bynum, 1987: 221, 227; Lawless, 1991; Mellor, 1991). This was not *all* they were doing – these women understood themselves to be finding ultimate truth, the reality and presence of God, through their bodies – but truth and sensual symbol were inextricably tied to one another.

Religious body regimes had as their main cultural context the social and political power of the Catholic Church in this period; a power which was concentrated initially in population centres, but which took strenuous steps to incorporate the rural hinterland in the early part of the thirteenth century (Cameron, 1991; McGrath, 1993). As the Church extended its reach over greater portions of Europe, ecclesiastical authorities sought to structure the volatility of medieval bodies by the use of certain practices, experiences and disciplines associated with religious ritual and knowledge. It is for this reason that the term 'body regime' describes these activities more accurately than 'body option' or 'body project' which assume a greater degree of voluntarism, choice and reversibility (Shilling, 1993a). Entered into on the basis of religious criteria, and saturated with sacred meanings, the value and purpose of these ways of managing the self were not subject to the fluctuations and changes associated with contemporary consumer culture.

The internal instability of the medieval body

The medieval Church also sought to sustain a more general, related approach to the body through the collective effervescence of sacred forms of sociality stimulated by religious ritual. In contrast to the Protestant focus on words (used to distance people from their surroundings and make language the route to individual knowledge and inspiration), medieval people often shared a less mediated relationship with their natural, social and supernatural environments. In this context, Church rituals stimulated a structured opening of the medieval body to its sacred surroundings, exhausted the meaning of discourse, and made the flesh into a route to religious experience.

Instead of dislocating individuals from their environments, then, the medieval Church sought to *manage* the immersion of people within the natural and supernatural world. Seeing itself as the Body of Christ, and having as its main cultic act the Eucharistic eating of Christ's Body, the Church sought to 'eat into' the identity of its adherents. It did this by stimulating the sensory and sensual experience of 'right/wrong' and 'good/ evil' categories through contact with the sacred. This involved minimising the importance of cognitive choice, and promoting the 'close contact' senses of touch and taste as paths to religious knowledge (Falk, 1994). Religious rituals were not merely 'symbolic' of more spiritual, cosmological concerns. Instead, they were meant to produce 'religious truth' by harnessing the sensuous experience of the body to the goals of an institution which had a highly developed awareness of the symbolic values of human and supernatural bodies (Asad, 1983). The promotion of experience over abstract thought did not, however, eradicate a sense of flux and change from the world of medieval persons.

If medieval identities were frequently bound up with acting on and monitoring the body, they also involved anxieties related to the *instability* of the body. As we have already suggested, the frequency with which people could suffer from disfiguring illness and disease never provided a basis for the widespread modern obsession with outer appearance. Issues relating to the reliability and predictability of the body figured prominently in the medieval imagination though, and could be exacerbated by the strong emotional responses stimulated by religious ritual.

Worms have, for centuries, been associated with sin and decay and in medieval times were often thought to live *inside* the body. As Ariès (1974: 42) notes, the 'worms which devour cadavers' were not thought to come 'from the earth but from within the body, from its natural "liquors"'. Disease and sin were frequently associated with the existence of worms and snake-like creatures in the body, and stories of their expulsion from various orifices were often seen as signs of healing. The association between worms and humans was also close in other ways. As Saint Augustine argued, what are all 'men born of flesh if not worms'? Worms were, like people, 'born of decay; man from fetid sperm, from stale blood, fed in the womb by the same putrid blood that also produced snakes' (Camporesi, 1988: 89). The fear of worms may not be such a pressing concern for modern people, but the issue of the body's stability (manifest, for example, in contemporary fears of HIV, AIDS, cancer and even ageing: Featherstone and Wernick, 1995) is obviously not an entirely modern phenomenon.

Concerns about the body's stability also extended to the area of gender identities. In contrast to the 'biology of incommensurability' dominant nowadays, a 'one sex/one flesh' model dominated thinking about sexual difference from classical antiquity to the end of the seventeenth century (Laqueur, 1992 [1990]). In many respects gender identities were not as strong in medieval times as they became in modern societies. The striking religious imagery of Christ as embodying both male and female, and the acceptance of flux and change in the body, meant that categories of sex were not opposites. This did not, however, eradicate sexual anxieties. If men used up too much of what was considered to be their superior heat and energy, for example, the concern was that their bodies could lose their maleness and become identified with the bodies of women (Brown, 1988; Laqueur, 1987; Miles, 1992; Sennett, 1994).

Anxieties were also closely related to the confrontation with death in the medieval era. Once again, though, this confrontation illustrates how identities of that era were bound up with immanence of sacred meanings within the fleshy body. The confrontation with death involved anxieties and fears surrounding one's own *bodily* resurrection (Bynum, 1991: 276–280; 1995), and the contrasting fates of bliss or torture awaiting those who had been saved or damned (Camporesi, 1988: 26–27). Not surprisingly, this resurrection anxiety contributed to the fear and terror which surrounded death in the medieval period. However, this was not a terror which could provide the basis for Peter Berger's (1990 [1967]) implication that reminders of death are required for the maintenance of civilising processes. While images and sermons of hell and damnation could shock people into conformity, the overriding precedence given to religious salvation and the afterlife in the Middle Ages provided a justification for forms of torture, interpersonal violence and war. These often linked the materiality of the human body to the sacred Body of Christ. As Anna Sapir Abulafia (1994: 134) argues, we can find this association in 'the fervour of the crusaders to win back for their Lord the land they believed he trod as a man'.

A close and often anxious association between the body and self-identity is not peculiar to the modern period. What is different about these medieval anxieties, however, is that they were often contained within religious meanings, and had a different, sensuous, focus. For example, public rituals provided a context and a pattern of expected behaviour from those facing death (Ariès, 1981 [1977]). The flexibility of the Church also allowed people to invest holy objects with powers which could assist them in the confrontation with death. A scapular or friar's coat, for example, was coveted as an object to be worn as protection from pestilence and buried as a short cut to salvation (Thomas, 1973 [1971]: 35). Furthermore, in the case of body regimes, John McManners (1981) has noted how one established medieval view held that God created a body to match the soul placed in it. Temptations, trials and other corporeal ordeals that confronted individuals were not arbitrary, then, or subject to the vagaries of 'high velocity fashion' (Baudrillard, 1993a; Tseelon, 1995), but were measured and structured precisely to match the capacities and durabilities of the individual.

The variation in these approaches to the body does not support simplistic readings of an open body/closed self model in which collective influence on the bodily habitus rules out individual differences. Nevertheless, medieval cultures did *not* encourage the development of what modern persons would regard as distinctive, individual selves. A person's taste, shape and nutritional intake tended to be structured by the social whole, and consumption was based upon the collectivity 'eating into' the individual's identity. The medieval body provided relatively little impetus for *individual* innovation or social change (Falk, 1994). It was not always the Church, though, that formed the basis of this collectivity; a point which is illustrated by the development of medieval carnival.

John Bossy (1985) has suggested that, despite certain appearances to the contrary, carnival was a thoroughly Christian phenomenon. As a period of time and a moral conception, 'Carnival was one half of an entity of which the other half was Lent' (Bossy, 1985: 42). Carnival usually occurred in the build-up to Shrove Tuesday or *mardi gras*, and was intended to represent and reveal the workings of sin in order that it might be got rid of before Lent. It included massive displays of consumption (in Nantes, Shrove Tuesday was dedicated to Saint Dégobillard – Saint Vomit) and sexuality (prostitutes were essential, as were symbols of lechery). Also central to these occasions were the symbolic overturning of hierarchies, collective expressions of envy and jealousy, and a carnival figure who dominated the feast and was tried and condemned at the end of it.

Carnival may have been closely aligned to religious purposes, to a carnal indulgence leading to a purging of the body, but the body's location within the festivities displayed a celebration of the grotesque which had a tendency to go beyond the goals of the Church. As Bakhtin's (1984 [1965]) analysis of *Rabelais and His World* shows, this intensified with the waning of the Church's power in the late Middle Ages. Carnival infused bodies with grotesque imagery and encouraged behaviour which reinforced this transcendence of the individual's bodily boundaries and the breaking of body regimes. The devouring, lascivious, laughing body was marked by open orifices which facilitated a merging with other people and with the wider environment and resisted categorisation. Instead of purging the body in preparation for a regime of denial during Lent, these carnivals were associated with an intensification of the body's loss in both itself and in the fleshy bodies that were other people.

Protestant modern bodies

The volatility, sensuousness, and dynamic religious potentialities of medieval bodies have not always been adequately accounted for in those sociological studies which have attempted to draw sharp contrasts between the modern and medieval eras (e.g. Giddens, 1990). In contrast, there has long been consensus on the dynamic nature of modern forms of embodiment, specifically with regard to the classical modern project's dependence on the 'disciplined individual' able to make rational decisions on the basis of 'autonomous self-interest' (Smith, 1950 [1776]), and to the prioritisation of cognitive thought expressed through the pervasiveness of plans, projects and designs (Bauman, 1995).

In tracing the development of the early modern body, it is important to note that the origins of the modern individual have been associated with quite different periods in history. For example, sociology has customarily associated the emergence of the modern individual with the Enlightenment and the development of industrial capitalism. In opposition to this, Colin Morris and other medieval historians have identified early but highly significant signs of individualism in twelfth-century religion (Morris, 1972, 1980; but see also Bynum, 1980), while Bryan Turner has produced a sophisticated analysis of how distinct components of the modern individual emerged in distinct eras (Turner, 1991). Taken together, these analyses suggest the inherent dangers of searching for the precise origins of modern, individualised bodies. The multiple processes which underpinned these bodies were both varied, and prominent at different points in time (Elias, 1978 [1939]). Nevertheless, Protestant attempts to re-form medieval bodies produced a significant acceleration and crystallisation of those processes. First, by seeking to dislocate people from their natural, supernatural and social environments, and in prioritising cognitive belief and thought as routes to knowledge, Protestantism made linguistic symbols and narratives (which could be thought with, spoken and read) a central source of people's self-identity.

Second, the Protestant flesh was something which had to be made subordinate to these (religiously justifiable) narratives; the body had, in other words, to be controlled by the mind. Third, the ultimate inability of these narratives fully to control human emotions and passions helps us understand the enormous degree of anxiety stimulated in Protestants over those sinful aspects of their bodily selves (and the bodies of others) which threatened to become grotesque and out of control.[3] The establishment of Discipline Ordinances serves as a manifestation of this; being enforced by courts while being mocked and ignored by sections of the population (Roper, 1994). Taken together, these three factors were essential not simply for the formation of a Protestant rationalised 'spirit', as Weber (1991 [1904–5]) has suggested, but for a more general (male-dominated) bodily form which could support contractual relations based on abstract ideas (Turner, 1992b).

The autonomisation of language

First, then, Protestantism was an important factor behind the formation of modern, individualised, bodies insofar as it encouraged people to lose their bi-directional relationships with nature and with sacred forms of sociality, and placed increased priority on 'the Word' as a source of self. The urban Reformers became separated from the 'natural world' by making nature, and the sensual experience of nature, suspect, robbing nature of its previous status as a source of religious inspiration. Protestantism was also associated with an intensified attack on magic, superstition and witchcraft (Turner, 1984). The world was divested of immanence of the sacred, so that any manifestation of the supernatural was liable to be interpreted as evil. In place of this immanence of sacred meaning, the significance of mind expanded as a recipient of the Word of God (Bussy, 1985; Thomas, 1973 [1971]). Finally, as Protestant believers stood alone before God, they also became separated from effervescent forms of sociality; a separation symbolised by the increasingly hostile attitude to ritual.

These conditions meant that Protestant bodies became 'closed' to tradition. Identity, consumption and routine were no longer given by a social group or sacred milieu, but had to be decided upon *individually* through an engagement with the Word of God. As Watt (1957: 92) notes, traditional social relationships were rejected, and networks of personal relationships had to be constructed on new, more conscious, patterns. The sacred communities of the medieval Church were deconstructed, and more self-conscious, profane associations took their place. In this context, the proliferation of diaries and biographies from the sixteenth century shows how significant the manipulation of linguistic symbols was as a means of sustaining and reflecting on narratives of self-identity (Haller, 1938). The individual, narrative journeys that Protestants embarked on contributed to the discursive symbolisation of religion brought about by the Reformers. To be made pure, religion was to be symbolised by words, or discourse, and alienated from sinful bodies and institutionalised sacred referents. The sight or sound of the word was meant to provide an inspirational source for the construction and maintenance of righteous self-identities.

As Pasi Falk (1994) notes, such developments represent an 'autonomisation of language'; a process which begins when the magical ties that bind words and things together are broken, and when words become detached from bodily states. Instead of being subordinated to social relationships, then, words were meant to be experienced in Protestantism as a liberated means of expression and representation (Falk, 1994: 32). Words, of course, were important ways of representing the world long before the Reformation. Medieval hagiographies, for instance, used words to illustrate holy lives and reinforce the sanctity of the Catholic Church. Nevertheless, the Protestant focus on the 'Word of God' was fundamentally different as it prioritised the linguistic signs of the Scriptures above all other sensory knowledge. Icons, paintings and even elaborate engravings and decorations were frowned on as 'graven images': their emotive character was viewed as implying a blasphemous portrayal of God (Gombrich, 1989). Reading or listening to the Scriptures, in contrast, involved Protestants in calm, considered thought which enabled them to conceptualise their lives as religious narratives; as possessing an origin, a development, and a goal which could sustain a sense of bodily self isolated in its relationship with God.

Cognitive narratives of the self

The emphasis placed on the word can be seen as part of a Protestant attempt to control the body through cognitive narratives of the self. By making the body individual, Protestantism helped remove it from the sensual experience of effervescent sociality and turn it instead into a vehicle for thought and belief. Deprived of institutional or sensual validations of identity, it was individuals' responsibility to discipline and cognitively reflect on their own embodied identity (MacIntyre, 1981). Instead of being driven by sensual desire, Protestants sought to ensure that their bodies would fit their narratives of self. In contrast to medieval bodies, this meant that Protestants gave priority to their 'distant contact' senses. These enabled individuals, distanced from their surroundings, to visually and aurally monitor, judge and anticipate natural and social phenomena *before* making close contact with them (Falk, 1994). To smell, to taste or to touch someone or something before this monitoring, in contrast, would run the risk of spoiling the integrity of one's identity by incorporating something 'impure' into the body; a danger which still exists in relation to the maintenance of self-identity (Goffman, 1968).

It is in this context that Protestantism sought to discipline and mould the flesh by engaging it in religiously justifiable activities (the status of which varied for Lutherans and Calvinists). So, while Reformers tended to be suspicious of natural desires, feelings, the arts, and nearly all forms of entertainment, certain 'industrious pastimes' and 'rational recreations' which were scripturally justifiable were encouraged (Hill, 1966). Approved activities could include the reading of historical works, gardening and the considered discussion of business matters (Weber, 1991 [1904–5]). In addition to these actions, the personal pursuit of healthy bodies became important to many Puritans. This was associated with the fact that dirt was symbolically linked with sin, while cleanliness and sobriety were markers of righteous living.

Removing our gaze from the immediacy of Protestant bodies for a moment, we can see that this early modern concern with *health* has been extremely durable. The Protestant concern with pure bodies has been associated with post-Reformation medical regimes, while Turner (1982) has pointed to a possible link between dietary management and the development of capitalism. Indeed, the idea that Protestant sectarianism unwittingly provided capitalism with a sober, honest and industrious labour force has become a general theme in historical sociology (Hobsbawm, 1964; Thompson, 1963). Individuals were responsible for their own spiritual and moral health, and this responsibility had to be discharged through a careful monitoring and control of the body (Rosenberg, 1979; Turner, 1982: 29). Such bodily concerns did not remain at the level of the individual, however, but became incorporated into the body politic. The relationship between food, calories and lifestyle, for example, emerged as a major issue in social policy (Rowntree, 1902), and ultimately informed the central principles of scientific management (Littler, 1985; Taylor, 1964).

The body becomes an object and, indeed, a project in Protestantism by being placed under the control of the active mind. The Protestant body has to be made healthy by being purged of sensuality. In place of heraldic forms of identity in medieval society (which indicated an affective bonding with the shield), Protestantism promotes the cognitive control of the flesh as a means to a worldly source of identity.

Grotesque passions

In contrast to the medieval body, the Protestant modern body was relatively dislocated from its surroundings and attempted to draw on the discursive Word as a central source of self. It also prioritised notions of cognitive control more than its medieval antecedent as a result of its efforts to subordinate the flesh to the mind through an engagement with religious narratives. Nevertheless, this could not prevent Protestants from experiencing a high degree of concern over their fleshy passions.

Words had to guide Protestant narratives of the self, but words alone could never encompass the stirrings and 'complaints' of a flesh which remained outside the control of reflexivity yet refused to be silent. The eye, the ear and the mind were validated insofar as they could access the Word of God. Fleshiness could not be owned entirely happily by Protestants, however, as it belonged to a 'natural', profane sphere of life which had been removed from the reassurances provided by the Catholic cycle of sin, repentance, confession and absolution. Furthermore, even when Protestants were able to still the flesh, they could never be certain that the particular ways in which they achieved this were entirely justifiable. As words and language had been removed from rituals and divested of ecclesiastical guarantees, the relationship between linguistic symbols, meanings and events assumed an inevitable degree of *contingency* (a contingency which could only be fought through belief) (Campbell, 1987). Protestants helped autonomise language from the flesh, then, but insisted that this flesh be contained within a potentially unstable language; a task which is, as Elaine Scarry (1985) has demonstrated, impossible.

The flesh was in constant danger of overspilling the boundaries of religiously justifiable narrative, but these dangers were more prominent for women than they were for men. Women were seen as more superstitious, more emotional, and more lascivious than men, and this made them particularly susceptible to the temptation of evil. During the period between 1563 and 1727, women constituted between 70 and 90 per cent of witchcraft suspects in northern Europe (McLachlan and Swales, 1980). Witchcraft had been common in the medieval era, but the Church had sought to deal with it by a syncretistic embrace of magical elements into its own ritual practices (Thomas, 1973 [1971]). Protestantism's cognitive orientation deprived people of this ritual containment of witchcraft, but it continued to spring up and to challenge this orientation (Turner, 1984). The extreme dangers of witchcraft and the more diffuse problems associated with women's embodiment tended to blur into each other. As Turner (1984: 132) notes, the prevalence of 'female witchcraft' suggests that men treated women as 'pre-social creatures whose lives were more determined by "natural" (or "unnatural") passions than by culture'. This was part of the environment in which women were made into objects of extreme suspicion by Calvin and other leaders of the Reformation (Prestwich, 1985; Wendel, 1965).

This attempt by Protestants to contain the flesh within discourse stimulated something of a subject/object split for these early modern individuals. Protestants were faced with a body which was sinful, but which could not be abandoned. They 'inhabited' a physical self which could not be absolved from sin and which provided a constant reminder of a corporeal path to damnation. In this respect, the confrontation with death proved a particular source of anxiety for the Reformers as it marked the ultimate limits of language.

Protestants were keen to remove the sacramental reassurances and public rituals surrounding death characteristic of medieval Catholicism (Duffy, 1992). However, the death of fleshy, breathing bodies was not sequestrated during the post-Reformation era, and dead bodies provided constant reminders to Protestants of the wages of sin. Indeed, instead of providing reassurances to believers in the face of their departure from this world, Protestantism encouraged the individual confrontation with death while leaving people with only linguistic or textual resources to deal with this prospect (Berger, 1990 [1967]: 112). As the Reformers rejected some of the sensuous dimensions of medieval beliefs in resurrection (Richardson, 1988: 274), believers were left trapped in, and alienated from, a body which had no future in this world or the next (MacIntyre, 1967).

To summarise, Protestantism proved well suited to people who were in the process of developing individualised bodies as a result of their participation in urban exchange relations. Its focus on the word and the mind shifted the boundaries of identity and control away from medieval collectivities, and towards the private body. Protestants could no longer immerse themselves in collective, sensual rituals (Bossy, 1985; Cameron, 1991), but were left as individuals to construct narratives of selfhood through an engagement with those textual sources containing the Word of God. An engagement in shared texts remained, but these had to be interpreted individually. So, while the Protestant body was progressively 'closed off' from others (Falk, 1994), the self became more open as a space to be filled according to 'personal inspiration' (Bossy, 1985; Cameron, 1991). The Reformation did not, of course, affect all bodies in this way, nor was it the only factor which stimulated these individualising developments (Elias, 1983; Manchester, 1992). Nevertheless, the influence of the Reformers belonged to a period in which people began to stand as *individual bodies* outside those sacred communities which had previously 'eaten into' their bodily identities.

This focus on reflexive thought and the text characteristic of Protestantism has much in common with the 'disengaged reason' of the Enlightenment (Lash and Urry, 1994: 51). Seidler (1994: 25–26) has discussed how in modern societies people, especially men, have been encouraged to construct forms of selfhood based on the 'clear voice of reason', in contrast to the troublesome emotions, feelings and intuitions which race around the body. He has, furthermore, emphasised the influence of Protestantism in this process, to the point of calling modernity 'a secular form of Protestantism'. Cognitive monitoring is at the very centre of this tradition of selfhood, which refuses to allow rationality to be impeded by nature or by the body. It is also central to the 'pure relationships' discussed by Giddens (1992), and, more generally, the 'talking revolution' discussed by Lawson (1988) and Habermas's (1987, 1989) notion of the 'ideal speech' situation.

It is our view, nevertheless, that theorists such as Giddens (1990, 1991, 1992) are wrong to imagine such patterns of self-identity and forms of knowing to be of overriding centrality in contemporary Western societies. They are an important *part* of contemporary forms of knowing, but are increasingly challenged by other forms. Consequently, we have to acknowledge that the Protestant modern form of embodiment which anticipates, in certain respects, the 'official face' of modernity is also subject to contemporary challenges. Indeed, debates centred on the ending or transformation of the modern project (Baudrillard, 1983; Lyotard, 1984; Turner, 1991; Touraine, 1995) point towards a further re-formation of embodiment which involves the reappearance of the sensuality that Protestant modern bodies sought to subjugate to cognitive control.

Baroque modern bodies

The bodily forms characteristic of contemporary Western societies are not simply *post* modern, but can be seen, metaphorically, as straddling the borders between the past, present and future. The disciplined, cognitively focused bodies of early modernity persist, but are increasingly accompanied by a resurgent sensuality which has caught the attention of a number of social theorists and sociologists. Buci-Glucksmann (1994), Turner (1991, 1994), van Reijen (1992), and Maffesoli (1996), have all associated this sensuousness with the 'baroque', indicating its similarities to the intense sensuality of the baroque cultures of Counter-Reformation Catholicism (Martin, 1977; Maravall, 1986; Rovelstad, 1993).

Our use of the term 'baroque modern bodies' is intended to capture something of both this 'recovered sensuousness' *and* the continuing importance of a modern prioritisation of the cognitive. Between these two dimensions of contemporary embodiment there are all sorts of fantasies and imaginings, related to technological developments and the contemporary dominance of the eye, which point towards further re-formations of embodiment. In contrast to Maffesoli (1996) then, who tends both to overestimate the extent of this resurgent sensuality and to underestimate the conflicts endemic to contemporary Western societies, we understand contemporary bodies to be *internally differentiated, prone to all sorts of doubts and anxieties, and to be arenas of conflict.*

Cognitively oriented bodies

There is nothing 'postmodern', about the middle class's continuing preoccupation with dieting, fitness, the perils of smoking, and the dangers of 'excessive' drinking: it reflects a neo-puritan desire to subject the body to cognitive control which has developed intermittently through the modern period, and is intimately tied to Christian attitudes to the care of the body (Ehrenreich, 1990: 233–234; Turner, 1991; 118-119).[4] Neither can the emergence of a highly paid 'cognitive elite' (Hernnstein and Murray, 1994), trained in the sophisticated mental work valued in Western societies (Webster, 1995), easily be associated with the notion of postmodernity. As Meštrović (1991) has noted, the modernisation process itself can be understood as promoting and valuing cognitive factors above emotional and sensual ones, while, as Ehrenreich (1990: 233) has suggested, this tendency allows the body to become a semi-autonomous zone in which a disciplined, 'hard body' can be worked upon.

Frank Webster's analysis of contemporary theoretical accounts of the increasing importance of information-management is worth considering with regard to this cognitive emphasis. He notes a general tendency amongst social theorists to attempt to conceptualise a major shift in modern societies, in terms of both their constituting practices and their manifest goals, through notions such as Daniel Bell's 'post-industrial society', Herbert Schiller's 'advanced capitalism', Jürgen Habermas's 'decline of the public sphere', Jean Baudrillard's postmodern 'explosion of signs', and various accounts of the 'information society' (Webster, 1995). Common to all, however, is an emphasis on the growing importance of the informational content of knowledge, coexisting with a decline in the 'direct experience' of this knowledge and a spiralling self-referentiality within modern cultures (Webster, 1995: 23, 36).[5]

Changes in the construction of self and contemporary culture arising from interactions (or 'interfaces') between bodies and new (or imagined) technologies are often associated with notions of postmodernity (Poster, 1995). The notions of cyberspace, cyborgs and cyberpunk certainly point towards a significant reconfiguration of embodiment, and imply the 'fragmentation of self' central to much postmodernist discourse (Robins, 1995). While cybernetics is already an established part of modern science (Tomas, 1995), and virtual reality technologies exist and are already beginning to transform the embodied experiences of certain groups of people (Heim, 1995), such developments point towards a *possible future* more than a present reality. It is also important to note that, despite the aesthetic and sensual possibilities opened up by these phenomena, they tend to take a certain Cartesian emphasis upon cognitive factors to new extremes. Inspired by the science fiction of writers such as William Gibson (1984, 1993), such imaginings of 'new disembodied subjectivities' (Featherstone and Burrows, 1995: 12) often reflect, rather than transcend, the culture of the 'head' which concerns Meštrović (1991).

Cognitive body options

Technology and science have for some time offered people the ability to alter the appearance or contents of their flesh, but they now confront individuals with an unprecedented range of 'body options'. Body options can be defined as technologically informed methods of radically restructuring human embodiment which extend the possibilities associated with *having* a body, by a direct assault on the limitations connected to *being* a body. The flexibility and variety of these options challenges the limits of more conventional body 'projects', such as those related to health and fitness programmes (Crawford, 1987; Fussell, 1991). While earlier body projects help us explore the possibilities of living in *one* body, the options associated with virtual reality and cyber-technologies promise us the potential of exploring and even occupying bodies which differ substantially according to time and place.

Many of these developments lie in the future, others may never happen, yet scientific and medical interventions into the flesh already hold out the possibility that a body may be radically reconstructed several times over a single lifetime. Nanotechnology has the potential to provide micro machines which can be injected into our veins to repair arteries or break down cholesterol deposits (Rucker et al., 1993), while the possibility of computer chip brain implants may ultimately provide us with new languages, the ability to undertake millions of mathematical operations in a split second, and the capacity to process and present large volumes of data in a flash (Tomas, 1991). Virtual reality may shortly be able to simulate this same degree of change in a *single evening* (Benedikt, 1991; Rheingold, 1991, 1994).[6]

The social potential of body options can be explored through Jean Baudrillard's (1993a, 1993b) discussions of the 'code', a term which signifies his view of technology's theoretical ability to remove finalities, absolutes and opposites. For our purposes, the code is best seen as belonging to a *possible* future scenario in which nature has been controlled by and absorbed into socio-technological procedures and institutions. Contemporary examples of what this means can already be found in the DNA code of biology, the binary code of computers, and the digital code of television and sound recording (Baudrillard, 1993a). Each of these codes possesses the potential to make anachronistic our ability to simply copy or counterfeit objects by production or imitation. Instead the code makes possible the reproduction of 'originals'.

This reproduction of originality, operating through such technologies as artificial evolution (Kelly, 1994), could ultimately make human life entirely self-referential; nothing would be outside our control because nothing would be outside our power to reproduce (Csicsery-Ronay, 1991: 192; Robins, 1995: 144). Even death, we are told, may one day become obsolete if science acquires the ability to regenerate life through cryogenics or a single human cell (Kimbrell, 1993). In this context, the options available to people in their daily lives could make malleable those evolutionary developments which have occurred over hundreds of thousands of years, and invalidate traditional sociological conceptions of 'reversible' and 'irreversible' time (Giddens, 1984: 35). In Braudel's (1973) terms, individual time could triumph over that of the *longue durée*. The spatial and temporal flexibility of body options could also challenge the conventional parameters associated with what it means to be an individual by undermining the 'singular body'. As Ian Watt (1957) notes, the principle of individuality accepted by Enlightenment thought depended on the possibility of identifying what was unique to a person across and outside the contingencies of date and location. Developed to their logical extreme, body options may remove any such continuities. An individual may, one day, no longer resemble herself or himself from one occasion to the next in terms of size, appearance, disposition or even gender.

The notion of body options is an umbrella term which refers to a variety of future-oriented methods through which it is possible to control, re-form and transform the body. We have concentrated here on some of the most spectacular cases, but it is important to take their potentiality seriously. These options may mean, for the first time in human history, that bodies can become transformed, rather than simply re-formed, in a manner that ruptures people from much of their evolutionary inheritance. Before we get carried away by the novelty of these body options, however, we should note than even the most spectacular cases that have been explored by sociologists (e.g. Featherstone and Burrows, 1995) build on *previous* inventions in architecture, temperature control and transport which distanced people from their climate, environment and neighbours, and increased the level of control they could exert over their bodily and social environment (Sennett, 1994). It may eventually become difficult to distinguish humans from machines, but people have long transformed themselves by transforming the environment in which they live (Marx and Engels, 1970 [1846]). Furthermore, the extent of these changes would have made them appear virtually unrecognisable to their ancestors (Elias, 1978 [1939]: xi).

Sensuously oriented bodies

Just as it is important to contextualise these cognitive fantasies of, and projects for, radical transformations of embodied humanity in a broad historical context, we must bear in mind that the sensuous dimensions of humanity persist in spite of dreams of cyborgs and a life in cyberspace. In fact, in contemporary Western societies these sensual dimensions are reasserting themselves. Maffesoli's (1996) account of the contemporary re-emergence of 'Dionysian values', expressed in highly sensual forms of embodiment, for example, points in another direction, away from the 'head' and towards the 'heart'. Analogous interpretations of contemporary bodies are also evident in Ferguson's (1992) discussion of a 'recovered sensuousness' and Lash and Urry's (1994) analysis of the emergence of 'aesthetic', rather than 'cognitive', reflexivity.

This reappearance of sensuality is related to the increasing importance and changing reception of images. The sensual dimensions of baroque modern bodies, which heighten visual sensitivity and tend to *tighten* and *sensualise* the relationship which exists between people's physical selves and images in consumer culture, can be both liberating (for individuals who feel restricted by their bodies), and deeply disturbing (for those who feel overwhelmed and even threatened by the body options available) (Kroker and Kroker, 1993; Tudor, 1995). Reactions such as these highlight the continued relevance of a paradox which has long marked the development of modern bodies. While modern people have the means to exert an unprecedented amount of control over their bodies, they are living in an age which has eroded their knowledge of what bodies are and undermined their capacity to make moral choices as to how they should control them (Shilling, 1993a: 3). This paradox is hardly new. What distinguishes baroque modern bodies from their Protestant modern counterparts, however, is the tendency towards an emotional and aesthetic framing of these conditions. Rather than being a matter of mainly cognitive doubt, the baroque modern body confronts and experiences this paradox through a resurgence of fleshy passions and somatic anxieties which are intimately related to sensual imagery.

Anthropologists of the senses have associated modernity with a growing importance of the eye, and a partial diminution of the body's close contact senses (Classen, 1993; Corbin, 1986). The baroque modern acquisition of a heightened visual sensitivity, however, involves both the dominance of sight and the channelling and experiencing of other senses via the activity of looking. As Pasi Falk (1994) notes, this post-traditional eye does not simply 'see' objects, but is a 'voracious eye' that anticipates, judges and consumes in a manner that involves other senses. Our mouths may water when seeing something sweet and forbidden (James, 1990), for example, but we can also become sad or angry when watching a movie, or aroused when viewing erotica (Falk, 1993; Williams, 1989). So, baroque modern bodies may 'read' and 'decode' images, but they increasingly experience these *sensually* (McLuhan, 1964; Ong, 1977, 1982; Meyrowitz, 1985).

This visual sensitivity has its commercial counterpart in the sensual imagery circulating in consumer culture. As Scott Lash and John Urry (1994) suggest, designers, marketing experts and image consultants have all been significant in reinforcing and exploiting this sense of sight. Vance Packard's (1981 [1957]) study of the advertising industry, for example, illustrates how advertisers promoted visions of the 'good life' to consumers who were seen as bundles of day dreams and yearnings particularly sensitive to image-based communication. These 'sensual images' have been produced and circulated at an ever faster rate since the Second World War and have come to pervade all aspects of our lives (Virilio, 1994). The multiplication and acceleration of sensual imagery is associated with advances in video and satellite technology (Spigel, 1992), and the growth of a television culture in which a small 'black box' can now be described as a 'Leading Object' in consumer culture (Silverstone, 1994: 87; Lefèbvre, 1984).

Psychologists have suggested that people are initiated into this tactile form of sight early in infancy and especially through the medium of television (Winnick and Winnick, 1979; Hodge and Tripp, 1986). Visual sensitivity can increase the influence of images of the 'body beautiful' which look good partly because they *feel* good. 'Healthy' and 'ill' bodies, for example, may remain important as ideas, but they are also attached to 'feel good' or 'feel bad' factors derived from *appearance* (Wolf, 1990). The consequences of this become much more significant as technologically informed body options weaken the boundaries which previously separated flesh and image. As this happens, people are more able to engage in what we might refer to as 'imaging their bodies': reconstructing their appearances and experiences in line with images in consumer culture. It is this imaging of the body that provides metaphorical support to the idea of the body as a 'screen' on which signs flicker, register and circulate (Baudrillard, 1983: 12; Featherstone, 1991). The body may never become an extension of network television, as Baudrillard suggests in his more ironic and playful moments, but images have become a significant source of the embodied self (Rojek and Turner, 1993).

The body images we see in consumer culture, then, appeal because they are made sensual. As Walter Ong argues, part of the reason for this is that these images are accompanied by voices, plots and narratives which seek to seduce and can be seen as part of a 'new collective culture' (Ong, 1971, 1982). This visual culture is still permeated by long-standing social distinctions. Images of black and white peoples tend to be permeated by different sensual charges (Dyer, 1986; Lyman, 1990), for example, while it remains easier for men than women to cultivate a visual sensuality at a time when women often remain the *object* of sensual looks (Berger, 1972). Nevertheless, the general effects of this culture differ from the individual-ising tendencies of print (Silverstone, 1994), as our bodies are *(re)opened* to collective influences. Baroque modern bodies differ, in this respect, from their early modern Protestant antecedents in that fast-changing 'images of self' have rivalled stabilising 'narratives of the self' as an important source of embodied identity.

Dangerous crossings

The full development of the baroque modern body remains a future possibility. Nevertheless, people's visual sensitivity, and their existing ability to change their bodies, is already creating greater space in their identities for the influence of collective factors. The consequences of this are difficult to specify with any precision. Unlike the 'past-oriented openness' evident in traditional societies (where people's identities were 'filled up' with rites and customs: Falk, 1994), baroque modern bodies are immersed in a fast-changing world of images which tends to be future oriented. That is, these images tend to speak to what people could become and refer mainly negatively to what they used to be. Nevertheless, this future-orientation has itself prompted very different reactions.

On the broadly positive side, people have used body options and sensual imagery to extend the possibilities of who they are, and sometimes to make themselves anew. Sexual radicals have sought to construct appearances and 'outlaw bodies' which escape the restrictive framings of heterosexual aesthetics and the conventional use of binary oppositions (Bell, 1993; Kroker and Kroker, 1993). Similarly, the potential of electronic communication allows people to engage in 'dangerous crossings' (Butler, 1993), to 'try out' new sexualiües in a 'game of masks' unconstrained by the limitations of convention (Wiley, 1995: 157; Russo, 1994). Combining technology with a visual sensitivity can, then, provide very real benefits. The flexibility and sensuality of baroque bodies may also predispose certain people toward contingent and creative 'tribal' forms of association (Maffesoli, 1996). However, this immersion in the world of images causes a number of general problems which can alienate people from both themselves and others.

On the negative side, image-directed, technologically informed body options can easily implicate people in the signifying practices of others (Pfohl, 1993). Images of the 'perfect female flesh', for example, continue to exert a massive influence over women (Wolf, 1990). While the gains of feminism and identity politics may have helped some women take advantage of the opportunity to develop new and more independent bodily selves, the influence of sensual images of the 'ideal body' is a reason why women embark on major programmes of cosmetic surgery. Furthermore, the quantity and velocity of choices body options make available to people threatens to leave individuals uncomfortable and uneasy, as well as dissatisfied, with the choices that face them and the choices they have made (Simmel, 1968). This does much to explain the contemporary sense of nostalgia evident in people who seek to 'lose their inhibitions' and express their 'natural feelings' as a way of escaping from a body they can no longer feel at home in (Featherstone, 1995a; Turner, 1987).

Taken to their extreme, it has been suggested that body options can stimulate a loss of 'basic trust' or 'ontological security' (Berger, 1990 [1967]; Giddens, 1991: 45–47) which can lead to the experience of 'paranoid horrors' (Tudor, 1995) and 'body panics' (Kroker et al., 1989). This is because the flexibility of body options disrupts conventional meanings associated with the flesh and can make the body internally nomadic – cut free from a stabilising centre (Zukin, 1988, 1990, 1992). So a reaction against certain forms of body options has become part of the conservative 'will to purity' in the treatment, punishment and categorisation of bodies (Kroker and Kroker, 1993). This consists of a repressive and potentially violent response to those who have transgressed conventional norms which Mary Douglas has suggested is based partly on a fear of the dissolution of body boundaries (Douglas, 1966, 1970).

More broadly, the spiralling of these body options casts further doubt upon the roles of both cognition and corporeality in what it means to be a human being. Baudrillard (1993b: 52), for example, notes how the cognitively focused interactions between people and technologies can make a person into a 'physical cripple', but also a 'mental cripple'. He may be exaggerating to say that the anthropological question 'Am I a man or a machine?' no longer has an answer (Baudrillard, 1993b: 57), but it is clear that such fundamental anthropological questions no longer have taken-for-granted 'answers'. This returns us to our earlier point about the aesthetic and emotional framing of the paradox which results when our ability to transform the body undermines our knowledge of what bodies are and how we should develop them. This paradox is not simply cognitive, then, but stimulates a sensual equivalent which travels through the senses and emotions and is manifest in feelings of desire, unease and even fear which lack an immediately corresponding object (Beck, 1992). Without such an object, this sensuality is turned both outward, to the bodies of others, and inwards to the embodied self.

Given these insecurities and instabilities about what the body is, it should perhaps come as no great surprise to learn that social theory is sprinkled with references to the 'death of the body' (in addition to the much heralded 'death of the subject' and 'death of the author') (Barthes, 1977b; Baudrillard, 1983). The prevalence and possibilities of body options has made the task of hanging onto a stable bodily referent increasingly difficult, which has given rise to this idea of the modern body's demise. This is exacerbated by the contemporary sequestration of actual death; something which robs people of regular encounters with that most intransigent of bodily referents (Mellor and Shilling, 1993), and encourages the concept of 'death' to be used as a flexible metaphor. Furthermore, as 'death' comes to assume the status of an image-laden metaphor used to describe certain aspects of the living body, such as its instability or its social or existential isolation (Kroker and Kroker, 1993), it is hardly surprising if our impressions of life become saturated with macabre imagery (Bossy, 1985).

This development contributes to a banalisation of contemporary culture, as humans begin to lose contact with something that has always been an essential part of themselves. The contemplation of actual death used to be considered an opportunity for self-revelation, a moment of contact with the sacred (Bataille, 1992 [1973]), but modern culture seeks to tame death by turning it into an image (Ariès, 1974). Yet it cannot rid this image of an uneasiness and a feeling that something is fundamentally wrong, out of place. As Baudrillard (1993a: 147) argues, 'death ceases to be the Grim Reaper', and becomes a much more general and diffuse 'anguish concerning death':

Pursued and censored everywhere, death springs up everywhere again. No longer as apocalyptic folklore, such as might have haunted the living imagination in certain epochs; but voided precisely of any imaginary substance, it passes into the most banal reality. (Baudrillard, 1993a: 185)

Similarly, the notion of 'evil' is banished from many areas of contemporary culture, but continues to 'bubble up' amidst the banality of everyday life (Baudrillard, 1993b: 81).

To summarise, baroque modern body options may well prove disruptive and disturbing to the conventional modern notion that humans possess *one self* which corresponds to *one body*. Their potential to alter the body rapidly, and to weaken the stability of any fixed habitus, also serves to increase the importance of individual-time to an understanding of modern bodies. The human potential to 'image the body' creates a space in which individuals are *potentially* able to construct and express their identities outside of an 'iron cage' (Tester, 1995a: 158–159), but can be also co-opted by consumer culture and may well create a degree of self-referentiality which stimulates unease and anxiety. Baroque modern bodies are still emerging and remain, at least in part, a future possibility. Bodies can be more or less baroque, then, and continue to exist alongside more classically modern forms of embodiment. Furthermore, in the 'two-thirds/one-third' societies that have emerged within the 'affluent West', issues of poverty, homelessness and basic civil rights are likely to remain much more visible for those struggling with the necessities of survival both in and outside of our 'brave new' global cities (Sassen, 1991).

Knowing bodies

The forms of embodiment we have described in this chapter illustrate how the conditions associated with humans both *being* and *having* bodies change over time. Baroque modern, Protestant modern, and medieval bodies are characterised by quite different organisations and hierarchies of the senses, for example, and these are related to contrasting ways of representing and gaining knowledge about the world. But what does all this add up to? What are the consequences of these forms of embodiment for how humans associate together, intervene in, and seek to organise their world? We analyse the broader religious, cultural and social environments that both shaped and were supported by these bodily forms in subsequent chapters. In the remainder of this chapter, we want to focus on how these bodies were involved in different ways of gaining knowledge about themselves and their worlds. This returns us to one of the themes that has been central to this chapter: the potential of linguistic symbols to orient people towards the world.

Each of the bodily types we examine was, as Elias (1991) points out, formed *after* the evolutionary lift-off provided by symbol emancipation. However, successive developments in the use of symbols (which could be thought with, spoken, written and read) reinforce our picture of how bodily identities were constructed for medieval, Protestant and baroque modern persons, and tell us much about how and why humans related to each other and to their surroundings in different ways. The terms carnal knowing and cognitive apprehension were used in Chapter 1 as a way of referring to different sensory ways of gaining knowledge about the world. We employ them here in order to develop our analysis of the varying relationships that exist between bodies, symbols and knowledge. Carnal knowledge and cognitive apprehension can coexist and intermingle, something which becomes especially clear in the case of baroque modern bodies, but their relative prominence varies across historical and cultural contexts, as we can see with regard to different forms of (auto)biography.

Hagiography

Carnal knowing refers to a form of gaining information about the world which is thoroughly embodied and connected to people's senses and sensualities. It is tied to specific social locations (Miles, 1992: 9), highlights the fusion that exists between experience and awareness, and reminds us of the mind's location within a fleshy body which is itself affected by material conditions and social relationships (Johnson, 1987). The 'open body' of medieval times tended to be immersed in, rather than dislocated from, its natural, social and supernatural environments, and this is reflected in its gaining of knowledge. Of course, there were different degrees of carnal knowing, and the Biblical interpretations of a learned clerical elite contained strong elements of cognitive apprehension, demonstrating that 'carnality' was not the only means of knowing the world in the medieval era. Nevertheless, women mystics, for example, pursued states of religious ecstasy through their bodies rather than through the cognitive interpretation of texts (Lerner, 1993: 66). More generally, the important point is not that linguistic symbols were made redundant in carnal knowing but that they were contained within wider contexts.

The consequences of carnal knowledge for the potential of linguistic symbols to orient people to the world can be clarified by looking at hagiographies. Hagiographies (biographies of saints) can be distinguished from modern biographies in the sense that they were not concerned with individualising their subjects in relation to various and changing social conditions, but with presenting them as purified Christians who had achieved sanctity (Head, 1990; Stauffer, 1930; Whittemore, 1988). Hagiographies were primarily resources used to promote the continuation of the Church and religiously approved forms of living. It is in this sense that Donald Stauffer judges biography as an art to be 'static' in the Middle Ages, and as something whose comparatively solid and unchanging characteristics served as a background 'for the diversity and richness of the biographies written in England after the Renaissance' (Stauffer, 1930).

Hagiographical texts were considered extremely important in the medieval era, but the status of discourse within them was subordinated to wider religious goals. It is in this context that hagiographies reflect an era of carnal knowing by appealing to a form of understanding dependent on a sensory and sensual contact with the sacred. This is why hagiographies make little sense as 'real life' representations to us now; they were reliant on a more general context in which words were surrounded by rituals which provided contact with the sacred through the experience of liminality (van Gennep, 1960). As Thomas (1973 [1971]: 37) notes, what stood out was 'the magical notion that the mere pronunciation of words in a ritual manner could effect a change in the character of material objects'. The Eucharistic eating of the body of Christ, for example, took place in a ritual context where words acted to help turn bread and wine into the flesh and blood of Christ (Bynum, 1987). Language was not self-referential, then, but provided people with a route to the sacred and the experience of sacrifice.

The hagiographical depiction of saints provides an immediate indication of the place of linguistic symbols in these texts, and the carnal form of knowledge presupposed by them. Hagiographies emphasised the holy dimensions of saints' corporeality; a corporeality that received sacred meaning through effervescent forms of religious sociality. The most extreme physical tortures could be withstood given the grace of God, and hagiographies contain stories of how saints were able to levitate, protect entire communities from physical disaster (Hamilton, 1986), and undergo lengthy periods of fasting (Bynum, 1987, 1991). In the story of Lidwina of Sciedam (who died in 1433), for instance, three-month-long fasts were accompanied by the loss of *sweet smelling* bits of skin, bone and entrails (Bynum, 1987: 124). Other hagiographies detail the holy resistance of Saint Lucy, who became immobile and could not be moved even by a thousand men, and the spontaneous rejuvenation of Saint Agatha's mutilated body (Burke, 1983). Saint George was eventually burnt to death, but not before his holy body had resisted poisoning, boiling oil, and being tortured on a wheel (Whittemore, 1988). In each of these examples, the bodies of saints assume an 'extra-discursive' quality as a result of their holy powers and 'magical' qualities (Thomas, 1973 [1971]: 29–57).

The emphasis on the physical body and the senses prominent in so many of these accounts has a much wider relevance because it meant that there was no need and little possibility for autobiography to serve as a constructor of self-identity. Literacy rates were low and one gains an account of medieval life much more by examining how life-styles were directly inscribed upon the body, than by looking at written accounts of individuals (Camporesi, 1988). As Peter Brown has pointed out (1988: 442) 'The pain of Christian asceticism consisted in the fact that the present human person was an unfinished block, designed to be cut into the form of an awesome model. The body required the deep chisel-bites of permanent renunciation, if the Christian was to take on the lineaments of the risen Christ.'

These medieval biographies are the product of a time in which bodily identities and the world are explored within the parameters of ritual structures and transpersonal meaning systems. They are associated with open bodies and carnal ways of relating to the world in which human physicality and the senses are embraced as an integral component of knowing oneself and one's world. In the case of medieval persons, words filled the profane world of everyday life, but were often at their most significant in terms of their status as things which facilitated contact with the sacred. They were often unintelligible (the language of the Church was Latin) but were also seen as having powers to act on the physical world (as in spells). Far from being an autonomous means of representing the world, then, words were often seen saturated with extra-discursive significance. In contrast to modern autobiography, where language is perceived as providing a key to the self, it is interesting to note the widespread suspicion with which discourse was treated in the medieval period outside of ritual context which provided it with a legitimate purpose (Duby, 1988: 306).

Biography

While carnal knowing tended to flow from medieval bodies, there was a gradual shift in the post-Reformation world to a position whereby the prominence of the word meant that people tended to orient themselves to the world through cognitive apprehension. This was not something which could be attributed exclusively to the Reformers, but they did much to accelerate the processes leading to this change. Cognitive apprehension is endemic to the Protestant focus on the text as a source of religious truth and is intimately linked to the Enlightenment's stress on the acquisition of scientific knowledge through reason and rationality.

While carnal knowing embraces the *body* as an integral element of adopting a relationship to oneself and one's world, cognitive apprehension rejects the body and autonomises the linguistic symbol. Cognitive apprehension assumes that valid knowledge is gained from mental activity freed from the bodily prejudices of emotions, and considers the mind and body to be fundamentally separate entities. It is the mind, cognition and symbols that can be thought with, that should serve to motivate action, and that mark off humans as 'noble' and autonomous creatures. Somewhat ironically, cognitive apprehension presupposes that one can increase knowledge only by losing a degree of sensory and sensual contact with that knowledge.

Cognitive apprehension is evident in those Protestant diaries and biographies which balanced an individual's spiritual books and lent a narrative coherence to their lives. It has been said that in New England 'almost every literate Puritan kept some sort of journal' (Watt, 1957: 75). Haller (1938: 37) suggests that the diary, the forerunner of the autobiography, was the Puritan's confessional where fear and weaknesses found in the heart could be offered to God in texts. Such an emphasis on the constitution of the self through narrative was not entirely alien to Catholicism, and the roots of such an autobiographical strategy can be traced to Saint Augustine's *Confessions* (Lerner, 1993: 47; Duby, 1988).[7] In Protestantism, however, this textual orientation became both widespread and normative. Diaries provided a way for Protestants to record their noble and baser deeds (Stauffer, 1930), biographies provided examples of lives lived properly (Whittemore, 1988), while the Reformers' individualised confrontation with death was eventually supported by 'consolation literature' (Douglas, 1977). As Haller (1938: 98) notes, a mass of biographical writings rapidly accumulated as the Puritan movement progressed, often explicitly encouraging others to record the good and bad things that had happened during the day, a 'daily posting of one's accounts with God', in order to find order and comfort in these events. According to Watts (1957: 49), by far the greatest category of books published in the eighteenth century was that of religious books, with Bunyan's *The Pilgrim's Progress* going through 160 editions before 1792, while at least ten devotional manuals had over thirty editions during the eighteenth century.[8]

The shift from carnal knowing to cognitive apprehension is usually said to result in an increase in knowledge, rationality, and the ability to control the environment. It is no accident that the autonomisation of language as a means of representation from the Renaissance through to the Enlightenment was associated with a massive growth in knowledge about science and society (Manchester, 1992). However, the processes involved in this shift were not unambiguously emancipatory. Focusing on 'the word' enabled people to become reflexively aware of their embodied selves and, indeed, gave rise to thoroughly modern forms of artistic expression such as the novel which broke 'with the earlier literary tradition of using timeless stories to mirror the unchanging moral verities', subordinating plot to the pattern of the autobiographical memoir, and linking truth to individual experience (Watt, 1957: 15–22).[9] For Protestants, though, this reflexivity was accompanied by several problems.

To begin with, the dominance of the word led to the body being viewed with suspicion, disgust and even fear. Partly because the ritual structures which allowed the body to become a route to transcendence had been done away with, the body became almost exclusively a vessel of sin which needed controlling. Many Protestants treated their own and other people's bodies as objects to be tamed and trained, but were confronted sooner or later with the realisation that the body could not be controlled fully by the mind (Campbell, 1987). Furthermore, the dominance of the word had its own problems. Words abounded but they had to be read with an appropriate depth of belief or they could mislead. This contingency of meaning (a contingency which postmodern theorists have mistakenly associated with recent times) informs Campbell's (1987) excellent analysis of the Protestant immersion in melancholy and despair that was stimulated by a search for divine inspiration via the Scriptures.[10] There was always the possibility that the meaning Protestants derived from words could be both misleading and infused with fantasy knowledge. Instead of providing direct contact with the sacred, words outside a ritual context came for Protestants to assume a contingent relation with the extra-human world.

Cognitive knowledge was not simply apprehended, then, but came coated in a layer of doubt derived from the evacuation of the supernatural from daily life. As Zygmunt Bauman argues (1995: 85–86), Protestants may have sought to strip the world of its fleshy and sacred contents, but they were left with the difficult problem of constructing their identity in this 'desert'. As a result, the importance of autobiographical work for many Protestants was matched by the difficulties associated with undertaking this work success-fully or with any great conviction as to its outcome (Campbell, 1987). The biography the individual held in mind was only one of many that could be constructed and the subjective recognition of this caused Protestants con-siderable doubt and anxiety. The establishment of a 'united' self required constant vigilance and continual work. Individuals had to continually integrate events that occurred in the external world, and sort them into the ongoing cognitive 'story' about the self. As Charles Taylor (1989) puts it, 'in order to have a sense of who we are, we have to have a notion of how we have become, and of where we are going'. This was made even harder for Protestants who existed through a sinful act, who were often unable to tell with any certainty whether their life's route was valid, who were unable to validate positively most of their fleshy passions and emotions, and who may very well already have been damned (Weber, 1991 [1904–5]).

Imaging words

Apprehending the world through cognitive, symbol-oriented thought con-tinues to occupy a position of immense importance in many sectors of the contemporary Western world. However, Protestantism was not simply associated with the promotion of cognition, but acted as its *defence* against the sensual forms of knowledge prevalent in the medieval era. In this respect, the decline of Protestantism has paved the way for a resurgence of fleshy means of knowing about the self and the world. This is not a simple reproduction of medieval forms of knowing, though it does show the affinity that certain modern developments have with their historical antecedents, but represents a more 'controlled' and mediated encounter with the senses through a heightened visual sensitivity.

The decline of Protestantism, and the gradual loss of faith in universal rationality, can be associated with a shrinkage in the power of discourse and a rise in the importance of images. It was not just that the word occupied a contingent relationship with the sacred, but that language couldn't even cope with the socio-natural world. As Scarry (1994) argues, the structure of language may be similar to the structure of life in certain ways but these are *ontologically distinct* phenomena. Furthermore, it is extremely difficult to impart meaning to experiences using a language that has become increasingly self-referential; which many suggest contains meaning only insofar as signs refer and relate to other signs. Images (which are themselves saturated with sensory and sensual information) become more important conveyors of meaning. These images inform the body options we discussed earlier in this chapter, and while the increasing use of sensuous images to portray and interpret life does not represent a simple return to carnal knowledge, it does herald a resurgence of sensual intimation within the human body.

The changing representational power of the word and the image is illustrated by the work of Marguerite Duras. Through film, drama and writing, Duras seeks to convey emotional, embodied experiences which can never be fully translated into representational forms. Loss, love and death are evoked, rather than discursively elaborated upon, through the style of writing employed, through the deliberate incorporation of absences, and through a refusal to construct her work around conventional oppositions (Duras, 1985, 1986). Duras's work has been read by Julia Kristeva as a 'commentary' on the crisis of representation that has followed such twentieth-century horrors as the Holocaust and Stalinism (Lechte, 1990), but it also seeks to represent life by tapping into some of those very bodily experiences which Protestant biography sought to deny, control and eradicate (Hill, 1993).

This same phenomenon is also reflected in what is rapidly developing as the flipside of autobiographical narratives: the writing of lives *through* or *on* bodies. Pasi Falk (1995) has highlighted some of the ways that this can occur by analysing permanent and temporary transformations. If the contemporary importance of imaging the body continues to increase, the 'autobiographical stars' of the future may not produce paper texts, but may write on their bodies. As Myers's (1992) and Vale and Juno's (1989) studies of 'modern primitive' tattooists and body piercers suggest, we may be entering an age in which the flesh and the symbol have once again joined forces as equal partners. Cognitive narratives may be all too fragile and subject to revision, but marking the flesh can potentially provide a design of the self which is more enduring and stable precisely because it draws for its support on a far wider range of senses and sensualities.

Knowing and civilising

The bodily variations we have examined in this chapter help us to understand the analytically distinct orientations to the world which can be associated with different forms of embodiment. Here it is worth engaging with Norbert Elias's (1978 [1939]; 1991) observation that the speed with which experience is translated into concepts and actions varies historically. Elias argues that in contrast to the volatility of medieval persons, generations from later eras developed self-controls manifest in 'rational thought' which interposed themselves between 'spontaneous and emotional impulses, on the one hand, and the skeletal muscles, on the other', and allowed for the deferral of action (Elias, 1978 [1939]: 257; 1983: 243). Self-control, foresight and cognitive reflexivity all vary between forms of embodiment. More specifically, the power of 'rational thought' to motivate is related to the importance of linguistic symbols (that can be spoken, thought with and written down) and the degree to which people are able to *restrain* other sensual forms of motivation.

This relation between linguistic symbols and human senses does not entail a direct correspondence between the importance of 'the word' and the consequences of physical restraint. As the administration of the Holocaust illustrates only too well, actions motivated by cognitive thought and planning can lead to bloodshed on a larger scale, and more systematic basis, than those propelled by rage, jealousy and emotional terror (Bauman, 1989). Nevertheless, the prominence and decline of linguistic symbols can tell us much about how particular forms of embodiment are oriented toward their social environments. Medieval bodies were frequently structured through an engagement with Catholicism which subordinated cultural ideas to religious experiences. Protestantism stimulated an explosion of the cultural sphere by emphasising the importance of texts at a time when the printing press was enabling these ideas to spread to a larger populace (Scribner et al., 1994). Having traced the main contours of these bodies, and their baroque modern successors, it is now time to examine how these religious, cultural and social environments were shaped by, and served to reshape, these forms of embodiment.

Notes

1. While being attentive to their differences, Maffesoli (1996: 42) draws an analogy between the villages, hamlets, communes and cantons of the medieval era, and the neighbourhoods, ghettos, parishes and tribes of the late modern metropolis.

2. This was based on an ontology of the inseparability of the soul and flesh – the two elements represented by the Hebrew words *nepesh* and *basar*, and was central to theological accounts of Christ's Incarnation and Resurrection and the sacramental character of communion.

3. This is particularly important in understanding the concern with which women's bodies were viewed. Immersed as they were in cycles of blood and birth, women had to be both protected from their own passions and prevented from inflaming the passions of men. Protestantism may have relieved women from some of the burdens of kinship relations, but it could also place even stricter confinements on their physical movements and legal status (Stone, 1977).

4. On this issue, Turner (1991: 118) suggests that the contrast between Catholic and Protestant approaches to health and diet was 'insignificant'. This view tends to underestimate the immense changes in forms of religious life apparent in the development of the Protestant Reformation (Chatellier, 1989; Delumeau, 1987; Elton, 1963).

5. The implicit marginalisation of embodied experience endemic to this informationally based self-referentiality is even evident with regard to warfare. As Frank Barnaby (1986: 2) notes, direct human intervention is no longer necessary, and wars could now be fought entirely with machines and computerised missiles (Webster, 1995: 54).

6. Linked up to others via a computer, stimulated by bodysuit responses connected to electronic graphics, one could slip into a 'virtual suit' to do battle as a Borg chasing the

Starship Enterprise before lunch, experience the thrill of being a champion ballroom dancer after dinner, and end up enjoying as Marilyn Monroe a quiet drink with Fidel Castro before retiring to bed.

7. As Duby (1988: 540–541) notes, the autobiographical narrative 'did not spring fully formed from the head of the now legitimate individual hero. It emerged gradually from other forms of narrative which centred on the individual in society. Authors felt an irresistible urge to put in a word for themselves, to indicate their presence at the side of the road when history passed, to remark on events, to place before the eye of God the example of their own tribulations. In other words, egocentric narrative sprang sometimes from the model of Augustinian confession, sometimes from the concern of prudent administrators to remind themselves and their families of the lessons of everyday experience, and sometimes from the habit of recording memorable events in conveniently accessible form.'

8. Haller (1938: 102–103) notes that these texts were always supplemented by a strong oral tradition, so that if a 'saint' had failed to write an autobiography, his deeds were often conveyed for many years through legend, reminiscence and anecdote. Nevertheless, Haller also details the vast numbers of spiritual autobiographies which became an important part of Protestant religious experience and were often collected in anthologies such as Samuel Clarke's *The Marrow of Ecclesiastical Historie, contained in the Lives of the Fathers, and other Learned Men, and Famous Divines, which have Flourished in the Church since Christ's Time, to this present Age.*

9. According to Watt (1957: 14), 'Defoe and Richardson are the first great writers of our literature who did not take their plots from mythology, history, legend or previous literature . . . from the Renaissance onwards, there was a growing tendency for individual experience to replace collective tradition as the ultimate arbiter of reality; and this transition would seem to constitute an important part of the general cultural background to the rise of the novel.'

10. The construction of meaning through such biographical narratives is still evident in contemporary discussions of autobiography which continue this early modern search for meaning through a text (Erben, 1993). For a further discussion see Shilling and Mellor (1994).

3

VOLATILE BODIES, SACRED COMMUNITIES

In the previous chapter we began examining the distinctive corporeal dimensions of modernity by identifying several forms of embodiment, and by looking at the contrasting ways in which these encouraged people to relate to their environments. We now focus on those wider patterns of sociality, and the relationship of these patterns to the sacred, that are associated with the formation and re-formation of these bodies. Before analysing how Protestants sought to redefine the structure and meaning of what constituted a human community, and thus helped establish the conditions conducive to the emergence of early modern bodies, we concentrate on how Catholic communities consolidated quite distinct forms of bodily being and knowing in the medieval era.

Medieval life was, in a number of ways, sensorially different from modern life. Surrounded by the noise of today's cities, it is hard to imagine the stark contrast between silence and sound that frequently characterised the medieval era (Huizinga, 1995 [1954]:10; Touraine, 1995: 91; Tester, 1995a: 91). More generally, this era was marked not only by the repetitious actions involved in rural and city life, but also by social spaces filled with violent passions, stark opposites and dramatic contrasts (Huizinga, 1995 [1954]:10; Elias, 1978 [1939]). The recurring cycles of the daily world of work were overlaid culturally by the presence of angels and demons, and by divine interventions in the everyday lives of persons (Thomas, 1973 [1971]; Kay and Rubin, 1994). The medieval world could be an enchanted and enchanting place to live in, if a dangerous and unpredictable one. The sacred, which Bataille (1992 [1973]: 52) refers to as a 'prodigious effervescence of life', was immanent within significant sections of everyday life and within the bodies of persons (Bossy, 1985).

The Church did not stand apart from these conditions, but addressed the bodily immersion in the natural, social and supernatural worlds of the medieval era by seeking to *harness* these somatic experiences to the development of its own, sacred, communities. This was quite different from the dominant strategy later employed by Protestants, and can be seen in the Church's syncretistic embrace of grotesque bodies. Instead of trying to eradicate the manifestations of grotesque bodies that appeared resistant to control and hierarchy (Bakhtin, 1984 [1965]), ecclesiastical authorities directed them towards the effervescent experience of religious issues through the Church's organisation of carnival (Bossy, 1985). Such carnivals, like the

Catholic religion in general and the Eucharistic sacrifice at the heart of its ritual and identity, took place on the basis of an embodied consumption of the non-individuating intimacy of the sacred (Bataille, 1992 [1973]: 55–57). The Church was prepared to accept this corporeal fluidity and intimacy as long as it thought it could be used for religious purposes; the dominant view was that meaning was to be found *through* the body, not in spite of it (Bynum, 1987; Mellor, 1991).

In this chapter, we examine a Catholic re-formation of medieval bodies which involved an incorporation of this physicality into a collective, sacred community. The Church's rituals and dogma, which developed within a plurality of magical, cultural and political contexts, helped *enchant* the natural and social world. In so doing, it promoted, in Durkheim's terms, a *collective* effervescence by binding individuals through their bodies into the ritual and dogmatic systems of Catholicism. What medieval persons understood to be the truth of God in Christ was not just a *message*, then, but an *embodiment*: the Church was the Incarnation of Christ continuing in sacramental form, and individuals were united with this Incarnate God through their incorporation into this religious body (Martin, 1980: 74).

Throughout this chapter we shall explore how such meaning was sought and maintained, concentrating especially on the tension between the volatility of bodies and the binding of individuals into sacred communities. Initially, we make a few methodological points about the character and importance of the Church's influence. Following this, we develop the notion of Catholic communities, and their relationship with human embodiment, by discussing how Catholicism constituted a sacred *eating* community. We then examine the broad conditions through which particular communities developed, before identifying their potential to shape medieval bodies and carnal ways of knowing the self and the world. The concluding sections point to those wider political and cultural conditions conducive to the profanation of much that Catholicism had sacralised. The Catholic Church may have been able to engage and structure people's sensory means of acquiring knowledge, yet these engagements became ever more precarious with the emergence of early modern forms of embodiment able to investigate and symbolise the world in a more sophisticated, cognitive manner. Catholicism may have developed partly through a forceful engagement with people's sensuality, yet it was eventually unable to contain the flux and change which is an essential characteristic of human embodiment.

Syncretism and sociality

The Catholic Church was a key social and cultural power during the medieval age. It occupied this position as a result of its relationship with other social forces, and because of its flexibility in incorporating elements of these forces into its own 'world view' and mode of operation. These comments should not be interpreted as an overestimation of the cohesion and cultural consistency of the era, but serve simply to highlight our focus on how the Church exerted its influence in a broader context marked frequently by social fracture and fragmentation.

Western studies of medieval life have often been based on unwarranted assumptions about the extent of socio-cultural coherence and consistency. Such assumptions have, however, been challenged. Daniel Bell (1980: 329) for example, has criticised the assumption that society is some kind of 'organic whole'. Margaret Archer (1988: 3) makes a similar criticism with regard to culture. She notes that a number of highly influential anthropological and social approaches have operated on a mistaken 'myth of cultural integration'. In opposition to this view, Archer (1988: 9) emphasises that 'pluralism is common, inconsistency is pervasive and syncretism is general practice', while Bell (1980: 329) makes the related point that, at most times, 'societies are radically disjunctive'.

We can see much of this pluralism, syncretism and volatility in the Catholic Church's operation within medieval society. This makes it important to be cautious about the romanticised image of medieval religion and society which has traditionally marked sociology (Nisbet, 1993 [1966]; Turner, 1987, 1992a; Touraine, 1995). The medieval period was no 'Golden Age' of religion, in which the Church exercised the hegemonic integrating function suggested by many secularisation theorists (who then go on to account for its deconstruction in the modern period) (Martin, 1966). As Turner (1992b) points out, the influence of the Church varied between different social classes and geographical regions.[1] On the other hand, recognising that the medieval period was marked by greater pluralism than has often been imagined should not lead to the assumption that the importance of the Church has been exaggerated but to the view that its nature has been misunderstood.

The Church was significant not simply because of its power and scope, but because of its openness to external relationships and because of the favourable 'tension balances' (Elias, 1983) characteristic of wider society. In contrast to Berger's (1990 [1967]) view of a medieval 'sacred canopy', which provided an all-embracing system of meaning, we should recognise the interactions between the sacred communities of Catholicism and other components of medieval life. While even Karl Marx suggested that Catholicism was *the* determining power during the Middle Ages (Marx, 1954 [1867]: 86 fn), this judgement was accompanied by the recognition that those Catholic communities which helped re-form medieval physicality were supported by other relationships. As Georges Duby (1977) has noted, the spiritual domination the Church wished to extend over the laity coexisted with the *economic* domination of lords over their labourers and the *political* domination of warriors over the unarmed. These conditions are obviously significant for the shaping of embodiment, even if the ideology of organic unity that tended to dominate this period (which saw the social body as a natural, interdependent whole, despite its many members) gave the Church a greater role than it might otherwise have occupied.

This notion of 'organic unity' does not rule out pluralism and diversity, for the two are intimately related in the medieval era. As Emile Durkheim (1977 [1938]: 25) noted, the Catholic Church had, for centuries, attempted to operate a 'one-sided syncretism' which drew alternative accounts of reality, meaning and experience into its own systems of practice and belief (Archer, 1988: 200). This syncretism may not always have been as 'one-sided' as the Church hoped, but its attempt to engage with medieval life draws our attention to the particular form of embodiment which made it possible, and which also facilitated the emergence of particular notions of community.

The strong 'sense-contact' with knowledge and meaning which existed as a result of people's immersion in social, natural and supernatural worlds of the time, was drawn on by the Catholic Church. Church authorities sought to place people 'in touch' with religious meaning by tying them to the sacred through the managing power of the Church. For this reason, it makes sense to talk about Catholicism as an embodied 'community'. If, as Maffesoli (1993b: 10) suggests, 'what is self-evident' creates community, then the Church's sacralisation of embodiment is simultaneously the creation of a sacred, communal expression of sociality. Individuals are not bound together simply by shared beliefs, but through the effervescent experience of having bodies which become incorporated into the Body of Christ.[2]

We might qualify Maffesoli's emphasis upon the 'self-evident' nature of community, however, by suggesting that community can be only *relatively* self-evident, since its corporeal basis is too prone to transformation to remain 'self-evident' for very long. As Keith Tester (1995a: 141) has noted, the 'body can never become entirely self-evident . . . [as it] always escapes social and cultural abilities to define it once and for all'. As the Middle Ages progressed, this self-evidence started to dissolve as people placed more emphasis on exploring the power of reflexive inquiry, and new, more cognitively focused forms of sociality emerged in place of communities centred on carnal knowing. Nevertheless, for much of the medieval era, and despite its variety and flexibility, Catholicism was underpinned by core religious practices and dogmas which nurtured a strong sense of community. These practices and dogmas may have contained within them a number of tensions and inconsistencies (Archer, 1988), but they lent a certain coherence to Christianity across geographical space (Cameron, 1991; Duffy, 1992), and bound people into the Church on the basis of a collective effervescence and enchantment of the world.

The development and variety of medieval Catholicism is, therefore, a highly complex matter. Nevertheless, some of its most central contours, and its relationship with other aspects of medieval culture and society, can be understood through the notion of Catholicism as a *sacred eating community*. This provides us with a heuristically useful way of approaching the development of medieval religion as a system of effervescent sociality which is both shaped by, yet which also 'eats into', its social and corporeal surroundings.

The sacred eating community

Pasi Falk (1994) defines an 'eating community' as a 'two-way order' which was shaped (or 'eaten into') by individuals during their daily lives, but which simultaneously 'ate into' and 'filled up' the identities of these people. If we add to this concept by viewing the Church as a *sacred* eating community, we can highlight the specific means through which Catholicism engaged with, and sought to harness for particular purposes, medieval bodies and their associated forms of carnal knowing. Touraine (1995: 304) has noted the close association between the religious construction of community and the cultural construction of a 'collective Subject'. The medieval Church was such a collective Subject: God was incorporated into the world through the Incarnation of Christ, while the world was incorporated into God through the Body of Christ, the Church. By organising activities through sacred and symbolically sacrificial rituals, by defining itself as the Body of Christ, and by having as its main cultic act the Eucharist, the Church was able to engage thoroughly with its constituents' fleshy sensuality, reactions and impulses.

In contrast to this emphasis on the sensual body, there was also a long-standing tendency within the Christian tradition to prioritise words and thought *above* the body. This was not the dominant tendency within medieval culture as a whole, however, even though it characterised certain monastic groups and became absolutely central to the most influential forms of the Protestant Reformation.[3] Medieval Catholic ritual drew heavily on the human body, and this engagement with the flesh was far from neutral in its effects. The Eucharist incorporated the Body of Christ *as food* into the body of the individual, and thereby incorporated the individual into the Body of the Church. This took place in an era marked by food shortages, plagues and physical conflicts which could make life nasty, brutish and short (Mennell, 1987; Watkins and van de Walle, 1985). As Thomas (1973 [1971]: 17) notes, helplessness in the face of disease was an essential element in the background to the beliefs and practices of the period. The Catholic tradition explored a dialectic between bodily suffering and the restoration of the unblemished body on the Day of Judgement which blurred the distinctions between the material and the spiritual, the soul and the body (Eade and Sallnow, 1991: 22). In this context it is, perhaps, not surprising that Christianity's promise of resurrection of the body and eternal life (conveyed partly through the effervescence stimulated by religious ritual) proved attractive to many.

This promise of Christianity, encompassing bodies, minds, natural and supernatural, can be understood with regard to Walter Benjamin's claim that 'the concrete totality of experience is religion'; a form of experience for which he coined the word *aura*, implying something akin to Rudolf Otto's concept of the 'numinous' or the Biblical conception of 'awe' (Bell, 1980: 347). For Benjamin (1973: 222), the aura is a form of enchantment which implicates both the universal and the particular, and is absent in the modern era of 'mechanical' reproduction. In the organic solidarity of the Middle Ages, however, the Church sought to constitute itself as a source of meaning and reality which *encompassed* and *transcended* the struggles and difficulties of everyday life through structuring and mediating human contact with, and responses to, the sacred (Berger, 1990 [1967]).

Benjamin's discussion of aura, nevertheless, has often been taken as part of his broader interest in the petrified, frozen or obsolete elements of civilisation which appear to lack the vitality of the modern world (Adorno, 1967: 233; Tester, 1995a: 37). Analysing Catholicism as a sacred eating community (which both 'ate into' but which was also *'eaten into'* by its constituencies) avoids the persistent sociological tendency to see it as either entirely homogeneous or as a static form of religious organisation. We can, in contrast, capture a sense of the dynamism in the generation of aura by looking at the two major means by which Catholic communities developed as a result of being immersed in their surroundings.

Catholic communities developed, first, through the growth and spread of their *doctrine* or *dogma* and, second, through their concrete *interactions* with the social and political world around them. It is the relationship between, and internal tensions within, these two factors which does much to explain the dynamism and flexibility of medieval religion. We shall say more about the development of Catholicism shortly, but here we should note that the syncretistic *flexibility* of Catholicism generally proved advantageous to the Church. It could also be disadvantageous, however, where its tolerance of pluralism did not result in an effective management of contradictions and challenges. This flexibility also, in any case, had limits which led to creation of 'established' and 'outsider' boundaries (Elias and Scotson, 1994 [1965]).

Flexibility proved to be a strength of the Church, on the one hand, as it tolerated a degree of pluralism in shaping communities according to local circumstances. By the middle of the twelfth century, the Church had evolved not merely a tolerance but an approval of the multiplicity of forms of religious life which characterised the medieval era (Constable, 1995). This meant that Catholicism could incorporate into itself 'a repertoire of inherited and shared beliefs and symbols, [which remained] capable of enormous flexibility and variety' (Duffy, 1992: 3). Evidence suggests that medieval persons both participated in religion and shaped it according to their own preferences (Warner, 1978 [1976]; Cameron, 1991: 17),[4] while the Church itself tended to tolerate local superstitions where it thought these might foster popular devotion (Thomas, 1973 [1971]: 56).

On the other hand, however, this flexibility also proved a weakness when it resulted in internal divisions and cleavages. Politically, for example, Catholicism was used by kings to further their own goals in a manner which opened the Church to charges of impurity and corruption. The Church's flexibility was also a potential liability socially. The centrality to popular devotion of the potency of the Church's 'magic' tested this flexibility to its limits (Thomas, 1973 [1971]: 57), while the Church's endorsement of carnival also encouraged the reappearance of a pagan legacy of hedonistic festivities (involving the symbolic overturning of hierarchies and the uncontrolled 'couplings' of grotesque bodies) which had the potential to resist and erode this Christian framing (Bakhtin, 1984 [1965]: 468; Gardiner, 1992: 54).

Catholic communities, then, developed by shaping but also by being 'eaten into' by their constituents; a two-way interaction which imparted to them their flexible character. But their flexibility had its limits. Catholicism was also *exclusionary* and promoted 'established' and 'outsider' categories. These reinforced various forms of social differentiation and contributed both to the early development of Orientalism, as the Church sought to make sense of the military successes of Islam (Rodinson, 1988; Said, 1978), and to the gendering of medieval identities (Lerner, 1993). In each case, the notion of 'outsiders' was expressed corporeally. With regard to Islam, Mohammed's assumed intention of dividing the Body of Christ was symbolised in Dante's *Divine Comedy* by the endless cleavages of his own body awaiting him in hell (Said, 1978). With regard to women, the immense value placed upon virginity became an almost sacramental representation of the intact boundaries of the Christian community itself, while the harlot and the heretic came to represent analogous threats to the penetration of the Christian Body/body by alien forces (Burrus, 1994).

For those recognised as full members of the Church, however, Catholicism helped promote particular forms of carnal knowing which provided the basis for civilising developments centred around communities of religious co-presence. These developments did not apply equally to men and women, and were restricted in other important ways. Nevertheless, they placed certain (if limited) walls around the use of violence, stimulated (largely localised) relations of interdependency, and encouraged people through confession and other rituals to take responsibility for (some of) their actions and to make amends for harm inflicted on (certain) others (Bossy, 1985). The Church was, in these and other respects, an important source of civilising developments during the medieval era (e.g. Bax, 1987). The strength and intensity of the boundaries which formed around these religious bodies also provided a basis, however, for the demonisation of, and confrontation with, outsider groups. This was exemplified by the spirit of holy warfare which marked the Crusades, and is also evident in the activities of the Inquisition (Moore, 1987; Hamilton, 1986). In each case, however, it is important to note that these are not solely the products of the hegemonic, ordering power of a clerical elite, but the results of a two-way interaction between the Church and a number of diverse contexts and influences. In order to understand some of these, we now turn in more detail to those doctrines and interactions which shaped the development of Catholic communities.

Catholic doctrine

In examining the development of, and tensions within, Catholic doctrine, Durkheim (1977 [1938]) has observed how Christianity both drew on, yet also sought to distance itself from, the heritage of the Graeco-Roman world. Caught up as it was in Roman culture and using the language of Latin, the early Church could not avoid being 'eaten into' by paganism. As Durkheim (1977 [1938]: 22) argued, 'in the literary and artistic monuments of antiquity there lived and breathed the very same pagan spirit which the Church had set itself the task of destroying'.[5]

This resulted in a tension which lay at the core of Catholic communities and their development. Catholicism was based on a culture and a heritage which it sought to go beyond, yet in which its codifications were inextricably bound (Archer, 1988: 150–151; Durkheim, 1977 [1938]: 25). The apostles Paul and John, for example, had been profoundly influenced by Neoplatonism. Of the seven cardinal virtues named by Pope Gregory I in the sixth century, only three were Christian (faith, hope and charity) while four (wisdom, justice, courage and temperance) were adopted from the pagans Plato and Pythagoras (Manchester, 1992: 8). Another example of these tensions is provided by the Church's teachings on the body. Peter Brown (1988) and Michel Foucault (1988 [1984]) have highlighted how pagan philosophers and physicians elaborated ethical systems, techniques of 'care for the self', that pre-dated yet were also associated with later Christian body regimes. The tension in these Christian regimes derived in part from their drawing on techniques which sought to achieve *harmony* with nature, yet developing these in a religious context which demanded that the flesh be *transformed* away from its natural state (see also Gouldner, 1965; Sennett, 1994).

These tensions were particularly evident in the Church's view of women, who were seen as being immersed in the natural world of blood and birth, and implicated in the Fall (Eve's seduction of Adam). Simone de Beauvoir (1972 [1949]) has condemned Christian doctrine as contributing in no small measure to the oppression of women. Alexandre (1992), in contrast, has shown how the Church drew on pre-existing forms of discrimination, but invested them with an ambivalence which is overlooked by de Beauvoir. Childbearing was a punishment for women, for example, but it was also a means of salvation. Women were condemned in Christianity, then, and the Christian religion has historically been the principal means of legitimising the control of women's bodies (Lerner, 1993; Turner, 1993: 236). However, women also occupied a special place within this religious system as a result of such factors as having looked after the crucified body of Christ, having witnessed and reported the Resurrection, and because of their association with the Virgin Mary's motherhood of Christ (Alexandre, 1992). More broadly, the Virgin Mary was an enduringly powerful religious model, while Mariology historically provided room for women to campaign for emancipation within the Church (Biezanek, 1964).

The tensions within Catholic doctrine show us one of the ways in which these communities both shaped and were shaped by their surroundings (in this case their Graeco-Roman intellectual heritage). The growing *scope* of this Catholic doctrine is another matter: it was a doctrine that encompassed growing areas of social life within the early Christian and medieval worlds.[6] The Christian body, for example, was surrounded by a web of morals, dangers and directions which made human flesh less ambivalent and indeterminate at the end of the early Christian period than it had been in antiquity (Brown, 1988). Having initially sponsored a number of diverse approaches to the transformation of the flesh (manifest by the divide in the early Church between the ascetics and moderates), the meaning of embodiment was increasingly codified and gendered by Christians concerned to anchor the body to stable moorings and solidify the role of the Church in society (Miles, 1992: 144; Synnott, 1993: 14). The Christian body had a definite physical, spiritual and mystical existence, and served also as a 'pervasive allegory of the hierarchies of society: church and family, and then state' (Synnott, 1993: 11–12; cf. O'Neill, 1985).[7]

The widening scope of Catholic doctrine can also be seen in its strictures on the position of women. Alexandre (1992) notes that nearly all of the aristocracy turned to Christianity after the Roman Emperor Constantine's conversion, and that social status became for the first time a major factor to be dealt with within the Church. The influential theologian John Chrysostom deplored the growing visibility and influence of certain women in the Church. Later, as the power of the medieval Church grew, so too did its doctrines seeking to diminish the influence of women. Prohibitions on women's activities were extended and clarified, for example, in Church attacks on heterodox movements (Alexandre, 1992: 426).

If Catholic doctrine placed greater strictures on the activities of women, its growing scope in the medieval era also tended to make illegitimate individual variations on authorised religious rule. For example, private and collective asceticism was supplanted by organised monastic communities 'governed by a rule, subject to an authority, and cloistered' (Alexandre, 1992: 413–414). This focus on doctrine, however, is bound to give us only a partial picture of Catholic communities, as these were built on *physical practices*. To gain a fuller view of the development of Catholicism, it is necessary to see how it was shaped by its interaction with, and location within, the political, supernatural and corporeally volatile contexts of the medieval era.

Medieval contexts

If the doctrinal aspects of Catholic communities developed in relation to their surrounding constituencies, so too did the practical influence of Catholicism. The Church nurtured ties of solidarity which sought to integrate blood, place and friendship, the three pillars of *Gemeinschaft*, into its religious system (Nisbet, 1993 [1966]: 75). The success of this syncretistic strategy was, however, sometimes incomplete, and often inherently precarious. Political and geographical considerations continued to shape the development of these Catholic communities, and to challenge Catholicism's re-formation of medieval bodies.

Political interaction

The influence of early medieval Catholicism was forged at a time when monopolies of secular power across large tracts of space were few, and when the Church's status as a representative of an other-worldly authority allowed it to prosper among a variety of local rulers. By engaging with the super-natural world, the Church could shape the lives of various people across large tracts of space without necessarily obliterating existing patterns of wealth and power. This was partly because the Church legitimised many existing social and political relationships by incorporating them into its own view of the cosmos (Gurevich, 1985: 288, 305). Kings were perceived as God's rep-resentatives on earth, for example, and could justify their actions on this basis.

The Church was also successful in promoting the view that ultimate political authority rested with *religious* representatives of God. As David Held (1992) notes, the political strategies of medieval secular rulers may have centred on the acquisition of wealth, territory and power, but the 'Christian world-view transformed the rationale of political action from an earthly to a theological framework; it insisted that the Good lay in submission to God's will' (Held, 1992: 81). With regard to the exercise of government over the lives of individuals, the Church was also intimately involved, as in the 'trial by ordeal'. Furthermore, the appeal to the supernatural was a common resource drawn upon in political government, and the churches were 'repositories for the instruments by which divine judgement was conveyed – the cauldron for the hot water, the brazier for heating the iron . . . and one of the commonest functions of the priest must have been the blessing of these instruments for their purpose' (Southern, 1993 [1953]: 101–102).

In practical terms the Church's location within, and promotion of, 'two worlds' meant there was 'no alternative' in medieval Europe, no competing 'political theory' to the theocratic positions of Pope and Holy Roman Emperor. The established authority of the Church had constructed what Agnes Heller has referred to as a 'natural artifice', a view of social arrangements which saw them as being prescribed by nature (Heller, 1990: 145). To call this authority into question, therefore, meant having to call into question what was natural and what was sacred.

Nevertheless, while the Church had considerable success in pursuing this strategy, it was not without its conflicts and failures. In this respect, Bernard Hamilton (1986) has highlighted the importance of the first Crusade, which took place near the close of the eleventh century. The struggle between the Papacy and temporal rulers was at its height, but the successful pursuit of this crusade did much to solidify the Church's earthly power. Knights who took the Cross withdrew their services from their lords and fought to regain land which was at a premium (the expanding system of primogeniture meant that lords needed to find land for both their family and for their vassals) (Hamilton, 1986: 21; Holmes, 1988: 119). The Church's success during this period was, then, assisted by its ability to help deal with surplus populations of landless knights (a benefit which was complemented by those nunneries which could provide a refuge for members of the female aristocracy) (see Elias, 1982 [1939]: 38–44; Turner, 1984).

These political conditions (which formed part of the context in which Catholic communities developed) show that it was not simply in terms of its doctrines that Catholicism stood Janus-faced in relation to its own priorities and those of the world in which it operated. Although we are focusing on the *opportunities* provided by this political context, the Church's powers were also limited by political considerations. Wars and conflicts fragmented power during the period Marc Bloch (1965) has referred to as the 'first feudal age' (AD 850–1050) (Koenigsberger, 1987). Survival was the primary aim and, as Elias argues (1982 [1939]), those refusing to engage in this struggle necessarily became weaker than those who had succeeded in appropriating the land of others. The medieval era which tended to be much more physically insecure than its modern counterpart. Economic trade was limited in a context where the struggle for power was such that the lives of merchants engaged in long-distance trade were at risk, while everyday violence and political insecurity were reflected in the actions and emotional structures of that time (Elias, 1978 [1939], 1982 [1939]). Even when the internal political situation was reasonably stable, the threat of Islam proved a lasting source of fear and trauma for Christian Europe (Said, 1978: 59).[8]

These political conditions did not, in short, provide any sort of secure basis for the development of rationalised, reflexive forms of bodily being in the world. There were few incentives for people to develop sophisticated means of self-control, and survival was the number one priority for the majority of the population. Catholic communities had to operate *within* these conditions; they were not immune to them despite their other-worldly concerns.

Identity and physicality

The notion of Catholic *eating* communities implies not just a two-way rela-tionship, but a mutual *devouring* of medieval religion and its surroundings.

If there is a certain violence to this metaphor, it would not be inappropriate. As Elias (1982 [1939]) has demonstrated, ready displays of emotion, aggression, and the quick resort to violence were often necessary and accepted modes of behaviour in a context full of physical insecurities. These insecurities varied according to social location and gender but they permeated medieval life. Jane Schulenburg (1986), for example, has examined how medieval women lived with constant warfare. This not only meant the possible loss of husbands, but the threat of rape from invading armies; a threat which was carried out even on cloistered nuns.

Violence may have been a nightmare for those on the receiving end, but torture and combat could be one of the 'joys of living' for its perpetrators in the medieval era (Garland, 1991; Peters, 1980). Hanawalt's (1976) study of death in fourteenth- and fifteenth-century England supports this view, observing a society ready to settle all manner of disputes with recourse to violence. Drawing on data from coroners' inquests, Hanawalt notes that medieval society had a very high incidence of homicide, tended to value fighting an enemy openly, and was marked by a remarkably low level of convictions for those accused of homicide (Hanawalt, 1976).

In engaging with this violence, medieval religion both *participated* in and *legitimised* a passionate physical intensity by locating and regulating it within a sacred context. A specific example of this, which we have already referred to but which is worth exploring further, was the popular 'trial by ordeal' which was common in north-western Europe in the early Middle Ages. One of several versions of the ordeal involved grasping a red hot iron accompanied by the solemn blessings of the priest. It was a device to achieve consensus in a dispute by allowing God to judge the rights and wrongs of a conflict (the judgement being apparent in the wounds on the hands of the participants in the ordeal). The nature of these grotesque wounds was often ambiguous, but this itself allowed the settling of a dispute without loss of face on either side (Brown, 1975). Such practices were concerned less with an abstract conception of truth and more with the resolution of conflict within the Christian community. Both ordeals and 'judicial combat' were rituals for regulating conflicts in order to redefine uncertain social relationships (Asad, 1983: 295). Here, we can see that the Church's involvement in this milieu of violence was geared towards its regulation within sacred orders of meaning. A similar process can be seen in the movement known as the 'peace of God'. In eleventh-century France, this sought to regulate the occasions in which knights engaged in war and killing. This justified certain acts of violence, but made others illegitimate (Duby, 1977).

The Church also engaged in the violent physicality of the era by promoting, as well as regulating force. It encouraged extreme ascetic flights into grotesque physicality such as lengthy fasts, flagellation, and hazardous pilgrimages and ordeals which ended in near certain death (Bynum, 1987; Mellor, 1991). These practices, which were accompanied at times by the Church's participation in persecution and torture (Cohn, 1975), may appear

shocking and incomprehensible to modern eyes. In the context of the
violence of the time, however, they may also be seen as consistent with the
embodied modes of expression characteristic of the Middle Ages. Less
religiously justifiable, if not socially unexpected, engagements with violence
were to be found in the running of the papal offices. William Manchester's
(1992) study of this period charges that popes and cardinals hired assassins
and sanctioned torture, and contains a report of how, at one Roman
banquet, 'a Holy Father "watched with loud laughter and much pleasure"
from a balcony while his bastard son slew unarmed criminals, one by one,
as they were driven into a small courtyard below' (Manchester, 1992: 38).

Superstition and the supernatural

One of the clearest ways in which the Catholic Church both 'ate into' and
was 'eaten into' by its surroundings involves the supernatural contexts in
which it developed. Medieval persons tended to be relatively ignorant of
the Bible which, like the Mass, was in Latin. Illiteracy was rife, the central
themes and stories of the Bible were taught through images on church
walls (Michalski, 1993), but Christianity coexisted with beliefs and
practices such as sorcery, witchcraft, black magic and the use of amulets:
'Everyone also knew – and every child was taught – that the air around
them was infested with invisible, soulless spirits, some benign but most of
them evil' (Manchester, 1992: 60–61).

In this context, the medieval Church found itself 'saddled with the
tradition that the working of miracles was the most efficacious means of
demonstrating its monopoly of the truth' (Thomas, 1973 [1971]). As Keith
Thomas's analysis of religion and the decline of magic shows, the essential
difference between religious prayers and magical spells was that only spells
claimed to work automatically. However, the sacred eating communities of
Catholicism weakened this distinction. The Church recommended prayers
for healing the sick, for example, or when gathering medicinal herbs. It also
encouraged the idea that there was virtue in the simple repetition of words.
Indeed, the role of words in the Eucharist could bring about change in the
character of material objects (Thomas, 1973 [1971]: 37, 47). So it was
hardly surprising that believers should 'eat into' and shape the supernatural
powers of the Church in a variety of ways. They sponsored Masses for
good weather, safe journeys and all manner of other purposes; said prayers
backwards to achieve evil ends; kept the Eucharistic bread in their mouth
as a source of magical power; and read the Gospels aloud to guarantee safe
childbirths (Thomas, 1973 [1971]: 37, 38, 51). This bi-directional
relationship between magic and the religion was not alien to Catholic
communities, but reflected their fundamentally two-way character:

> Theologians further enhanced popular belief in the existence of the Church's
> magical powers by stressing the mystical powers available to the faithful as a
> means of preservation against the assault of evil spirits. The leaders of the
> Church thus abandoned the struggle against superstition whenever it seemed in

their interest to do so. Throughout the Middle Ages their attitude to the credulities of their simpler followers was fundamentally ambivalent. They disliked them as gross and superstitious but they had no wish to discourage attitudes which might foster popular devotion . . . Such practices as the worship of relics, the recitation of prayers, or the wearing of talismans and amulets, could all be taken to excess, but what did it matter so long as their effect was to bind the people closer to the true Church and the true God? (Thomas, 1973 [1971]: 56)

This close relation between magic, religion and ordinary people was especially clear in the case of saints. The relics of saints were the object of pilgrimages, their shrines were associated with miracles, while even the image of Saint Christopher was meant to offer a day's protection from illness or death (Duffy, 1992). As the above quotation implies, it was not just the people who drew on the magical powers of the Church, but the Church which drew on the superstitions of the people. The motivation for people to fight in the Crusades, for example, was bolstered by the demonic images of Mohammed fed to people. In the first half of the twelfth century, Mohammed became a sorcerer whose magic and deceit destroyed the Church in Africa and the East. As Rodinson (1988) notes, by supposedly sanctioning sexual promiscuity, his success was seen as assured. Images such as these gave free rein to the 'triumph of creative imagination' as religious figures freely admitted that they had made up stories about a leader whose 'malignity exceeds whatever ill can be spoken' (Southern, 1962: 28–31).

The flexibility of Catholicism's approach to the supernatural facilitated its success but also proved part of its undoing. The magical powers attributed to images led the Renaissance humanist Erasmus, anticipating Luther, to suggest that 'people should be taught that these are no more than signs; it would be better if there were none at all, and all prayer were addressed only to Christ' (quoted in Manchester, 1992: 185). We will return to this type of criticism later. For now, it is worth noting that it is not simply an attack on certain aspects of Catholicism as a system of ideas, but is levied at the two-way character of its sacred eating communities.

Sacramental relationships

The sacraments lay at the heart of religious sociality for ordinary people. These were central to the capacity of Catholicism to 'eat into' and impart coherence to the diversity of local practices and innovations. Indeed, the sacraments used by the Church to encourage ascetic practices and penances were associated with an elementary rationalisation of the body and a degree of internalised control. In this respect, Catholicism was involved in an early civilisation of the body. These civilising processes were, however, self-limiting.

Medieval religion made all sorts of associations between the natural, the social and the supernatural, while the Church encouraged the view that the divine existed *within* the body. These linkages encouraged people to direct their emotions into particular activities and to treat their bodies, and the bodies of others, with reference to certain sacred practices. This helped forge interdependencies within religious communities, but could also stimulate the emotionality, unpredictability and loss of control which has been associated with many medieval people's actions. For example, visions, trances and states of religious ecstasy stimulated encounters with the divine but could also produce a loss of self-control. The Church's existence as a sacred community, then, involved a balancing act. It could exacerbate volatile behaviour, but also sought to direct behaviour through a religious structure in which sacred knowledge was encountered *through* the body.

At the heart of the sacraments was the development and maintenance of a relationship with the Church, which was itself defined sacramentally, and which was a thoroughly embodied phenomenon. The theology of experience developed by the influential theologian William of St-Thierry expressed this embodied character. He placed 'feeling' (*sentire*) and 'tasting' (*gustare*) at the centre of his spiritual doctrine, arguing that being a Christian is to do with *having a taste* for God, and that Christ makes things *savoury* for humanity. The Church, the Body of Christ, had, furthermore, the *eyes* (of the Angels), the *ears* (of the Patriarchs), the *nose* (of the Prophets), the *touch* (of the people), and the *taste* (of the Incarnate Christ) (von Balthasar, 1982: 289). This 'touch' of the people, meaning the 'common sense' of the Catholic community, and the 'taste' for God were expressed through the communal character of the sacraments.

The seven sacraments, formalised in the twelfth century, sought to Christianise crucial life stages, so that participation in the Church and the pattern of life itself became inextricably integrated. Thus, baptism marked birth and the entry into the Church (and community); confirmation marked the movement to adulthood and thus full participation in the Church (and community); marriage marked the coupling and procreation of humans (and thus the continuance of community), while extreme unction marked the preparation for death (and leaving community).

The remaining three sacraments had a slightly different nature, being concerned with the incorporation of people into this ritual meaning structure. The Eucharist involved those taking communion entering the body of Christ, the body of the Church and, at this time, the body of society. The sacrament of penance allowed for the confession of sins and thus the continued participation in the Church's communion. Together with the relative rarity of excommunication, penance also signified the Church's desire to keep as many as possible within its fold. Finally, the sacrament of holy orders identified those who could administer the other sacraments, represent Christ in the Mass, and represent the Church at other times.

Of all the sacramental activities of the Church, the Eucharistic Mass was clearly the most important. It was the one which expressed much of what it meant to be a Catholic in the Middle Ages, and provides us with a key to the communal forms which both shaped medieval bodies and provided a context for religious civilising processes. The elements of the Mass, bread and wine, were taken from nature to become the body and blood of Christ to be consumed by the communicants. The incorporation of nature into the sacred is therefore represented by the substances of the natural world being 'transubstantiated' into religious redemption (Martin, 1980: 76). Through the consumption of these transubstantiated natural elements, people became incorporated into the body of the Church, which was itself understood to be both natural (a human community) and supernatural (the sacramental continuance of Christ's Incarnation).

The Mass constituted a bond of love rooted in a sense of charity and manifest in a commitment to works of mercy. Furthermore, although the Mass was used to endorse existing community power structures, this was only possible because it drew on a more general collective imagery. This imagery both endorsed the authority of the Church and, as Duffy (1992: 92–93) has suggested, was often deeply felt by the individual Christian. Unofficially, the Mass was also used as a form of 'poison ordeal', with the suspect required to communicate risking damnation, but taking an opportunity to demonstrate innocence in front of the Christian community (Thomas, 1973 [1971]: 50). This association of the Eucharist with the constitution and maintenance of a community is a major defining feature of Catholicism and medieval society.

The Catholic Church, then, not only sought to harness and direct medieval forms of embodiment to its own agenda, but structured the sacraments in a way which organised and gave meaning to life. The power of the Church to forge particular links with persons can be understood best with regard to its privileged role as the creator and maintainer of a community which engaged *all the body's senses*. Eating God during the Mass, for example, is thus an oral signifier of the Catholic emphasis on the transformation of the body through its incorporation of Christ.

This organisation of the senses had important consequences for the Church's ability to engage in medieval persons' physicality and to maintain particular forms of religious practice and meaning. The Church both based itself on this vigorous medieval physicality and sought to direct it in a specific manner. Making abundant use of the taste for blood, torture and violence through the Crusades, the Church also utilised the physical senses via visual imagery, chants, incense and oral penetration through the Eucharist (Bossy, 1985; Bynum, 1987). Words were most definitely not generally prioritised over food or other aspects of bodiliness. Far from being primarily the mental, cognitive, phenomenon religion was to become after the Protestant Reformation, the medieval Church was instead a matter of sensuous 'taste'.

The bonds of interdependence

The French religious and social philosopher Lamennais's contentious and influential *Essay on Indifference*, published in 1817 as a challenge to the rationalism and Protestant individualism then dominant, would not have been remarkable in the Middle Ages. His point was this: the relationship between 'God and man', and between 'man and man', is not grounded in the 'word', but in *community* (Nisbet 1993 [1966]: 54). Our emphasis upon the Church of the Middle Ages as an '*eating* community' focuses attention on the embodied basis of community in this period, while our emphasis upon the *sacred* nature of this eating community signals the incorporation of bodies into a system of meaning which encompasses both the natural and the supernatural. For Durkheim, the sacred appeals to feelings and desires in a spontaneous fashion (Meštrović, 1991: 42), but it also shapes not merely the substance but the forms of knowing characteristic of each community (Nisbet, 1993 [1966]: 243).

It is worth paying some attention to a few examples of how particular communities within the broader community of Catholicism sought to harness the medieval body by marking it with sacred meanings and rituals. Communities central to Catholicism included Catholic 'confraternities', communities of the dead, marriage, communities of knowledge and of friendship. The sacred character of these communities was reinforced by their embeddedness in the large number of sacred festivals, entertainments and theatrical events associated with the Church calendar (Cameron, 1991: 16). By structuring the ways in which people related to each other, and to the wider world, each of these communities contributed to the shaping of bodily identities and the acquisition of knowledge and meaning. It is also worth noting that in each case they were bound together by eating God in the Eucharist.

Catholic confraternities

Catholic 'confraternities' (or brotherhoods) were forms of sociality made up of people who had a bond with others such as a similar trade. They had been present since the time of early Christianity, but spread throughout the West during the thirteenth and fourteenth centuries. By the later Middle Ages, one-fifth of the adult population was likely to be a member of at least one confraternity. As Bossy notes, these forms of sociality 'often recruited the majority of a local community, sometimes the whole of it' (Bossy, 1985: 58–59). Furthermore, memberships of confraternities overlapped, so that it was not uncommon to belong to half a dozen at a time (Cameron, 1991: 15).

Catholic confraternities developed as an expression of Christian charity (meaning, at this time, social integration or solidarity) which was the principal end of the Christian life. Anyone claiming to be a Christian was obliged to embody this aim 'somehow, at some time, in this world' (Bossy, 1985: 57). Confraternities have been 'embryonic forms of welfare organis- ation', but Bossy has suggested that they were far more than self-help or substitute kinship groups as they 'embodied sacred Christian kinship, as opposed to profane consanguinity' (1985: 58). The members of Catholic communities were directed through *sacred ties* to provide support for each other. For example, within each fraternity the rich had a responsibility for looking after the poor. Support for the costs of burial was provided, while collective funds were used to alleviate poverty, and interest-free loans of food, goods and livestock were used to support those who had fallen on hard times (Bossy, 1985: 61). In these and other ways Catholic confraternities managed to mitigate some of the unpredictabilities and extremities of medieval life.

As well as helping to assist in the bodily well-being of their members, confraternities affected how people gained knowledge about themselves and the world by linking the natural with the supernatural. For example, when confraternities met they had Mass together. They would also pray together for the souls of their members in purgatory. Bringing together their bodies in such collective rituals stimulated carnal forms of meaning and knowledge acquisition. It also served to solidify the sometimes fragile relations of interdependence existing within these communities and also signified their essential unity with all Catholics.

The development of Catholic confraternities can be seen as a manifestation of civilising processes in that they stimulated a certain lengthening of the chains of interdependence and responsibility between people. Elias links such an expansion of chains of interdependence to greater reflection upon the long-term effects of one's actions and words on others, and to the development of foresight and the increased acquisition of knowledge. But such dependence was stimulated, legitimised and maintained in medieval confraternities through an overarching frame of meaning joining natural with supernatural and centred on Catholic ritual practice. Interdependence was neither merely a functional necessity for survival, nor a rationalised assessment of social or human interrelations, but a religiously legitimised reality signified by the idea of the 'Body of Christ'. This is demonstrated by the fact that joint celebration of the Mass was central to the activities of the confraternities. Consequently, while these confraternities lengthened chains of interdependence, they tended to do this *within* the bounded frame of meaning generated by the Catholic Church. Furthermore, while confraternities did not always exclude women, they tended to be dominated by men and helped structure a public/private division which was to be made much stronger in succeeding centuries.

Communities of the dead

The religious bonds of interdependence stimulated by Catholicism are evident even in the organisation and images surrounding death in the medieval period. Theologically, the eschatological transformation of the body was signalled by doctrines concerning the resurrection of the tortured and broken body of Christ (Eade and Sallnow, 1991: 22). Liturgically, this transformation was indicated by the breaking of the bread during the Mass, as it is today: 'The act of breakage is the point of communion. The fracture of the body is the healing of the body, and the body of Christ is brought together by being torn apart' (Martin, 1980: 76).

Socially, however, the Church sought to contain death within those ritual structures which have been explored by Phillipe Ariès (1974, 1981 [1977]). Ariès notes that the supernatural framework of meaning surrounding death was allied to a strongly communal focus for Christians' belief and practice. He argues that death was a social phenomenon in the medieval period, an event which produced communal responses and which was contained by collective signs and rituals. Indeed, Turner (1991: 230) has suggested that deaths were hardly individualised at all, with burials being communal and graves unmarked. As Bossy notes, after flesh had rotted the bones were usually 'dug up and added to the anonymous mass in the charnel-house', under the care of the Church (Bossy, 1985: 31).

The treatment of the dead reflected in certain respects the communal experiences of the living. While early Christians buried their dead away from inhabited places, medieval burial places were usually in the middle of dwelling places of the living (the churchyard was a centre for social activity, festivity and trade) (Bossy, 1985; Duby, 1988). The dead also served as a model for the living. This was evident in the images of the *danse macabre* (the dance of the dead) which developed in the fourteenth and fifteenth centuries:

> Painted on the cloister wall of a number of celebrated churchyards . . . [the *danse macabre*] portrayed a circle where the dead alternate, holding hands, with the living, and lead them in a dance around the graves. The skeletal dead, an undifferentiated community of equals, dance keenly, the living reluctantly: weighed down by robes, possessions and thoughts about status, they have to be dragged in by the dead, polite but firm. (Bossy, 1985: 31)

Death was presented as a passage into a supremely collective existence. There was order, meaning and knowledge about death, while the relationship between the living and the dead was one of community. All Souls' Day, for example, was an opportunity for children to lay cakes on the graves of their deceased ancestors, and for the souls of the dead to enjoy respite from their situation and come out of their graves for warmth and succour. Those with friends among the living would make for the domestic hearth where fires would be covered in order to guard against the possibility of burning (the soul visited naked from its grave). In this respect, the Church stimulated chains of interdependence not only within localised confraternities, but between generations past and present. Deathbed reconciliations had an important place within Catholicism, while the prospect of a common fate could stimulate mutual affinity between people (Duby, 1988).

Catholicism was firmly exclusionary as well as inclusionary, though, and this is illustrated in the case of communities of the dead. Catholicism regarded Islam as a schism from, and a misguided version of, Christianity. Christian scholars may have encompassed inaccurate versions of Islam within the Christian world view, but there was also a strong element of differentiation here (Rodinson, 1988). In Dante's *Inferno*, for example, we find Mohammed in eight of the nine circles of Hell. After Mohammed, there are only the falsifiers and the treacherous (such as Judas) before arrival at the bottom of Hell, where Satan is to be found. As Said (1978: 68) points out, Mohammed thus belongs to a rigid hierarchy of evils. Being responsible for a schism within Christianity, his punishment involves being endlessly cleft in two from his chin to his anus.

These traditions are of interest for two main reasons. First, the religious organisation of death had itself resulted from interaction of the Church with the pagan practices of local communities. Second, they illustrate the Church's shaping of bodily volatility. As Bossy (1985) suggests, there was a considerable amount of fear and superstition surrounding death, yet religious organisation anchored that fear to a ritualised meaning system.

Marriage

The structuring of marriage promoted by the Catholic Church provides a quite different example of how the body was linked to forms of carnal knowing in the medieval era. We have already noted how the Christian account of the Fall linked women's bodies to desire, temptation and sin (Miles, 1992). This supernatural emphasis on the body of woman also reflected the wider social responsibilities placed on women's 'natural selves' in medieval society.

Within the aristocracy, women's bodies were often immensely important in the sealing of alliances between medieval ruling elites. Women were, for example, given as brides to families with whom reconciliation was sought (Klapisch-Zuber, 1990: 287). These women were not only the objects of trade, but had a responsibility to maintain the alliance through blameless conduct and repeated childbirth. Thus, women were used 'to guarantee social bonds and found cohesion on the "charity" and love that allies owed one another' (Klapisch-Zuber, 1990: 288). This illustrates the fact that the volatility and emotionality of medieval bodies was highly gendered: women frequently shouldered a much greater responsibility for managing their emotions than men, and for solidifying pacts of non-violence. This unequal burden can also be seen in the medieval treatment of sex and childbirth.

The sexual fidelity of women was a source of great concern in this system of exchange, since the children of an adulterous wife might 'pollute' the blood lineages at the heart of family alliances and disrupt the system of primogeniture (Turner, 1984). 'The sexual fidelity of women was solidly at the heart of family structure, and women's bodies required unflagging surveillance' (Klapisch-Zuber, 1990: 292).[9] The role of women in forging social solidarity through the body was not, however, confined to medieval elites. Women in general were married young, usually before the age of eighteen, and were often subject to closely spaced pregnancies up to the age of about forty (if they managed to live that long). In some parts of Europe, there is evidence to suggest that many women were pregnant for nine months out of every eighteen (Klapisch-Zuber, 1990: 299).[10]

Catholic 'communities of marriage', celebrated sacramentally in the Church within the Mass, were shaped by this interaction but also sought to structure behaviour according to their own teachings. This is why Turner (1984) and Davies (1993), among others, have pointed to the lack of total fit between the needs of the male aristocracy and Catholic dogma. So, while the use of women's bodies to maintain and reproduce social solidarity was reflected in the teachings of Catholicism, the Church also sought to regulate the use of women in family alliances. It insisted, especially firmly though not necessarily especially successfully from the late eleventh century onwards, that women had to give their free assent to marriage, and that women should not be forced into marriage at such an early age that this consent be meaningless (Klapisch-Zuber, 1990: 292). Marriage, a sacrament within the Church, had to have the equal consent of man and woman in order to be true to the principle of Christian solidarity.

In incorporating medieval marriage practices into its communities, the betrothal of couples also became subject to the Church's control. In Normandy, for example, the transfer of the bride from the father to the husband, which had been a private home-based ceremony, was moved to the church. The priest welcomed the couple to the church and witnessed their exchange of statements of consent. Marriage thus became more public, and had attached to it a certain solemnity due to the presence of a priest.

The Catholic Church's incorporation of marriage into its structures may have given what was then considered an 'unusual weight to the woman's voice' (Klapisch-Zuber, 1990: 293). However, the Church also encouraged a view of women which saw them as potentially threatening to males because of the particular character of their embodiment.[11] Sins of the flesh were an unavoidable part of community life (Bossy, 1985: 35), but men still had to be on their guard. Women's bodies were marked by a sensuality and instinctual nature. This both *required* the authoritative control of the more rational male, and *threatened* that authority and rationality: 'Poorly governed by women's incomplete reason, the body required that its lord, the husband, use it to satisfy his appetites with prudence and regularity and without abandoning himself to any vertigo of the senses that might diminish his authority' (Klapisch-Zuber, 1990: 305).

Catholic communities of marriage placed women in a highly disadvantaged position in relation to men (even at this time the Church condemned the use of contraception, which meant that the only way many women could avoid the dangers of childbirth was by embarking on, often equally dangerous, careers as holy mystics). Nevertheless, it would be wrong to conclude that the Church merely reproduced women's subordination in the identical form in which it had existed previously. The Church's strictures on consent were likely to have at least mitigated, for some women, one of the most coercive practices associated with medieval marriage. As such, they represented something of a civilising development in relation to what had gone before.[12] Catholicism also provided the alternative of 'holy careers' for women eager for an alternative to the rigours of marriage and repeated childbearing (Bynum, 1987).

Communities of knowledge

We examined in our previous chapter the minor role played by gaining knowledge through linguistic symbols in the Middle Ages, the general prevalence of carnal knowing, and the gendered structuring of this form of knowing. These ways of knowing were not simply incorporated into Catholicism, however, but were reinforced by their own 'communities of knowledge' within the broader Eucharistic communion of the Church. Biblical interpretation, for example, was based on philosophical and theo-logical arguments which required scholastic progression and the ability to engage with sophisticated linguistic symbols. As Lerner (1993) argues, this form of knowledge acquisition was not only a minority pursuit in the medieval era, but tended to be the province of a learned male clerical elite. While a number of women undoubtedly engaged in Biblical criticism, various techniques existed to prevent their participation, deny their authorship, and exclude their work from the public domain.

Mysticism provided an alternative route to knowledge that was more open to women, holding as it did that transcendental truth came not from rational thought but through inspiration and revelatory insight. The nun Hildegard of Bingen (1098–1179) may have been one of the best known mystics, but there was throughout the Middle Ages a significant rise in the numbers of women who gained the status of saints through this form of carnal knowing (Weinstein and Bell, 1982). Indeed, Weinstein and Bell's (1982: 220–221, 229) analysis suggests that the most striking characteristic of female saints seems to be their immersion in supernatural signs and communications (Lerner, 1993: 71). This increase in women saints took place from the eleventh to the fifteenth centuries and affected Holland, Germany, England, France and Italy in the fourteenth century.

Mysticism could be a dangerous activity, however, and Bynum (1987) has illustrated how female mystics could be accused of witchcraft and demonic possession in the absence of male protection and sponsorship. Furthermore, even the most powerful medieval women writers felt it necessary to announce their unworthiness to the reader. It is interesting that women's claims to *sacred* carnal knowledge were often tied to the somewhat safer experience of their status as mothers whose duty it was to give advice and instruction in morals (Lerner, 1993: 51, 116).

Friendship and the communion of saints

Just as confraternities can be seen as social arrangements which expressed Catholic community, so too can the communion of saints be approached as an expression of the importance of Christian friendship, which was for

Tönnies one of the pillars of *Gemeinschaft*. This communion, embodied in the Mass, linked existing patterns of friendship to religious rituals and supernatural knowledge, but also encouraged the development of social interdependency built around the Church.

The cult of saintly friendship grew out of an engagement with the social and supernatural structures of the medieval era. Rituals commemorating saints, for example, tended to dramatise relations between peasants and landlords (the peasants–saints relation reflected the client–patron model that characterised peasant–landlord interactions) (Wuthnow, 1989: 27). However, the saints were also valued as friends who embodied above all the ideals of Christian friendship, and who made positive interventions in human affairs. As Bossy notes, the power of living saints

> was illustrated by their power to bring about the reconciliation of enmities, to induce powerful, if temporary, states of amity and concord in such faction-ridden cities as Sienna and Barcelona; or, like St. Roch, by their heroic determination to maintain the bond of charity with victims of the plague. Among dead saints it was evidenced by their patronage of the innumerable collectivities of fraternity, craft, parish, city, country, religious house or order of which Christendom was composed. (Bossy, 1985: 12)

These social and supernatural features can also be seen in the means by which saints were sought and honoured as helpers and friends. The frequency with which saints appeared on the altar screens of late medieval parish churches indicates the very public attempts that were made to enlist their help. Events such as pilgrimages to the shrines of saints illustrate the visible ways in which they were honoured. Indeed, the religious importance of saintly interventions was such that beneficiaries of their help had to make this known publicly (Duffy, 1992: 166, 178, 199).

Saints were not just channels for God's favours, then, or even exemplars of the ideal of friendship with God. They were also models of the ideal of friendship and help which encouraged the cementing of social relations. As Bossy notes, 'The friend of God was the friend of man, and vice versa' (1985: 13). Furthermore, Duffy (1992) has suggested that the saints were possibly never better loved than in the fifteenth and sixteenth centuries. On the eve of the Reformation there was a 'luxuriant flourishing of devotion to the saints', partly imposed by the Church (which solemnly dedicated over fifty days in the year apart from Sundays to the saints), but also enthusiastically supported by the laity. This popularity of the saints was also apparent in the hagiographical accounts of saints' lives which flourished in this period (Head, 1990; Stauffer, 1930; Whittemore, 1988).

Bodily guarantees of the supernatural

We hope by now to have demonstrated that the various forms of community promoted by the Catholic Church were not simply imposed by the clerical hierarchy upon medieval people, but were also shaped by medieval persons who 'ate into' the structure, organisation and resources of Catholicism. The patterns of interaction which followed these two-way exchanges highlight the links that existed between religion and the body, the natural and the supernatural, and the living and the dead.

Such linkages stand in marked contrast to the main tendencies of the modern era, and point our attention to the carnal forms of knowledge that permeated medieval times. The forms of community promoted by the Church underline the fact that medieval self-identities had much less to do with individualised, reflexive narratives of the self, and much more to do with a form of embodiment in which the fleshy body and its senses were experienced as integral to the gaining of knowledge about oneself and one's world. People were immersed in the sensations of the flesh, in all that was 'natural', while the importance of these sensations and experiences was reinforced and guaranteed by the supernatural dimensions of religious practice. Action, rather than thought, was prioritised:

> In general, all the most popular activities of late medieval religion were based on doing something, on participation, activity, movement, essentially on experiencing an event more than on learning or understanding a message. (Cameron, 1991: 16)

It is clear, then, that the medieval construction of identity was generally characterised by a marked absence of that choice and reflexive monitoring associated with modernity (Beck, 1992; Giddens, 1990, 1991). For most people, indeed, even being a 'Catholic' was not necessarily a conscious decision but a given part of their identity. On the other hand, the absence of pervasive cognitive reflexivity does not imply the absence of dynamism imagined by Giddens. Religious life (like social life in general) developed on the basis of a dynamic form of embodiment in which the natural and supernatural mingled within and outside of the body. This is best demonstrated by the sacraments of baptism and the Eucharist, wherein water and bread, two staples of the human diet, acquire supernatural referents (entry and participation in the Body of Christ) and social consequences (entry and participation in the Church and society).

The links between the natural and the supernatural are also illustrated by the dominant ethical system, which was centred around the 'seven deadly sins': pride, envy, anger, avarice, gluttony, sloth and lechery. Its focus on the body was, however, tied to an acceptance of the excesses of the consuming flesh. As Bossy notes, 'the seven deadly sins were a system of community ethics making more excuse for the sins of concupiscence than for those of aversion. The sins of aversion destroy community, but without some flirtation with the sins of concupiscence there is unlikely to be any community at all' (Bossy, 1985: 35). Jocelyn Wogan-Brown (1994: 48) makes a similar point about the ambivalence of flesh as the territory where 'the senses and the volition can be led astray – it is the border zone to a body which is both sinful and capable of redemption'.

This linking of natural with supernatural, and the social with the religious, is the main feature of Catholic communities. Its major consequence was the provision of a certain assurance of meaning and security for many, if by no means all, medieval persons which did not operate at an abstract level, but which was integrated firmly into daily life. As Thomas notes, the medieval Church acted as a repository of sacred power 'which could be dispensed to the faithful to help them in their daily problems' (Thomas, 1973 [1971]: 35).[13]

In saying this, we are not following those secularisation theorists who have pictured the medieval period as one of unparalleled order and psychological security (Martin, 1966). This period was a violent, often insecure one. The threat of natural and human violence, disease, starvation and hardship was frequently much more extreme than they are for modern Western persons (Elias, 1982 [1939]: 202–203). Nevertheless, Catholicism offered a context within which these insecurities could be mitigated and, to some extent, relativised through their location within supernatural orders of meaning. Furthermore, the sacred eating communities promoted by Catholicism shaped corporeality in particular directions which promoted particular types of interdependence and connection between people. In other words, Catholicism can be seen as exerting an important, if limited and under-recognised, influence on medieval civilising processes.

Catholic communities were an integral part of society. As the medieval era wore on, however, the flexibility that had been a strength of Catholicism began to become a liability. This did not necessarily weaken the popularity of religious practices among most local people, for whom it remained centred around native traditions and a local church, but it did lead to a growing dissatisfaction with the *institutional hierarchies* of the Catholic Church, which were seen by many as needing reform.

The challenge to Catholic communities

In examining the political conditions which shaped Catholic communities, we noted that the early medieval fragmentation of power, and its later concentration, presented the Church with both problems and opportunities. Having concentrated on the opportunities, it is time to say something about those problems which became especially significant in the late Middle Ages.

Elias's (1982 [1939]) long-range study of state formation processes has demonstrated that as territories became very gradually more stable and secure, competition for economic and political rewards moved slowly away from force and conquest, and inched toward the more regulated realms of trade and diplomacy. By the twelfth century, reasonably stable hierarchies of power had been established which facilitated an increase in the number of chains of interdependency which bound people together. As Mennell (1989: 65) argues, this built on the gradual extension of towns, trade and the use of money during the ninth to eleventh centuries which stood as a counterpoint to the main processes of feudalisation and the fragmentation of effective power (see also Duby, 1988). With a relatively secure power and taxation base, secular authorities could contemplate long term alliances and economic agreements, and begin to build an infrastructure which assisted trading links. Planning thus became more important both for secular authorities and for many individuals.

Koenigsberger's (1987) analysis of the changing political environment of the late medieval period highlights how certain political rulers became dissatisfied with the Church's legitimacy and international power, and how the flexibility of Catholic communities became a liability. Exploiting this flexibility, a number of kings argued that adherence to Catholicism and obedience to the Pope were separable. For example, in a dispute in 1508, Ferdinand of Aragon threatened to withdraw his kingdoms of Spain, Sicily, Naples and Sardinia from obedience to the Pope. The importance of this incident was that a Catholic king thought that 'the papacy, and hence the unity of the Church, were expendable without detriment to the Catholic religion'. Similarly, Henry VIII of England (1509–47) disavowed obedience to the Pope, who had refused to annul his marriage. Henry 'declared himself "supreme head" of the English Church, but expressed the wish that this should not change one iota of Christian belief' (Koenigsberger, 1987). Disputes within the Christian West even led to alliances with the previously demonised Ottoman Empire (Rodinson, 1988: 34).

These political cleavages ruptured the position and integrity of Catholicism within the West, a situation which was reinforced by the growing influence and power of urban secular elites. Wuthnow has pointed out that, at the close of the Middle Ages, much of Europe was still predominantly rural. Secular government was often underdeveloped in these areas, and Catholicism was an integral part of the moral economy of rural life (Wuthnow, 1989). Nevertheless, this period also marked a time when cities grew in population, prosperity and political organisation. This was important for two main reasons.

First, the growth of cities encouraged territorial rulers to rely on the influence of political assemblies; assemblies which acted frequently against the interests of aristocratic and ecclesiastical estates (Wuthnow, 1989: 33, 47). One obvious strategy for power-hungry princes was to co-opt the support of newly emerging lay elites in order to gain for themselves some of the spoils acquired by the Church (spoils which grew as the Church expanded through large tracts of west and south-west Europe) (Bax, 1987: 3). Second, the growth of medieval towns stimulated a more general process which threatened the two-way character of Catholic communities. This is illustrated by Weber's (1958) comparative study of city life. Weber argued that medieval cities were, from their origin, associations of individuals. Allegiance was sworn to the city as an *individual* and not as a member of a kindred group. This had a religious basis, as citizenship was dependent on participation in the Mass (the factor used to exclude Jews from the status of citizens, and one of the bases on which existing anti-

Jewish propaganda flourished: Abulafia, 1994; Sennett, 1994). However, it also contained strains toward individualism in which the rights of individuals became more prominent and the *associational* character of medieval cities became more evident (Nisbet, 1993 [1966]: 81–82). These political and economic developments increased the size and influence of secular elites and stimulated the beginnings of a form of bodily being in the world dependent on foresight, planning and reflection, rather than volatility and violence. These events had important implications for the long term social and cultural influence of Catholicism as they led to the growth of secular authorities able and willing to challenge the power of the Church.

The rise of cognitive association

These political developments were not the only ways in which the power of the Church and the prevalence of carnal ways of knowing came under challenge. We stressed at the beginning of this chapter that since Catholic communities developed out of a two-way interaction of Church and locality, and on the basis of a particular engagement with the body, the cultural power of the Church would always be partial. In this respect, the Renaissance and court society cultures were especially significant in shaping the consumption of Catholicism, and in generating new forms of embodied identity among the educated elites of Europe.

Historians have suggested that many aspects of the modern individual, which used to be attributed to the Renaissance, are more aptly located in the twelfth century (Ferguson, 1948; Burkhardt, 1935 [1860]). These include the appearance of the individual as author and hero in poetry and romance (Dronke, 1970), the discovery of an 'inner landscape' of self (Benton, 1977), and more choice in religious lifestyle. Real though these changes were, Bynum (1980) has argued that far from heralding the appearance of the modern individual, these were signs that people were more able and willing to scrutinise and judge whether their behaviour and intentions fitted religiously and publicly justifiable types, roles and models. As Bynum argues, 'In the twelfth century, turning inward to explore motivation went hand in hand with a sense of belonging to a group which not only defined its own life by means of a model but also was itself . . . a means of salvation and of evangelism' (Bynum, 1980: 14).

Those signs of early 'individualism' remain pertinent to our concerns, as they illustrate a tendency toward introspection and the development of an inner life which served as a counterpoint to the more direct forms of carnal knowing common to most medieval people (Duby, 1988). They were also developed in more significant and secular directions by the later Renaissance and court society cultures. These developments did not eschew the Church entirely, but derived a significant portion of their meaning from codes and cognitive considerations based on extra-religious considerations such as personal status.[14] They also encouraged forms of interdependency that were based less on (potentially volatile) *doing*, and much more on *interpreting*, *monitoring* and *evaluating* the self and others.

As Peter Burke (1987) has pointed out, the Renaissance represented a wholesale attempt to revive a classical culture, which meant the rejection of elements of the Middle Ages, and this had an important impact on Catholic communities. Humanists attempted to broaden and deepen the scope of education, for example, emphasising speaking and writing as well as reading. It was concerned, in other words, with a much greater attentiveness to linguistic symbols, their autonomy, and their representative accuracy.[15]

This partial dislocation of culture from religion was reinforced by certain developments within those court societies which operated in Europe from the fourteenth to the eighteenth centuries. Court societies were hardly irreligious arenas, as the fourteenth century Avignon papal court illustrates, and were also involved in the Crusades (Elias, 1983).[16] Nevertheless, they promoted 'arts of consumption' driven by a search for aristocratic distinction. This involved learning ways of seeing, dressing, interpreting, and ultimately *experiencing* the body which could not be contained entirely within the parameters of Church culture. As Elias (1978 [1939], 1983) demonstrates, it was in these arenas that the *courtois* codes of behaviour took shape in a form which enabled it to spread through the later Middle Ages, and to exert an influence on the manners and personality not only of court members but of significant members of the wider society.[17]

To be successful in the search for distinction at court society, Elias has suggested, individuals had to develop an 'armour-plating of self-constraint' in which reflections intervened 'more or less automatically between the affective, spontaneous impulse to act and the actual performance of the action in word or deed' (Elias, 1983: 242–243). People had to 'meticulously weigh the gestures and expressions of everyone else', carefully fathoming 'the intention and meaning of each of their utterances' which were indicative of personal status and contributed to the formation of court opinion (Elias, 1982 [1939]: 271; 1983: 104). Affective outbursts were dangerous as they revealed unguarded feelings and signified a loss of control (see also Keen, 1984).

If we accept this view, we can see how the pressures of court society brought about significant changes in how some people related to themselves and their social environment; changes which ran directly counter to the volatility, emotionality and violence of the body built upon by the Church. Expressed at its most general, people could not afford to live through their sensuous bodies at court, but had to make the *mind* the controlling agency in order to comply with the demands of court etiquette. Court society turned the body into a surface on which the self was managed, spoken and made visible. Self-restraint was prized and courtly etiquette sought to marginalise or suppress bodily similarities between animals and humans. While the monastic regimes of medieval religious orders may also have placed constraints on the management of the body, courtly competition represented much less of a flight into physicality, apparent in certain monastic and other religious orders (Bynum, 1987; Delumeau, 1990), and much more of a conscious *distancing* of the sensuous, potentially grotesque, body from the mind.

More specifically, the pressures of court society not only encouraged individuals to manage the impressions they made on others, but to develop a reflexivity in evaluating the effects of these impressions. In a context where 'a single unconsidered utterance could have a permanent effect' (Elias, 1983: 110), court society required the ability to plan ahead and anticipate the possible consequences of actions. The reflexivity required for these tasks also promoted a growing degree of mutual identification between people based in the mind rather than in religious ritual. As Johan Goudsblom puts it, preserving or improving one's position within court society required a 'psychological' view of others which involved precise observation of others' actions and expressions (Goudsblom, 1987).

The skills required to function as an adult in court society also tended to increase the bodily and psychological distance between adults and children. As the degree of self-control exercised by adults grew, so did the amount of learning children had to accomplish before they were accepted as full members of society. This civilising development was in marked contrast to the relations between adults and children that scholars have suggested was characteristic of most sectors of medieval society (Ariès, 1979 [1960]; Gurevich, 1985; Flandrin, 1979). It also exerted some effect on the position of women. Renaissance court societies provided more, if still limited, opportunities for upper-class women to be considered 'learned'. While these women would usually have to give up their education on marriage, they continued as 'patrons of learning' for others (Lerner, 1993: 195).

Given their emphasis on the conscious control and careful representation of the body, it would be wrong to view these Renaissance and courtly developments as secular celebrations of the fleshy, sensual body. The body's shape, size and symmetry were frequently idealised in Renaissance paintings, sculpture and clothes; religious images of the body remained influential (Bottomley, 1979; Delumeau, 1990); and religious movements (such as the civilising campaigns of the clergy in Italy) rivalled the influence of court societies (Duby, 1988; Kempers, 1982; Mennell, 1989). Nevertheless, courtly culture and Renaissance art did much to make bodies locations for increasingly refined codes of distinction. These codes were formalised in those works on etiquette and manners penned by fifteenth- and sixteenth-century humanists such as Erasmus. They also show how relations of interdependency began to move away from the limitations of religious ritual and sensual emotion, and towards the human capacities associated with self-control and the mind released (relatively speaking) from the immediacy of the affects. This partial liberation of the mind from emotional volatility was eventually to create its own contradictions, but it represented the beginnings of an important departure in terms of how people came to know themselves, other people, and the world in which they lived.

The transformation of body pain and truth

Talal Asad's (1983) analysis of the transformation of medieval patterns of producing truth through the infliction of bodily pain draws our attention to a further example of the emergence of a more cognitive experience of the world, which also had a destructive effect on the corporeal unity of the Church. The starting point for Asad's analysis is a recognition of the consensus amongst historians concerning the growing appeal to human, rather than supernatural, sources of judgement as the Middle Ages progressed. Southern (1993 [1953]: 101–102), for example, has discussed how the study of Roman Law made people aware of elaborate systems of purely human proof in settling disputes. The Catholic Church's Lateran Council of 1215 expressed this shift towards human patterns of proof when it forbade priests to take part in the trial by ordeal, which the Church had previously encouraged and regulated, so that people 'were forced to prefer the probability arrived at by human agencies to the certainties of divine judgement' (Southern, 1993 [1953]: 102).

The Church's actions thus marked a partial shift away from the syncretistic flexibility with regard to popular superstitions and magical practices, reflecting not simply a rationalist, more human-centred perspective, but an underlying transformation in the experience of embodiment. Asad notes that many historians have praised the medieval critics of the ordeal for their rationalism, failing to understand that it was 'changes in the practices defining truth which led to the "recognition" of superstition, and not the other way round ... the reforming Church didn't *rediscover* rationality, it *redefined* it' (Asad, 1983: 291). The forbidding of priests to become involved in the trial by ordeal thus gives rise to the emergence of torture, as part of the inquisitorial system; a strategy of inquiry which aimed to produce *information*, making *verbal discourse* the medium of truth rather than the marks or position of the defeated body in the trial by ordeal (Asad, 1983: 296). In shifting truth away from the body and into the mind, represented by this inquisitorial method of working upon the body in order to produce a verbal confession, the Church's actions prefigure the Protestant emphasis upon the word above the embodied community of Christians. As Asad (1983: 298) expresses it, 'the truth is both the author of the word and the word authorised'. Through this increasingly cognitive emphasis, and an attendant encouragement of processes of disenchantment, the Church itself had begun to open up the possibilities of experiences of truth and reality which were no longer closely tied into the embodied bonds of the sacred eating community.

Preparing the ground for reform

These cultural and political developments encouraged a more critical and sceptical approach to the Church's authority by educated elites and many of those in power. While the state of religious practice may have remained healthy in certain respects (Bossy, 1985; Duffy, 1992: 132, 479; Chadwick, 1990 [1964]: 11), emerging changes in the embodied basis upon which truth and meaning were established allowed an increasingly reflexive scrutiny of the institutional hierarchies of the Church. The Church faced widespread charges of corruption and a number of territorial powers were no longer prepared to subsidise a 'foreign power' (Elton, 1963; Scribner, 1994). It is highly questionable whether the Church was any more corrupt in the later Middle Ages than it had been in previous centuries, but the point is that many people were now in a position to become *aware* of this corruption and to use it as an opportunity for restructuring their relationship with the Church. The social and corporeal ground for reform had been prepared, and new forms of sociality and meaning construction were able to emerge. New patterns of embodiment were developing, assisted by the Renaissance and court society, while the religious contexts which had re-formed medieval bodies were themselves being undermined.

In summary, we have seen in this chapter that the nature and place of human embodiment across large segments of medieval Europe was shaped by the beliefs and ritual cycles of Catholic Christianity. This stimulated a sense of interdependence and reciprocity in human relationships, and located the reality and meaning of social and natural worlds in the corporeal bonds of a sacred eating community. Catholic communities were shaped by their constituents, but were also responsible for a partial re-formation of medieval forms of embodiment. They 'ate into' the bodies of their members by structuring their contact with the sacred, and by directing this toward the cementing of particular patterns of sociality.

Notes

1. The distinction between the laity and 'clerical elites' was not as firm nor as clear in the Middle Ages as it came to be in subsequent eras. Many monks and nuns did fulfil the roles of 'religious specialists' and had access to the Bible and other sources of the Christian tradition which most of the laity did not. The extent to which priests had access to, and knowledge of, these sources varied considerably, however, and became a source of controversy during the Protestant Reformation (Thomas, 1973 [1971]; Chadwick, 1990 [1964]; Cameron, 1991; McGrath, 1993). In fact, the professionalisation of the clergy was an important consequence of the Reformation and Counter-Reformation (Cameron, 1991).

2. In this respect, however, Durkheim's (1984 [1893]) contrast in *The Division of Labour* between premodern 'mechanical' and modern 'organic' solidarity lacks a certain descriptive power: the brittle, utilitarian and undynamic qualities implied by 'mechanical solidarity' hardly do justice to the corporeal dynamism of community, as Durkheim himself seemed to realise: he quickly abandoned the term in his own work (Nisbet, 1993 [1966]: 85). Interestingly, in pursuing a basically Durkheimian analysis of modern and postmodern forms of sociality, Maffesoli (1996) understands modern forms of solidarity to be more 'mechanical' than the 'organic' forms of pre- and postmodernity.

3. Such an attitude was evident, for example, in Saint Augustine's argument that 'the separation of spiritual and bodily appetites involves . . . a sublimation of food into words' (Kilgour, 1990: 52; Falk, 1994: 35).

4. This applies to the emergence of the doctrine of the Immaculate Conception of Mary, which became dogma only in 1854, and to the development and popularity of the Rosary and Marian devotion. It has been noted that the 'Christianity of the later Middle Ages was a supple, flexible varied entity, adapted to the needs, concerns and tastes (with all their undoubted, crude, primitive features) of the people who created it. It was not an inflexible tyranny presided over by a remote authority. It left room for personal preference and private or local initiative. It threatened but it also comforted; it disciplined, but it also entertained' (Cameron, 1991: 19). This picture of medieval religion calls into question the judgement of those who see pre-Reformation Catholicism as both authoritarian and unresponsive to the laity (Mellor, 1993a).

5. There were several means by which this cross-fertilisation occurred. The formative years of Christian thought were, for example, influenced by a Stoic thought which itself promoted specific regimes of caring for the body (Stoicism was the dominant philosophy in the Roman Empire at the turn of the millennium). The Emperor Constantine's adoption of Christianity as the official imperial religion in AD 312 affected the moral and legal climate of Rome, and did much to cement a gap between the practice and institutionalisation of religion. Finally, the Church itself became the chief bearer of Roman culture after the fall of the Empire (Chadwick, 1990 [1964]), and thus carried with it certain ancient dispositions toward the flesh. Despite this cross-fertilisation, there remained important points of difference between early Christian and Graeco-Roman views of the body. While the dominant emphasis in Graeco-Roman society was on *disciplining* the body (in order to maintain vital bodily heats and minimise the links humans had with the animal world), early Christianity was concerned with *transforming* the fallen human body.

6. Peter Brown (1988) has rightly highlighted the differences and discontinuities between early and medieval Christianity. Nevertheless, the development of early Christianity remains pertinent to our analysis as its legacy emerged from the Dark Ages to achieve a fuller elaboration and influence within the Catholic communities of the Middle Ages.

7. The conversion of the Roman Emperor Constantine is especially significant in relation to the further religious codification of bodily practices as it transformed Christianity from an illicit faith to the favoured religion of the Emperors. According to many Christians, some of whom took flight to the desert to be 'alone with the alone' and practise a purer form of faith, this corrupted and polluted their religion. It is certainly true that the Church effectively incorporated or sanctioned many pagan rituals and practices based on various aspects of carnival and involving various excesses of the flesh (Brown, 1988). In so doing, the Church interacted with its community, helped shape and impart a new meaning to local traditions, and provided the conditions for a growing gap between religious practices and their formal codification; processes which continued in the Middle Ages (Bossy, 1985). Whatever other effects this change in status had on Christianity (Bottomley, 1979: 74; Brown, 1988: 23–25), it did help to provide a supportive context for the codification of the religious body in the work of two of the most influential early Christian figures, Saint Ambrose of Milan (339–397 AD) and Saint Augustine (354–430 AD).

Saint Augustine was enormously influential within the Catholic Church, yet also inspired Reformation theologians (Bottomley, 1979: 82). He adapted and widened Saint Ambrose's important vision of a humanity transformed within the Catholic Church by placing the human body, and particularly human sexuality, within a highly detailed and penetrative net of prescription and explanation. This revolved around the notion of corporeal order, applied to *both* sexes (Brown, 1988: 349), and held that the misery of the human race consisted in the loss of harmony that it was condemned to after the Fall. Saint Augustine made a place for marriage in the Church, but also viewed the dead body as the most visible sign of human frailty. Death could never be welcomed as freeing the soul from the body as it prevented the soul's deepest wish: to live at peace with the body.

8. According to Said (1978: 59): 'After Mohammed's death in 632, the military and later the cultural and religious hegemony of Islam grew enormously. First Persia, Syria, and Egypt, then Turkey, then North Africa fell to the Muslim armies; in the eighth and ninth centuries Spain, Sicily, and parts of France were conquered. By the thirteenth and fourteenth centuries

Islam ruled as far east as India, Indonesia, and China. And at this extraordinary assault Europe could respond with very little except fear and a kind of awe. Christian authors witnessing the Islamic conquests had scant interest in the learning, high culture, and frequent magnificence of the Muslims . . . What Christians really felt about the Eastern armies was that they had '"all the appearance of a swarm of bees, but with a heavy hand . . . they devastated everything": so wrote Erchembert, a cleric in Monte Cassino.'

9. The common, male-centred view of conception and pregnancy at this time was that paternal 'blood' was merely 'baked' in the mother, and it was therefore essential that there was absolutely no doubt that a pregnant wife was carrying only her husband's child (Laqueur, 1992 [1990]).

10. Even at this time the Catholic Church condemned contraception, and its attacks on the 'mortal sin' of those couples who sought sexual pleasure in marriage without the attendant goal of procreation indicate that some couples did seek to limit the size of their families. Klapisch-Zuber (1990: 301) notes, for example, the condemnation of sodomitic practices between spouses in Bernardino's warning to women not to obey their husbands if they should seek to impose upon them a sexual position that 'breaks the order of God' and makes the woman 'into a beast or into a male'. This is a notable example of the Church seeking to mediate the relationship between women's bodies and social solidarity by encouraging women to prize its teachings above the authority of their husbands.

11. This view may have been derived from the role of Eve in the Fall, but assumed an intense form in the institutional hierarchies of Catholicism. Jean Delumeau (1990) has addressed these images of women by suggesting that the medieval taste for the macabre was an 'antifeminism' in that it associated women's bodies with sin and death. To support this, he quotes from a poem composed at the beginning of the fifteenth century, 'Der Ackermann aus Bohnen' (The Plowman from Bohemia), where 'Death' describes the female body as 'a repulsive object, a bag of filth, a foul food, a stinking sink, a repulsive bucket, a decaying carcass, a mildewed coffer, a threadbare sack, a pocket with a hole' (Delumeau, 1990: 47). Such images were, however, mainly the products of monastics anxious to maintain their celibacy and counter their own sexual feelings towards women. These images of women's bodies are also commonplace in other religions, such as Buddhist monasticism, where they serve much the same purpose (Ling, 1981).

12. The community of medieval marriage was located with a family-based economy. This contrasted greatly with the restriction of women to the home in the period following the Reformation. The medieval household was an important centre of economic production at the time and women invariably found themselves carrying out functions, such as the supervision of agricultural work, which had long been thought of as 'male' tasks (Howell, 1988: 11; Pantel, 1992).

13. In the case of sin, for example, this was manifest in the practice of indulgences (which allowed people to purchase a reduction of time spent in purgatory) and in the public and visible organisation of forgiveness. Sin was regarded as a visible and social matter, something which had to be forgiven in a visible and social way. In many ways the development of the theory of the sacrament of penance in the Middle Ages may be regarded as an attempt to consolidate the social grounding of forgiveness. Forgiveness was not simply a private matter between the individual and God; it was a public matter involving that individual, the Church and society (McGrath, 1993: 102). Although there are grounds for noting an increasing privatisation of penance in the medieval era (Asad, 1988), this social orientation remained central due to penance's sacramental character.

14. According to Duby (1988: 556–557), 'A new conception of private life developed imperceptibly in the midst of the gregarious family. From now on privacy meant being oneself among others, in one's own room, at one's windows, with one's own property, one's own purse, and one's own faults – recognised and pardoned – as well as one's own dreams, inspirations, and secrets.'

15. Based on the cultural revival of antiquity, the Renaissance rediscovered the body as an object of aesthetic beauty. Artists like Botticelli and Leonardo da Vinci, and sculptors like Cellini, invested the flesh with a form and attraction which went far beyond the parameters of

dominant religious codifications (Burke, 1987). This was reinforced by philosophers, such as Castiglione, who praised the body as an object of *secular* worth and whose work contributed to a renewed focus on the body as a location for social codes (Bottomley, 1979; Synnott, 1993).

16. Forms of court culture can be seen as early as the twelfth century among the courts of major territorial lords through France, Germany and Italy. However, in referring us to Sombart's (1967 [1913]) *Luxury and Capitalism*, Mennell suggests that the papal court at Avignon in the fourteenth century can be seen as the first court which attracted a cultured and leisured elite with some expertise in the *'arts of consumption'*. The Avignon court was followed by the courts of Renaissance Italy, before the royal court of France 'attained undisputed leadership of Europe in matters courtly during the C17th and C18th' (Mennell, 1989: 81).

17. A person's rank within court society was determined first of all by their house – their official title. Permeating and altering this hierarchy, however, was an order or rank dependent on the favour a courtier enjoyed with a king. This was based on the power and importance an individual enjoyed within the field of court tensions, and competition within this field placed great demands on the management of the body. Displays of 'bad manners', defined as such because they offended prevailing behavioural codes, were likely to bring the offender into disrepute, and success in this status competition demanded a finely honed set of impressions management skills.

4

SINFUL BODIES, PROFANE ASSOCIATIONS

Marshall Berman (1982) has argued that Marx's vision of modernity as a state where 'all that is solid melts into air' represents a generally encountered experience of living in modern societies. It is our suggestion that this experience of flux, change and instability has its cultural archetype in the sixteenth-century Protestant attack on, and reconstruction of, medieval Catholicism. This attention to the transformative effects of the Reformation is not, in itself, new. Durkheim (1951 [1897]) and, most famously, Weber (1991 [1904–5]) were greatly concerned by these effects, while sociology had from its origins what Nisbet (1993 [1966]: 230) calls a 'preoccupation with Protestantism' and its depreciation of ritual and promotion of individualism. Comte, for example, traced what he saw as 'the present dislocations of society' back to the 'spiritual disorganisation of Europe' which followed the attacks of Luther and Calvin upon the 'organic fusion' of religion and society in the Middle Ages (Nisbet, 1993 [1966]: 228–229).

While there are elements of nostalgia in such analyses (Turner, 1987: 151), this sociological preoccupation with Protestantism included a concern with its bodily effects. The Protestant Reformation, which was really a series of reformations, was not merely a transformation of religious *beliefs* which had an important role in encouraging the deconstruction of relations between Church and state, and in promoting the individualism and rationalism which came to mark the Enlightenment project. It also involved a *re-formation* of embodiment. We have already analysed medieval Catholicism as a sacred eating community which ate into its members but was also eaten into in a mutual devouring of the sacred immanent within natural and social worlds. Instead of restructuring the *immersion* of people within their various surroundings, however, Protestantism sought to *abstract* people from the natural, supernatural and social environments, and encouraged believers to apprehend and actively structure their lives as individuals through a committed and fundamentally cognitive engagement with the Word of God (Cameron, 1991).

This reformation of religious community contributed to a sense of both social and corporeal change across much of Europe. Socially, Protestantism helped undermine the view that hierarchies were fixed according to 'divine right', and was also associated with political upheavals and military conflicts, some permanent and some temporary in their impact (Kantorowicz,

1957; Scribner et al., 1994). In this respect, Luther's dismissal of the idea that the Catholic Church enjoyed a privileged position in political affairs provided a justification for lay rulers to challenge and take control of religious affairs in their territories. Indeed, it is the spread of this idea and practice which has frequently been associated with the end of medieval Christendom and the beginnings of the modern secular era in which individuals strove to force their *own* designs on the world (Berger, 1990 [1967]; Cameron, 1991).

If Protestantism stimulated its followers to adopt a critical and inter-ventionist approach to the social world, it also promoted a sense of *corporeal flux*. This was because its doctrines and practices made it difficult for believers to make positive sense of their passions, emotions and desires (Elton, 1963: 103). Human relations and personal actions had to be established and justified on the basis of rational considerations (rational insofar as they were formed on the basis of God's Word), while affective desires tended to be cut free from religious rituals. This is not to say that certain forms of Protestantism, such as the much later development of Pentecostalism, did not come to be characterised by an intense emotionality. This emotionality, however, was constrained and mediated by a thoroughgoing cognitive control manifest as theological conservatism and a strong commitment to the authority of the Bible (Rosenberg, 1988; Lawless, 1991). Unless derived directly from carrying out God's will, strong emotions tended to be seen as a sign of sin or moral laxity rather a necessary counterpart of social bonds (Campbell, 1987: 102; Thomas, 1973 [1971]; Weber, 1991 [1904–5]: 119). This is illustrated by the counsel of Richard Baxter, a prominent Puritan who argued that 'everything is sinful which is contrary to the reason given by God as a norm of action. Not only passions which have a sinful content, but all feelings which are senseless and intemperate as such. They destroy the countenance and, as things of the flesh, prevent us from rationally directing all action and feeling to God' (Weber, 1991 [1904–5]: 236).

The problem with these sentiments was that they called for the elimina-tion of human enfleshment. Emotions may have been largely superfluous to the Puritan project, but they continued to 'race round' the body and caused growing concern and anxiety whenever they 'bubbled up' to obstruct rational thought. Luther may have been relatively relaxed about the pleasures gained from eating and drinking (rejecting only those activities specifically forbidden by the Bible), for example, but Calvin and later Reformers made a much stronger link between physicality, sin and evil (rejecting anything not approved by the Bible) (Friedenthal, 1970; Synnott, 1993: 20–21). These features of Protestantism, which sometimes reached the extremes of a paradoxical cognitive obsession with the dangers of the flesh, could, as Colin Campbell (1987) suggests, lead individuals to a melancholy and despair prompted by a basic inability to 'make sense' of their sensual bodies.

Centred upon an essentially individual and cognitive engagement with a radically transcendent God, Protestantism made the sacred sublime insofar as it could only be apprehended indirectly, through the Word of God, and not directly through the fleshy body. Despite the superfluousness of emotions to the Puritans, other forms of Protestantism may have seen some religiously legitimised emotions as being of importance, but here too they were often filtered through processes of cognition and the medium of texts. In place of a thoroughly embodied devouring of religious meaning, Protestantism undertook a *discursive symbolisation* of religion closely associated with individualism, self-reflexivity and a tendency towards the *production* rather than *consumption* of religious meaning. In so doing, it also encouraged patterns of sociality more 'secular-associational' than 'sacred-communal' (Tönnies, 1957 [1887]). As Alain Touraine (1995: 26) argues, the importance of Protestantism rests not so much upon the expressed contents of religious faith, but upon its rejection of the enchantment of the world, previously defined by both the sacraments and the temporal powers of popes.[1]

Although Protestantism has often been associated with the emergence of democratic ideals within Western societies, it was Alexis de Tocqueville (1945 [1840]) who first pointed out that Protestantism tends to make people independent rather than 'equal' (Nisbet, 1993 [1966]: 236). In the light of this, and the Protestant rejection of enchantment, it would be inappropriate to talk about Protestant 'communities', despite the fact that the Puritans themselves placed some importance on this term. The Reformers promoted 'associations of faith', based on the shared commitment to particular beliefs, rather than communities of bodily interaction bound together through ritual eating. In Tönnies's (1957 [1887]: 64) terms, these associations were 'essentially separated in spite of all uniting factors'. Association was dependent upon the clarification of correct beliefs and the *commitment* of individuals to these beliefs, both of which reflect a prioritisation of cognitive dimensions of human experience above sensual aspects. In Maffesoli's (1993b: 10) terms, there was nothing 'self-evident' about Protestant associations.[2]

The first part of this chapter clarifies what we mean by Protestant 'associations of faith', and from here we go on to explore the transformation of the sacred into a 'sublimated', radically transcendent form, and the attendant profanation of large areas of social life. Following this, we examine how the profane associations of Protestantism informed reconstructions of the family, charity and death. These religious reconstructions helped promote cognitive modes of apprehending social life over carnal ways of knowing the world. However, they did little to make positive sense of people's fleshy desires, and tended instead to perceive these as 'bodily guarantees of sin'. We concentrate on this view of the body as sinful in the concluding sections of this chapter and suggest that the Protestant reformation of the body was associated with civilising and decivilising developments which differed from those characteristic of the medieval era.

Profane associations of faith

Earlier we observed that medieval Catholicism was characterised by a syncretistic flexibility which sought to incorporate into itself a plurality of beliefs, practices and symbols. This incorporation was based on an engagement with the fleshy body and expressed through a ritual engagement with the immanence of the sacred which constituted community. In this section, we consider some of the implications of the Protestant attempt to turn Christianity into an 'association of faith'. This involved not only undermining the corporeal bonds of community and the status of the Church as an institution, but also radically devaluing ritual and promoting the quest for a 'pure' form of Christianity. In short, the emergence of Protestant associations marks not only the appearance of an alternative way of organising and understanding religion, but a new account of how human beings could experience themselves and their relationships (Dumont, 1982; McGrath, 1993: 104; Turner, 1991: 155–156).

Protestant associations of faith were to be constructed on the basis of two, closely connected, principles. First, by distancing religion from people's embodied relations and close contact senses, both faith and the sacred were to be made more cognitive. The Reformer Zwingli, for example, argued that those things 'which indulged the senses starved the spirit' (Michalski, 1993). Second, the Reformers invested faith and the sacred with a linguistic and textual character, and thereby contributed to the 'discursive symbolisation' of religion.[3] From this point onwards, then, associations of faith were to be reconstructed on the basis of a cognitive engagement with religious discourse. Anything that could not be justified on the basis of this symbolism was construed as a threat to these Protestant associations (O'Neill, 1985: 67).

Alienating faith from sensual communities

It has been suggested that a tendency to break the link between religion and human community, by giving the Christian Church an essentially non-social meaning, has always been inherent in Christianity (Touraine, 1995: 35). We have already seen that this was not the dominant tendency in Catholicism during much of the medieval era, but such a rupture lies at the very heart of the Protestant Reformation. Protestantism alienated faith from large areas of lived experience by a radical idealisation of the 'religious community' which abstracted it from everyday social interactions. For example, while the Reformers continued to express a belief in the 'Holy Church' of the creeds, this 'community' was no longer an earthly institution, but was unknowable, invisible and thus *purely* a concept of faith (Althaus, 1986 [1966]: 290–293; Cameron, 1991: 146). This distinction between an actual and a 'virtual' community was expressed by the radical Reformer, Sebastian Franck, who argued that the 'outward Church of Christ . . . went up into heaven' 1400 years ago, and that the ecclesiastical forms which now claim to embody it are therefore 'parodies' (McGrath, 1993: 191; Littel, 1958).[4]

The Protestant 'community' of the Church came to be understood as the 'aggregate of all those who *truly* believed', regardless of their separation by time and space. Mere associations of embodied people, in contrast, could only be examples of profane social interaction (Cameron, 1991: 145).[5] What began as an attempt to 'purify' Christianity quickly evolved into a *reinvention* of Christianity. This prioritised the cognitive commitment of individuals, and rendered profane those embodied social bonds the Catholic Church had sacralised. From this point onwards, Protestant forms of Christianity ceased to be fully embodied or sensually experienced social realities; religion became an altogether more abstract phenomenon.

It was not simply in matters of doctrinal belief that the Reformers sought to alienate religious community from sensual experience; they also reduced the scope, character and significance of the sacramental ritual apparatus. Rejecting the Catholic pattern of seven sacraments mirroring various life stages which had been established during the Middle Ages, Luther initially recognised three (baptism, the Eucharist and penance), but then only two (baptism and the Eucharist) (McGrath, 1993: 165). Furthermore, Protestantism's repudiation of 'transubstantiation' (the doctrine which held that bread and wine turned into the Body and Blood of Christ when consecrated during the Mass) meant that even the Eucharist lost its magical and bodily connotations (Elton, 1963: 99). This began when Luther argued that Christians should believe Christ is present in the Eucharist, but not *physically* present in the actual substance of the bread and wine. It was taken much further by Zwingli, who argued that the bread and wine are not altered in themselves: what alters is their *signification* (McGrath, 1993: 176; Michalski, 1993: 51). This symbolisation of religion reflects a clear prioritisation of mind over body. The presence of Christ is 'spiritual', and therefore to be experienced psychologically, while the 'body' of Christ becomes a mere signifier, a way of speaking.

Given the Protestant rejection of earthly community, consolidated by a transformation of the sacraments and directed toward eradicating the idea of the 'stranger' who does not fully belong (Simmel, 1971 [1908a]), it is hardly surprising that many Protestants eventually rejected *any* form of sacramental practice. The Quakers, for example, eliminated all sacramentally based ritual, and evolved church services characterised by a silent waiting-on-the-Spirit. This 'unsacramental quietism' was very much apparent in the personal character of George Fox, the founder of the Quakers. At the age of nineteen, Fox had abandoned going to church, choosing to wander around with his bible, waiting for the inspiration of the Holy Spirit (Chadwick, 1990 [1964]: 241). As Bauman (1995) notes, this early modern wandering was associated with a 'freeing' of the mind from the familiarities and constraints of specific locales, and a refusal to attribute bodily social relationships with sacred value (see also Sennett, 1994; Tester, 1992).

To summarise, Protestantism abstracted religion from much of people's everyday lived experiences by dislocating faith and the sacred from ritual forms encountered through the sensuous body, and turning them into *cognitive ideals*. The sacred resided in the mind, while bodily relationships were, at best, a matter of profane association rather than religious community. As Bataille (1986 [1957]) suggests, this sensual separation of people minimises what they share in common and emphasises their isolation as individuals. Touch, smell and sacrifice are divested of much of their meaning as media for communication, while individuals are encouraged to engage in a form of 'monadic communication' via religious symbols.

The discursive symbolisation of religion

As well as distancing religion from earthly communities and sensual experiences, Protestant associations sought to reconstruct faith according to the Word of God. This valued Scripture, linguistic symbols and reflexivity above human relations and sensuality. Instead of being dissolved into a unity through the collective effervescence stimulated by religious ritual, Reformers were linked together as individuals through shared use of, and obedience to, those symbols which revolved around the issue of individual *belief* (Falk, 1994).

Central to this development was the Puritan view that the will of God was revealed to all, on an equal basis, through the *Scriptures* (Haller, 1938; Hill, 1966). As Luther (1955 [1520]) argued in *On the Babylonish Captivity of the Church*, 'we are all equally priests, that is . . . we have the same power in the Word' (Reardon, 1981). Of course, religious discourse was not unimportant to medieval Catholicism. In the thirteenth century, for example, William of Auxerre saw the *words* in the Mass as having the power to turn bread and wine into the Body and Blood of Christ (Rappaport, 1979: 201). Compared with the degree of autonomy that linguistic symbols gained within Protestantism, however, these words were *words-within-a-ritual-context*; a context which was itself seen as an integrated part of social community.[6] As John Bossy notes, in the pre-Reformation Church, the word 'was the deposit, not the creator, of a common history, and in its written form neither the original nor the most important such deposit' (Bossy, 1985: 99). The tradition of the Fathers, common religious custom, and the sacramental mysteries were seen as more important than language. Protestantism, in contrast, invested religious discourse with an ontological existence and social importance over and above earthly communities and sensual experiences. This can be seen in the case of both religious texts and preaching.

Texts had always been important to the Catholic Church but they became qualitatively more so within Protestantism. One striking manifestation of this was Luther's recommendation that the walls of cemeteries be painted with texts rather than images (Burke, 1983: 229).[7] Another important example concerns the Bible. Before the Reformation, the Bible was a text-in-context, a text which was revered, maintained and read in the Church. The Bible had been put together in the Church, and the Church had sole authority to be able to interpret it. Although there had been many pre-Reformation attempts to quote the Bible against the Church these had never succeeded (Congar, 1972).

Nevertheless, the Reformers broke from this consensus concerning the Church's authority and introduced a new way of reading the Bible. The Bible was now the inspired Word of God, and was to be validated and interpreted by the power of personal 'inspiration', not by the authority of the Church (Cameron, 1991: 139). This served to cut loose this sacred text from community, and make it an autonomous source of authority; a status expressed theologically in the phrase *sola scriptura*. The Protestant rejection of the doctrine of purgatory and the practice of praying for the dead, for example, were based on the argument that there was no basis for these in Scripture. As with other Protestant rejections of Catholic practices, it is notable that *communal* activities are rejected on a *textual* basis.

If the discursive symbolisation of religion was evident in the Protestant treatment of texts, it was also manifest within *preaching*. Preaching became separated from ritual and locality and became extremely important to the Reformers' cause; a judgement which should, perhaps, come as no great surprise given the levels of illiteracy of the time (Heimert and Delbanco, 1985: 13; McGrath, 1993: 15). A typical example of this can be seen in the well-known 'Sermon of the Plowers' by Hugh Latimer (a prominent leader of the Protestant Reformation in England). Latimer's sermon begins by emphasising the value of the written word, and the importance of individuals increasing their knowledge to better understand that word (Latimer, 1974 [1549]: 1031). He proceeds to criticise earlier (Catholic) priests who had 'long customs' and many 'ceremonies', on the basis that they spiritually starved people by failing to preach God's Word. According to Latimer, those who participate in the 'popish Mass' are actually being 'drawn to the Devil' (Latimer 1974 [1549]: 1038–1039). This approach to preaching reflects a more general Protestant view that the role of a Christian 'minister' (displacing the notion of 'priest') has little to do with the performance of sacramental rituals, but concerns the expression of Christian discourse and the education of people in a sound knowledge of Christian doctrine.

The centrality of preaching to the Reformation is another example of how religion was progressively transformed into a form of discourse which tended to stimulate greater levels of individual reflexivity (Lerner, 1993). In contrast to the Catholic Church (in which the volatile dimensions of the medieval body were directed through ritual to the sensual experience of religion), Protestantism was more subjective and introspective as it was tied to the individual interpretation of discursive symbols. It gave individuals more authority over their religion, but was also characterised by a strong emphasis on the need to acquire 'proper' knowledge of religion, which tended to limit the 'empowerment of the laity'. Consequently, while there may have been a theoretical emphasis on the equality of all believers, the weight placed on correct doctrine resulted in a strong professionalisation of the Protestant clergy (McGrath, 1993: 206–207).[8]

As Haller (1938) has suggested, the influence of this discursive symbolisation of religion had much to do with its ability to provide moral values in a time marked by flux and change. Once removed from ritual contexts, words could provide individuals with direction in a world where medieval social relations were breaking up, where commercialisation and urban areas were growing (Haller, 1938: 117). This discursive symbolisation was closely associated with male authority, and was informed by that patriarchal organisation of households which featured in Protestant theology (Power, 1975; Stone, 1977; Turner, 1984). In this context, it tended to be men who had authority to speak and interpret while women were expected to listen.

Nevertheless, Lerner (1993) has suggested that the Reformers' apprehension of religion through linguistic symbols (which stimulated communicative talk, but also internal thought) had the general impact of 'opening up' the identities of both sexes to the contingencies of reflection, interpretation and conversation. Reality was no longer 'given' by a social order, but was represented by symbols amenable to rearrangement and reconstruction. This meant that instead of being defined by their embodied contexts, people could develop a more flexible interpretation of events and orient themselves more actively toward the future. As Elias's (1991) discussions of the emancipation and development of symbols suggests, new scenarios and new identities could be envisaged, while social change could more readily be conceptualised.

The transformation of the sacred into the sublime

Protestantism's associations of faith and discursive symbolisation of religion are closely related to a fundamental change in the perception of the sacred. Writing when the development of modernity was well advanced, the French Catholic philosopher Chateaubriand (1856 [1802]) argued that the power of religion lay not in its *ideas* but in the rituals and *mysteries* through which individuals are integrated into community. This was a response to the alienation and disintegration that he and others such as Comte believed Protestantism had encouraged in Western societies (Nisbet, 1993 [1966]: 231). Chateaubriand was reflecting the developing concern with the disenchantment of many areas of social life, and the attendant reconstructions of human sociality, which were to become central to the work of many sociologists such as Weber. We will now consider this disenchantment and the opening up of the world to human intervention.

For Weber (1991 [1904–5]: 13), disenchantment developed with the emergence of Protestantism and expresses the idea that 'there are no mysterious incalculable forces that come into play, but rather that one can ... master all things by calculation'. This was a slow and gradual process.

As Roper (1994: 125–144) demonstrates, merchants were not averse to using magic as a way of helping their business activities by, for example, employing 'crystal ball gazers' in order to gain useful information. Nevertheless, the Reformers demonised these activities; a process which can be related directly to the modernist vision of a world whose character can be discovered through reason (Touraine, 1995: 33), and to the emergence of a corrosive, relentless glare of suspicion concerning all claims to meaningfulness (Tester, 1995a: 52). In a study of the emergence and decline of 'scientific consciousness', Morris Berman (1981: 113) notes that these developments were accompanied by a new type of personality. This was because disenchantment results in markedly different conceptions of identity, relationships and values to those of the medieval era. Nevertheless, although Protestantism rejected the medieval Catholic enchantment of human, natural and social worlds, it expressed an idealism and a tendency towards abstraction which made relationships with the world double-edged in their consequences.

Discussing societies dominated by the ritual construction of meaning, Clifford Geertz (1973: 112) has commented that 'In ritual, the world as lived and the world as imagined . . . turn out to be the same world.' With the emergence of the profane associations of Protestantism, these two 'worlds' not only diverge, but the 'world as imagined' comes to dominate over 'the world as lived'. The somewhat paradoxical effects of this deconstruction of ritual meaning are a devaluation of lived experience and a tendency towards social activism.

The development of the sublime

Lived experience became devalued for Protestants, irrespective of how fearful or joyous it was, since the 'real' was a pale reflection of the 'ideal'. As the Anabaptists and Quakers illustrate, religious life became an attempt to grasp something beyond earthly existence. God was no longer immanent within a magical, unpredictable world, but was radically transcendent of His fallen creation (Berger, 1990 [1967]). Knowledge of God could be apprehended through the Scriptures, but this placed Protestants in a highly abstract relationship with God (Bataille, 1986 [1957]). The sacred was not only removed from large areas of the social and natural worlds, then, but to some extent changed its nature. The sacred, the very essence of religion, became something more *sublime*; existing but defying satisfactory representation, and encouraging estrangement rather than incorporation (Lyotard, 1991).

Bryan Turner's (1987) discussions of nostalgia clarify the consequences of this situation by suggesting that the experience of estrangement stems from being alienated from one's surroundings. Although religious anxiety and depression have been associated with the spiritual and intellectual 'dryness' of medieval monks (Jackson, 1981), these experiences are also relevant to the Protestant removal of the sacred from the human world and its transformation into the sublime. In the Protestant philosophy of Kant (1951 [1790]), for example, the melancholic personality is explicitly related to a concept of the sublime precisely because of the vast gulf between the sublime and the painful, lonely and finite world of humans (Turner, 1987: 149; Cassirer, 1926). Right from the start of the Reformation similar sentiments are evident. Luther's aim was to eliminate all intermediaries between humans and God, to the point where the human world and the divine world are not only completely distinct, but in *conflict* with each other (Touraine, 1995: 37).

The transformation of the sacred into the sublime expresses what Jonathan Z. Smith (1986: 223–224) has called a devaluation of the everyday in favour of 'direct cognition' of religious meaning. Social life is 'external activity', contrasted with an 'inner' search for God, so that even religious practice is understood as 'applied' religion rather than an expression of its essence (Davis, 1994: 48). Thus, what Touraine (1995: 213) calls 'the demise of the sacred' can better be understood as the transformation of the sacred into the sublime. This presupposes an emphasis on cognition and a devaluing of sensual experience, and is connected to the profanation of large areas of social life and the transformation of human sociality. The emergence of the sublime also makes possible, however, the development of an individual subject, and a scientific knowledge that had previously been constrained by religious cosmogony (Touraine, 1995: 213), and is therefore also associated with the appearance of a new social activism.

Intervening in the profane

While the Protestant transformation of the sacred into the disembodied transcendence of the sublime led to the experience of estrangement, it also stimulated a reshaping of that estranged world. Peter Berger has pursued this theme by examining how Protestantism objectified the world as a profane environment, emptied it of its magical content, and thereby made it a place conducive to rational intervention. As Berger (1990 [1967]) puts it, once God is made transcendent, and the status quo cannot be justified by divine will, the world opens to the plans of humans (see also Bauman, 1995).

In Calvin's Geneva of the sixteenth century, for example, social life was subjected to major reconstruction. Sumptuary laws were established, leisure and entertainments were carefully controlled, church attendance became a legal matter, and punishments for adultery included execution (Hill, 1966). Furthermore, the Reformers' alliances with the lay authorities in Germany led to the establishment of Discipline Ordinances and Discipline Courts which filled the concept of order with evangelical fervour, creating a 'compelling and integrated vision of a disciplined society' which could set the purified Christian city apart from the 'Godless outside' (Roper, 1994: 147). The reforms were harshly enforced in an attempt to create 'a republic prostrated before God'; a goal which was attempted elsewhere through the promotion of strict rules of purity and bodily discipline (Greyerz, 1994: 38). People may, perhaps, have known about the Reformation's arrival not when they 'received the sacrament in two kinds', but when they found themselves 'hauled up before the Discipline Lords for swinish drunkenness' (Roper, 1994: 148). As Weber (1991 [1904–5]: 36) notes, the Reformers did not simply reduce Church control over everyday life but sought to regulate 'the whole of conduct which penetrated to all depths of private and public life'. The vigour with which this task was pursued should not, however, be confused with the importance Puritans placed on earthly life. In line with the defining features of Protestant associations, fleshy human interaction paled into insignificance, irrespective of its policing, next to private belief. The strict organisation of social life was seen by Protestants as a *means* to encourage righteous relationships with God.

Individual faith may have been the ultimate concern of the Reformers, but it is important sociologically to clarify how Protestantism opened the world to more rationalised forms of human intervention. First, the Protestant rupturing of people from their traditional surroundings involved an attack on both pagan and Catholic magic and superstition. Ozment (1993) and Turner (1993) locate this as a source of the modern impulse to intervene in and control the world. In this respect, Weber (1991 [1904–5]: 265) has argued that magic was potentially a major obstacle to the rationalisation of economic life, while Thomas reinforces this point by arguing 'It was the abandonment of magic which made possible the usage of technology, not the other way around' (Thomas, 1973 [1971]: 786). This attack on magic helps explain the iconoclasm which was a defining feature of the Reformation. Protestantism associated earthly images with idolatry and sensuality, and while art had been largely religious before Luther (Michalski, 1993: 2), this changed rapidly during the sixteenth century. The Reformers pulled down statues, painted over or smashed stained-glass windows, and whitewashed walls before covering them in texts; an act which returned them safely to the realm of discourse (Duffy, 1992: 454).

A key point to bear in mind, however, is that the Protestant distinction between 'religion' and 'magic' or 'superstition' is itself dependent upon a re-formed experience of embodiment. As Talal Asad (1983) has noted, in the development of Christianity certain phenomena only became classed as 'superstition' once the immanence of the sacred had started to ebb away and a more human-centred interpretation of experience had emerged. We could say, in fact, that there was just no room for magic in the Protestant world view: since God was radically transcendent, the world was necessarily profane. Faith and reason became strictly separated, removing the bridge between them that magic had constituted (Elton, 1963: 99). The Protestant attack upon magic is therefore closely tied to the abstraction of individuals from the corporeal bonds of medieval communities, and the transformation of the sacred into the sublime.

The attack on magic is also related to the stress placed upon the importance of discursive knowledge, the second factor which opened the world to human intervention. The emphasis placed on the Scriptures could boost education and people's abilities to use linguistic symbols as a way of representing the world around them more accurately (Lerner, 1993). Luther may have been seen as an enemy of humanism, but had himself received a classical education and was sympathetic to the scholarly revival of ancient learning. He believed this to have been 'encouraged by God as a preparation for the reform of the Church' (Burke, 1987: 40). More generally, it is commonly recognised among historians that the Reformation opened the door to humanist principles in education and learning (Elton, 1963: 103). Furthermore, the Protestants may have associated education with religion, but the consequences of this education had a much wider impact on people's ability to represent and engage rationally with the world around them (Lerner, 1993).

Third, the ordered and disciplined life-styles that Weber (1991 [1904–5]) associates with Calvinists can be seen as an aid to the pursuit of religious truth through the mind, and an incentive to the development of *rational labour*. As Weber argues, Protestantism did not merely place a religious value on labour, but saw this resting in *rational* labour; a priority which he held was to play a major part 'in building the tremendous cosmos of the modern economic order' (1991 [1904–5]: 161–162, 181). The Calvinist view of rational labour was bound up with the doctrine of predestination (while an individual's eternal fate had already been determined by God, this did not prevent them from seeking 'signs of election' in the fruits of their labour). Nevertheless, these general qualities of mind and body were not confined exclusively to Calvinists but, as William Haller suggests, tended to unite many Puritans otherwise separated into Presbyterians, independents, separatists and Baptists (Haller, 1938: 17).[9]

Early modern contexts

Protestantism continued to be marked by the doctrinal contradictions which derived from the Christian legacy of both drawing on, yet seeking distance from, the heritage of the Graeco-Roman world. Given the importance the Reformers attributed to religious discourse, however, they sought to minimise these tensions by identifying 'authentic' and 'inauthentic' Christian writing. Despite the theoretical primacy accorded to the individual engagement with the Scriptures, the Reformers also reconstructed Biblical Scripture. In one dispute between Luther and the Catholic Church (concerning the question of whether people were justified before God by faith and works – the Catholic position; or faith alone – Luther's position), Luther translated Romans 3: 28 to read 'a man is justified by faith *alone*', but he had actually added the word 'alone' (Cameron, 1991: 141; emphasis added). As Weber comments, 'Luther read the Bible through the spectacles of his whole attitude' (Weber, 1991 [1904–5]: 84; see also Cameron, 1991: 141).[10] This emphasis on discursive consistency meant that while Protestant associations of faith were open to all 'true believers', they did not contain the 'real world' flexibility of Catholic communities. This helps explain the multiplication of Protestant sects, and the hostile political reception that often met intransigent Protestant leaders when travelling between territories (Rupp, 1969).

Political conditions

Protestant leaders had frequent cause to lead a relatively isolated and nomadic existence (Fife, 1957; Lohse, 1987). This was exemplified by Luther, who had occasion to flee, seek refuge, and even be 'smuggled away' from the Diet of Worms in 1521 (after appearing in front of the Holy Roman Emperor, and having been placed under the Imperial ban). Nevertheless, the world was becoming a relatively hospitable place to Protestantism. In the years prior to the sixteenth century, for example, there were major conflicts between the Pope and the rulers of France and Spain. The sack of Rome in 1527 was generally seen as a sign of the corruption that had infested the Catholic Church, and there were moves by political leaders to distance themselves from the Papacy (Manchester, 1992).

The Reformation assumed different forms in different countries and, as the examples of Spain and Italy illustrate, was far from fulfilling its ambitions for change (Scribner et al., 1994). Broadly speaking, the Protestant Reformers were most likely to find receptive audiences amongst those living in urban areas, and engaged in market-based activity sharing least affinity with the 'bonds of Catholic community' (Wuthnow, 1989). Nationalism was another important factor in establishing conditions conducive to the expansion of Protestantism and this can be seen in the Lutheran Reformation in Germany.

As Holy Roman Emperor from 1519 to 1555, Charles V inherited the responsibility of defending the interests of the Catholic Church, but this was complicated by the struggle for European supremacy he was engaged in with the Valois kings of France. France was prepared to ally itself with the Lutheran states in Germany as a way of applying pressure to Charles. This pressure was reinforced by various princes and city councils who were contemplating ending allegiance to Rome. Such a move would mean they could stop subsidising the Papacy and divert some of the Church's wealth into their own coffers. These distractions on Charles were exacerbated by his having to direct resources to prevent the Ottoman expansion which was threatening portions of the Holy Roman Empire (Rodinson, 1988).

Conditions such as these added up to what Elias has referred to as a set of 'tension-balances' favourable to Lutheran Germany; a situation replicated elsewhere in early modern Europe (Cameron, 1991). In Germany, though, the competing demands on Charles's time and resources led to him pursuing a strategy of appeasement with the Protestants This eventually resulted (despite subsequent military successes against the Protestants), in the Peace of Augsburg (1555) and the recognition that Lutheranism would continue to exist (for a detailed analysis of the German Reformation, see Scribner, 1994).

The development of printing

The development of printing was of great importance to the Reformers across much, if not all, of Europe (Rupp, 1969; Chrisman, 1982; Eisenstein, 1979; cf. Scribner, 1994: 218–219).[11] Indeed, Burke (1987: 47) has gone so far to suggest that 'The Reformation succeeded where medieval heresies failed because it had a mass-produced means of propagating new ideas.' This point remains valid despite the levels of literacy during the Reformation. Books spread the Word not only through reading, but on the basis of people *listening* to preachers. Printing meant that religious propaganda could be produced quickly and cheaply. It also allowed for the principal theological sources of the Reformation (the Bible and the writings of the early Church Fathers), to be produced more accurately and in far greater numbers (McGrath, 1993: 13).[12]

These developments have major implications for Benedict Anderson's (1991) writings on the importance of 'imagined communities'. Anderson (1991: 16) has associated the emergence of the 'nation', as a secular imagined community, with the decline of 'religiously imagined communities' bound together by the Latin of the Catholic Church, and the consequent development of the fragmentation, pluralisation and territorialisation of languages. It is certainly true that the Catholic Church strove to defend what Anderson calls the 'citadel of Latin' against the Reformers (Anderson, 1991: 40), and that the spread of an ever increasing amount of books, pamphlets and texts is intimately related not only to the success of the Reformation, but also to Protestantism's inherently diverse character in contrast to the comparative unity and coherence of Catholicism (Durkheim, 1951 [1897]). Nevertheless, the spread of printing cannot be associated simply with secularisation. Anderson himself notes the development of a shared Protestant world view, centred upon language and faith, in early modern societies (Anderson, 1991: 188). Despite tendencies towards the fragmentation of earlier models of community, then, Protestantism encouraged new ways of imagining community. Printing allowed the Reformers to stimulate a common cognitive idea of Protestant sociality as the ideal model of human association. This included clearly defined models of those people living within and those existing, as strangers and demons, outside these Protestant boundaries (Rodinson, 1988).

While printing affected the development of the Reformation, the Reformation exerted a reciprocal influence on the progress of printing and the reception of texts. By subjecting religion to a process of discursive symbolisation, Protestantism placed a massive new emphasis on the *written* Word of God.[13] The development of printing took place at a time when demand for original texts, translations and commentaries on texts was stimulated by their centrality to the acquisition of religious knowledge and meaning (Cameron, 1991: 141).

Identity and physicality

The Reformers' approach to the written word provides us with one manifestation of how the 'Protestant body' displays a different ordering of priority to the senses, and to the fleshy experience of religion, than that evident in the medieval era. In the case of carnival, for example, the medieval 'grotesque body' was characterised by openness and flexible boundaries. Protestant physicality, in contrast, tends toward an accentuation of the Renaissance closing of the orifices (Bakhtin, 1984 [1965]). In place of the 'collective effervescence' stimulated by rituals based on earthly images, it was the ear, the mind and the eye that could provide unsullied access to God's Word. In Calvinist thinking, the ear was the organ which formed this route to God (Michalski, 1993: 2). For Luther, it was the mind's ability to apprehend and reflect on the discursive symbols of religion that was crucial. This was because mental images of Christ could avoid the effects of earthly icons which 'played upon people's senses' and led to a 'suspicious', fleshy experience of religion. The senses of touch and smell were frequently implicated in the Protestant view of the body as sinful, while the eye was (with appropriate education) able to read the Word of God (Michalski, 1993).

This orientation to the flesh may have represented a stark contrast to the volatility and emotionality associated with medieval forms of embodiment, yet Protestantism was not alone in promoting these type of changes (Elias, 1978 [1939]). The struggle for distinction in court society placed pressure on people to control and monitor their emotions and pay careful attention to the 'presentation of self'. This management of the body was directed towards very different ends than those sought by Protestantism, but these approaches to the body had certain affinities with each other, and both frequently viewed as unacceptable the immediate translation of affects into actions.

Protestantism enjoyed other successes based not simply on its own strength, but on the wider conditions undermining the authority of the Catholic Church. However, despite achieving converts throughout Europe, Protestantism only became dominant in a minority of territories. The partiality of its religious success, though, should not lead us to underestimate its promotion of political, social and corporeal change across Europe. As the sometimes very similar reforms introduced by the Catholic Counter-Reformation illustrate, the Protestant challenge to the establishment stimulated a degree of reflexivity, self-scrutiny and change even when failing to establish its own institutional base in a particular nation

(Cameron, 1991: 422). We can gain some idea of the Protestant contri
bution to these changes by examining how they sought to reconstruct three
key areas of social organisation (the family, charity and death), according
to their own associations of faith. In each case, the Reformers attempted to
prioritise faith over earthly communities, and to stimulate a mental
engagement with religious discourse rather than bodily effervescence
through ritual.

The reconstruction of the family

The Protestant reconstruction of religion not only turned collective rituals
and earthly icons into discursive symbols, but used this cognitive apprehension of religion to *shape* and *control* people's lives. The spheres in which
people actually lived were now to be ordered, far more than previously, by
abstract ideas about how they should live. This is particularly clear in the
Protestant approach to the family. The Reformers enhanced the family's
importance, but also subjected family life in general, and the position of
women in particular, to a series of rules and obligations.

We noted in Chapter 3 how families were shaped by the relationships
which existed between Catholicism and medieval modes of property
inheritance. These links accorded women's bodies a special importance in
the reproduction of community, the transmission of wealth, and the forging
of political alliances. In practice, many marriages continued to be driven by
the force of necessity under Protestantism (Lerner, 1993; Davies, 1993;
Roper, 1994). However, in line with their attempt to rupture religion from
earthly communities, the Reformers emphasised that marriage should
constitute a *voluntary contract* between men and women. This was associated with Luther's opposition to the Catholic Church's acceptance of
'secret' marriages of the young which 'indicated a cavalier approach to the
most serious of life's decisions and the most important of human
institutions', and failed to manifest the interior commitment and seriousness
appropriate to married life (Ozment, 1993: 156, 158). The contractual
character of marriage was not confined to its point of entry but was
promoted by Reformers' interventions into families to ensure the proper
conduct of family life.

If the Reformers began to dislocate marriages from earthly communities,
they also changed the relationship between marriage and the Church. Their
attack on the Catholic Church radically reduced the authority of the priest
in society. It also dismissed the confessor, as a mediator between the
individual, Church and God, from his traditional position of authority
within the family. As a result, Protestantism invested the family, and more
particularly the father, with a different importance and a new set of
responsibilities, but this did not entail a *laissez-faire* approach to domestic
life. Urban councils in Reformation Germany, for example, frequently
found themselves involved in marital conflict, 'imposing contracts on each

side' (Roper, 1994: 110). Ironically, as Roper (1994: 46) notes, the council's powers to punish 'led it to intervene in the domestic sphere – often at the wife's insistence – thus undermining the master's household rule which it claimed to uphold'. Husbands may have been the route of authority to the family, but they could not always be trusted to act in a manner supportive of Protestant sociality. This could not be tolerated as domesticity was elevated to a lay vocation within Protestantism, and the family was meant to play a significantly greater role in educating children as well as subjecting them to strict moral standards and discipline (Davies, 1993; Zaretsky, 1976; Turner, 1984).

This familial discipline was essential for the home-based (and sometimes school-based) education which was to follow; an education which held that 'initiation into Christianity was not really achieved by symbolic rituals but by instructing children in their faith' (Bossy, 1985: 117).[14] Such instruction required an ability to control bodily impulses and urges, and to manage discomfort in order to hear the Word of God. It was, in short, an essential part of the Protestant civilisation of children.

These family responsibilities frequently focused on disciplining the fleshy desires and 'uncontrolled movements' of young people. Nevertheless, they also served to make valid the discursive symbolisation of religion for the next generation. We have already seen how the Reformers rejected collective rituals and tended also to reject the external 'voice of authority' of the Church for a direct confrontation between the Word of God and the internal 'voice of conscience' of the individual (Davies, 1993: 75). For this to be successful, however, required both an appropriately rationalised body and what might today be referred to as an appropriately moulded 'superego'. In other words, it was the family's task to instil in their children a habitus suited to life in the symbolic associations of Protestantism.[15]

This harsh disciplining of youth was informed not only by the discursive symbolisation of religion, but by the Protestant view that children were marked by original sin and needed to be instructed out of it. For example, the Nuremberg *Catechism* or *Children's Sermons of 1533* (possibly the most popular catechism of the Reformation) emphasises the extent of sin even in newborn infants. Infants are seen as manifesting 'evil desires' and physical indulgence in the act of crying for food, milk or warmth. This crying was a sign that instruction should begin as soon as possible, because it indicated the emergence of an 'independent will' which could develop into a 'cunning to plot against God' (Ozment, 1993). Such views generated a highly authoritarian approach to youth in general. This was reflected in the behaviour of Luther himself, who once punished his eldest son for a moral lapse by forbidding him to be in his father's presence for three days. The son was required then to write a letter begging for forgiveness, to which Luther replied saying he would sooner see his son dead than ill-bred (Ozment, 1993: 166).

Paternal authority was not a law unto itself, however, nor was it isolated from other social and political developments in the family during the

Reformation. Insofar as there was increased regulation of family life during this period, it was to some extent nurtured by the Reformers. Ozment (1993: 151), for example, acknowledges that 'Protestant clerics became self-styled marriage counsellors and child psychologists, as free spoken in domestic matters as in the divine'. Newly created marriage courts, also under the influence of Protestants, rigidly supervised domestic relations. These were ostensibly concerned with the stability of the family (Ozment, 1993: 158), but they were also informed by the Protestant seriousness with which marriage was viewed, the theological legitimations associating women with domesticity, and the encouragement of greater state regulation of domestic life and morality. As such, the marriage courts were indicative of an attempt to impose an idealised vision of Christian living on populations. The family had, in short, become the object of interpretation through the 'autonomous' holy Word of God.

This idealised family was not, however, ideal for women. While the position of paternity was elevated within the family, maternity was rather too closely associated with the Catholic promotion of carnal knowing, and the medieval Church's attachment to the Virgin Mary, the Mother of God (Bossy, 1985: 116; Warner, 1978 [1976]). Indeed, the Protestant attitude in general towards women can be summarised as one of men seeking to regulate and control women's lives rather than to elevate their importance. Luther may have had a high regard for 'women's abilities' as wives and mothers, but he also declared that 'Eloquence is not to be praised in women; it is more fitting that they stammer and babble' (Ozment, 1993: 158).

Luther's attitude is particularly significant as it reflects the Reformers' exclusion of women from full and equal membership of their religion on the basis of their overly close association with the body. In the family, men should speak, while women should listen. Men, in fact, had an obligation to speak and *keep* speaking in order that they educate their children. Women, in contrast, had an obligation to *produce* children. According to Luther women were created to conceive and bear children. This was evident in their narrow shoulders and wide hips which were signs from God that 'he intended them to limit their activity to the home' (Ozment, 1993: 152).[16] Luther also encouraged wives to be constantly pregnant, saying that if women wore themselves out in the process, 'this is the purpose for which they exist' (Ozment, 1993: 164–165). The dangers of women not wearing themselves out in this way is illustrated by the high numbers of witchcraft accusations made against women who were past their childbearing years (Trevor-Roper, 1969; Hester, 1992). Furthermore, it would be a mistake to think that accusations of witchcraft were always made by men. As Roper (1994: 203) suggests, many were made 'by women who experienced child-birth', with the most common target being 'a post-menopausal, infertile woman who was caring for the infant', projecting fears of ill health, misfortune and evil onto targets who fitted the vision of witches as 'dry' and parasitic on the vulnerable and newly born.

This view of women's role was accompanied by a new restrictiveness on their activities prompted by fears that educational opportunities might lead them to jettison their roles of wife and mother (Lerner, 1993). In this context, 'constraints on women's behaviour became an accepted part of the argument for their intellectual emancipation', while women's education was itself portrayed as a means for the creation of 'better wives and helpmates' (Lerner, 1993: 198). It was fairly common for women to work outside the home in the medieval era, yet became less so with the advent of Protestantism. Furthermore, Protestantism's attack on convents, often resulting in their enforced closure, created a great deal of poverty, hardship and restriction of opportunities for women. Those 'holy careers', which offered women a means of escape from the dangers associated with marriage and repeated childbirth (Bynum, 1987), were 'an unnatural and unchristian attempt on the part of women to escape their God-given responsibilities in life' (Ozment, 1993: 154, 159).

The Protestant reconstruction of the family also had consequences for its viability. Marriage as a relationship had been both profaned and exalted by Protestantism's insistence that this institution should be entered into with due thought and consideration. In making the decision of whom to marry subject to reflexive scrutiny, however, the Reformers brought to the foreground not only the importance of the individual in forming a marriage, but also raised in the long term the issue of the dissolubility of marriage. For a long time divorce remained unacceptable as a solution to an unhappy marriage (Turner, 1984: 134). However, as the focus on marriage as a relationship was accompanied by its removal from the sacraments, theological reasoning against divorce became more problematic. Furthermore, with the ultimate acceptance of divorce, the importance of marriage was reduced to what was practically, emotionally and psychologically sustainable between two consenting adults. From being set apart from the everyday, through its status as a sacred institution, marriage had started its shift towards the profane world of everyday life.

The reconstruction of charity

The Protestant view that faith and the spirit were more important than bodily relations of interdependence shaped the organisation and perception of charity. For Catholicism, charity served primarily as a means of integrating communities of embodied people. The medieval confraternities, the communion of the saints, and the sharing of the Body of Christ at Mass were all, in different ways, expressions of the *direct* bonds of charity understood to unite people (Duffy, 1992: 133). In Protestantism, however, charity became associational (a more impersonal phenomenon which reduced contacts between benefactors and recipients), and a form of social and corporeal engineering.

The Protestant transformation of the sacred into the sublime, and its abstraction of faith from earthly communities, made unacceptable the Catholic view that salvation was assisted by works of charity. By downgrading charity, however, the Reformers left themselves vulnerable to accusations that they were 'drying up the springs of Christian charity altogether' (Bossy, 1985: 146–147). They responded by reconstructing charity according to their belief that Protestant associations should facilitate the individual's relation with God. This meant distinguishing between the 'deserving' and 'undeserving', and dispensing charity through projects rather than through close interpersonal relationships (on the relationship between charity and society see Simmel, 1971 [1908b]).

As 'charity' became abstracted from its medieval context it became a means through which potential recipients could be categorised into the deserving and the undeserving. Since intense work could discipline the emotions and sensuous flesh, and release the mind to concentrate on religious truth, the *willingness* to engage in such work served as a logical means of categorising people. Hard work was God's 'special remedy' for people's sin, constituted a way back to God, and was to be encouraged (Ozment, 1993: 73). Those who chose not to work were seen as wallowing in their sin, a judgement which increased the moral stigma attached to poverty. The Lutheran Reformer of Altenburg, Wenceslaus Linck, carefully distinguished between 'professional' itinerant beggars and the 'deserving poor'. Linck advised Altenburg's magistrates not to assist the former category, which included (Catholic) mendicant friars. Members of the latter category, in contrast, could be assisted but only if they were 'truly needy' and 'gave clear evidence of a will to work but were unable to do so because of circumstances beyond their control' (Ozment, 1993: 73).

The Reformers' redefinition of charity also entailed an abstraction and rationalisation of the help that was given to the 'deserving poor'. Protestants became involved in shaping legislation on the poor, for example, and the Reformer Linck's view gave a Lutheran blessing to welfare legislation in Germany. As Ozment notes, 'New ordinances created moral and need tests for applicants, identifying badges for the qualified poor, and a system of loans for the temporarily unemployed, the underpaid, and those who had become economically paralysed because of too many children' (Ozment, 1993: 74). This introduction of calculation, rules and tests acted as a form of what Foucault refers to as 'biopower' (Gordon, 1980). It served to *individuate* the poor by identifying them as different through marks, numbers, signs and codes. It also supports Bryan Turner's (1993: 163) claim that this individuation 'is paradoxical in that, by making people different and separate, it makes them more subject to control'. In this case, the poor were subjected to control through the compulsion to work.

This reconstruction reflects Protestantism's belief that faith was more important than charity, and that social bonds were less important than the individual Christian's conscience. 'Charity' began to adopt its more modern meaning, signifying a more *abstract* benevolence towards the needy. There was, for example, a general discouragement of giving to beggars, and a prohibition of begging in many parts of Europe which marked the end of the notion that reciprocity and some kind of personal relation were characteristic parts of an act of charity (Bossy, 1985: 146).

A good summary of Protestant and Catholic attitudes to charity appears in a pamphlet written by the Reformer Hans Sachs in the early sixteenth century (Sachs, 1524). Two speakers appear in Sachs's dialogue: Romanus, the Catholic critic, and Reichenburger, the Protestant critic. Romanus criticises the unprecedented fear of unemployment, the exploitative wages given to workers and the harsh treatment given to the indebted poor (Ozment, 1993: 84). Reichenburger, however, although critical of those who seek 'unconscionable profits', argues that much of what Romanus criticises is for the greater good. He finds nothing wrong in harsh treatment, and strongly opposes unrestricted charity to the poor, as such policies 'create many idle and useless people'. He argues that the kingdom of God is invisible and not to be found in society, which merely needs to be ordered in the best way possible in order to encourage people to become aware of where God's kingdom really lies – which is within the individual (Ozment, 1993: 85–86).

Such views reflect the particular form of individualism associated with Protestantism. God's kingdom was no longer to be found in the social body of which a person was a member, but in the introspection of the individual. As Watt (1957) points out, these differences between Catholic and Protestant views of work and poverty had much affinity with economic developments which contributed to the rise of a work ethic:

In the Middle Ages the examples of Christ and St. Francis gave sanction to the view that poverty, far from being a disgrace, might well enhance the individual's prospects of salvation. In the sixteenth century, however, as a result of a new emphasis on economic development, the opposite viewpoint came to be widely accepted: indulgence was both shameful in itself and presumptive evidence of present wickedness and future damnation. (Watt, 1957: 95)

It has been suggested that these Protestant reconstructions of charity were the product of a century predisposed to risk dismantling the *actual* relations of Christians in the hope of achieving some more general benefit for the Christian community as a whole (Bossy, 1985: 147). Commentators such as Ozment (1993: 16–17), however, have been strongly critical of this view and have suggested that it romanticises traditional Catholicism and caricatures Protestantism. Recent studies have given partial support to this view by highlighting the stark limitations of medieval charity. Nevertheless, they have also shown how Christian relationships and categories were indeed reconstructed through the Protestant concept of charity. This is a development which points us to the double-edged effects of Protestant civilising processes.

The redefinition of charity, and the dissolution of those bonds central to the pre-Reformation understanding of that term, helped lengthen in certain directions the chains of interdependency characteristic of religious benevolence. People who may previously have been at the borders of, or even outside, Catholic communities could now receive material assistance. In this respect, the more abstract conception of 'community' incorporated within Protestant charity represented a civilising development (one that was extended considerably during the Counter-Reformation by the Jesuits' large charitable projects). By apprehending people through the use of the prescriptive categories of 'deserving' and 'undeserving', however, the Reformers did much to change and expand the stereotypes associated with poverty. The poor may not have been known to the individual, but that did not stop the individual 'knowing' about the poor as 'Others' existing outside the boundaries of religious association and deserving to be treated as fundamentally different (Simmel, 1971 [1908b]).

The reconstruction of death

The Reformers' attempt to reconstruct Catholic communities through processes of discursive symbolisation and individuation also permeate developments in the organisation and experience of death. In this respect, the work of Phillipe Ariès (1974, 1981 [1977]) has been influential in mapping those changes which the Reformers sought to bring about. Protestantism helped privatise death by shifting its organisation away from the social body and towards the individual body. Ariès argues that during the medieval period dying and death were *social phenomena* in that they constituted an integral part of daily life. Insults were traded over the deathbed, disputes continued and were settled there, and people frequently witnessed death in daily life and public spaces (Duby, 1988). Death was an event which produced communal responses and was surrounded by a multiplicity of practices which harnessed the body's senses to the expression of collective rituals:

> The death of a man still solemnly altered the space and time of a social group that could be extended to include the entire community. The shutters were closed in the bedroom of the dying man, candles were lit, holy water was sprinkled; the house filled with grave and whispering neighbours, relatives and friends. At the church, the passing bell tolled and the little procession left carrying the *Corpus Christi*. (Ariès, 1981 [1977]: 559)

For Weber (1991 [1904–5]: 105), in contrast, the genuine Puritan 'even rejected all signs of religious ceremony at the grave and buried his nearest and dearest without song or ritual in order that no superstition, no trust in the effects of magical and sacramental forces on salvation should creep in'. This Protestant particularisation of death was facilitated by a reduction in those social rituals designed to ensure the continuation of the social body. As Berger (1990 [1967]) notes, one example of the Protestant reduction of the Catholic sacramental apparatus was the disappearance of the Requiem Mass, with the 'living praying for the dead', and the 'dead in heaven interceding for the living', which maintained contact between generations.

The Protestant emphasis on the individual was also associated with a focus on those forms of body management that would enable the dying person to achieve a 'good death', in control of their speech, emotions and actions. Death made it impossible for the Reformers to ignore the fleshy corporeality of believers, but they still sought to maintain that individualisation and rationalisation of the body which underpinned their approach to life. The development of 'consolation literature', which helped individuals manage their own deaths through texts, offered mental/spiritual assurances rather than collective responses. Comprising detailed accounts of 'good deaths', this literature recounted brief life-stories of individuals before dwelling on their moving, and usually protracted, ends (Douglas, 1977: 200ff.).

Guided by such literature, the search for a 'good death' sought to calm those dramas associated with the medieval deathbed. This Protestant 'model of dying' wanted to limit the pain, mess and anguish which accompanied death. It also illustrates how the Reformers' legacy promoted the development of affect control, which was necessary to achieve a socially approved departure from this world, through the discursive symbolisation of religion. Anxieties were to be calmed, and bodies stilled, through the reading and interpreting of texts.

As well as individualising death, these reforms sought to isolate the living from the dead in a way that would have made little sense to the medieval culture of the *danse macabre* (Bossy, 1985). While religious orders and ritual structures sought to 'contain' the terror of death in medieval Catholicism, Protestants were left *alone* with the task of interpreting and investing these events with meaning (Berger, 1990 [1967]). After death, the individualisation of the body (as corpse) itself continued to be manifest in post-Reformation funerary inscriptions which recorded the Christian virtues of the deceased and helped personalise memories of the dead (Duffy, 1992: 332–333).

The isolation which marked the Protestant confrontation with death could not overturn the popular insistence on maintaining Catholic death rituals after the Reformation (Bossy, 1985: 26). Indeed, Protestant theologians and pastors had a huge job on their hands in seeking to reconstruct this area of medieval life. The Reformers not only had to encourage people to reject the hugely popular Catholic ritual containment of death, but had to construct a sense of death's meaningfulness outside of these structures. Even Luther found this difficult. Writing to a friend in 1542, he noted that he should be thanking God for the recent death of his thirteen-year-old daughter Magdalene (as she was now free of the flesh and the Devil) but found he could not. Far from consoling Luther, Magdalene's death overwhelmed him 'to the point that his faith in God failed' (Ozment, 1993: 167). This is one example of the difficulty Protestantism had in making sense of the emotions and passions through religious discourse; the 'pure' Word of God was unable to contain the emotions of fleshy people.

The Protestant approach to death is far from the complete 'privatisation' of dying that has been talked about in relation to contemporary society (Mellor and Shilling, 1993; Walter, 1991). Furthermore, in examining the Protestant re-formation of death it is important not to romanticise the pre-Reformation organisation of death. Protestantism can, in fact, be seen as civilising death. Giddens (1991) has argued that the sequestration of death can allow people to concentrate on the tasks of living relevant to *this* world. As death became hidden from public life, Giddens's suggestion was that people could cope more easily with a future-oriented society. Plans for the future and the implications of present actions could all be considered without having their value thrown into doubt by the prospect of mortality (Berger, 1990 [1967]). Nevertheless, the Protestant privatisation and sequestration of death is not a straightforward civilising development.

To begin with, this reorganisation serves to separate the living from what they have in common with the dead. In Bataille's (1992 [1973]) terms, Christianity had long ruptured human experience of the shared fate of death by abstracting sacrifice through the Eucharist. Protestantism took this much further, by making the Eucharist symbolic. By rupturing the dead from the living, Protestantism also helped separate people from the *dying*. As Elias (1985) notes, once death becomes privatised, people become unused to speaking with the terminally ill (feeling, perhaps, that they have no further need for language), and the end of life can become a period of loneliness (not, perhaps, mitigated by the hordes of professionals who appear to believe they ease dying and bereavement through a 'talking cure'). While certain cannibalistic societies paid homage to the dead by eating them, and thus symbolically preventing their escape from the social order, modernity all too often excludes the dying from the realm of life (Baudrillard, 1993a).

The anomic body

If Protestant associations of faith stimulated people's ability to engage with the social world (and to help reconstruct the family, charity, death and other areas of society) they also made humans vulnerable to the experience of anomie (Durkheim, 1951 [1897]). In making God radically transcendent, thus transforming the sacred into the sublime, they removed the possibility of directly encountering the sacred in this world. Furthermore, the individual's cognitive relation with God's Word became more important than their fleshy relations with other people. Salvation was to be gained, ultimately, by a discursively oriented *faith*, rather than by *good works*. The world of people and passions could easily become meaningless, to be left behind in a pilgrimage for religious truth. In John Bunyan's *Pilgrim's Progress* (1768), for example, Christian embarks on his travels by abandoning his family and setting forth with the cries of his wife and children still 'ringing in his ears' (Davies, 1993).

This individualism is, then, closely associated with the experience of being physically separated from the sacred. While the Reformers emphasised the importance of the Scriptures, God's Word was to be listened to, read, or contemplated; activities which provided believers with a far smaller scope of bodily contact with the sacred than was common in the Middle Ages. Believers 'lost touch' with the collective effervescence of religious ritual, and focused instead on individual engagements with the Scriptures, and leading a disciplined and righteous life on earth. This was not a peaceful life, though, as the world of objects, relationships and senses had been significantly emptied of their sacred content, and of their ability to provide secure reference points for action. Only the 'wicked' were at peace on this earth (Haller, 1938: 153, 160), while critical scrutiny of life against the Scriptures could promote regular changes and movements. Ozment, for example, has suggested that Protestants embarked on an unceasing search for religious perfection through cognitive certainty, which meant they could never be 'at home' in their bodies:

> In the quest for a religious life that works, they unhesitatingly change churches and denominations, shedding the spiritual truths of yesterday as if they were just another bad investment or failed love-affair. No other modern religious communion is marked by such variety and mobility. (Ozment, 1993: xiii)

Protestant associations can be seen as paradoxical in their implications, since they facilitated human intervention in the world, but also made it difficult for believers to 'make sense' of their fleshy desires and relationships. Already alienated from their surroundings, the Protestants' experience of ungodly emotions could pose a threat to their sense of identity. The ordered and disciplined life styles that Weber (1991 [1904–5]) associates with Calvinists can be seen as an aid to both the pursuit of religious truth through the mind, and to the struggle against emotions which made little religious sense and were easily associated with sin.

Bodily guarantees of sin

We have been concerned in this chapter to examine the Reformers' attack on Catholic communities and their promotion of 'associations of faith'. Instead of following the Catholic path of harnessing the fleshy volatility of the medieval body to religion (by engaging with the senses through ritual activity and stimulating carnal knowing), the Reformers were concerned to civilise the body on the basis of a cognitive approach to religion. Having suggested that this focus on a faith in the sublime made it difficult for believers to make positive sense of their fleshy impulses and passions, we shall examine how this situation was exacerbated by the Protestant linking of the fleshy sensuality of human embodiment with *sin*.

The 'sinful body' has a long history in Christianity (Brown, 1988), but took on a new intensity within Protestantism. This was partly because of the Reformers' unwillingness to invest the flesh with positive qualities and their refusal to allow people to be absolved from their bodily sin through confession. It also had much to do with the flesh's status as an impediment to the Word of God. Protestant notions of the sinful body are expressed most clearly in Luther's comment that 'both flesh and blood, having been corrupted by Adam, are conceived and born in sin' (Delumeau, 1990: 27). The 'sinful body' was also evident in the Methodist John Wesley's conviction that the guilty body must be mortified, and in the Baptist belief that God speaks only when the flesh is silent – when all the natural passions and everything impulsive, irrational and sinful have been overcome (Weber, 1991 [1904–5]: 148).

These views highlight the fact that religious knowledge was not just based on an ordered body, but actually *promoted* an opposition to the flesh as sinful. The emergence of catechism, for example, increased the ways in which Protestants should be concerned about their bodies as sinful. Catechism concentrated on the Creed and the Ten Commandments and has been seen as one way in which Protestantism tended to reduce 'Christianity to whatever could be taught or learnt' (Bossy, 1985: 120). Catechism provided people with a set of ethical rules to guide an individual's behaviour, was designed to instil obedience, and was complemented by a great deal of instruction concerning behaviour and deference to civil authorities (Bossy, 1985). A consequence of this was that large areas of day-to-day life became subject to rules and guidelines concerning sinful behaviour and civility. Lyndal Roper (1994) makes the important point that this concern does not indicate an eradication of ungodly behaviour and there is plenty of evidence to show that 'drinking, whoring and gorging' continued in Protestant areas. Furthermore, a 'literature of excess' was vigorous in its mobilisation of those pleasures of 'defecation, alcoholic excess, fighting and vomiting'. Nevertheless, this opposition does not just represent the fact that negative and positive attitudes to the body are held simultaneously (Roper, 1994: 157). It developed in early modern contexts where there was indeed a slow and gradual control exerted on the affects (Elias, 1978 [1939]).

Catechisms had an affinity with those writings on manners penned by the humanists and others expert in the field of etiquette (Elias, 1978 [1939]). Secular elites, for example, came to experience bodily slips as embarrassing and as potential threats to their social standing (Elias, 1983). However, the combination of these religious and civil strictures promoted increased monitoring and apprehension about the body and its sinful failings. All that was uncontrollable about the body, all that was 'animal' about bodily functions, could become a source of sin and embarrassment. Indeed, when discussing the growing Protestant antagonism towards the flesh, Delumeau (1990) notes that there developed a hatred of the body which had its basis in *shame*. He considers the example of Cotton Mather, one of the most influential pastors of late seventeenth- and early eighteenth-century New

England, who was shamed by the resemblance between the natural functions of people and animals. Cotton Mather called people 'mean and vile' because of their 'mortal state', and bemoaned how 'natural necessities abase us, and place us, in some regard, on the same level with the very dogs!' (Delumeau, 1990: 507).

These developments associated the body with both sin and uncivilised behaviour, neither of which were acceptable to the rational Protestant. This was reflected in the almost Apollonian concern with internal control found in the Protestant catechism. Establishing interior restraint was meant to serve the dual purpose of *limiting* that disruption understood to be created by animal passions and self-will, while *stimulating* 'a sense of shame for immoral behaviour and fear of its consequences' (Ozment, 1993: 105). Thus, fear and shame had 'a positive role' to play in the catechistic education of persons *into* truth faith and civility, and *out of* any sense of ease with the anthropological fact of their embodiment (Ozment, 1993: 111).

The Protestant desire to live an ordered and rational life, then, was closely associated with an antipathy and anxiety towards human embodiment. As the Reformation progressed, the sensuality and volatility characteristic of the medieval body, and the carnal knowledge gained from a mind immersed in the body's senses, were both stigmatised. In their place, the Protestants promoted a form of cognitive apprehension which required the guilty, sinful body to be disciplined and stilled. In the medieval era, the sacred could be encountered through and within bodies. For Protestants, bodies symbolised the vast gulf between humanity and the sublime, and were therefore stigmatised as 'sinful' and subjected to increasing cognitive scrutiny.

The reformation of self-identity

The Protestant reconstruction of religion is summarised by two major slogans of the Reformation: *sola scriptura* and *sola fide*. 'Scripture alone' elevates the importance of text and diminishes the importance of tradition, while 'faith alone' increases the value of mental commitment while diminishing the importance of physical 'works'. Instead of 'doing things', based upon a location within a religious community, religion becomes an interior disposition in relation to texts and beliefs. These reforms had bodily as well as religious consequences, as we have already seen, and also posed specific problems in relation to the construction of religious self-identity. The difficulties Protestants had in making sense of their emotions and passions, and the tendency for these to be associated with sin, contributed to an existential uncertainty and decentring of the self that is frequently and mistakenly associated exclusively with the postmodern rather than the early modern era.

The Reformers made the teachings, writings and practices of other Christians *resources* for the *individual*, instead of integral components of

traditional religious practice. Coupled with the Protestant focus on predestination, these resources encouraged individuals to authenticate their
status with regard to salvation, while simultaneously denying them the
possibility of achieving such an assurance. The Catholic ritual cycle of sin,
repentance, confession and absolution had been removed, while salvation
could never be assured to Protestants because of their sinful, mortal bodies
(Delumeau, 1990: 30).

This shift in the understanding of religion makes it a necessarily more
cognitive phenomenon, something which is mediated by and located in the
mind, yet also serves to *problematise* the stable construction of self-identity.
Identity becomes something the individual has responsibility for, but this
responsibility has to be exercised in a context where meaning is likely to
shift as a result of its location in a text. As a consequence, people have a
responsibility for constructing their own identity which overruns the
resources they have to achieve this task. There are, in particular, two major
difficulties associated with the business of identity construction in the world
forged by the Reformers. These are, the *despair* of being unable to escape
from a sinful world 'emptied of angels', and the *bodily isolation* and
personal insecurity associated with living in a world devoid of sacred
reassurances.

First, Jean Delumeau has noted that volumes could be filled with
sixteenth-century Protestant texts that despair of people, their sin and
unhappiness. This attitude was hardly unknown to the medieval world.
However, while certain aspects of medieval Catholic monasticism had
articulated such a despair, the monastery and the convent were also
understood to be refuges from the outside world. Protestantism removed
these refuges. The Reformers not only brought a monastic asceticism into
lay life but, in their opposition to monastic separatism, denied the possibility of a social refuge from sin and unhappiness. While the Reformers
may have shut down the possibility of *social escape* from the sin of the
world, they provided for the possibility of *spiritual escape* by emphasising
the healing power of God's grace. Even this, however, could be a source of
despair for individuals. God's grace was totally gratuitous, and was visited
on people at random, irrespective of their worldly actions.

The second problem which accompanied the re-formation of self-identity
concerned the bodily isolation and personal insecurity that accompanied
Protestant individualism. The Reformers' reduction of religion from a vast
corpus of ritual, social and sacramental practices to an interior disposition
resulted in a new objectivication of the world. Rather than being immersed
in a world alive with the sacred, individuals came to stand apart from a
world which had been largely divested of its sacred qualities. Protestants
may have been joined through symbol communities to the 'Word of God',
but there was little which linked their emotions and flesh other than a
shared concern with discipline. This tended to make the embodied self a
lonely and uncertain place. For Catholics, the sacraments of the Church,
the intercessions of Mary and the saints, and evidence of the supernatural

in miracles, all helped stimulate emotional states which were communally experienced and validated. Calvinists, in contrast, were left in a world where emotions and identity had to be invested with *personal* meaning.

This feature of the Reformation has been explored by Weber (1991 [1904–5]) who recognises the psychological conflicts, anxieties and insecurities stimulated by Calvinism. He argues it was impossible for the broad mass of Calvin's followers to accept the consequences of the doctrine of predestination. Instead, it became incumbent upon Calvinists to regard themselves as 'chosen' and to treat all doubts as temptations of the Devil. Thus, a lack of certainty as to one's election was taken to be a sign of insufficient faith (Delumeau, 1990: 547). Despite this emphasis on *faith*, then, Calvinists still sought to find evidence of their election in the fruits of their *worldly activity* (Hill, 1973; Peacock and Tyson, 1989: 216).[17]

These problems associated with the Protestant re-formation of embodied self-identity bring us back, full circle, to the development of new forms of textuality under the influence of Protestantism. In place of Catholic models of sanctity (which were frequently woven into common understandings of holy days, and expressed in the highly ritualised form of hagiography), Protestants developed an overriding concern with the workings of 'providence'. The role of the providential hand of God in the events of an individual's life had become an increasingly prominent theme in the writings of Luther (Weber, 1991 [1904–5]: 85). Its importance also spread through Protestant understandings of the self. Thus, as we noted in Chapter 2, the Puritan was expected to keep a record of the mercies bestowed by providence. This created a vogue for diaries, journals and autobiographies, which detailed such things as childhood illnesses and providential preservation from a variety of mishaps (Thomas, 1973 [1971]: 108).

The fact that modern forms of autobiography (i.e. writings marked by reflection, introspection and narratives about the self as an individual) start to emerge with the Reformers is particularly important (Shilling and Mellor, 1994). It signifies clearly the shift from *church-centred* accreditation of one's status as a Christian to a form of *self-accreditation*. Diaries detailing providential interventions into a person's life served to reassure individuals of their status as Christians and became crucial ingredients in any tests of suitability for membership of the Church of true believers (Campbell, 1987: 128). The spiritual autobiography came to be an essential tool in what became a 'cult of spiritual self-help' (ibid.: 130), in the sense that the organisation of a person's life experiences into the structure of a text allowed the creation and validation of a particular identity as well as having the potential to offer the assurance of salvation. This multiplication of texts mirrors the multiplication of sects, cults and persistent rearticulations of Christianity which came to characterise Protestantism. Thus, we could say that the institutional entropy of Protestantism is due not only to the individualism of the Protestant religion (Durkheim, 1951 [1897], 1961 [1912]), but to the partial 'disembodiment' of Christianity during the Reformation.

Separating the mind from the body

The developments considered in this chapter add up to a Protestant re-formation of the religious body. This was stimulated by the Reformers' tendency to make the construction of meaning a reflexive, individual task. The abstraction which lay at the heart of the Protestant approach to religion, and to the body, brought about the beginning of a psychologisa-tion of Christianity. More broadly, it also led to a wider process of psychologisation within Western societies. Indeed, we would suggest that the recurrent ideas of the 'self in the case' in Western philosophy (Elias, 1978 [1939]: 257), and of the body as 'an empty tube which is simply inflated by the mind' (Wittgenstein, 1953: 11), have their archetype in Protestantism. Furthermore, Protestantism went a long way to making the body what Baudrillard (1993a) refers to as a material for 'sign exchange' in which emotions were senseless and irrelevant.

The transformation of the sacred into the sublime, which divested it of its immanence in social and natural environments, both reflected and encour-aged this re-formation of the body. The Protestant body was 'sinful' because it was so far removed from all that was sacred. While cognitive appre-hension tended to become exalted as a means through which this sublime form of the sacred could be encountered, it also encouraged patterns of greater reflexivity and critical scrutiny which resulted in a fragmentation of Protestantism into competing faith communities. The transformation of the sacred into the sublime itself, however, also renders Christian faith a difficult phenomenon to maintain. As Anton Zijderveld (1986) has com-mented, Protestantism's removal of the sacred from these environments meant that faith was dependent upon the 'thin thread' of a commitment to a radically transcendent, far away God. By the nineteenth century, in fact, this dependence had already manifested its vulnerability 'as the reformed religions began to deteriorate into an ethical liberalism in which faith in God to all appearance played no essential part' (Elton, 1963: 101).

Historically, Protestantism's specifically religious influence was necessa-rily self-limiting, since its pursuit of doctrinal purity and the cognitive suspicion it directed toward human communities made it unpalatable to many people, on the one hand (Cameron, 1991), and, on the other, encouraged patterns of sectarianism and institutional entropy amongst its most devoted followers (Durkheim 1951 [1897]). More broadly, however, it helped bring about the profanation of many areas of social life (Weber, 1991 [1904–5]; Berger, 1990 [1967]; Bell, 1980), which allowed its influence to resonate throughout modern societies. In the following chapter we explore some of the major social and corporeal influences of Protestantism, focusing especially on how cognitive modes of apprehending self and society became incorporated into the agendas of subsequent social move-ments and institutions. We also examine the Catholic Church's response to the individualistic and thoroughly cognitive challenge of the Reformation, and its own attempt to reconstruct carnal knowing.

Notes

1. Touraine (1995) implies that the specific *contents* of Protestant faith are not that important alongside the broader process of disenchantment promoted by Protestantism. Our position is rather different. We consider the contents of the Protestant faith to be important for two reasons. First, these contents develop upon the basis, and express central characteristics, of a form of embodiment which encourages and reflects processes of disenchantment. For this reason they are worth examining closely. Second, one of the defining features of Protestantism is precisely its intense focus on the *correct contents of the Christian faith* in contrast to the more ritually focused emphasis of medieval Catholicism. We can hardly be in a good position to examine the effects of Protestantism without being attentive to this. On the other hand, Touraine is right to draw attention to the transformative effects of Protestantism *as a whole*, regardless of differences within its many sects. Over the course of this chapter we are not inattentive to variations within Protestantism, but believe that our focus on its underlying re-formation of the body also allows us to deal with it in broad terms.

2. This privileging of the mind over the body, and the deconstruction of traditional patterns of social relations, also had particular implications for the position of women; implications which anticipated the later position of females within social contract theories (Pateman, 1988). Women were formally included within Protestant associations, but were effectively excluded from full participation because of their relationship with temptation, blood and birth. This threatened their ability to engage rationally with the Scriptures, or to utilise rationally any learning they may have acquired (Lerner, 1993).

3. By 'discursive symbolisation' we are referring to the Protestant tendency to turn religion into language, thought and text. In comparison with medieval Catholicism, there is a shift in Protestantism away from ritual and tradition towards the apprehension of religion through symbols which can be thought with, spoken, read and written. In order to prevent misunderstanding of our use of this term, it is important to make several additional points:

Our use of 'discursive symbolisation' is not to be associated with Foucault's notion of discourse, which is far too wide and unspecific for our purposes. Foucault's term also carries with it connotations of discursive reductionism whose usefulness for analysing historical change is strictly limited.

Our use of discursive symbolisation assumes a difference and opposition between language and ritual. While ritual has often been associated with an avoidance of explicit speech and narrative (Lévi-Strauss, 1981: 670–672; Bell, 1992: 111), it would be a mistake to view ritual as a language (Bell, 1992: 112) as they have very different implications for the construction of meaning. Bourdieu (1977: 106, 120, 156), for example, emphasises that ritual is pure *practice* on the 'hither side of discourse'. While ritual within the Catholic Church frequently incorporated language, language never assumed sufficient autonomy to constitute a 'ritual' in its own right.

Our use of discursive symbolisation is also tied to an analysis of the translation of Christianity into a cognitive system of beliefs and values into which people needed to be instructed (or into a 'speaking association'). As we argue in this chapter, this itself marks a rejection of the 'eating community' of the medieval period.

4. For the Anabaptists, this orientation became manifest socially as separatism, exile and a desire for self-sufficiency in a condition of permanent alienation from their social surroundings (Cameron, 1991: 336).

5. In fact, Calvinism has often had an apparently positive appreciation of community relative to other forms of Protestantism, but even so betrays a deep ambivalence about the embodied communities that people actually live in, while simultaneously nurturing a view of community which is both idealised and abstract. This tendency to abstraction endures within Calvinism even today. We can see it for example in the ambivalence towards community which recurs continually in a recent study of the Primitive Baptists of the Blue Ridge area of the Appalachian mountains in the southern USA. As Peacock and Tyson (1989: 4) point out,

these Calvinists treasure community whilst suspecting it, love it and yet deny 'the ultimate morality and authenticity of any human community'.

6. For example, as Bell (1992: 112) points out, the words of consecration only achieved such an important position within the Mass in the standardised rite established by the Council of Trent in 1570. Up till then the emphasis within the rite had been more obviously focused on *action*, 'specifically those thought to have been done before by Christ himself' (Dix, 1983 [1945]: 12–15; Bell, 1992). Thus, discourse came to be more central within Catholic practice only following the Reformation, in the Church's *Counter*-Reformation, but, even then, remained located in the constraints of ritual practice.

7. This recommendation resulted in the plastering of texts over the walls of churches and temples in both Lutheran and Calvinist areas.

8. In some forms of Protestantism, however, the theoretical empowerment of the laity was taken to an extreme practical conclusion. The Quakers dispensed with the priesthood altogether, for example, while 'in Gerard Winstanley's Digger utopia anyone who professed the trade of preaching and prayer was to be put to death "as a witch"' (Thomas, 1973 [1971]: 80). The crime here consisted of the attempt by someone (or some group) to appropriate for themselves a *particular* expertise and authority in interpreting God's Word. This view illustrates just how much importance Protestants could place on the relationship between the individual and God.

9. Protestant associations of faith encouraged believers to engage rationally with the world around them, yet this rationality remained firmly tied to the Scriptures and the Reformers' attempt to purify the Catholic Church. Given the Protestant emphasis on pursuing the truth through an individual and cognitive engagement with the Scriptures, it is not surprising that their associations of faith were highly exclusionary. This was evidenced in the proliferation of competing Protestant sects, and also in the Reformers' tendency to multiply the number of 'dangerous Others' they had to deal with. Calvin, for example, thought that anyone who disagreed with him was an agent of the Devil. Women were marginalised within Protestantism because of their 'irrational natures', while some of the Reformers sanctioned the beating of women as a means of discipline. Muslims remained a threat for Protestants because of false beliefs and their association with the flesh, but were not necessarily any worse than Catholics. Similarly, anti-Semitism continued to flourish, both because of the 'overly literal' Jewish readings of Scripture and because of the inhuman qualities attributed to Jewish bodies (Abulafia, 1994; Sennett, 1994).

10. Another illustration of this is provided by the Reformers' rejection of the doctrine of purgatory for its lack of scriptural basis. The Catholic Church gave its scriptural basis for this doctrine as 2 Maccabees 12: 40–46. Thus, in order for the Protestants to reject purgatory on the basis of *sola scriptura* they had to exclude 2 Maccabees from the canon of Scripture, which they did by judging it to be 'apocryphal' (McGrath, 1993: 141).

11. Although early Protestantism was characterised by a marked anti-intellectualism which encouraged an unprecedented spate of book-burning, this did not signal a hostility to learning or texts as such, only to *particular forms* of learning (Campbell, 1987; Manchester, 1992: 183; Watt, 1957).

12. The spread of Protestant ideas at Cambridge and Oxford, for example, was tied closely to the importation of new editions of such texts together with the Protestant commentaries on them (Rupp, 1969).

13. Discussing the English Protestant William Tyndale, who became Luther's first translator, Bossy notes that for him 'the Word' of God was an 'it' rather than a 'him', and instinctively conceived as something written. The written word's revelatory power to convey God's message also informs the importance many commentators attach to the development of printing for the Reformation.

14. Luther's *Short Catechism* of 1529 had been framed as a dialogue between father and child, where the child was instructed in the correct details of faith. Nevertheless, the responsibility for catechism rested principally with the clergy rather than the laity (Bossy, 1985: 118). The underlying conviction was that 'initiation into Christianity was not really achieved by symbolic rituals but by instructing children in their faith' (Bossy, 1985: 117). This shift is

signalled by the mutation in meaning of the word 'catechism' itself, which had originally meant an exorcism performed before baptism, before coming to mean a course of instruction in faith (Bossy, 1985: 118). It is also reflected in the enormous significance placed on religion by the Reformers.

15. The attention directed towards the family was consistent with the Protestant interpretation of the Bible. Catholics had interpreted the fourth commandment, 'Honour thy father and thy mother', in metaphorical terms so that paternity was understood to reside with the authorities of the state and, especially, with the Church. In line with the priority they placed on the 'Word of God', Protestants took the injunction more literally, elevating paternity and paternal education in the process (Bossy, 1985: 116). Indeed, the importance of this task of socialising the young was such that Calvin recommended that those who violated the authority of the father should be put to death (Davies, 1993: 76).

16. Ozment sees this comment by Luther as being no more than jesting. Jest or not, we suggest that it betrays a wider approach to the treatment of women within Protestantism.

17. Although worldly activity provided opportunities for signs of election, as the early Puritans believed that God had instituted market processes for just such a purpose (Hill, 1973), the doctrine of predestination created a state of psychological anxiety concerning religious salvation. Whatever successes in worldly activity were achieved, this anxiety could never be calmed, since the Calvinists did not have the sacramental apparatus which assured Catholics of their relationship to God and of their own salvation. Thus, although Calvin himself had a deep-rooted hostility to indulgence in feeling and emotions, and emphasised the importance of rational, ethical conduct, this was not true for all subsequent generations of Calvinists. As Colin Campbell (1987: 126) argues, given the importance attached to the state of grace, the precise attitudinal and emotional nature of that experience became an almost inevitable focus of concern.

5

JANUS-FACED MODERNITY

Sociology has a heritage of writings which suggest it is possible to talk of *two* modernities (Levine, 1995: 315; Meštrović, 1991, 1993). On the one hand, there is the modernity with which we are perhaps most familiar: that of Cartesian dualism, Kantian reason, Corbusier's *machine à habiter* and Habermas's 'ideal speech' situation. On the other hand, however, is another modernity: that of Schopenhauer's 'senseless will', Nietzsche's 'will to power', Baudelaire's *flâneur*, and the reassertion of sensuality in baroque culture (Lash and Friedman, 1992). While the former modernity lends itself to the 'organic' sociality and contract mentality Durkheim (1984 [1893]) talked of as increasingly important to modern life, the latter reminds us that contracts cannot contain embodied human relationships in their entirety. Instead, they rely on bodily foundations and more somatically oriented forms of sociality which may, *or may not*, be supportive of these rationalistic and corporeally abstract channels for interaction.

In this chapter we argue that the corporeal consequences of both the Protestant Reformation and the baroque cultures of Counter-Reformation Catholicism provide central, if markedly divergent, sources for these 'two' contrasting and potentially conflicting modernities. Various commentators have noted that the seventeenth century assumed a 'Janus-like' aspect, with the emergence of scientific developments coexisting with intense theological controversies (Martin, 1977: 12). In relation to the encouragement of scientific developments, Protestantism's stimulation of modernity's profane, objectified and interventionist view of the world is captured well in Berger's (1990 [1967]: 112–113) phrase: 'A sky empty of angels becomes open to the intervention of the astronomer and eventually the astronaut' (see also Merton, 1970). The form of embodiment which facilitated this 'emptying of angels' was, however, vulnerable from the start to 'heretical' knowledge, to the sensual experience of the sacred, and to melancholy, unease and anxiety (Campbell, 1987). This vulnerability was manifest not only in the difficulties of maintaining that cognitive control of the body analysed in Chapter 4, but by a Catholic challenge to the Protestant re-formation of the body in the early modern period.

This challenge will be traced in what follows by opposing the Counter-Reformers' model of 'voluptuous corporeality', their seductive justifications for earthly rule, and the close association of melancholy and baroque culture, with the Protestant promotion of 'ascetic corporeality', their demonisation of the sensual flesh, and the approach to civil society contained in Luther's 'two kingdoms'. While the Protestant emphasis on mind over body shared an affinity with early modern institutions, its subordination of the flesh and the sensual experience of the sacred proved highly precarious. Despite the fact that the official 'face' of modernity came to define itself in terms of reflexivity and rationality, then, it is also the case, as Baudelaire (1964 [1863]), Durkheim (1951 [1897], 1961 [1912]), Weber (1991 [1904–5]) and Bataille (1986 [1957]) have suggested, that the origins of modern culture are not as far removed from an extra-rational sensuality as is often imagined.

What is especially significant about the Counter Reformation's use of baroque culture is that its manipulation of the sensuous experience of the sacred was accompanied not only by attacks on certain forms of discursive belief, but by an increasing emphasis on others. This reintroduced a greater level of cognitive apprehension and visuality to carnal knowing within Catholic communities, and provided another reason for early modern Protestants to be concerned by, and fearful of, the 'shadow kingdom' of human sensuality. While the Protestant focus on the individual provided a basis for the extension of contractual arrangements built initially around the Word of God, the Counter-Reformers' incorporation of the Word into the flesh constantly threatened to stain, muddy and bypass these abstract channels for human interaction. From the viewpoint of Protestantism, the Counter-Reformers were not simply opposed to the discursive symbolisation of religion but were, in Mary Douglas's terms, trying to pollute the purity of their religious discourse by associating it with a sensuality which was, most definitely, 'matter out of place' (Douglas, 1966, 1970).

The Janus-faced character of the early modern world is considered in three major ways in this chapter. First, while Protestantism helped create a bodily basis for modern modes of knowing self and society, it was challenged by the Catholic reassertion of a sacred carnal knowledge within baroque culture. The Reformers' focus on cognitive modes of apprehension became incorporated into the agendas of subsequent social movements and institutions (especially with regard to contractarian conceptualisations of social relationships), and was facilitated by an 'elective affinity' between religious idealists, emerging social classes and changing political orders.[1] The form of embodiment this was based on was limited in scope, however, and did not go unchallenged. It tended to be associated with white urban European males across important parts of Europe, but by no means all of these lands, and encouraged the view that women lacked the rationality to manage their bodies effectively (Fanon, 1970; Pateman, 1988; Rose, 1976; Seidler, 1994; Walvin, 1982). Furthermore, in the evolution of Western cultures following the Reformation, there emerged an influential baroque form of bodily-being-in-the-world associated with the new 'Catholic' Europe promoted by the Council of Trent (1563) (Chatellier, 1989).[2]

Second, these competing forms of embodiment can be distinguished not only by their religious characters, but because they manifest divergent attempts to manage the tension between being and having bodies. These expressed what Georges Bataille (1986 [1957]) has called the 'voluptuous' and the 'ascetic' potentialities of the human spirit. It was Bataille's view that these are not necessarily in contradiction (something we explore in Chapter 6 through our analysis of the baroque modern bodies which have emerged within the contemporary West). Historically, however, these potentialities have often been conflictual rather than complementary, though the baroque celebration and manipulation of sensuality contains elements which rule out a simple opposition of the two.

A third manifestation of the Janus-faced character of the early modern world is that these competing bodily forms are prone, in different ways, to what Simmel and Bataille have referred to as cultural 'tragedies' of modern life. These are the immersion of humans in the profane world of objects following the retreat from the sacred (Bataille, 1986 [1957], 1992 [1973]), and the enduring sense of personal incompleteness that follows from being immersed in a culture which can never be wholly assimilated (Simmel, 1968). In certain respects, the post-Reformation world subjected both Protestants and Catholics to these circumstances by the ways in which they scrutinised and reconstructed those religious orders of meaning which shaped people's corporeal experiences of the Middle Ages. While the Protestant response to being alienated from the fleshy experience of the sacred was to *institutionalise* this alienation, by developing contractarian notions of the 'good' civil society, the Catholic response to the Reformers involved an absolutist manipulation of the senses based on *nostalgia* for the medieval sacred order and 'divine rule'. Baroque contact with the sacred was experienced less through the immanence of the close contact senses and collective effervescence, and more through a seeing which was experienced as sensual but also as mediated and individualised in relation to the medieval era.

These two responses manifest a tendency to 'lose touch' with the world. This 'loss' takes rather different forms in each case, although both exemplify what Baudrillard (1993a) describes as an 'emptying out' of community from successive modes of representation, allowing all that is natural to be conceived of as separate from humans, as artificial, or as subject to human intervention and domination. In Protestantism the per-fection of nature was pursued through rational intervention, while in the baroque it was sought through art (Martin, 1977; Maravall, 1986). As Taylor (1978: 8) points out, the assumption that the world is open to these forms of manipulation rests on a vision of its disenchantment: individuals no longer have to make themselves thoroughly 'in tune' with a meaningful order, but have to construct meaning through the manipulation of apparently contingent, mutable events and circumstances.

In examining these Janus-faced features of the early modern world, our discussion also looks back to the Protestant re-formation of the body, and forward to the 'baroque modern' corporeality of the contemporary West. This bi-directionality draws attention to the stubbornness of bodies: the re-formations discussed here build on the persistent fleshiness of humans. Protestants were not able to extract large chunks of human sensory capabilities from the body and, despite their emphasis on cognitive apprehension, there was always the danger that touch, taste, smell, sight, and even hearing, could lead to heretical knowledge. Similarly, the modern emphasis upon rationality and the regulation of passions has an equally vulnerable basis, expressed in a persistent anxiety about the fleshy body, and the uncontrollable reappearance of passions in the form of modern anomie.

Voluptuous corporeality

The Catholic Counter-Reformation vigorously promoted its own forms of embodiment and sociality in opposition to the Protestant reduction of the scope of the sacred and its ascetic rationalism. One example of this is provided by the battle over exorcism which raged in sixteenth-century Germany. As Lyndal Roper (1994) argues, exorcism dramatised a series of questions concerning the relationship between the body and soul. Since Protestants could sometimes seem to represent a religion 'utterly divorced from the bodily', the 'evidence' provided by possession and exorcism could be particularly significant. In another, later, context, seventeenth-century Massachusetts actually had courts of law conducting experiments to test claims regarding possession and exorcism (Weisman, 1977).

The 'miracles' of Protestantism (such as the endurance of Lutheran teaching, the futile resistance of the Pope, and the hindering of the Devil's work) were abstract in the extreme and involved 'no intervention of the divine in the bodies of human individuals' (Roper, 1994: 178). The body of the possessed individual, however, was no abstract matter. Sickening smells could be emitted as demons left the body, limbs of the possessed could be endowed with unnatural strength, and exorcisms could be accompanied by torments of agony and grotesque swellings. Possession had long provided spectacular validations of the power of carnal knowing. In the 'dance frenzy' of 1374, for example, a monastic eyewitness attested to the hysterical dancing, crying and pain which marked these events, and reported that those cured of the affliction 'said that they seemed to have been dancing in a river of blood, which is why they jumped into the air' (Rosen, 1992). During the Counter-Reformation, however, exorcisms were employed much more self-consciously as a weapon against the 'sterility' of the Protestant mind.

Protestants might interpret physical distress not as the 'outpourings of a body in the grip of Satanic power, but as the toiling of the soul weeping over its sins' (Roper, 1994: 179). For Catholics, though, exorcisms enhanced priestly authority, 'vindicated the efficacy of holy water, showed that fasting worked, and demonstrated that relics, blessings and the sign of the cross were effective against the Devil' (Roper, 1994: 181; see also Walker, 1981: 6). The importance of these 'demonstrations' was such that

Pope Paul V's *Rituale Romanum* of 1614 sought to standardise the procedures of exorcism (Walker, 1981).

If exorcisms provided a vivid opportunity for Catholics to verify their theology of the body, their use of baroque culture was even more significant. Rather than placing trust in the intellect, baroque culture was preoccupied with the 'passions in the soul', and 'preferred to appeal to extrarational means that moved the will' (Martin, 1977: 13; Maravall, 1986: 228). Its marked sensualism contrasts sharply with the cognitive emphasis of the Reformation. As Turner (1994: 13) has commented, the 'glittering worldliness' of the baroque suggests a very different way of knowing oneself and one's world than the profane asceticism of Protestantism.

It is misleading, however, to imagine the baroque as simply the *contrary* of ascetic Protestantism, as it too was conscious of 'a sky empty of angels' (Berger, 1990 [1967]: 113). In baroque art a new emphasis was placed upon naturalism and visual realism: Caravaggio argued that 'to imitate natural things well' is the mark of the competent painter (Martin, 1977: 13). This interest in naturalism expressed a developing secularisation of knowledge under the impact of scientific developments, and a new sense of the importance of human intervention in the world which is not entirely dissimilar to that found in Protestantism. Both groups were aware of what we may now refer to as the *homo duplex* character of people, and both sought to regulate the passionate sides of humanity. For Protestants, a radically demythologised natural world could be understood and utilised through the rational interventions of humans. For baroque culture, the very truth and beauty of nature could not reveal itself without the *artful* interventions of humans to perfect it (Maravall, 1986: 231).[3] In other words, Protestant and Catholic bodies were beginning to compete on the same terrain. While the 'disciplined bodies' of the Reformers dislocated themselves from their natural environment in order to prioritise the mind, baroque culture was similarly distanced in attempting to seduce the flesh to a renewed experience of the sacred.

Tendencies towards the secularisation of knowledge were constrained, however, by the development of post-Reformation Catholicism. Baroque naturalism can be distinguished from its Protestant counterpart, for example, by its continued espousal of a fundamentally metaphysical and sensual view of the world, so that even the most apparently naturalistic paintings contained layers of allegorical and emblematic meanings (Martin, 1977: 13). Secularisation, in fact, was fought with a sensualisation manifest in the scrutiny of human actions, physiognomy, emotions, and the fascination with carnal passions (Martin, 1977: 73ff.), which can be related to the Church's attempt to limit Protestant influence and to renew religious experience through carnal knowing.[4] The coexistence of this seductive sensualism with a more distanced approach to nature, marked by the Counter-Reformation's emphasis on 'correct belief', helps explain Protestantism's heightened suspicion of sensual experience, and shares an affinity with the later theorists of civil society who viewed passions as undemocratic and facilitative of authoritarianism.

Religious seduction

In opposition to the Reformers' iconoclasm, Catholicism intensified its positive attitude to images during the Counter-Reformation as a way of seducing people toward religious righteousness (Michalski, 1993: 6, 56). The ostentatious splendour and ornate elaboration of church architecture and decoration was one way in which the ecclesiastical authorities sought to inspire people toward Christian truth (Wright, 1982). While Protestant churches were 'stripped to their white walls', baroque churches overflowed with 'the frolics of bucolic, chubby cherubim' (Turner, 1994: 13).

Seducing the senses constituted part of the Church's attempts to encourage people to attend confession and partake in Mass more frequently, and to stimulate during these sacraments an intense *emotional* and *mystical* response to religion. Indeed, the veneration of artistic works was encouraged by the Church *insofar* as it enabled people to strengthen belief by contemplating beauty, as can be seen in the blatant eroticisation of religious ecstasy in Bernini's *Ecstasy of St Teresa* (Turner, 1991). As Michael Mullett (1984: 44) notes, baroque art 'played an indispensable part in the fostering of a deeply felt Catholic piety', while Maravall (1986: 90) suggests that 'Everything which belongs to the baroque emerges from the necessities of manipulating opinions and feelings on a broad public scale.'[5]

This desire to manipulate the flesh expresses two important assumptions: that passions are an integral part of being human; and that they have a utilitarian value which can be stimulated for religious and political goals. The Jesuit Senault expressed both these assumptions, noting that those who sought to remove passions from the soul diminished our humanity, and that 'there is no passion in our soul that cannot be usefully manipulated' (Maravall, 1986: 76). This expresses something beyond the simple facts of manipulation, through its association with a re-forming of the sensory body. In contrast to the medieval Christian engagement with the close contact senses, the Counter-Reformation tended to become ever more centred upon *visual* stimulation.

The baroque is enchanted with all the senses, but the eye has a central place in consuming material images designed to produce religious ecstasy (Buci-Glucksmann, 1994). As such, the baroque can be examined as expressing an 'imperialism of seeing' (Barthes, 1977a: 62–66; Buci-Glucksmann, 1994: 140–141) in which the value of visual resources was sometimes unquestioned (Maravall, 1986: 252). This contrasts with the Protestant evaluation of the ear, as well as the eye, as a route to religious truth (Michalski, 1993). The Counter-Reformation's different ordering of the senses in relation to the sacred is illustrated by the work of Van Dyck, Seghers, Rubens and Callot; artists who assisted the Church in moulding the religious sensibilities of Catholics (Chatellier, 1989: 254). It is also worth noting the Jesuit scholar Claude Clement's promotion in 1627 of a baroque model of the ideal library. Words and artistic images were equally important; *both* were used to guide visitors in their search for spiritual truth (Rovelstad, 1993).

This baroque fascination with images is not a simple association of visuality with sacred truths. Rather than adopting a 'seeing is believing' mentality, the baroque was alive to the deceptiveness of the visual. While baroque illusionism had the persuasive purpose of directing persons towards eternal values (Martin, 1977: 14), it coexisted with the spread of a relativism inclined to suggest 'perspective is truth' (Maravall, 1986: 194–196). It was in this potentially corrosive context that the Catholic Church was concerned to reinforce its sensual 'propaganda' (a term coined during the Counter-Reformation period) with a growing emphasis upon correct belief. While the *raison d'être* of Protestantism was to purify religion, the Catholic Counter-Reformation reasserted its own version of religious purity (Bossy, 1985; Delumeau, 1987). The content of Catholic belief may have been different (e.g. an acceptance of the real presence of Christ in the sacrament of the Mass), but the importance of cognitive conviction began to mirror that of the Reformers.

The Church's struggle against 'Protestant pollution' encouraged a reaction against medieval pluralism, but the Counter-Reformation was most definitely not just defensive. In Italy and Spain, Catholic renewal was concerned mostly (once the relatively minor Protestant incursion of the sixteenth century had been repelled) with raising levels of piety and instruction. In other areas, such as Germany, the need to fight Protestantism was much clearer. This was manifest in attempts to preserve and protect Catholic areas through such repressive measures as the Inquisition and the Index of prohibited books. It was also manifest in the Counter-Reformation's concern to attack Protestant gains, and to spread its own doctrines through missionary activity (Koenigsberger et al., 1989; Scribner et al., 1994).

The Council of Trent (1563) did much to shape this Counter-Reformation insistence on correct belief. The decrees of Trent confronted and contradicted the beliefs of the Reformers. They held that the Protestant appeal to Scripture *alone* was misconceived, and that written and *unwritten* religious traditions were equally important. Trent defended the authority of the Church to interpret Scripture against the individualism of Protestant interpreters, and decreed that no Catholic was allowed to publish any work relating to the interpretation of Scripture unless it had been approved by the Church (McGrath, 1993: 156).[6]

These actions illustrate how Trent attempted to control the discursive symbolisation of religion; an aim which had extensive educational implications. Trent ordered the bishop of every diocese without a university to establish a seminary to train men for the priesthood. This was designed to ensure that the clergy were educated in correct theology and developed disciplined devotional habits (Chadwick, 1990 [1964]: 279). It also assisted the Catholic Church in competing with the Protestant Reformers to impose alternative systems of belief (systems which were becoming increasingly well defined) (Delumeau, 1990; Wright, 1982). Contrasting approaches to the body persisted into the Counter-Reformation, then, but these systems of *belief* indicate the importance that both Protestantism and Catholicism came to place on the religious mind.[7]

Magna civitas, magna solitudo

As well as confronting the discursive symbolisation of religion, the Counter-Reformation brought about a partial *abstraction* of Catholic forms of sociality. Indeed, the emphasis on communal, co-present solidarity central to the medieval Church was to some extent transformed by the Counter-Reformation's engagement with the baroque, a culture in which the development of egoism and individualism coexisted with a concern with the anonymity of the masses (Maravall, 1986: 104).

Fernand Braudel has argued that the baroque was a product of the imperial mass civilisations of Rome and Spain, and it is in cities that much baroque architectural and artistic work was concentrated; as in Vienna, Prague, Paris, Madrid, Seville, Valencia, and Rome (Maravall, 1986: 104–105). Thus, while the baroque epoch is marked by an increasing appeal to the individualisation of experience, it is also marked by a new sense of isolation which flows from urban life and is expressed in Francis Bacon's 'Magna civitas, magna solitudo' – the greater the city, the greater the solitariness of the individual (Maravall, 1986: 122).

This partial atomisation of public life forms an important part of the context in which the Counter-Reformers' attempts to extend and reorganise their institutions, in line with a purified doctrine, altered the structuring principles of Catholic sociality. The importance of existing relations of co-presence declined, while there was an increasing emphasis on cognitive notions of what Catholic communities *should* be like. Indeed, Roper (1994) suggests that in some areas Catholic and Protestant reforms were barely distinguishable. The priority given to the efficient management of charitable and medical work, for example, weakened direct relations between beneficiaries and benefactors. This was reinforced by the growth of religious orders specialising in particular forms of charity, and by the Church's attempts to encourage fraternities to extend their help to non-members (Wright, 1982: 100).

These reforms illustrate how medieval Catholic social solidarity became subject to rational planning, requiring a heightened ability to distance emotions from ritual, and decisions from tradition. In this respect, the Counter-Reformation was not opposed to, but was *part of* wider civilising processes of the age. Planning was prioritised, and links of interdependency between people stretched over time and space (Elias, 1978 [1939], 1982 [1939]). Despite these reforms of community, however, the Catholic Church did not become a 'symbol association' in the manner of Protestantism. It may have placed greater emphasis on rationalising, ordering and widening the scope of its community structures, but Catholicism could still be seen, at least in part, as a sacred 'eating community' (Chatellier, 1989).[8] The Church continued to defend the sacrificial and sacramental character of the Mass, and its baroque reliance on the power of images to stimulate spiritual knowledge and contact with the sacred continued to 'eat into' the identities of its adherents. The Counter-Reformation's restructuring of symbols and communities, then, promoted a relationship between religion, the body and meaning which both engaged with and *opposed* the agenda of Protestantism.

Sensuous justifications for earthly rule

The Counter-Reformation's opposition to Protestantism, and use of baroque culture, was bolstered by its alliance with a particular type of political authority – royal absolutism. Indeed, it is impossible to understand the Counter-Reformation without appreciating the links that developed between Catholic orthodoxy and absolutist states. Both promoted and relied on the seductive powers of baroque culture to regulate the passions and desires of bodies and, through them, people's minds. Both relied on visions of the 'supernatural body' (of Christ and the king) to justify their authority. However, by projecting the doctrine of the mystical Body of Christ (which suggested that Christ possessed a natural and supernatural body) onto the king,[9] absolutism gradually helped undermine its own legitimacy.

Promoting the sacred body

The Catholic Church established a view of the 'natural artifice' during the Middle Ages; a view of social arrangements and human bodies as prescribed by nature and legitimised by God (Heller, 1990). As Protestantism challenged this view, the Counter-Reformation did what it could to counteract the individualist and rationalist challenge of the Reformers (Turner, 1991: xvii). By seeking to reassert tradition and prevent the march of the modern, the Catholic Church and absolutist powers had much in common. So it is not surprising that they became closely allied in their use of baroque culture, which was deeply conservative, both religiously and politically. It championed the rights of divine kings, and sought through fantastic images, colour and elaborate music to reassert ideologically 'the authority of the old order over various social classes emerging in the new urban economy' (Turner, 1991: xvii, 1994; Vierhaus, 1988: 65).

It was in this context that the opposition between Catholicism and Protestantism became mapped onto an opposition between *absolutism* and *liberalism*, and between the *sacred* and *profane* body; an opposition which was expressed through the body's location within ideologies of divine authority (Ullman, 1975). The doctrine of the 'mystical Body of Christ' was used to justify the authority of the Catholic Church, while the form of this doctrine was transferred into the 'king's two bodies' in order to justify the status of absolutism.[10] This held that the monarch's legitimacy was based on divine right, and manifest in the king possessing a natural body (subject to decay and death) and a sacred political body (in which resided incorruptible sovereignty) (Kantorowicz, 1957; Delumeau, 1990: 96–99). As Tester notes, this ideology drew a direct line of authority from God, to the Church, to the king and, indeed, on to the family through the male head of the household. The Word of God 'was communicated to subjects through the monarch, who in his turn communicated to all other individuals through their fathers' (Tester, 1992: 29).

The allegorical understandings incorporated in the 'king's two bodies' may appear strange to those familiar with death as the decay and destruction of an indivisible, fleshy body. The influence of this doctrine as a principle of political legitimacy, however, can be seen in the idea of the king leading a bodily existence which is at once both visible and invisible. For example, Blackstone's *Commentaries on the Laws of England* (1765) states that while the king may never judge, despite being the 'Fountain of Justice', he retains legal ubiquity: 'His Majesty in the eye of the law is always present in all his courts' (Blackstone, 1765: 1270).

This doctrine is also apparent in the 'royal utopia' works, published after the interregnum caused by the English Civil War of the seventeenth century. These suggested that the harmony of society was dependent on the king's role as head of the social body (Davis, 1981; Turner, 1991). Monarchical systems of punishment, for example, illustrate how an attack on the fleshy body of the king was also an assault on the social body as a whole (a logical assumption, given the metaphorical structure of this doctrine) (Foucault, 1979 [1975]). Such an attack was dealt with by a public display in which the body of the king and society obtained justice by obliterating the body of the offending individual.[11]

The prevalence of violence and cruelty in baroque art reflects these assumptions and indicates how the authorities sought to structure violent passions through spectacles of blood, pain and death. The *consciousness* of violence, and a fascination with its potentialities, reached the point of inspiring what could be called an 'aesthetics of cruelty' which, though utilised as a means of repression and subjugation, could also be experienced as pleasurable, entertaining and morally enlightening (Maravall, 1986: 162–163). Indeed, spectacles of punishment were even considered suitable for the education of young children. In one case, town authorities insisted that all young people watched two 'diabolical good-for-nothings' being punished (Delumeau, 1990). These fourteen- and fifteen-year-olds had been found guilty of poisoning their drunken father and uncle:

> They began by stripping the two boys, then they whipped them in such a way that their blood abundantly covered the ground. Then the executioner stuck red-hot irons on their wounds, at which they screamed such screams that it is impossible to describe them. Next they cut off their hands . . . In this torture, one

and all admired the last judgements of God and learned from this example.
(Jannsen quoted in Delumeau, 1990: 107)

This spectacular ritual was a 'learning experience' precisely because it
engaged and stimulated the body towards a sensuous appreciation of truth.
It was also a learning experience which contrasted with the Protestant
apprehension of truth through the mind's confrontation with the *Word* of
God.[12] Punishment for Protestants served the purpose of *stilling* the body,
while in baroque culture it *directed* bodies.

Undermining the sacred body

Justifications of religious and political rule based on the 'king's two bodies'
assaulted the senses in an attempt to link earthly authority to the supernatural. Baroque spectacles of coronation, celebration and punishment
were all central 'collective representations' which bound absolutism to
Counter-Reformation Catholicism (Meštrović, 1993: 122–123). The
absolutist attempt to consolidate power through the sacralisation of the
king's body and a development of baroque culture was not, however,
without its problems.

First, despite incorporating the 'sacred body' within its rationale, the
'king's two bodies' also stimulated a reflexive, secular approach to the
understanding, and rule of the body. This was because the idea that the
king had two bodies was itself a somewhat profane and secular version of
the 'mystical Body of Christ'. It has been suggested that the age of the
baroque was one in which divinity was brought down to earth, but when
humans also sought to become divine (Martin, 1977: 140). The transfer of
sacredness involved in this doctrine was certainly a vital step towards the
secular understandings incorporated in the terms 'body politic' and 'social
body'. Furthermore, while the 'king's two bodies' allowed the absolutist
monarch to claim to be the source of human law, this legitimacy was based
on the principle of 'divine right' which also placed political authorities
under the law (Benn and Peters, 1959). This supported the monarch's power
while the doctrine retained its sacred content – while the king was the
recipient of law through Christ – but undermined it as the law became
secularised.

The second problem with the absolutist assertion of power through the
'king's two bodies' concerns the social and economic contexts which shaped
the development of baroque culture. The baroque was designed to seduce,
but was marked by the change and uncertainty of its era that it was
employed to combat. It is true that absolutist monopolies of violence within
a territory increased the civilising potentialities of the time (Elias, 1982
[1939]). However, economic changes and the absolutist involvement in
political and military conflict (conflict which was bound up with the
Reformation and Counter-Reformation) gave rise to a pervasive sense of
political catastrophe and collapse of tradition. This led to a view of the
present and of the king's body as both uncertain and destructive. In this

context, baroque culture expressed not just a *celebration* of the sacred and of absolutism, but reflected a *rupture* between the image and reality of these phenomena: 'a deep sense of alienation from society, self and nature' and, indeed, from the sacred (Turner, 1994: 23).

Baroque knowledge and uncertainty

If baroque culture and political absolutism helped the Counter-Reformation promote a voluptuous form of corporeality which could be seduced towards religious righteousness, it also gave rise to a melancholic fatalism about the frailties of the flesh and the location and depth of the sacred (van Reijen, 1992: 1–8; Buci-Glucksmann, 1994: 135). This fatalism was related to an awareness of inconstancy, transience and mutability, combined with a strong nostalgia for sacred medieval *Gemeinschaft* communities (Maravall, 1986: 179; Martin, 1977: 15).

This sense of change, flux and melancholy is why the baroque is both the culture of the Counter-Reformation and 'the culture of the *crisis* of seventeenth-century absolutism' (Turner, 1994: 22; emphasis added). The alienation stimulated by baroque culture is expressed in two of its most potent themes: 'the artificially, socially constructed nature of reality (its hyperreality) and the precarious, catastrophic, uncertain and hazardous nature of all human existence' (Buci-Glucksmann, 1994; Turner, 1994: 8). The idea of the labyrinth (expressed in the baroque passion for the maze and the hall of mirrors), and the image of the ruin (as a sign of the transience of human endeavours), expressed this awareness. They did this by articulating a nostalgic desire for the resolution of oppositions between sacred and profane, while simultaneously opening up the possibilities for new experiences (and new conceptualisations of these experiences) which make such a resolution thoroughly problematic.

Increasingly inclined to think of perfecting humankind (Jensen, 1976: 3), yet also urging people to deepen the interpretation of feelings (Martin, 1977: 73), baroque cultures were acutely conscious of the tension between knowledge and uncertainty, objectivity and subjectivity, between the importance of acquiring knowledge and the futility and precariousness of human endeavours.[13] Pascal, for example, thought of humanity as plunging into a whirlwind of amusements to avoid the suffocating ennui of life. Expressing baroque disillusion, but also the neo-Protestant influence of Jansenism, Pascal saw man as 'a chaos' suspended over 'an abyss', whose very survival depended on prevailing over the passions, and yet who knew that reason would finally have to submit before the God who was to be found in the 'heart' (Pascal, 1962 [1670]). In contrast to the Cartesian emphasis on the unitary subject able to control a unified discursive field or 'point of view', Pascal's *Pensées* point towards a divided subject of modernity, yearning for transcendent truth yet sceptical of the possibility of truth in a disenchanted world (Cascardi, 1992: 133–134). This subject was not only located in a 'realm of worldly signs' which could not be assimilated, but was aware of the difficulty of finding a 'firm footing' on which to reach out to the sacred (Cascardi, 1992: 131).

Pascal's 'sacred horror' (Lefèbvre, 1956), and the baroque focus on ambiguity, ambivalence and a blurring of categories can, nevertheless, be differentiated sharply from Protestantism: it has been noted, in fact, that Protestants and their modern cultural heirs were involved in a 'flight from ambiguity', manifest in their commitment to the language of precise propositions (Levine, 1985). It was also a flight from fantasy. For Protestants, the 'mechanism of fantasy' was considered 'the site of communication between demon and man' (Couliano, 1987: 203). It was the imaginary world (*mundus imaginalis*) which lured people into sins of the flesh through seductive images (Falk, 1994: 190). In contrast, while the Counter-Reformation involved an increased discursive codification of Catholicism, this was matched by a reassertion of carnal knowing that recognised the desires and passions which race through human bodies and defy cognitive management. Catholicism, then, sought to stave off an anomic confrontation between carnal passions and cognitive regulation, by manipulating the senses towards religious righteousness. Nevertheless, Catholicism's association of meaning with seductive images tended to promote the relativism that its Counter-Reformation systematisation of religious thought intended to eliminate.

Ascetic corporeality

So far in this chapter we have seen how the Catholic Counter-Reformation promoted forms of embodiment and sociality in opposition to those of Protestantism, but distanced from the medieval immersion of humans in their (super)natural environments. These forms of enfleshment and 'being together' continued to influence the development of the early modern world, but we now concentrate on how it further encouraged Protestantism to place itself on a war footing against sensuality and somatic manifestations of the sacred; a stance which historians have suggested shaped the early modern state (Roper, 1994: 147).

Given the baroque association with Catholic absolutism, it is not surprising that Protestantism encouraged the continuation of a distrust of the sensuous body. This involved an elevation of reason as that which defines our species as human, and a corresponding attempt to exercise power through the education of the *mind*, rather than the sensual education of the fleshy body. In so doing, it promoted a thoroughly reflexive, deconstructionist 'spirit of free inquiry' which meant that modern persons began to 'lose touch' with the world (in that greater knowledge about it entailed a loss of sensory touch with this knowledge).

Meštrović (1991: 14) has argued that the official face of modernity encourages humanity to suffer from an excess of 'mind' at the expense of the 'heart', stimulating a 'virulent abstractionism'. This view is also evident in the work of Simmel (1971 [1903]) who associates modernity with a view of humanity which degrades the passions, Nietzsche (1993 [1871]) who understood it as the imposition of Apollonian order upon Dionysian passions, and Durkheim (1951 [1897], 1961 [1912]) who associates its rationalistic spirit of free inquiry with the stimulation of an anomic abstractedness from the essentially *irrational* basis of human sociality. This 'excess of mind' is particularly evident, as Durkheim and Mauss (1975 [1902]) suggested, in Kant's focus on the importance of duty at the expense of desire (Meštrović, 1991: 104); a stance inherently suspicious of any sensually effervescent contact with the sacred which threatens rational control.

This Kantian emphasis upon the mind is also central to Seidler's (1994) discussion of the separation of modern persons from 'somatic life', and his argument that Protestantism encouraged the view that people had to be saved from their 'animal selves' (1994: 25–26). Modernity, for Seidler, is a 'secular form of Protestantism' which teaches people, especially men, to distrust their bodies, emotions, feelings and intuitions and, instead, to listen only to the clear voice of reason. Maffesoli (1993b: 12) has discussed how this Apollonian prioritisation of reason has been manifest not only in the interior lives of modern individuals, but in the contractarian, rational constitutions of modern societies: modernity has been about 'fighting and then conquering the dark forces of irrationalism'. Thus, in the philosophies of Enlightenment thinkers such as Voltaire, Montesquieu and Diderot, reason could shake off the yoke of tradition, liberate people from supersitition, and enable the constitution of a society which promoted the greatest possible freedom for the individual (Levine, 1985: 143).[14]

In contrast to the voluptuous exploration of sensuality in baroque culture, Protestant modernity expresses an ascetic attitude: humans cannot allow themselves to become immersed in nostalgia for the sacred but must dominate nature and constitute societies on the basis of rational criteria and active interventionism. The baroque became associated with 'decreptitude' and the 'grotesque' (Osbourne, 1970: 108), while modernity became future-oriented, rational and vigorously interventionist in both nature and society. The alienation from medieval sacred order and the forms of community associated with it, could be overcome through the reflexive construction of a 'good' society; a construction which is rooted in Protestant opposition to the 'king's two bodies'.

Ascending and ascetic justifications for earthly rule

The cognitive individualism inspired by Protestantism threatened not only traditional religious orders of meaning and authority, but political orders too, resulting in the gradual distancing of political authority from religious legitimacy (Wright, 1982). While the Catholic Church held onto a 'descending', theological legitimacy for earthly power (which maintained that authority descended from God, through the sacred body of the Church, to the sacred body of the king), 'ascending' justifications for earthly rule (which maintained that people had important rights by virtue of belonging to a profane body politic) grew increasingly influential.

The Reformation did far more than challenge papal jurisdiction and authority across Europe, then: it also stimulated a reflexive questioning of political obedience which complemented the Protestant focus on discursive knowledge. It was on this basis that a vision of civil society, in which rational persons shared common interests, was able to emerge: the 'king's two bodies' gave way to Luther's 'two kingdoms'. Luther's social ethic suggested that two totally different moralities existed side by side: a private Christian ethic, based on the doctrine of justification by faith alone, and a public morality, based upon coercion (McGrath, 1993: 208). This emphasis on coercion was connected to concerns about the possibility of society in the absence of a natural, divine order, while the removal of the specifically 'Christian' element to the private sphere meant that the source of political legitimacy moved away from religion, explicitly at least, and became the object of rational planning and reflexive, secular thinking. As political and religious conflicts progressed, during and after the Reformation, a growing number of rulers recognised that, to be effective, the powers of the state would have to be separated from the authority of the Catholic Church (or, indeed, from the duty of rulers to uphold *any* particular faith) (Skinner, 1978).

These developments highlight why the sixteenth century has been seen as a particularly important period in the relationship between state formation processes and the state's acquisition of supreme coercive power (MacKenny, 1993). As Held (1992) notes, the recognition that divine rule and the Catholic Church could no longer guarantee power was accompanied by a focus on the idea of state sovereignty; the view that supreme and indivisible power resided in the state. This provided a potential path for rulers who had to confront religions competing to secure for themselves the kind of privileges enjoyed by the medieval Church.[15]

This rupture between legitimacy and established forms of authority involved a shift away from the flesh toward reflexivity and the mind. No longer could governance simply be felt and trusted to be valid as a result of the weight of tradition. The limited reflexivity of the consumption of religious orders of meaning, associated with what Bataille (1992 [1973]: 48–49) calls the 'intimacy of the sacred', was displaced by a thoroughly cognitive emphasis upon the production of new orders of meaning, value, authority and legitimacy. Thus, with regard to politics, emerging theories of sovereignty sought a modern, cognitive basis which was *solid* in its foundation, *universal* in its scope and *indisputable* in its rationality (Bauman, 1992b).

Civil society

As religious political authority waned from its medieval heights, political elites recognised the need for a new, legitimate basis on which individuals could be controlled, managed and educated for the 'collective good'. If people were being cut asunder from the disciplinary ties of the sacred cosmos, they needed to be re-attached to profane bonds located in the secular state. Furthermore, in place of the volatility of medieval persons, who were ordered through the patterning power of the Church, new models of authority required a new humanity.

In the seventeenth and eighteenth centuries, theories of 'civil society' attempted to explain how a specifically secular and human society was possible, and within what forms of sociality individuals could be expected to coexist peaceably (Bauman, 1992b: 1–25: Tester, 1992: 7). By promoting a view of 'man' as both the object and subject of knowledge, and by having at their focal point the rational minds of individual citizens, these theories assumed that cognitive reflexivity had been released from the parameters of religious tradition. Society was no longer immanent with the 'prodigious effervescence' of the sacred: it was a profane 'order of things', to be constructed upon the rational deliberations of its citizens (Bataille, 1992 [1973]: 52).

Theories of civil society may have provided ruling elites with a resource to help them distance themselves from the Catholic Church and other religious interests. Nevertheless, the notion of 'civil society' was not religiously neutral: it drew on some of the underlying assumptions of Protestantism (Hill, 1966). The term 'civil society' was first mentioned in a sixteenth-century text by Martin Luther (Colas, 1991), while Calvin's view of 'natural man' and Thomas Hobbes's view of nature had striking similarities (Hill, 1966).[16] In countries such as France, which remained predominantly Catholic, such ideas were developed outside the Catholic Church and in *opposition* to it (Groethuysen, 1927; Chatellier, 1989). As well as being indebted to the Reformation, however, theories of civil society contained fundamental problems traceable to the abstraction and reflexivity stimulated by ascetic Protestantism. This can be illustrated through the writings of Hobbes.

Thomas Hobbes wrote against the background of the English Civil War and his work illustrates the central dilemma facing those who sought to replace one supreme authority (the Church) with another, be it 'the people', or 'the state'. The central dilemma is this: once the 'natural artifice' has been emptied of dominant conceptions of power and authority, how does one justify a replacement? What is the point at which reflexivity, having challenged the ground on which divine rule stood, can and should stop deconstructing sources of authority? Hobbes sought to avoid this dilemma by suggesting that human life in a state of nature was nasty, brutish and short (Hobbes, 1957: 82). In the state of nature, individuals enjoyed a natural right to everything which would assist self-preservation yet could not, given the conflictual character of this 'pre-social' state, guarantee the realisation of *any* of these rights. Hobbes argued that because humans were a rational species, they would agree to forgo their natural rights and submit to absolute and undivided sovereign authority. It was only such an authority that could establish the conditions for social peace and civil rights (Hobbes, 1957).[17]

For Hobbes then, the 'Leviathan' or 'State' could overcome those destructive desires and passions which inhibit the creation of the good society. Like Habermas's more recent theory of 'communicative rationality' and Giddens's model of 'pure relationships' (where passions pose a threat to the rational subject's struggle for pure discursive communication), Hobbes's theory of society reflects a thoroughly Protestant attempt to construct forms of symbolic association upon an ascetic repression of carnal knowledge.

Uncivil bodies

Visions of civil society, in which rational persons shared common interests, reveal two key features of the increased importance attached to reflexivity. The first, as we have already mentioned, is connected to deep-seated concerns about the actual possibility of society in the absence of a natural, divine order. Second, as the source of political legitimacy moved away from religious orders and towards rational orders, the assumption was that the secular mind could be both separated from, and used to control, the body. Humans may have been *born* natural within contractarian interpretations of civil society, but these theories also assumed they could be *made* social (Meštrović, 1993; Tester, 1992).

Those features of humanity associated with the natural needed suppressing in order for the mind to be released into society and made available for educating. The threat posed by irrational, sensuous bodies had to be subjugated and controlled, and the citizens of a state had to be made rational in order to achieve this goal of a secular civil society. This making rational of embodied humans was partly an extension of the Protestant project and provides a context for Durkheim's (1977 [1938]) observation that the sixteenth-century focus on learning was accompanied by whips becoming a regular part of college life. As this new asceticism grew more widespread, fears of 'dangerous' passions, desires and impulses grew, threatening to 'break the dikes, to confront productive activity with the precipitate and contagious movement of a glorious consumption' (Bataille, 1992 [1973]: 52). The mind could be controlled, with enough education and surveillance, while fleshy sensuality had far too many negative connotations to do with an experience of the sacred which might undermine these conceptions of the new society.

The growth of the modern state, then, was accompanied by a more sophisticated view of *homo duplex*: the rational human whose animal nature needed civilising before it was fit for social existence. This threat of 'unconquered physicality' was seen as *internal* and *external*; as irrational experiences which could be regulated successfully by certain groups. If the body was not already profane, it could be made profane by the reflexive control of individuals and the regulative power of the state. Externally, this fear of unconquered physicality was also projected onto and perceived in the ubiquitous 'stranger'; the person who existed beyond the boundaries of civil society yet constituted, as a result of his or her difference, a threat to social order (White, 1978). In this time of political and religious change, and given the ubiquity of the physical body as a location for classification systems, it is hardly surprising that there arose a heightened concern about the bodies of individuals (Douglas, 1966, 1970; Sennett, 1994).

Fearing the unruly flesh

Visions of civil society contained universalistic assumptions about the rationality of humanity. Nevertheless, some groups were considered to have a much greater potentiality for rationality than others and this made them, and them alone, suitable for civic roles. While geographical discoveries, global patterns of trade and a fascination with 'exploration' awakened a new interest in distant lands and peoples (Martin, 1977: 15), this interest also aroused fears and desires of uncontrolled sensuality which were projected onto African and Eastern bodies (Said, 1978). Black African bodies were seen as the bodies of slaves or subordinates, and as bodies that had sexual relations with apes (Walvin, 1982; Fanon, 1970; Rose, 1976). David Hume's visions of social order, for example, were accompanied by the argument that non-white races were created separately and were innately inferior to their white counterparts (Popkin, 1974).

These perspectives bore a resemblance to those popular in Renaissance writers' portrayals of happy, contented, but idle natives of foreign lands (Delumeau, 1990). Furthermore, they maintained the view that the bodies of black peoples were associated with much that was uncontrollable and animal about humans, while Africa became the continent in which one could travel in order to be an adventurer. White Europeans could have an adventure here which reminded them of what they had repressed *within themselves*. As Georg Simmel puts it, such adventures were both alien yet also connected to the adventurer. They involved travel, distance and mental reflection, yet were ultimately associated with the 'inside' of the adventurer. Images of foreign bodies were intimately connected with the adventurers' experience of their own embodied self (Simmel, 1971 [1911]: 188).

Views such as these informed the thought of subsequent generations of intellectuals and politicians in both Europe and America. One of the more influential examples of this can be found in the work of Francis Galton. Galton coined the term 'eugenics' in 1833 and argued that both marriage and family size should be regulated according to the hereditary endowment of parents; variables closely related to racial stereotypes based upon these visions of social order (Gould, 1984 [1981]: 76). Similarly, Louis Agassiz held that white and black peoples were separate biological species and that while the *rational* white race was able to make use of education, the *irrational* black race was naturally fitted to engage in manual labour (Agassiz, 1895). Both Thomas Jefferson and Abraham Lincoln also wrote about the intellectual inferiority of black people (Gossett, 1965; Sinkler, 1972).

The Protestant subjugation of sensuality was, then, carried forward in a distinct direction and shaped in the writings of civil society theorists. It also influenced subsequent views of social difference. Protestantism sought to suppress the fleshy body in order to modernise and purify religion, while theorists of civil society provided a rational basis for the suppression of the unruly flesh. Fear and distrust of the bodily incorporation of the sacred had become a fear and distrust of the flesh itself. Such a relationship illustrates how the Protestant Reformers gave impetus to a long term civilising project which developed in opposition to the fleshy body. In seeking to suppress the sensual body, however, Protestantism and visions of civil society did not eradicate social relationships based on fantasy knowledge of other people, but provided a basis for their reconstruction.

Irrational women

The view that people were unequally capable of achieving the rationality necessary for participating in cognitive life is striking in the case of gender. As Carole Pateman (1988) suggests, the emergence of civil society deconstructed one meaning of patriarchy, associated with divine right, only to reconstruct another based upon the unequal distribution of rationality. While men's rational minds were meant to be able to control and direct their physical bodies (even if male rules of bodily conduct were long observed more in the breaking than in the making) (Roper, 1994: 145–167), women's relationships to blood and birth meant their 'fragile minds' were ruled by their demanding, unpredictable bodies. Women's bodies had long been thought weak, natural homes to the Devil (Roper, 1994: 190), and residues of this view lingered on through women being placed firmly at the margins of civil society. They were part of the social contract, yet their relationship with (super)nature meant their proper place was in the *private realm* of civil society. Men no longer had 'body-obsessed-bodies' but lived more in their minds, while women suffered from an incapacity to absent themselves from their bodies (Starobinski, 1970).

The emergence of modern patriarchy (or what Turner, 1984 refers to as patrism), therefore, begins with the political defeat of paternalism by contractarians: women are no longer subject to their fathers, but to men *as men*. It is they who dominate a civil society constructed out of contracts, from which women are marginalised through their association with the privatised realm of the home, or through male violence, or through the connection between women and a carnality which precludes the rationalism inherent in the contractarian approach (Pateman, 1988: 3; Beck, 1992). Chatellier (1989: 255) suggests that this contrasts sharply with Counter-Reformation Catholicism, where the paternalism of the medieval period was replaced by a growing emphasis on the partnership and joint responsibilities of men and women. Based upon a possessive individualism which associates ownership of the body with ownership of material property, contractarianism not only precludes women on the basis of their insufficient rationality, but on their insufficient *individuality*. Women were unable to exert individual control over bodies suffused with what Rousseau called 'unlimited desires' (Pateman, 1988: 55, 97).

Baudelaire (1964 [1863]) observed that the association of women with mystery and desire had continued into modernity; a view also expressed by Simmel and Durkheim. Meštrović (1991: 146) has attributed this to the enduring association of women with fertility and, despite feminism, the persistence of traditional rather than modern values. This assumption of women's irrationality has served as a vehicle of their subjugation to men, but has also been the source of challenges to male order. The series of 'apparitions' by the Virgin Mary in the nineteenth and twentieth centuries, for example, can be understood as 'anti-modernist' eruptions of female power, and the power of the sacred, within the predominantly male, Protestant culture of modernity (Meštrović, 1991: 147–148).

Pateman's vision of a modern contractarian mentality which expresses an ideology of equality and action through mutual agreement, yet which also serves to subjugate women, is to some extent evident in early Protestant developments. As discussed in the previous chapter, the Reformers progressively emphasised that marriage was a *voluntary* contract between man and woman, yet also encouraged the enforced marriages of former nuns. Marriage was sacred because it was a religious relationship entered into by individuals as a result of free choice, yet, as Pateman observes, the 'individual' upon whom contractarianism rests is actually male (1988: 41). So more emphasis was placed on marriage as a relationship but the gender inequalities characteristic of married and family life in the medieval era were not transcended, merely transformed. In the great moral tracts of Protestantism it was invariably *men* who embarked upon mind-expanding journeys, while women stayed at home caring for the more immediate needs of the family. Women and children usually appeared in these tracts only as what we might term 'people baggage'.[18]

The specific *ideology* of patriarchy (as a theory of male authority over women and children) emerged from the Protestant Reformation's repressive treatment of female sexuality, its view of priests as an interference in the natural rights of fathers, and its virtual elimination of the Virgin Mary from the theological economy of Christianity (Stone, 1977; Turner, 1984; Meštrović, 1991). Despite the establishment of this ideology, however, the Protestant promotion of individualism and individuality stood somewhat uneasily beside the continued treatment of women as a *category* of people subordinate to another category of people, men. This can be seen as indicative of Protestantism's concern to promote disciplined bodies and forms of sociality removed from the irrationalities associated with sensual contact with the sacred; a goal which came to exclude women. Nevertheless,

Lerner (1993) suggests that those features of Protestantism concerned with introspection, reflexivity, and the importance of achieving 'good works' on earth, permeated women's consciousness and experiences in a manner which has been highly liberating. Reacting against the exclusion of women from civil society, however, certain forms of feminism have challenged women's exclusion from the contractarian possibilities of modernity without challenging the cognitive apprehension and fear of sensuality upon which such possibilities are constructed (Pateman, 1988). As Meštrović (1991: 161) expresses it, feminism has often sought only to make both sexes 'equal in relation to Protestant, abstract, subjectivist values'.

Managing the cognitive life

Theories of civil society tended to be predicated on the suppression of the sensuous flesh. As Max Weber's writings have shown, this concern was carried into the establishment of modern systems of governance. The modern state's promotion of effective and efficient rule was based on an attempt to subdue the body and make it manageable; an attempt which has significant affinities with Protestantism, even though it was progressively shaped by other influential forces. The body was to be controlled through the exercise of legitimate force (via the intermediaries of the police or army) which treated embodied persons according to a universalised model of the rational individual. Once the body was brought under control, however, the state needed to access the minds of its citizens. In comparison with previous eras, for example, contemporary education places much less emphasis on the training of the physical flesh, and directs much more attention to the moulding of consciousness, intentions and language (Shilling, 1993b).[19] The ability to govern, and to levy taxation over a territorial area, also required a highly rationalised mode of planning, monitoring and accounting; a system which again had a very limited place for passions, impulses and outbursts of emotive behaviour (Weber, 1968 [1925]: 973; Martin, 1989 [1987]).

Forming the mind

The state's ability to plan and promote particular ways of living received a great boost with the development of statistical means of gathering information (Rowntree, 1902). Statistics allowed the state to focus on and manage a differentiated *population* instead of a relatively homogeneous *people*. Individuals could be classified, for example, according to specific categories of 'need', 'control' and 'criminality'. Being able to derive norms through the calculation of averages (and deviants through their distance from these norms) was boosted by the work of Francis Galton (who formulated the concept 'normal distribution'), and provided an agenda for the education of populations. The meanings of sex, for example, could be harnessed to a view of national planning, once ruptured from religious control, which focused on the reproductive fitness of both the social body and of individual bodies (Foucault, 1981 [1976]).

These developments meant that governance was able to focus on managing life (in contrast to the medieval concern with discipline through the threat of death). The modern prison system sought to stimulate among prisoners 'useful' and 'productive' ways of living by encouraging inmates to reflect upon, monitor and eventually control their own behaviour (Foucault, 1979 [1975]). The army, hospitals and other institutions made similar attempts to regiment people's bodies in order to educate their malleable minds (Ball, 1990; Honneth and Joas, 1988: 144; Theweleit, 1987 [1977], 1989 [1978]).

This focus on the classification of populations allowed states to engage in processes of individuation which were not possible in the medieval age. Once knowledge of the population was gained, norms could be constructed. Individuals could then be identified and separated from others by marks, numbers, signs and codes. As Bryan Turner (1991) notes, this is paradoxical in that it consists of a set of practices which make people more individual, yet more controllable. As well as contributing to the care of individuals, for example, teaching hospitals became involved in monitoring the health of the nation. This implicated them in the construction of medical norms against which individuals could be compared and classified (Armstrong, 1983, 1987). Similarly, in plotting the relationship between individual and aggregate productivity, governments, industries and businesses could construct norms against which individuals could be compared and differentiated, rewarded or punished.

Despite these successes, modern modes of governance were unable to escape from the paradox evident in theories of civil society. In seeking to control the body, in order to release the mind for education, this rationalist approach to planning and management gave rise to great concern about the body and its disruptive potentialities. As the fleshy self could disrupt the proper education and moral growth of the individual, attention was directed towards how this could be prevented. While this attention was negative, it did not prevent the flesh from becoming the target of procedures and technologies directed at disciplinary goals. In Victorian Britain, for example, a whole panoply of procedures were employed to prevent boys and girls from indulging in dangerous sexual practices considered injurious to their mental health (Haley, 1988).

The relationship between governance, individuation and the mind/body order can be seen in the history of intelligence testing. This illustrates how people were individuated on the basis of cognitive criteria, and how these tests were used to reinforce concerns about undisciplined flesh. Intelligence testing also shows how the individuation of people was used to *reinforce* the relationship between fantasy knowledge and existing patterns of social inequality.

Mindful bodies

The history of intelligence testing is well known, but commentators have yet to clarify the importance of this history for the relationship between forms of embodiment and patterns of sociality. In the nineteenth century, 'intelligence' was measured by craniometry (the calibration of skulls). In the twentieth century this method gave way to mind-focused psychological testing.

Scientists were generally agreed in the nineteenth century that intelligence was a single entity, found in the brain, and amenable to measurement. Calibration focused on the container for the brain, the skull, and it was assumed that skull size, brain size and intelligence were related. Just as writers of civil society held that some people were more rational than others, craniometry reinforced this picture of corporeal inequality. Paul Broca, for example, concluded that 'the brain is larger in mature adults than in the elderly, in men than in women, in eminent men than in men of mediocre talent, and in superior races than in inferior races' (Broca, 1861: 304). While white men were rational guardians of the realm of civil society, women and black peoples were too irrational and emotional (Gould, 1984 [1981]).[20] Emphasising the intellectual distance that had been travelled between medieval and modern times, Broca also claimed that there had been a steady increase in European brain size between the two epochs (Broca, 1862).

This focus on intelligence had a dual effect: it elevated the importance of the mind, but contributed to a certain resurgence of the flesh. The body may have been 'dumb' and 'dangerous' but it was a sign of, and gateway to, the mind. Bodies, passions and sensualities were vital precisely because of the 'secrets' they contained about fitness for civil society. Cesar Lombroso's late nineteenth-century theory of *l'uomo delinquente* (the criminal man) held that criminals were 'evolutionary throwbacks' whose bodies displayed their irrationality and inherited criminality. Skull thickness, low and narrow foreheads, long arms, large feet and heavy wrinkles were just a selection of those criminal signs involuntarily imprinted on the body (Gould, 1984 [1981]: 129).

The twentieth century sought to bypass the body completely by suggesting that *psychological testing* could uncover the secrets of the mind. Such tests were used to identify children with special educational needs, assess the mental fitness of recruits during the First World War (over 1.75 million American recruits were tested in this way), and differentiate between students both within and between schools and colleges (Douglas, 1967 [1964]; Gould, 1984 [1981]: 149, 177). While the physical body was no longer implicated directly in these classifications of intellectual worth (though the inability to sit still long enough to take these tests was a sign of intellectual feebleness), intelligence tests were still used to shape the bodies and social interactions of those subjected to them. Tests were used to differentiate between people in education and employment, and even justified the forcible sterilisation of the 'feeble-minded' in Virginia, USA, from 1924 to 1972 (Gould, 1984 [1981]: 335). The mind now said so much about the potential dangers of the body (to the reproduction of the next generation) that it justified surgical removal of the ability of women to procreate.

The example of intelligence measuring shows how techniques of governance promoted individuation. Carnal knowing was invalidated and the fleshy body was to be managed according to information revealed about the quality of the brain. This approach to the body was also evident in the broader development of psychology. The work of Sigmund Freud is particularly significant here, in that it marked a shift in Western societies from the body to the mind. In the course of his psychiatric practice, Freud moved from a focus on the *physical traumas* of his patients to the workings of the *unconscious*. By developing a theory of repressed desires, Freud gave birth to psychoanalysis and switched from 'an essentially somatic explanation . . . of the aetiology of mental disturbance, to one located merely "in the mind"' (Porter, 1991: 215). This reflected a distrust of the body, yet also a concern to tame the body through discourse.

Modern knowledge and uncertainty

The development of Janus-faced modernity provides us with a narrative concerning how people can come to believe in the Enlightenment project of the mind's domination of the body. This involves the mental fantasy of being able to shut down human sensuality through the extension of profane, rational forms of sociality, and to embark as a consequence on an unprecedented form of human self-assertion (Cascardi, 1992: 127; Rochberg-Halton, 1986: 230). Abstracted from community, from the sacred, and from their bodies, Protestants did not succumb to the nostalgia of the baroque, but sought to counter the alienation of the early modern habitus by searching for rational foundations on which a social order could be constructed. The emergence of the 'official face' of modern society is, therefore, made possible by the displacement of individuals from a web of obligations and communally generated ritual orders of meaning, and becomes a symbolic association of what are essentially dissociated subjects (MacIntyre, 1981).

This contractarian devaluation and repression of human sensuality, while further developing the Protestant emphasis upon discourse, also tended to encourage a renewed focus on, and cognitive colonisation of, the visual. This tendency was 'carried' within Protestantism from the start, despite its distrust of images, by its attention to texts (which are *read* as well as heard) and its promotion of the 'autonomous subject'. What we mean by this can be clarified by referring to Berger's (1990 [1967]: 112–113) image of disenchantment as a process whereby a 'sky empty of angels becomes open to the intervention of the astronomer and eventually the astronaut'. The emergence of modernity is also the emergence of a particular way of *looking* at the world. Both the invention of printing, itself tied very closely to the emergence of Protestantism, and the invention of the telescope encouraged this privileging of the visual as *science* rather than baroque art (McLuhan, 1964; Ong, 1982; Eisenstein, 1979; Jay, 1992).

Scientific notions of 'objectivity' (Simmel, 1968) and the prevalence of surveillance in modern societies (Foucault, 1979 [1975]) reflect what has been called the 'scopic regime' of modernity (Metz, 1982; Jay, 1992). This regime expresses not just the tendency to locate sight at the top of the sensual hierarchy, but the *colonisation* of the visual by the cognitive (Lash and Friedman, 1992), through what Cascardi (1992: 185) calls 'the fiction of the subject as a sovereign Observer or Judge'. Elements of this colonisation can be found in the baroque's utilitarian manipulation of sensuality for specific ends; however, baroque seduction does not pre-suppose a world of sovereign observers and dissociated cognitive subjects, but a world of inherently sensuous beings who can still be manipulated into collective orders of meaning through their bodies. Thus, the baroque emphasis upon the visual presupposes bodies nostalgic for the sacred, while the visual emphasis of Protestant modernity presupposes profane bodies.

With regard to the birth of modern science, Simmel (1968) noted its abandonment of the search for the essence of things, and its reconciliation to merely 'stating the relationships that exist between objects and the human mind from the viewpoint of the human mind'. This accords with Heidegger's (1977) view of modernity as a culture in which man becomes the centre and measure of everything, but raises the question of how sustainable this extreme form of self-assertion can be. The prioritisation of the cognitive not only polarises an abstract, 'cold science' and the embodied, 'hot-blooded' sensuality of humans, but also points towards an inevitable sense of personal incompleteness and the difficulties of 'keeping in touch' with knowledge and meaning which follow from this modern estrangement from the body.

The evolution of Janus-faced modernity can therefore be understood as related to, if by no means entirely reducible to, the development of the Protestant re-formation of the body. Whereas in the Middle Ages the sacred expressed a tension between the productive activity of humans and the 'glorious consumption' of a religious order of meaning which was both transcendent, in its cosmic scope, and immanent, in the bodies of humans (Bataille, 1992 [1973]: 52), the Protestant Reformation's rejection of embodied immanence promoted instead the value of human production. Protestant asceticism valorised the 'self-made man', the product of his own labour and responsive to his 'calling', and for whom the call to labour became a moral imperative. This Protestant self-made man became Kant's autonomous subject (Cascardi, 1992: 170), liberated from ties to groups based on birth and free to participate in those that issue from 'conscious reflection and intelligent planning' (Simmel, 1971 [1903]: 137; Levine, 1985: 202).

It would be mistaken, however, to associate this increased emphasis upon reflexive scrutiny and rational calculation with a simple disappearance of the body. We have already noted various ways in which modern societies showed an intense interest in bodies, expressed primarily through a desire to manage them (and, in the case of women, a concern with the incapacity of some bodies to be managed effectively). Furthermore, the modern concern with stigmatising what is animalistic in people, and promoting the importance of the mind, also facilitated a selective resurgence of the body. Indeed, the rise of cognitive apprehension, as one face of the modern world, contains within it the story of how the body assumed a new importance in Western culture.

The resurgent body

This resurgence of the body within Western culture is not necessarily in contradiction to the process of prioritising the mind. The same social and technical innovations (such as the invention and location of the toilet and bedroom, and the development of the nightgown, cutlery and handkerchief) which allowed those bodily functions uniting people to be hidden from public view, also allowed the body's *appearance* to assume a new prominence (Elias, 1978 [1939]). Furthermore, the treatment of bodies as mannequins in Paris and London of the eighteenth and nineteenth centuries, for example, is essentially a reflection of social elites seeking to display their class (Sennett, 1992 [1974]).[21]

Somewhat different are those nineteenth-century theories of character and criminality which emphasised the body as an indicator of individuality and moral worth.[22] Character could be derived from behaviour and skull shape, clothes were considered to be 'emblems of the soul', and emotions were imprinted on the body. In this context, the display of the body became less important than the *cloaking* of appearance. As Sennett (1992 [1974]: 173) notes, 'One shielded oneself from the gaze of others because one believed that they could read the innermost secrets of one's feelings at a glance.' While these theories reflect a thoroughly modern attempt to establish meaning through reflexivity, they nevertheless show an attentiveness to the body far removed from Descartes's view of the desirability of being able to say 'I shall consider myself as having no hands, no eyes, no flesh, no blood, nor any senses' (1973: 101; Synnott, 1991: 70).

The resurgence of the flesh can express itself, however, in forms not so easily contained within the cognitive orders of modernity. Earlier in this chapter, we noted that the Reformation's rejection of carnal knowing was inherently problematic: there was always the danger that touch, taste, smell, sight and hearing could lead to the acquisition of heretical knowledge. Similarly, modernity's promotion of cognitive apprehension cannot eliminate the passions and sensations of bodies, however much it has tried to manage or repress them. If the voluptuous sensuality of the baroque reflects a partial alienation from, and nostalgia for, the carnal knowing of the Middle Ages, the modern asceticism which has sought to subjugate the corporeal to the cognitive expresses a deeper alienation which has stimulated patterns of anomie, malaise, depression and cynicism (Meštrović, 1991). Baudelaire's (1964 [1863]) dandy, Simmel's (1971 [1903]) blasé urbanite and Durkheim's (1951 [1897]) anomic type all suggest a tendency for the modern person to be 'out of touch' with the emotions, feelings and sensations of themselves and others (Meštrović, 1991: 12). But they also point towards the continuing strength and importance of embodied experience.

Baroque sensuality may have reached its peak in the Counter-Reformation, but it did not disappear along with the royal absolutism associated with it.[23] Post-Tridentine Catholicism contained elements of this sensuality at least up to the Second Vatican Council of the early 1960s, and its influence can still be felt in Europe (Chatellier, 1989), and many parts of South America (Moser et al., 1993; Lopes, 1993). More broadly, however, the decline of absolutism did not signal the demise of baroque sensuality but an opportunity for its reappearance in other forms. Releasing the sacred potentiality of flesh from absolutism, in fact, has allowed it to be taken up elsewhere. This is not to imply that it is an unchanging constant throughout history, but that the sensory experience of humans persists, in different forms, and will manifest itself in fresh ways once previous social and cultural expressions and instrumentalisations of it have declined. The tension between cognition and carnality which shaped the post-Reformation era is at the heart of the advanced modern experience of the world: seductive images have returned in the modern information age, and it is even possible to talk of the emergence of a form of embodiment which is both 'baroque' and 'modern'.

Notes

1. We have already argued that by promoting the discursive symbolisation of religion the Reformers helped reconstruct medieval bodies, and that in seeking to return Christianity to its Biblical roots, and break the control of ecclesiastical authorities over religious tradition, the Reformers also reduced the power of the medieval Church. Following from this, it is not surprising that the Reformers' agenda for change shared an affinity with those seeking social and commercial freedoms (Ozment, 1993: 20–22). As cities and towns became more commercially active in the late Middle Ages, newly emerging elites came into conflict with the Catholic Church. The Church was resented for its power as a landowner, for its control over poor relief, for the support it received from the aristocracy, and for its status as a force which transcended the interests and boundaries of the emerging city-states (Wuthnow, 1989: 54–63). Powerful alliances grew between the interests of urban and commercial elites on the one hand, and the agenda of the Reformers on the other. The individualised, cognitive and future-oriented bodies promoted by these groups conflicted directly with the traditional, communal and carnal mode of embodiment associated with Catholicism.

2. The influence of Protestantism remained marginal in certain countries such as Spain and Italy, while the Catholic Counter-Reformation asserted its authority in lands – such as France, Belgium, Bavaria, Bohemia and Poland – which had wavered between Protestantism and Catholicism during the sixteenth century.

3. This interventionism is also apparent in the macabre iconography of the baroque which expresses a tension between a kind of awe in the face of human decay and mortality and, simultaneously, a developing fascination with scrutinising the composition of the human body, the spread of anatomical knowledge, and an interest in the transformations of cadavers. This tension can be seen in visual representations of the death of Christ, where Christ's dead body is no longer the glorified body of medieval art but a 'dramatically humanised' corpse (Maravall, 1986: 65).

4. Rembrandt's *Naked Woman Seated on a Mound* (1631), thought offensive by some when first exhibited, is a good example of this naturalism; it depicts a woman with sagging breasts, lumpy legs and a swollen stomach (Martin, 1977: 52).

5. On a wider level, the Church played a significant role in the emergence of new art forms. As Wright (1982: 234) notes, the 'splendour of liturgical and non liturgical religious ceremonies after Trent . . . provided the model for the seventeenth-century employment of scenic and musical effect in the evolving masque, opera and related court ballet'.

6. As the Council of Trent was meeting, there were rumours that Protestant armies were marching on Trent. Indeed, in 1552 a Protestant army under Maurice of Saxony was only a few hours' march from Trent, but the Council persisted and reinforced the Catholic understanding of the Mass in the face of Protestant reinterpretations (Chadwick, 1990 [1964]: 275). As McGrath (1993: 187) notes, the Council 'vigorously defended both the doctrine and the terminology of transubstantiation'.

7. This can be illustrated with regard to the changes to Catholic confessional practice introduced after the Council of Trent. These changes undoubtedly included a move *away* from actions and *towards* intentions, words and thoughts (Foucault, 1981 [1976]: 19). Nevertheless, in contrast to Foucault's conclusions on the matter, the Catholic confession remained a sacrament, placing a new value on *sacramental* confession and not on confession in general. The stimulation of emotional penance through ritual remained central, and contrasted with the Protestant tendency towards written and spoken confession. Foucault suggests that changes in Catholic confessional practice after the Council of Trent (1545) reduced the need for an 'entire painstaking review of the sexual act in its very unfolding' (Foucault, 1981 [1976]). Instead, emphasis moved away from actions and toward intentions, desires, dreams and memories. While details about specific sexual acts became vaguer, the scope of sexuality and sexual sin increased (Foucault, 1981 [1976]: 20). Desire was turned into discourse, as people became obliged to speak about the most internal aspects of their lives. For Foucault, this marks the beginning of both the modern practice of talking about sex exhaustively and, more generally, the development of Western society into a 'confessing society' (see also Turner, 1991). However, this conclusion fails to consider the limited ritual contexts in which confession became more important during the Counter-Reformation. As noted earlier, the Reformers dislocated confession from ritual and expressed it instead through the highly personalised literary forms of diaries and autobiographies.

8. It is true that the Council of Trent placed a greater priority on the conscious and discursive knowledge of religious truth. Nevertheless, the route to this truth was quite different, and much more corporeal, than that offered by Protestantism. Jacques Lacan has focused on this baroque concern with materiality. He notes that in a Catholic culture where the display of the body evokes infinite *jouissance*, the importance of Christ is established through his body. In such a culture it also follows that the body of Christ assumes importance for the Catholic through oral incorporation or devourment (Lacan, 1975; Buci-Glucksmann, 1994).

9. It has been noted, in fact, that some of the most impressive artistic creations of the period were devoted to the glorification of monarchy (Martin, 1977: 14).

10. Deriving from the 'mystical body of Christ' (a phrase which suggests the natural and supernatural existence of Christ's body), the Christological version of the doctrine of the 'king's two bodies' originated in a treatise written around 1100 by an anonymous cleric from Normandy (Turner, 1993: 180).

11. The best-known example of a regicide is Foucault's Damiens, an unfortunate who had his flesh torn from his body with red-hot pincers, had molten lead, boiling oil and sulphur

poured on his wounds, had his limbs stretched by horses and then cut off with the aid of the executioner's knife, before finally having his torso thrown on a fire (Foucault, 1979 [1975]).

12. This is not to say that Protestantism didn't engage in all sorts of spectacular and bloody punishments (Scribner et al., 1994). Nevertheless, these punishments were justified on the basis that offenders had gone against the *Word* of God.

13. This is evident with regard to the fascination with time. While the sacred can be associated with a timeless continuity and immanence, the growing profanation of human experience can be linked with a growth in processes of differentiation, especially with regard to time (Bataille, 1992 [1973]: 19). The baroque, consumed with nostalgia for the disappearing medieval sacred order, was simultaneously obsessed with time. As Panofsky wrote, 'No period has been so obsessed with the depth and width, the horror and sublimity of the concept of time as the baroque', an obsession reflected in innovations in clock making and a zeal for measuring time (Maravall, 1986: 187). As Maravall notes (1986: 186), the measuring of time was an attempt to reduce its terrible, unknown power to the world of human objects.

14. Seidler also discusses the influence of a Protestant moral culture upon socialism, particularly with regard to a Calvinistic ethic of self-denial. He observes, for example, that socialism has often combined a heroic ethic of self-denial with a variation on the Protestant conception of the corruptness of human nature, expressed as an attack on 'bourgeois' feelings (1994: 65). Identifying the self with reason, socialists have discounted emotions and feelings as 'temptations' and 'distractions' that lead to error. This Protestant influence is also apparent in the way in which socialism has so often tied its visions of self-realisation to *work*, implicitly subordinating other areas of life (1994: 105). Similarly, socialism tended to follow Protestantism in the idea that nature had to be subordinated to the control and intervention of humans (1994: 106).

15. 'When established forms of authority could no longer be taken for granted it was the idea of sovereignty which provided a fresh link between political power and rulership. In the struggle between church, state and society, sovereignty offered an alternative way of conceiving the legitimacy of claims to power . . . it became a theory about the possibility of, and the conditions for, the rightful exercise of political power' (Held, 1992: 106).

16. Hobbes's state of nature has frequently been seen as a reflection of bourgeois society without the police, while Calvin's 'fallen man' can only be reduced to civil subordination (failing regeneration) by a discipline imposed by secular authorities (Hill, 1966).

17. The work of Thomas Hobbes was accompanied and succeeded by that of other theorists of civil society (Campbell, 1981). Jeremy Bentham, John Locke, Jean Jacques Rousseau and others sought very different grounds on which to project their views of secular authorities. Nevertheless, what these and other theorists of civil society shared in common was the construction of a secular realm of rationally justifiable order. This was not only to be based upon rational foundations, but should be able to be recognised as such by those subject to its authority.

18. In *Robinson Crusoe* (1678–84), for example, a man has a quarrel with his father, runs away to sea, and becomes as self-sufficient as possible.

19. This contrasts with those forms of 'religious education' characteristic of the Middle Ages, and also with baroque absolutism. Here, governance was concerned with the individual's fleshy, physical body, and with the sins and threats posed by virtue of humans being bodies. Authorities were concerned with controlling the bodies of relatively anonymous crowds and, as we have seen, punishment was concerned with repression and the ultimate annihilation of the body.

20. Paul Broca was the best-known exponent of craniometry, but it would be a mistake to assume that craniometry was influential among just a small group of scientists. Ideas about the relationship between skull size and intelligence were disseminated widely and gained a significant degree of public currency (Gould, 1984 [1981]: 82). Craniometry was used to support slavery, and to reinforce the subordinate position of women in European and American society. Gustave le Bon, for example, was horrified by the proposals of some American reformers to provide equal opportunities for women in the sphere of higher

education. Such reforms should never be made, as women 'excel in fickleness, inconstancy, absence of thought and logic, and incapacity to reason' (Le Bon, 1879: 60–61).

21. They began this period by smearing red pigment on the nose, forehead, or around the chin, by painting their skin apoplexy-red or dull white, and by wearing enormous and elaborate wigs. As the body signified more and more about an individual's *social* position, its *appearance* became more important while evidence of its natural fleshiness became hidden from view. The body's position as a location for the expression of social codes was reinforced by statute. In England and France sumptuary laws assigned to each station in the social hierarchy a set of 'appropriate clothes' which could be worn by them and them alone (Sennett, 1992 [1974]: 65).

22. Theories of intelligence were part of a much broader change in dominant orientations to the body that occurred at the end of the nineteenth century and were indicated by a number of developments. John Stuart Mill conceived of a science of 'ethology' (concerned with ascertaining character from behaviour) which was popularised in such practices as phrenology (deducing character from the shape of the head). Carlyle constructed a theory that clothes could be seen as 'emblems of soul', and Charles Darwin published *The Expression of Emotions in Man and Animals* (1955 [1896]), a work on psychology which suggested that emotions had specific correlates in physical appearance (Sennett, 1992 [1974]).

23. Baroque culture is generally understood to have decayed with the emergence of the eighteenth century (Martin, 1977). The 'holy alliance' between Counter-Reformation Catholicism and absolutist states was, ultimately, unable to hold at bay the modern project it had opposed. Ironically, the large territorial areas created by the rise of absolutism – facilitating the establishment of monopolies of violence and the application of a more 'unitary, continuous, calculable and effective rule' by a single sovereign head – meant that while seeking to reassert tradition, absolutism was actually creating part of the foundations on which modern states could be built (Poggi, 1978: 60–61; Held, 1992). More broadly, however, it is hard to see how a culture which was so thoroughly nostalgic could have sustained itself for very long.

6

AMBIVALENT BODIES

Over the last decade or so, the question of whether we are living in a modern or a postmodern society has preoccupied a number of social theorists. Some of these theorists have taken the view that the modern project, which aimed to conquer nature and to transform people's relations with each other upon the basis of rationality, has come to a halt (Baudrillard, 1983; Lyotard, 1984). Others, disputing the nature and the very existence of 'postmodernity', have reconsidered the nature of the modern project itself, drawing attention to the centrality of 'reflexivity' throughout its history, and to the unprecedented pervasiveness of reflexivity in contemporary Western societies (Giddens, 1990, 1991; Beck, 1992). Theorists such as Bauman (1991, 1992a, 1992b) have attempted to draw on both these perspectives, seeing postmodernity as a development of certain aspects of modernity, rather than a complete break from it.[1]

Despite Bauman's efforts, however, one of the problems with the question of whether we are living in a modern or postmodern society is that it tends to discourage attention being directed to the ambivalent, Janus-faced character of the contemporary world, and to those phenomena which permeate, overlap or erode the distinctions between contrasting epochs. In this chapter, we address this problem by suggesting that the dualities of early modernity have been reshaped within those divergent forms of sociality which are associated with the emergence of a *baroque modern body*. This argument adds to the already commonplace themes of 'fracture' and 'contradiction' pervading recent descriptions of the modern world. In our analysis, this 'fracturing' is best understood not just as 'modern reflexivity's' confrontation with 'modern metanarratives' (Giddens, 1990), nor as 'modern culture's' confrontation with 'modern society' (Bauman, 1992a), but as the elaboration of an internally differentiated relationship between human embodiment and the sacred which is tied to the divergent development of *banal* and *sensual* forms of sociality.

Crucial to our analysis, then, is a conceptualisation of the changing character and location of the sacred in relation to social life. This focus on the sacred is becoming evident in the work of a number of theorists. Bryan Turner's (1991: xvi) growing emphasis on the important role of religion in contemporary social changes, for example, has led him to question his previous reliance on conventional secularisation theories. Harvie Ferguson (1992) has suggested that advanced modern forms of sociality are characterised by a 'recovered sensuousness' which reflects a developing *consecration* of the profane world. The relationships surrounding the internally fragmented character of the baroque modern body are, however, more contradictory than this argument implies. It is our view that contemporary social changes cannot be addressed merely with regard to the 'return of the sacred' (Bell, 1980); both the reappearance of sacred forms of sociality in certain spheres of social life *and* the increasing elimination of the sacred must be considered. These can be associated with the further development of Protestant, profane forms of sociality in other social spheres.

These changing relationships with the sacred, and the development of divergent forms of sociality, are intimately tied to the baroque modern re-formation of the body. In what follows, we argue that while the declining socio-cultural influence of certain aspects of Protestantism has indeed led to the increased visibility of the sacred (in what we refer to as sensual solidarities), it has also contributed to profane forms of sociality becoming *banal* (operating on the basis of a formal rationality and an internal referentiality which excludes and ignores broader issues of morality and social cohesion). Certain aspects of the disciplined and individualistic body of early modernity are being *extended* (through banal forms of sociality, the individualisation of contracts, and within particular dimensions of people's bodily selves). Elsewhere, however, these 'disciplined bodies' are giving way to a further re-formation, centred on an involvement in sensual forms of sociality which echo the seductive, sacred corporeality of the baroque period, and which prioritise what we refer to as *tribal fealties* over individual contracts. In Weber's terms, then, the 'formal rationality' of advanced capitalism is not confining people entirely within an amoral and spiritually impoverished 'iron cage'. Instead, sensual forms of sociality coexist with, and sometimes threaten to overwhelm, the contracts underpinning banal associations existing, as they do, within a habitus which is both *modern* and *baroque*. From conflicting individual affects, to the 'breakdown' of male/female relations within the family, to the fragility of inter-state civilising processes, the discipline and order presupposed by Enlightenment narratives of rationality have shown themselves to be insufficient in relation to the effervescent intimations and experiences of sensual physicality.

Our concentration on the relationship between re-formations of the body and changing types of sociality is also highly relevant to certain concerns addressed by many policy analysts and political commentators. Before examining banal associations and sensual solidarities in detail we can, in fact, usefully ground our analysis by summarising recent laments for the 'disappearance of discipline' and the 'decline of community'. While these suggest that overarching social contracts have been replaced by volatile and rampant individualisms based on choice, sensuality and irresponsibility, it is our contention that these 'dangerous' sensibilities are manifestations of those coherent and related forms of sociality that form the focus of this chapter.

The disappearance of community?

Social critics from various political positions appear to have difficulty in specifying the particular character of advanced modern forms of sociality, and their implications for identity-construction and the apprehension of meaning. No longer structured by rituals which 'eat into' their members' bodies, nor by a (Biblical) discourse invested with a sacred ontology, many 'communities' are often understood to be invested with no more solidity than that implied by Bulmer's (1989: 253) concept of 'intermediary structures'. Closely allied to this view of community has been a lament for the disappearance of the contract mentality which provided the traditional context for American individualism, and whose apparent decline has resulted in what is envisaged as a state of 'moral confusion and social anarchy' (Etzioni, 1993: 12).

In charting the decline of community and contract, these critics look back, implicitly or explicitly, to the Protestant traditions that shaped modern America. Despite its individualistic focus, for example, John Locke's eighteenth-century Protestant ideal of the autonomous individual was 'embedded in a complex moral ecology that included family and church . . . and a vigorous public sphere in which economic initiative . . . grew together with public spirit' (Bellah et al., 1992: 265; Bloom, 1988). It was *within* this morality that limits on the individual were rejected other than those freely and rationally consented to in the social contract (Bellah et al., 1992: 67, see also 27–28; 234–235; Dunn, 1969, 1984).

When considering contemporary America, however, these critics question whether the social contract is any longer possible. They see enthusiasm for unbridled individualism and hedonistic pursuits, but little taste for rationally defined common interests (Bloom, 1988: 27). In *Habits of the Heart*, Bellah et al. (1985) argue that the language of achievement, self-fulfilment and aggressive individualism which pervades America makes it difficult to sustain any commitment to the Protestant and civic traditions that have been so important for the development of American society (see also Bellah et al., 1992). Against this, Etzioni (1993: ix, 12) argues that it is time once more 'for people to live up to their responsibilities and not merely focus on their entitlements'.

Morally vacant communities

The concern with the degeneration of a Protestant, contract mentality has several manifestations in the work of these critics. First, a strong valuation of *choice* without responsibility dominates American society: 'America has no-fault automobile accidents, no-fault divorces, and it is moving with the aid of modern philosophy toward no-fault choices' (Bloom, 1988: 228, 236; see also Etzioni, 1993). Second, economic and educational effectiveness cannot exist while young people are unable to value discipline and planning (Bellah et al., 1992: 261), and suffer from that 'deeper deficiency: insufficient self-control' (Etzioni, 1993: 92; see also Bellah et al., 1992: 267; cf. Ehrenreich, 1990). Third, there is general concern about the 'decline of the family' and the 'irrelevance' of fathers to family life (Blankenhorn, 1995; Davies, 1993); part of a situation in which marriage 'has become a *disposable* relationship . . . entered into like a rental agreement – with an escape clause' (Etzioni, 1993: 27).

Concerns about social degeneration are nothing new; they ebb and flow throughout history. In late modern societies, however, these concerns are more evident and influential. Associating moral value with cognitive commitments to overarching social contracts, politicians in North America and Europe complain that 'communities' are now morally vacant spaces marked by fast moving populations cycling in and out of 'single-stranded' relationships (Etzioni, 1993; Baumgartner, 1988). In the absence of an overarching social contract that can be agreed upon by people of different classes, ethnic backgrounds and genders, individuals make their way on the basis of transient, individualised contracts. Made in writing, orally, or even in the mind, these contracts link employer and employee, husband and wife, student and college, individual and church, through a reciprocity which is easily agreed and easily broken.

If the decline of an overarching social contract has caused concern, in 'closing the mind' on a selfish individualism, so has the '[re]opening' of the body. Bloom's (1988) critique of the liberation of 'bodily desires', for example, identifies a cultural shift which has lifted 'sexual restrictions', condoned drugs, and promoted hedonists as heroes. As Bloom argues, never before 'has there been such a marvellous correspondence between the good and the pleasant' (Bloom, 1988: 328–329). 'Sex, drugs and rock 'n' roll' may provide a sensual 'basis of association' via 'shared feelings [and] bodily contact' (Bloom, 1988: 75; Stivers, 1994: 145), but we now live in a society where 'There is no printed word to which [the young] look for counsel, inspiration or joy' (Bloom, 1988: 62).

Not enough religion?

This concern with the degeneration of a Protestant contract mentality, which implies a kind of secularisation, has developed at a time when sociologists are increasingly concerned with the apparent *strength* of religion, including its Protestant forms, and are inclined to question conventional secularisation theories.[2] Warner (1993), for example, questions whether secularisation ever occurred at all, at least in the USA. In contrast to many conventional sociological assumptions, it is increasingly recognised that modernisation here went hand in hand with an immense expansion of religion (Herberg, 1960: 47–50; Caplow et al., 1983: 28–29; Finke and Stark, 1986; Stark and Finke, 1988; Warner, 1993). Warner points out that Parsons's (1960, 1967, 1969) emphasis on the abstraction of religious values and Berger's (1990 [1967]) and Luckmann's (1967) on their privatisation are representative of a sociological tendency to ignore the extent to which modern religious pluralism is connected not only with individualism, but also with the development of particular notions of community. Warner suggests that religion in America is constitutively pluralistic, structurally flexible and, though inherently individualistic, can serve as a vehicle of empowerment for minorities and otherwise subjugated people (Warner, 1993: 1044).[3]

In the light of Warner's arguments, it is important to distinguish between the declining influence of a Protestant social contract mentality, and the apparent strength of many Protestant religious organisations which is evident not only in the USA but in Britain too (Beckford, 1992). In failing to do this, laments for the Protestant social contract mentality which framed American individualism tend to misconceive the nature of the changes they are seeking to understand. Instead of representing a simple *negation* of Protestantism, the emphasis on choice and sensuality observed by critics such as Bloom can be seen as an elaboration and uncoupling of two of Protestantism's major features. As Stivers (1994: 30– 31) notes, while 'The United States was from its inception a . . . religious experiment in community building', the intersection of Protestantism with a national project involved *two* notions of community. These were an intensely personal commitment of individuals to a religion, and the commitment to a much wider contract of rationality grounded in the Word of a radically transcendent God. What has happened in advanced modern societies is not that these components have disappeared, but that they have become dislocated from each other and from their traditional referents.

Individual commitment continues to be valued in societies such as America, and words still play a key role in helping people structure their priorities and interactions (the market for self-help literature and chat-based entertainment/advice shows, which bears a resemblance to the Protestant practice of testifying before the community, provide examples of this). Commitment often escapes the boundaries of institutionalised religion, however, and words need no longer be anchored in the sublime Word of God. Criteria for the construction both of knowledge and of human relationships proliferate without reference to the sublime, and without the guidance and security of its nomic properties (Berger, 1990 [1967]), though more fragile sources of meaning and identity are increasingly plentiful.[4] Similarly, *contracts* have not disappeared from sociality, but have become ruptured from overarching normative criteria and based instead on the individualising tendencies of law and choice.

If our analysis is correct, it would be wrong to associate recent laments for the loss of 'community' with the absence of structured relational forms. Information, contract and choice are central to the proliferation of banal associations in contemporary life, while these forms of sociality have developed alongside sensual solidarities.

Banal associations

Banal associations are *productive* forms of sociality, bound up with formal rationality and the creation of goods, services and relationships in advanced capitalist societies. The ideal typical 'rational organisation' provides a good example of such an association; dedicated to the instrumentally efficient pursuit of a goal without needing or being able to justify that goal (Weber, 1948 [1919]). Banal associations continue to be structured by rationality and cognitive apprehension, but are entirely dislocated from Protestantism's discursive symbolisation of the sacred and other, more sensually visible, manifestations of the sacred; a situation which erodes previous limits on, and certainties about, how people should relate to their environment and to themselves. Criteria of efficiency and reciprocity replace standards of ultimate truth and morality, and there is nothing which cannot be subjected to scrutiny, nothing which cannot be explored or reconstructed, and nothing which remains 'out of bounds' because of its 'other worldly' status. In this respect, banal associations have much in common with the 'iron cage' of modern life so central to the concerns of Weber (1991 [1904–5]).

Information is central to the operation of these associations, then, but circulates outside any sacred ontology in a quantity and at a velocity which threatens its status as meaningful knowledge (Baudrillard, 1993a). Furthermore, while banal associations are based on discursive communication and have grown with the development of information technologies, they are not confined to formal organisations. Giddens's (1992) analysis of 'pure relationships', which we consider in more detail later in this chapter, provides us with one example of an 'intimate' but banal form of sociality.

The gathering, organising and exchange of information has grown in importance since the establishment of the nation state (Giddens, 1985), but most analysts would agree that information now plays a historically unprecedented role in society. Just as the electricity grid 'links every home, office, factory and shop to provide energy', so the information grid connects people to communications networks which promise to be as important as the industrial development of roads, railways and sea ports (Lash and Urry, 1994; Webster, 1995: 7). Mark Poster (1995: 82) suggests that increases in transmission capacity will enable us to transmit audio, video or text based information 'real time' (24 frames of video per second with an accompanying audio frequency range of 20 to 20,000 hertz), while the development of telephone linkages in the forms of computers, telex, TV and video has begun to eliminate the need for everyone to be physically present 'at work' (Abbott, 1987: 70). Thus, Keller (1977: 296) has suggested that people could become 'stationary nomads . . . going everywhere without moving from a spot, in instant contact with any and everyone, armed solely with ourselves, our personal computers and our portable telephones'.

As Frank Webster (1995) argues, it is one thing to analyse how greater information flows have shaped and layered existing economic relationships, but quite another to suggest it has *transformed* these relations. Concerning the 'layering' of these relations, Max Weber (1991 [1904–5]) discussed how the Puritans' search for signs of salvation became linked to, and then disconnected from, production. It is Jean-François Lyotard (1984), however, who has traced the increasing banality of the information saturated relationships of the contemporary cultural world.

Once information proliferates outside of any stable sacred/profane division, there is a tendency for it to become uncoupled from certainty, and for its utility to be determined by principles of performativity and profitability. In other words, information becomes commodified and separated from consensually shared notions of truth. As Lyotard puts it, information-based 'phrase regimes' become meaningful signifiers only to their specific 'user groups' (Lyotard, 1984). Pressure groups and lobbyists, for example, provide a political manifestation of this use of 'knowledge', gathering and presenting data solely in terms of its ability to further sectional interests. These developments are exacerbated by the ways in which people have 'lost touch' with the world around them. People tend to acquire their information, irrespective of how much of it they have access to, through highly mediated forms which provide them with limited sensory contacts with the objects they learn about. This is one reason why the manipulation of news by the press, and the distortion and hiding of statistics by government, is both corporeally feasible and appears so commonplace (Fiske, 1987; Iyengar, 1992; Katz and Liebes, 1990).

Alain Touraine's (1995) analysis of modernity claims that information is more multi-layered and complex than Lyotard suggests (see also Stehr, 1994). Nevertheless, economic associations frequently operate without reference to ultimate values or to large numbers of human beings. As Baudrillard (1993b) points out, millions of dollars can be won and lost in the 'economy of the stock market' without a single thing being produced and without a single meeting between an employer and employee, while the economy of football can dictate that soccer matches are played behind 'closed doors', away from the prying eyes of ill-behaved fans. We can explore this progressive loss of 'sense' from banal associations, and the loss of publicly shared meanings, with reference to the work of Bataille, Baudrillard and Simmel.

Losing the sublime

According to Georges Bataille, and to the related work of René Girard, the most important act of 'exchange' within tribal societies was the act of sacrifice (Bataille, 1992 [1973]; Girard, 1977 [1972]). The sacrifice was an offering to a god (the sacred representation of society) which provided people with a recognition of their continuity in death and a chance to displace conflict through a ritual act of violence. The immanence of people within 'exchange' was continued outside sacrifice, however, as the giving and receiving of objects was saturated with status-based relationships structured round sacred/profane divisions. The 'gift relationship' was reciprocal and the exchange of goods was subordinated to the sacred or profane status of embodied individuals within a community.

This analysis of tribal societies contains some features which are also apparent in the medieval era, as we explored in Chapter 3. It is as the 'sacred communities' in these societies disintegrate that the functional utility of goods (and then their exchange value) as a criterion of exchange becomes profane and begins to marginalise the sacred, interpersonal significance of gifts. Furthermore, with the decline of Protestantism's civic influence, the world of economics loses its 'sublimated' sacred referent. As Weber (1991 [1904–5]: 180–811) argues, rational conduct on the basis of the idea of 'the calling' has declined, while the spirit of religious asceticism has escaped from the system of capitalism. Markets operate and goods circulate on their own terms, with even less reference to the sacred ties that once existed between known persons. This is compounded by the shrinkage of time and space characteristic of capitalism (Harvey, 1990: 260–307) and by the tendency of consumer culture to absorb any utility goods may have into the rapidly changing *images* and *signs* attached to them (Featherstone, 1991), and the arts of consumption associated with them (Bourdieu, 1984). In his more recent work, Baudrillard has identified a further stage in this 'removal' of the sacred and of enfleshed people from exchange relations. We have now reached a 'fractal stage', he suggests, where value circulates without reference to people, objects or any logic save for its own momentum (Baudrillard, 1993b).

If Baudrillard is talking metaphorically about the inability of people to gain full contact with, or control, processes of signification in the contemporary world (Clark, 1995: 130), he also points to the double-edged character of information and its association with cognitive doubt. On the one hand, information (whether commodified or not) has been linked to a growing human capacity to exercise control over the environment (Bell, 1979). 'Informational cities', for example, constitute a nodal point for sign systems which allow managers to control production from afar rather than being reliant on local conditions (Castells, 1989; Sassen, 1991), while computer-mediated communications enable people to form personal relationships without having to conform to particular norms of sexuality or appearance (Goffman, 1969; Wiley, 1995). On the other hand, however, it has become common for social theorists to examine how the association of information with certainty has weakened (Beck, 1992; Giddens, 1991). Multinational companies spend large sums of money seeking to identify misinformation and insuring themselves against the risks associated with 'information breakdowns', while individuals can only ever assess a small percentage of the options made available to them through electronic communications (Wiley, 1995; for an analysis of this paradox, see Turner, 1996).

Doubting the world

These paradoxical effects can, according to Giddens (1991), result in a chronic reflexivity that produces in individuals a cognitive sense of the precariousness, uncertainty and artificiality of contemporary life. At its most severe, these circumstances are linked to the difficulties of maintaining 'ontological security', a basic trust in reality (Giddens, 1991: 39). Whilst based on the psychological work of Erikson (1950) and Winnicott (1965, 1974) (which contains a bodily basis insofar as it is concerned with basic trust and the presence/absence of parents), Giddens's use of the term is irredeemably cognitive. For Giddens, it is the basic contingency of knowledge (which assumes the status of facts only 'until-further-notice') that can lead to a chronic reflexive revisionism. Individuals who experience this must either take advantage of the empowering and liberating opportunities it offers, or succumb to the 'radical doubt' which threatens disorientation, fragmentation and, ultimately, the collapse of self (Giddens, 1991, 1992). In facing these options, people are surrounded by a growing number of experts, counsellors and advisers ready to proffer guidance in all aspects of life (Rueschemeyer, 1986). So, the boom in the therapy business may be caused partly by its fashionable status (Gellner, 1993), but is also reflective of the doubt and disorientation widespread among the very people who enjoy financially rewarding jobs (Pahl, 1995).

The information which permeates banal associations, and the cognitive doubts it can engender, is not wholly oppositional to human sensuality, however, as it can 'spill over' to stimulate a certain resurgence of the flesh. Simmel's (1990 [1978], 1971 [1903]) analysis of the growth of the information-proliferating money economy and its metropolitan milieu shows how banal associations can liberate people from bodily ties, but also *stimulate* in them a distinctive emotional response to modern life. The forms of sociality facilitated by money have tended to liberate people from groups based on ascribed factors such as birth, and made them dependent instead on 'conscious reflection and intelligent planning' (Levine, 1985: 202). So far, so cognitive. This move from determination to choice, though, has paradoxical implications for the social habitus. On the one hand, it promotes reflexively constituted group associations as part of a broader valuation of 'the purely cognitive dispositions of actors at the expense of their emotional or sentimental dispositions' (Levine, 1985: 202). On the other hand, these same developments create a highly intellectualised relation between people and their culture which, in its tendency to turn everything into objects to be rationally assessed, surpasses the ability of persons to absorb it (Levine, 1985: 203). This is the context in which 'the rapid telescoping of changing images, pronounced differences within what is grasped at a single glance, and the unexpectedness of violent stimuli' can create a resurgence of sensual responses to modern life (Simmel 1971 [1903]: 325). While one response to this may have been the production of a blasé attitude, another may derive from a 'spilling' of all this information over the mind's eye into the body's sensualities.

Lash and Urry (1994) are probably correct to suggest that the proliferation and acceleration of information flows are likely to have been accompanied by an increase in people's abilities to assimilate and decode signs and messages. There are limits to this, though, and modern societies both promote and continue to *overwhelm* people's cognitive abilities. As Baudrillard (1993b: 32) says: 'So many messages and signals are produced and disseminated that they can never possibly all be read. A good thing for us too – for even with the tiny portion we do manage to absorb, we are in a state of permanent electrocution' (see also Heim, 1995).

Redemption through consumption?

Banal associations promote 'reflections on reflections'; a situation which has, as we have seen, been linked by Giddens (1991), Beck (1992) and others to the state of radical doubt. As Lash and Urry (1994) point out, though, the priority attached to discourse, openness and perpetual dialogue has also been associated with the stimulation of *carnal* responses and an *aesthetic reflexivity* toward our environment. These are promoted by images in consumer culture which seek not simply to inform, but to encourage appetites, emotions, sensations and fantasies. As information about the world becomes dislocated from certainty about the world, then, it is not always possible to separate rationality from sensuality. Modern people can find themselves dealing not only with an 'assault on the mind', but an 'assault on the senses.'

Banal associations are not only characterised by a surfeit of discursive signs, but by a surfeit of sensual *images*. John Fiske (1991) has suggested that the 'sign saturated' character of our society distinguishes our present epoch from its predecessors: 'In one hour's television viewing, one is likely to experience more images than a member of a non-industrial society would in a lifetime' (Fiske, 1991: 58; Webster, 1995: 177). As Alison Landsberg points out, the potential of images in film has long been recognised (by cultural critics of the 1920s such as Walter Benjamin and Siegfried Kracauer) as being able to arouse the 'material layers' of 'the human being: his nerves, his senses, his entire physiological substance' (Kracauer, 1993 [1940]: 458; Landsberg, 1995: 180).

This stimulation of the senses informs the attempts of marketing companies to saturate goods with images that will produce a desire for the fantasy world of consumer society (Lash and Urry, 1994). Tourists, for example, draw on these fantasies as a way of turning sights into places of 'oriental exoticism', 'Hollywood fantasy', or 'natural beauty' (Urry, 1990). The diner at McDonalds, or at the Indian or Chinese restaurant, is prompted to undertake a similar imaged or semiotic work of transformation. The leisure industry also draws on sensory reception in promoting the experience of escape (Cohen and Taylor, 1992). Paint ball hunting (where tourists shoot big game with 'harmless' ink pellets), and dare-devil fun park rides (which propel people in secured 'seats' upside down at speeds of over eighty miles an hour) are just two activities which give rise to a temporary reordering of the priority attached to people's senses (see Rojek, 1995).

The effects of these developments have been evaluated in contrasting terms in relation to consumption and morality. In the case of *consumption*, it has been suggested that the influence of images renders redundant the rational self-control of early modern persons, so that 'the duty of the individual is to consume, not as a process of self-education and self-understanding, but simply in the hope of being excited' (Ferguson, 1992: 172). Ferguson (1992: 170) has suggested that while early capitalist consumption was driven by a passionate individualism, contemporary consumption occurs on the basis of a rediscovered sensuousness. Whereas early capitalism tended to leave decisions about consumption to 'sovereign individuals', whole industries now seek to create, control and organise appetites and their satisfactions. An alternative analysis of consumption associates this 'seduction of the senses' with a sense of disillusionment and melancholy. Colin Campbell (1987) has argued that cycles of desire, acquisition and dissatisfaction are central to a sign- and image-based culture. The gap between the object of consumption and the images associated with that object can lead to disappointment and insecurity. People continue to consume, but consumption can be marked by a loss of purpose; there are no overarching guidelines about how to consume, and the promise of 'redemption through consumption' soon wears thin (Campbell, 1987; Falk, 1994).

This ambivalence about images has also been identified in relation to the moral implications of *the* image-based medium of modern society, namely the television. Michael Ignatieff (1985) has argued that television images can be powerfully stimulative in making people morally responsible and active subjects in relation to the suffering of war and starvation. As he argues, 'Millions of households look out through the screen in search of their collective identity as a national society and as citizens of the world' (Ignatieff, 1985: 71). An alternative perspective has been provided by Keith Tester (1995b). Developing the work of Benjamin, Tester argues that television images may not be able to forge moral solidarity on an unreceptive terrain, and that frequently repeated, technologically repro-duced, images of suffering others forces us to do absolutely nothing (Tester, 1995b: 474–475, 481). In the case of violence, for example, Bauman (1995: 149, 150) suggests we may be insensitised to cruelty as a result of the huge volume of images we see of human suffering: 'to stave off the "viewing fatigue", they must be increasingly gory, shocking and otherwise "inventive" to arouse any sentiments at all or indeed draw attention'. This is a view shared by Kevin Robins (1995) in his analysis of the moral bankruptcy of virtual environments; milieux in which the 'speed of thrill substitutes for affection, reflection and care', and where, as 'hallucinations and reality collapse into each other, there is no space from which to reflect' (Csicsery-Ronay, 1991: 192, 190; Robins, 1995: 144). It is reinforced in a different way by Michael Heim's (1995) intensified experience of images within a virtual reality centre. Hours after his experience, Heim could still recall flashing images and continued to experience a touch of 'perceptual nausea', the cumulative effects of which he termed 'Alternate World Syndrome' (Heim, 1995: 67).

Some commentators continue to see elements of Protestantism within this image assault on the senses. Ferguson, for example, notes that the psychological position of the contemporary consumer is not unlike that of the early Puritan (Ferguson, 1992: 173). The insecurity and doubt, together with the responsibility for validating one's own identity, which burdened the Puritan, remains potent for the contemporary consumer. For the baroque modern body, however, such insecurities cannot be reduced to the category of cognitive reflexivity, but can express themselves in *sensuous* forms. Stivers (1994: 143) has noted how the pervasiveness of the media and its heavy coverage of violent attacks, wars, natural disasters, personal tragedies and deaths heightens widespread fears about safety and security. Similar observations have been made by Richard Sparks (1992), who also implies that it is not only doubt, but unease and even dread, that can 'seep through' even the most affluent banal association.

These observations do not, however, mean that Lash and Urry (1994: 41) are entirely correct in assuming that 'fear has a clear object', or alternatively that Giddens is completely right to follow Durkheim's concept of anomie in associating 'high modern anxiety' with undifferentiated feelings. A more appropriate way to make such a distinction is to note the relation of each of these reactions to bodies. Fear is not always a cognitive phenomenon but can be a carnal one. It can also initiate processes of resacralisation which cannot easily be explained with regard to reflexivity. This point can be illustrated with reference to Beck's (1992) discussion of the endemic insecurities of late modern life.

Beck's (1992: 72) analysis of 'risk societies' suggests that the very quantity of risk information bombarding people means that individuals are becoming aware of a new 'shadow kingdom'. This kingdom is hidden behind visible reality and threatens not only the quality of life, but the fact of life itself. Danger lurks everywhere, in microbes, people, machines, telegraph wires and walkways, and is often concealed behind apparently harmless façades. Nothing can be taken at face value, while even things basic to human life such as breathing and eating are potentially fraught with unknown dangers: 'Everywhere pollutants and toxins laugh and play their tricks like devils in the Middle Ages' (Beck, 1992: 73). Beck calls this 'risk consciousness', but this is too restrictive and cognitive a term for the phenomena he is examining. For example, everyday thought and imagination are removed from their 'moorings in the world of the visible', and engrossed in anxieties about what people cannot see, touch, taste or hear: controversy over risks, he argues, threatens to turn into 'a modern seance' (Beck 1992: 73). In a similar vein, Hans Morgenthau (1970: 38) suggests that the Enlightenment view of knowledge as liberation has become very different when people feel they live in 'something approaching a Kafkaesque world, insignificant and at the mercy of unchangeable and invisible forces . . . a world of make-believe, a gigantic "hoax"' (Stehr, 1994: 258).

The thoroughly carnal imagery these writers use, together with their similes of 'devils' and metaphors of the 'shadow kingdom' and the 'modern seance', capture something of the relationships between (risk) information, the reappearance of the carnal and its association with sensual experiences. In this respect, Vivian Sobchack (1995: 207) makes an important point when she says 'there is nothing like a little pain to bring us back to our senses'. With this 'shadow kingdom', though, we are dealing here with something less than pain and more like Sartre's somatic imagination of slime, 'a gluey substance, compromising and without equilibrium, like the haunting memory of a metamorphosis' (Sartre, 1956: 610, in Wilson, 1995). The hoaxes and devils of the contemporary world stimulate not doubt, but sensual imaginings of contamination and pollution: 'Slime suggests the transience and drift of things. Imagine a loved one's eyes or tongue falling wetly into your hands, or that person's blood thickening into verminous sludge around your fingers' (Wilson, 1995: 249).

This analysis points to some of the carnal uneasiness and fears which can face even those occupying the upper echelons of information work (Hirsch, 1976). What it does not account for is the more active reappropriation of carnal forms of knowing which is increasingly evident in Western societies. It is this development which moves us away from the cognitive orbit of banal associations and places us within the carnal terrain of sensual solidarities.

Sensual solidarities

If the declining influence of certain aspects of Protestantism, and the attendant disappearance of the sublimated experience of the sacred, allows for the development of banal associations, it also facilitates the resurgence of the sacred as a sensually experienced, this-worldly phenomenon. Information may have become banal, expressing a self-referentiality so thorough that even evil can mutate into a transparent, fleeting image for those removed from its immediate effects (Baudrillard, 1993b), but it has not yet absorbed people's sensualities into its circuitry. Banal associations may dominate the formal institutions of contemporary society, but they cannot contain the human body in its entirety. This is the context in which the modern body's protection from the magical breaks down and sensual solidarities are able to arise (Buci-Glucksmann, 1994; Turner, 1991, 1994; van Reijen, 1992).

If banal associations are productive, sensual solidarities can loosely be described as *consumption*-oriented forms of sociality; bound up with corporeal absorption and immersion. They are based on the feelings, emotions and the effervescence which can derive from *being with* others (as opposed to simply discursively communicating with them). Sensual solidarities do not exclude the information flows and technological interventions which have surrounded and altered people's bodily selves. Indeed, Featherstone and Burrows (1995: 11) have suggested that the assembling and reassembling of bodies made possible by technology forms the basis for groups resembling Maffesoli's (1996) 'postmodern tribes'. Nevertheless, it is more usual for sensual solidarities to emerge from the immanence of the fleshy body within situations of co-presence and interdependence; a situation which can even result in a carnivalesque 'loss of self' (Bakhtin, 1984 [1965]). More usual than a complete loss of self, though, is a one-sided syncretism of the grotesque, in which people can lose their individuality and cognitive control insofar as they choose to 'open' certain aspects of their sensuality to flux, interaction and absorption.

Simmel (1971 [1903]: 324) has suggested that the deepest existential problems of modern life flow 'from the attempt of the individual to maintain the independence and individuality of his existence', yet sensual solidarities turn this cognitive problem into a carnal opportunity. In this respect, sensual solidarities both mirror and diverge from Simmel's 'pure form' of sociability. They may not involve 'talk for talk's sake' but they do involve 'flesh for flesh's sake'. They are, furthermore, ambivalent in relation to the exclusion of personal properties. While Simmel suggests that the most personal facets of character and mood have no place in sociability, sensual solidarities may be forged around the very 'light and shadow of one's inner life' (Simmel, 1971 [1910]: 131).

Sensual solidarities may appear at first glance to represent a resurgence of traditional *Gemeinschaft* relations, but this would be a mistaken impression (Nisbet, 1993 [1966]: 75; Tönnies, 1957 [1887]). People are united within these forms of sociality, yet frequently remain divided outside their parameters. Religious 'charismatics' are tied together through the effervescence provided by their 'miraculous' services, football crowds through their emotional involvement in the ritualised combat of the game, and certain radical feminists through the effervescence provided by their relation to blood and birth. The performance artist Carolee Schneemann (1975), for example, shows how the body can be central to the stimulation of a sensual solidarity: 'In some sense I made a gift of my body to other women: giving our bodies back to ourselves . . . joyful, free, bare breasted, skilled women leaping precisely from danger to ascendancy' (Hunt, 1991: 67). Nevertheless, the characteristics of kinship, neighbourhood and friendship these solidarities are built on can soon disappear from their specific contexts.

Drawing as it does on Durkheim's analysis of collective effervescence, and Simmel's analysis of sociability, our account of sensual solidarities has certain affinities with Maffesoli's account of 'neo-tribes' (Maffesoli, 1996). As Rob Shields (1996) notes, Maffesoli theorises the break-up of mass culture into a proliferation of 'affinity'-based groups with overlapping memberships. Whereas social contracts provide a basis on which people can interact, Maffesoli's tribes provide an opportunity for people to 'keep warm' together. Their analysis requires, as he puts it, 'that less weight shall be given to what each individual will *voluntarily adhere to* (contractually or mechanically) than to that which is *emotionally common to all* (sentimentally and organically)' (Maffesoli, 1996: 18).

Retouching the sacred

Sensual solidarities are formed in response to the banalities of those formal associations which traverse important parts of economic and social life, and their existence illustrates the fact that Weber's 'iron cage' has yet to cover the whole of social life. Their various and diverse manifestations are resistant to formal regulation, but when they do become 'fixed' and structured as cultural forms they are vulnerable to becoming associational in character (Simmel, 1968). This fluidity does not diminish the sociological importance of sensual solidarities, though, as it is they that provide people with those corporeal intimations and representations of sectional groupings or a larger social whole long recognised as central to the ongoing cohesion of society. It is these manifestations of the sacred which help 'bind' societies together, cementing conflicts, division and violence but at least providing a vantage point from which these phenomena can be kept in dialogue with each other. Having lost their sacred referent and having become internally referential, in contrast, banal associations have a rather dubious ability to represent anything *meaningfully*.

In the case of sensual solidarities, even the most fleeting sensory contacts made in daily life can provide experiences which reveal something beyond the participants. The expressions of sympathy and empathy made between two parents struggling with their babies in a shopping mall, the buying of rounds between friends in a bar, and the sharing of laughter; it is these events which may appear to display an 'empty nature', but which can also possess a transcendent character (Simmel, 1971 [1910]: 139). There is a momentary 'recognition of other' and partial 'loss of self' here which is evident in Bataille's analysis of sacrifice and of eroticism (1986 [1957]), and which illustrates Simmel's (1971 [1918]: 391) argument that 'Life wishes to express itself directly as religion, not through a language with a given lexicon and prescribed syntax.'

If banal associations leave our senses and sensualities with energies to expend (Bataille, 1986 [1957]), the sensual solidarities of Maffesoli's tribes provide for an expenditure of that energy which, in Simmel's terms, can reveal the deeper nature of sectional groupings of society 'more completely and meaningfully than any attempt to comprehend it realistically and without taking distance' (Simmel, 1971 [1910]: 139). The mass society theorists recognised this in their analysis of the authoritarian and fascistic potentialities of 'the crowd' (Richman, 1995). Maffesoli's tribes do not, however, have this mass basis. Instead, they usually emerge from the opportunities provided by custom to engage in fleeting contacts and Dionysiac outbursts which connect us to 'collective frameworks of memory' and the lived 'tides of experience' (Maffesoli, 1996: 25).

Maffesoli (1996) refers to this sacred binding as a process whereby people 'keep warm together' within localities and against the impersonality and 'cold winds' of modernity. Referring us to the work of Peter Brown (1976, 1981, 1982), Maffesoli traces this development to early Christianity; a time when small groups held their rituals and services and shared their beliefs in secret and away from the threats posed by Roman society. As he notes, 'The idea of "keeping warm together" is a way of acclimatising to or domesticating an environment without it becoming in any way threatening . . . Thus even if one feels alienated from the distant economic-political order, one can assert sovereignty over one's near existence' (Maffesoli, 1996: 42, 44). In their analysis of graffiti in New York, for example, Atlanta and Alexander (1989) inform us that the origins of this painting are to be found in the foreign language graffiti of the immigrant areas: 'The manifestation of the home tongue and written language of the displaced community, set against the walls of the huge city with its alien public language and sign system, was an assertion of ethnic cultural identity' (Atlanta and Alexander, 1989: 157).

Maffesoli's description of what sensual solidarities provide for their members is suggestive, but one-sided. The recognition of the sacred comes not only in keeping warm together, but, to continue the metaphor, in getting burnt together and, moreover, in burning others together. We could extend the comparison with early Christianity, for example, but would need to follow Christians to their slaughter. We would also need to recognise that it was not just they who were experiencing the sacred through 'getting burnt' together, but that the sacrificers may well have been experiencing a similar phenomenon (Bataille, 1992 [1973]; Girard, 1977 [1972]). As Shields (1996) suggests, these solidarities can also assume a violent, shocking and divisive manner which stretches to breaking point Durkheim's view of society as 'always already' embracing conflict (Nisbet, 1993 [1966]; Richman, 1995), and takes his work firmly into the province of conflict sociology (Collins, 1975, 1988). The effervescence produced by the *Freikorps*, by gangs, by paramilitary survivalists and by the Ku Klux Klan, for example, is based on a hatred and fear which is highly destructive and inimitable to society as a 'whole' (Elias, 1988; Gibson, 1994; Richman, 1995; Theweleit, 1987 [1977], 1989 [1978]). Most modern, civilised 'sacrificers' tend to pick on animals rather than humans but, as Don Atyeo (1979: 69) reports, they too are 'kept warm' through the 'joy of killing'. The sacred can be nasty, unpleasant and terrifying, as well as glorious and salvational. If life is generally brutish and short, then intimations of the totality of that life, through the collective effervescence of the sacred, are likely to reflect that reality. Echoing Robert Hertz's distinction, then, sensual solidarities can represent either a deviant, virulent and threatening *left sacred* concerned with death and malevolent forces, or a consecrated *right sacred* aligned with power and order (Hertz, 1960; Richman, 1995: 69).

Individual contracts and tribal fealties

The precise forms and distributions of banal associations and sensual solidarities vary and, despite the impression we may have given so far, their appearance as opposites is misleading. Just as the seventeenth century contained a Janus-faced relation to ascetic discipline and voluptuous corporeality, these contemporary forms of sociality are *related* sensory reactions to paradoxical features of the contemporary Western world. Nevertheless, people have responded to the doubts, anxieties and hazards of banal associations and sensual solidarities in contrasting ways, and the existence of individual contracts and tribal fealties may become especially significant ways of managing the cognitive and corporeal flux of modern life. Individual contracts are marked by openness, reciprocity, rationality, commitment and agreement, while tribal fealties are marked by secrecy, initiation, allegiance and loyalty.

Conditions conducive to the establishment of overarching social contracts may have declined, but this has not diminished the importance of individualised and particularised contracts; agreements which provide people and organisations with a means of pursuing a path through the overwhelming mass of discursive information which fills everyday life. This is apparent in Roland Robertson's (1992) analysis of globalisation in which he traces a growing tendency for previously excluded groups of people to seek rights which provide them with access to the benefits of modernity, but also to reject any overarching system which refuses to recognise their specificity as a group. Parents in the southern USA have, for example, sought to reassert their rights as a cultural group by banning the teaching of values and scientific perspectives with which they disagree (Robertson, 1992). A further example of this can be seen in the attempts which have been made by women to 'contract out' of patriarchy.

In the centuries following the emergence of Protestantism, the ideology of patriarchy and the material conditions involved in the marginalisation of women from the cognitive life of modernity have been both strengthened and undermined. The continued dependence of economic and social policy on unpaid domestic labour has reinforced women's attachment to their early modern roles of wife and mother (Charles and Kerr, 1988; Walby, 1989). As feminist political theorists and historians have shown, it is this unwaged work that has long provided a material precondition for the development of rationalised industrial production and the organisation of a public economy (Clark and Lange, 1979; Coontz and Henderson, 1986;

Harding, 1991). Despite remaining inequalities, however, many women have countered this 'partial modernisation' through their adoption of an individualistic contractarian mentality (Beck, 1992; Turner, 1984: 153). The future for significant numbers of women is no longer constrained in the way it once was by traditional roles. New identities and new contracts are being forged by those who have been successful in the education and labour markets.

Carol Gilligan's (1982) work on the relationship between gender and morality has examined some of the psychological correlates of these changes. Drawing on child development literature, such as the work of Chodorow and Piaget, Gilligan rehearses the argument that girls' and boys' upbringing tends to be marked respectively by intimacy and separation. The significance of this for Gilligan is that women's moral judgement has developed on the basis of *protecting relationships* rather than conforming to elaborate *rules*; a situation which is reversed for men, and which contributes to the subordination of women within patriarchal contexts. The growth of 'second wave' feminism in the 1970s, however, contributed to a significant change in this relationship by placing women's rights on the agenda of women's morality. According to Gilligan (1982) this encourages a rights-based mentality 'by enabling women to consider it moral to care not only for others but for themselves. The issue of inclusion first raised by the feminists in the public domain reverberates through the psychology of women as they begin to notice their own exclusion of themselves' (Gilligan, 1982: 149; cf. Collins, 1988).

This general situation confronts women with choices – which educational route to follow, how to present oneself in public contexts, where to work, what to work at, which lifestyle to follow – and enables many to construct identities significantly different from those available to their antecedents confined by the effervescence and discipline of sacred communities and profane associations. Marriage has the potentiality to become more voluntary and personal. It is an option, even if it remains a massively popular option, available to women who have the potential to be independent and the means to demand, and negotiate, a relationship that is personally fulfilling and satisfying (Beck, 1992: 112–113; Beck and Beck-Gernsheim, 1995 [1990]; Mansfield and Collard, 1988).

If individual contracts have become more important within marriage and other forms of association, they can provide women and men with ways of negotiating routes through the multiplicity of options made available to people in modern society. However, these contracts are necessarily based on cognitive assessments which prioritise *evaluation* over feeling, and the *mind* over the body. It is even possible to negotiate and sign contracts that remove organs from our bodies in return for a financial payment (Wolf, 1990). Carole Pateman (1988: 214) has argued that feminist notions of 'intimate contracts', where women seek to participate equally with men in the construction of social relationships upon a contractarian basis, are signs of a widespread alienation from the body which seeks to reduce women to the 'empty vessels' modern men have imagined themselves to be (Pateman, 1988: 214).

Contractual agreements (between firms, employer and employee, consumer and retail outlets, and husband and wife) may represent a paradigmatic means of coping with the opportunities and uncertainties produced by banal associations, but these are not manifestations of Durkheim's (1984 [1893]) 'cult of the individual'; a recognition and respect for individual differences based on a contextualising organic solidarity. Having lost their sublime referent, and having eschewed sacred ritual, the internal referentiality of banal associations rarely gives them the ability to stimulate any sort of collective effervescence.[5]

The spread of banal forms of sociality represents a highly problematic situation because these forms deny the significance, or even existence, of those supra-individual forms of sociality which frame them and thus have the capacity to render social life itself devoid of any manifest meaning: 'If the idea of society were extinguished in individual minds, and the beliefs, traditions and aspirations of the group were no longer felt and shared by the individuals, society would die' (Durkheim, 1961 [1912]: 347). Durkheim's analysis led him to express doubts about the very continuation of a cohesive social organisation in the face of modern tendencies toward such a process of extinction. As Nisbet (1993 [1966]: 85) points out, while analytically separating modern and premodern forms of solidarity, Durkheim, like Weber, believed that organic solidarity had to be rooted in the achievements of mechanical solidarity. Just as contract could not be sustained on the basis of self-interest, since this would result in a war of all against all, so too the division of labour could 'be produced only in the midst of pre-existing society. There is a social life outside the whole division of labour, but which the latter presupposes' (Durkheim, 1984 [1893]: 277). Banal associations therefore threaten not only the very foundations of modernity itself but, more generally, the possibility of a meaningful social life.

While individual contracts prioritise evaluation and the mind, tribal fealties are all about 'blood commitments' which tend to reject rationality as a basis for sociality. Malise Ruthven (1989) has observed this prioritisation of commitment over rationality in his analysis of the proliferation of cults in modern America. Freedom of worship not only means freedom from public scrutiny, but 'freedom to shut out the corrosive effects of Enlightenment' thinking (Ruthven, 1989: 307).

Maffesoli uses the Mafia to illustrate his modern 'neo-tribes', and this organisation provides an example of the fealties that underlie this relational form. Gangs provide another, with their use of initiation rituals, blood oaths, violence and drug use; examples of behaviour which echo those forms of transcendence contained within Bataille's analysis of religion. The rejection of orthodox individualism also runs through contemporary descriptions of life in inner city American ghettos. Indeed, some commentators have implied that in certain American ghettos there has been a wholesale displacement of individual contracts in favour of identities which are constructed through the consumption of clothing, dance, sport, music and drugs (Wilson, 1991a, 1991b). This has nothing to do with any notion of 'race' *qua* 'race', of course, but is related to the removal of businesses from such areas and the subsequent collapse of employment opportunities.

Having used women's attempts to 'contract out' of patriarchy as an illustration of the individualisation of contracts, the 'return' of sections of the American men's movement to bodily immersions in masculinity provides an interesting case of sensual solidarities. One example of this is the 'Wild Man' movement popularised by Robert Bly's *Iron John*, and a proliferation of weekend retreats for men. These have sought to create an environment which contests the modern 'shaming of men' (resulting from the sequestration of premodern models of maleness) and allows males to regain contact with their 'hairy selves' (Bly, 1992: 2–6). A central argument of Bly's is that there is 'not enough father' in modern societies, a general description used to denote the absence for men of traditional ritual and support structures. In particular, Bly is concerned with the idea that men now suffer from an absence of 'mentorship' and initiation in modern life, that economic changes mean sons no longer work with their fathers, and that fathers no longer have a valued teaching role in the community. The destruction of sacralising, mythological depictions of fatherhood has left modernity without a 'positive' appreciation of patriarchy (Bly, 1992: 92–122). Bly contrasts this modern 'grief in men [which] has been increasing steadily since the start of the Industrial Revolution' (1992: x) with the positive patriarchy of 'traditional cultures' where fathers, uncles, grandfathers and other men taught young males about women, weaponry, discipline and ritual (1992: 93). As Connell (1995: 211) notes, however, such forms of 'masculine therapy' are often predicated on an attempt to resolve men's 'private troubles', while leaving alone the 'public issues' associated with continuations of male power over women.

Religious initiation rituals and the bonding of fathers and sons in the shared construction of weaponry are not, of course, parts of most everyday life-patterns.[6] However, the popularity of these and similar cult movements may well represent a longing for such things in a milieu where they are generally absent, and an attempt to find meaning in the body (Gibson, 1994). Theological attempts to explore the carnal dimensions of spirituality, such as Nelson's (1992) discourse on the spiritual meanings of men's genitals, clearly serve a similar function. Like Bly, Nelson is attempting to help men deal with what he views as a widespread anxiety about what it means to be male in modern society (Nelson, 1992: 4; for a female-based equivalent, see Estes, 1992).

These tribal fealties can be seen as mere additions to the vast array of self-identity options opened up by the modern information economy. However, the degree to which they are underpinned by anxiety, and by a partial rejection of the present, suggests they are at least as much an expression of unease with modern life (Cohen and Taylor, 1992). So, sensual solidarities may *appear* to be reminiscent of Durkheim's call for a resurgence of rituals and associational forms which could allow people to escape from the anomie engendered by modern society. However, sensual solidarities not only represent the 'ties that bind', a recognition that feelings and senses are bound not only to the individual but to the social whole, but also a rejection of the huge numbers of modern ties that *fail to bind*.

Exercising the mind, indulging the senses

We have outlined some of the general features of banal associations and sensual solidarities, but the characteristics of each can be clarified by focusing on a few illustrative examples of the embodied processes of meaning construction which are representative of each of them. A consideration of these reinforces the above points regarding individual contracts and tribal fealties, and contrasts the importance attached to communicative relationships, therapies and schooling, with tendencies towards eroticism, exorcism and 'dropping out'. These examples have been chosen because of their ability to provide us with illustrations of the potentially diverse ways in which people can relate to distinct aspects of their environment, even if these diversities are more usually manifest in terms of less spectacular contrasts.

Pure relationships / erotic dissolutions

Although a number of sociologists have concluded that we know relatively little about the nature or meaning of 'love' and 'intimacy' in contemporary society (Jackson, 1993; Dunscombe and Marsden, 1993; cf. O'Connor, 1995), Giddens's (1992) notion of 'pure relationships' is meant to represent a democratic form of intimacy supposedly typical of certain developing features of modern relationships (for a sympathetic consideration of this work see Jary and Jary, 1995). Pure relationships are entered into as the result of individual judgements in terms of a person's own life plans. The fear of economic hardship, or the pressure exerted by a society marked by sacred communities and mechanical solidarities, no longer exerts the influence on relationships it once did. *Choice* plays a central role in pure relationships: while the importance of external anchors diminishes, so the value attached to ongoing (and potentially revocable) decisions to continue and invest in this 'intimate contract' increases.

Pure relationships are centred on the 'mutual growth' of partners through what Lawson (1988) terms the 'talking revolution'; a revolution in which 'knowledge has become the new commodity of exchange between intimate partners' (Lawson, 1988: 29; see also Gray, 1992; Berger and Kellner, 1964). In this context, 'confluent love' requires self-revelation and a capacity to share, and there is a tendency for *authentic* intimacy to be achieved less through touching, cuddling or the vigorous exchange of bodily fluids, and much more through the revelation of 'secrets' and the knowing of the intellect (Giddens, 1992; Lawson, 1988). Here, the breaking of sexual fidelity within a marriage matters not only, or even primarily, in terms of physical action, but because of the lying and other *betrayals of discursive trust* it represents (Askham, 1984; Lawson, 1988).

If pure relations have resulted largely from women's demands for equality and independence, they are none too easy to maintain. In instances where the pursuit of two careers becomes impossible, Johnson and Johnson (1980: 146) have noted how some individuals 'cycle in and out of marriages'. A more usual option to the pressures faced by 'dual career couples' has been the increasing number of 'commuter relationships' (Zinn and Eitsen, 1987), a relational form which highlights the more general importance of talk in modern intimate relationships where so much – careers, leisure, children, shopping and even sex – has to be negotiated and scheduled.

Pure relationships can be seen as the latest flowering of the ideology of 'companionate marriage' (Cate and Lloyd, 1992; Stone, 1987). In our terms, however, they represent a banal form of association based on talk and transient contracts (pure relations are based on an intimate contract which can always be revoked by moving out, or divorce). Giddens even retreats from the emphasis placed by Berger and Kellner (1964) on the nomos-building potentialities of marriage, preferring instead to view 'mature adults' as already invested with a large inoculation against ontological insecurity. It is interesting that Giddens's analysis finds it difficult to cope with manifestations of sex which cannot be justified through democratic discourse. Pure relationships are clearly insufficient in relation to human embodiment; being unable to cope with sweaty, heaving and breathless bodies, animalistic urges and sexual fluids which might colonise the mind and interfere, however temporarily, with the reflexive and democratic processes of talk work central to 'confluent love'. Bataille, rather than Giddens, is better able to analyse the 'other side' of close relationships.

If pure relationships are based on a dialogue concerned with enhancing the individual self, Bataille's writings on eroticism provide us with a view of 'intimacy' that is sensually rather than cognitively based (Shilling and Mellor, 1996). Eroticism refers to a heightened experience which transgresses the self, wipes away the discontinuities that separate individuals, and accomplishes a temporary fusion of selves. As Bataille (1986 [1957]: 15) notes, eroticism can be physical, emotional or religious, but the intensity and attractions of each lies in its ability to substitute for individual isolated discontinuity a feeling of profound continuity: 'the unity of the domain of eroticism opens to us through a conscious refusal to limit ourselves within our individual personalities' (Bataille, 1986 [1957]: 24). The talk central to pure relationships may result in a 'crisis of communication' (Tannen, 1990), but the fusion of selves promoted by physical eroticism can result in a *crisis of being* (Bataille, 1986 [1957]).

Eroticism can never be reduced to talk: it exists apart from purposive reason and productive work, but it does provide fleeting contact with the 'sacred world' which unites people otherwise made different by social and occupational structures. While reason is bound up with work and relationships which threaten to turn us into 'mere things', erotic pleasure 'mocks at toil' (Bataille, 1986 [1957]: 168). While eroticism provides us with an intimation of how the world could be, the talk of 'pure relationships' ruptures people from this world and promotes the 'closed body' characteristic of banal forms of association. For Bataille, it is our erotic, sexual exuberance which can rupture us from the world of things and put us back in contact with an experience of dissolution that allows us to regain touch with the sacred.

Therapy / exorcism

Conventional therapy depends on choice, involves an attempt to reconstruct the self through discourse, requires a decision to enter into a contract which can be revoked at any time, and is directed towards reconciliation and reform rather than transcendence. Michel Foucault (1981 [1976]) regards therapists and therapy as the modern equivalent of priests and confession. Control and 'cure' are accomplished by an agreement and an insistence that every experience and thought be turned into language and made subject to control. What we have in therapy is an exchange of words which denies the immanence of meaning within the fleshy body. As Gellner (1993: 138) notes, 'nothing actually *happens*. An intense relation and a revelation are not danced out, as primitive religion was . . . In fact, the static physical positions of the two participants are virtually prescribed and almost mandatory.'

Gellner's damnation of the psychoanalytic movement is taken in a very different direction by Giddens's (1991) evaluation of therapy. Focusing on the positive features of therapy, Giddens follows Rainwater's (1989) analysis of therapeutic practice by suggesting that 'therapy can only be successful when it involves the individual's own reflexivity . . . For therapy is not something which is "done" to a person, or "happens" to them; it is an experience which involves the individual in systematic reflection about the course of her or his life's development . . . Self-therapy is grounded first and foremost in continuous self-observation' (Giddens, 1991: 71). This autobiographical work involves 'corrective intervention into the past' which is cognisant of the body but assumes that experience and emotions can be placed in new frames of reference to produce new life stories which 'empower' the self (Giddens, 1991: 72, 143). As with all banal associations, the fleshy body is relegated to a position beneath information and talk.

If therapy eschews 'physical dances' of revelation and transformation, exorcism is based on the body's potential for volatility. Seen largely as a primitive relic to be enjoyed for entertainment's sake in horror films, exorcism's heritage is based firmly in the practices of the medieval Christian Church. Catholic exorcisms were designed not only to demonstrate transubstantiation, but also to vindicate 'other practices and beliefs under attack from Protestants as magical superstitions: exorcism itself, relics, holy water and other blest objects, the sign of the cross, the power of names' (Walker, 1981: 6). In certain parts of Europe, exorcism was an important tool of the Catholic Counter-Reformation. The practice has not died out entirely, but remains alive and well among 'technicians of the sacred' within religious minorities in the West, and continues to be practised by the occasional, and stubbornly 'medieval', Catholic priest (Lindholm, 1990).

According to André Goddu (1992: 3–4), Christian exorcism assumes 'that the person from whom the Devil is to be expelled is either possessed physically by a demon or is ethically or spiritually within the power of Satan'. The subject of an exorcism is not always willing, and the coercion involved in this activity is complemented by the violent rupturing of the body from itself brought about by the ritual practices associated with this event. In the case of compulsion, exorcisms might be viewed as sensual solidarities only insofar as they involve the exorcists. The point of this practice is not to change the self from 'within', as in conventional therapy, but to remove that which is evil and inhabiting the body from without.

If exorcisms are not common in the contemporary West, if they no longer provide people with protection from superstition and evil, we should probably not be surprised at the resurgence of fears about 'Satanist' activities. As Richardson et al. (1991) note, anti-Satanist crusades have their roots in several social movements including religious fundamentalism, the anti-cult movement, child abuse carers, and the survivor/recovered memory movement. Long a staple of religious broadcasts and talk shows, reports of Satanism have received confirmation (if little critical examination) from these groups and have crept onto network news and prime-time programming, with news stories and documentaries about Satanic cults. These Satanic solidarities may or may not exist in the forms often portrayed in the media, but their image has heightened fears which have been met with an alarmed response by modern expert systems. Growing numbers of 'police officers, child protection workers, and other public officials attend workshops supported by tax dollars to receive formal training in combating the Satanist menace' (Richardson et al., 1991: 7).

Schooling / dropping out

Schooling is crucial to the viability of banal associations as it seeks to initiate young people into the forms of discourse and conversation which lie at the heart of our 'information societies'. This is why both liberal communitarians and conservative cultural critics place such enormous emphasis on the importance of school as a means of harnessing the mind to the formally approved world of talk. The hope is that properly managed and executed, schooling can introduce children from any background into the universal or elaborated linguistic codes that have long been the object of sociological analysis (e.g. Bernstein, 1971, 1973, 1975), and which will help integrate young people into the 'community' (Etzioni, 1993).

Schooling has the body as a constant official referent, but mainly insofar as it seeks to discipline or direct it into cognitively approved programmes of activity and learning. This applies to 'physical education' just as it does to the more academic components of school work (Evans, 1990). Once the flesh is under control, through appropriate forms of discipline and organised experiences, the mind is released into the formally approved world of talk; a combination of effects which can successfully introduce children to shared values (Etzioni, 1993: 88).

Fears concerning the effects of unsuccessful schooling and the 'sensual child' have a long heritage, as illustrated by Clement Duke, the physician to Rugby School in England. Duke observed in 1883 that the 'boy who does not join in games, but swaggers and lounges about, should . . . be weeded out and got rid of, before he has the opportunity of corrupting others through his idleness and the evil it engenders'. The problem of 'sensualism', associated in this context with homosexuality and masturbation, was regarded as a problem of 'unsurpassed importance in Victorian schools' (Haley, 1988: 167).

Dropping out is one, very common, response to the cognitive demands made by schools. If an earlier generation of 'lads' came to school in order to play, smoke, fight and oppose the 'effeminacies' of mental work (Willis, 1977), many youngsters from the most deprived neighbourhoods have now given up on schools and indulge in extra-school solidarities. These may involve 'joy riding', drugs, gang activities, stealing, or the less spectacular activities of escaping constraint through merging with the crowd (Carlen et al., 1992: 154). In relation to those young men who have become immersed in crime, it is interesting that Bea Campbell (1996) should suggest that in England 'nothing works with these boys, not reform school, not prison, nothing'. The rush of adrenaline they get from car stealing and being chased by the police, coupled with their inclination to keep the boredom at bay by drugs, provides a sensory orientation to the world which is not easily changed. While boys may keep their extra-school solidarities in public space (Hall and Jefferson, 1976), however, girls are frequently immersed in less spectacular sensual solidarities based on caring for others (David, 1993).

Current debates on schooling and dropouts reveal fears about a general breakdown in the structures which have traditionally facilitated the transition to adulthood (Hendry et al., 1993: 183), and which have helped young people to achieve the high demands of civilised behaviour expected in contemporary society (Elias, 1978 [1939]: 140–141, 169–176). Permeating this 'moral panic' is a concern with the sensual dangers that await young people outside formal institutions. Drugs and violence are the two most visible examples of these dangers, but music and even games which overly 'absorb' the imagination and senses of children are suspect (Bloom, 1988). The net of suspicion has even extended to the popular fantasy game 'Dungeons and Dragons'. Daniel Martin and Gary Alan Fine (1991) have suggested that such games have a 'vacation appeal' and may lead to a temporary 'reenchantment of the world'. The sensory immersion required by the game, however, has led sections of American society to associate it with mind control, violence and even Satanism.

Fractured bodies, fractured relationships

The coexistence of banal associations and sensual solidarities is closely related to the development of the baroque modern habitus and helps us to understand the sociologically 'schizophrenic' nature that this contemporary bodily form can sometimes assume. Baroque bodies are associated with a new 'epiphany of the senses' in which information, signs and images no longer lead to just factual knowledge, but to doubt, unease and excitement. These changes in the social habitus are partial and incomplete both in, and between, different sectors of Western society, but they are centred around a sensory reorganisation which has a particular impact on the meaning and experience of *seeing*.

As we have already noted, 'to see' and 'to know' became conflated in an early modern era which privileged cognitive activity and the text, and regarded sight as a direct highway from the 'outside' world to the 'inside' mind (Jay, 1992; Jenks, 1995; Slater, 1995).[7] However, as the idea of 'rational knowledge' came under intensified attack in the twentieth century (O'Neill, 1995), and as sensual images came to constitute a central part of consumer culture, sight regained something of its potentiality as a sense to be cultivated for sensuality's sake. Information no longer always travels a straight and unproblematic highway through the eyes to the mind, but often spills over the eyes to provoke human sensuality. The volume and velocity of images and words in contemporary life can thus stimulate appetites, emotions, sensations and fantasies, and are implicated in how individuals relate to their bodies, other people and the world. Indeed, instead of being a highway for 'knowledge', seeing something may do little more than spark a sensual reaction which bypasses much in the way of cognitive containment. We could say, in fact, that the real 'information superhighway' of contemporary societies is the body itself.

This sensory reorganisation, and the partial decline of the Protestant body associated with early modern societies, is one possible reason for why themes of fracture, inconsistency and uncertainty are so popular in contemporary social theory. If knowledge and seeing have become uncoupled, and if new generations are beginning to experience their senses in novel ways, there may be good reason for following Lash and Urry's (1994) argument that we are witnessing a rise in 'allegoric sensibilities' (in sensual solidarities) and a decline in 'symbolic unities' (in banal associations). The resurgence of the baroque involves a loosening of the body's fleshy sensuality from the Protestant taint of sin. This 'liberation' of sensuality may bring certain people together, but it can also divide people on the basis of sensuality. In other words, people may be committed to a search for experience, difference and novelty but, outside of banal associations, they are less willing and less able to find overarching grounds for communication between diverse groups.

Given the violence associated with modern rationalities – rationalities which have legitimised slavery, colonialism and systems of patriarchy – this rejection of universality has been greeted with relief by theorists who have welcomed the neo-tribal basis of 'postmodern' sociality (Maffesoli, 1996). The rise of an allegorical celebration of difference, however, has also been associated with decivilising processes. As Bauman argues, this celebration tends 'to render human relations fragmentary and discontinuous' and can 'bar the construction of lasting networks of mutual duties and obligations' (Bauman, 1995: 155). This is the basis on which communitarians such as Etzioni have criticised the unbridled pursuit of individuality, and called for a return to the values of a social contract. The problem they face is that while many people have embraced a rights-based culture, they no longer seem interested in living on the basis of overarching social contracts. This situation applies not only to oppressed minority groups, but to those 'cognitive elites' who appear to have benefited most from the information economy.

Underpinning the arguments of the communitarians and conservative cultural critics is an assumption that it is possible to engineer a shared phenomenology of bodily experience; that we can forge a form of embodiment which can transfer those dispositions that are general within a *particular part* of the environment into the bodily selves of each and every one of us. The existence of banal associations and sensual solidarities, in the context of societies which are also divided on economic and social grounds, throws a certain amount of doubt on this by suggesting that people do not, and do not want to, walk on the same phenomenological terrain.

Banal relational forms demand much in terms of cognition and work, yet provide little opportunity for people to establish a bodily state they are satisfied with. Furthermore, given their rupture from the sublimated sacred of Protestantism, these relations are devoid of the 'ultimate values' which historically helped secure people's allegiance to specific forms of association. In this respect, sensual solidarities provide a release for those bored and made stale by the formal. Others, however, have rejected banal relational forms in favour of a complete immersion in the sensual. While this usually applies only to either the idle rich or to those robbed of decent employment opportunities, it is a scenario which strikes not just cognitive concern, but carnal fear into those who have assumed the responsibility of resurrecting the social contract. There are just too many people around who refuse to participate fully in the formal institutions of modernity, who refuse to have their lives ruled by contracts. As Richard Sennett (1994: 359–370) argues, this is part of the same situation in which the wealthy and influential seek safety and comfort rather than social engagement. People may live 'together', but they have as little as possible to do with each other.

Notes

1. 'Postmodernity' is often associated with the growth of incommensurate truths, values and ways of living, along with the decline of any convincing overarching narratives which can explain 'reality' (Lyotard, 1984). As reality becomes fragmented, so too does self, as self-identities get caught up in a 'simulational world' where fleeting images and experiences disappear as quickly as they alight on people; a simulational world best exemplified by television's transformation of reality into a series of disparate images which defy any distinction between appearance and reality (Baudrillard, 1983). Discussing the culture of MTV, for example, Pat Aufderheide (1986: 135) notes the playful postmodernism of music videos, expressed through their premise that identity is a constantly shifting phenomenon in a world without formative social relationships. Similarly, theologians who have embraced post-modernism have suggested that coherent and consistent self-identities are no longer possible, and that a pluralistic celebration of difference and discontinuity is our only approach to contemporary social and cultural life (Cupitt, 1992).

Critiques of the notion of postmodernity have taken a number of forms. Jürgen Habermas (1989: 6) has sought to defend the modern project by arguing that postmodernism is often the expression of an *ideological* opposition to modernist principles of authentic self-experience and self-realisation. Ernest Gellner has argued that postmodernism is merely a contemporary form of *philosophical relativism*, caused by the difficulty of making sense of such a complex social world (Gellner, 1992). Anthony Giddens (1990, 1991) has argued that postmodernity is really *high modernity*, the working out of a deconstructionist, chronically reflexive dimension of the modern project which had been present since the emergence of the modern period. In a similar vein, Zygmunt Bauman (1992a, 1992b, 1993) has suggested that postmodernity is really modernity coming to terms with itself, 'the victory of modern (that is inherently critical, restless, unsatisfied, insatiable) culture over the modern society it aimed to improve through throwing it open to its own potential' (Bauman, 1992a: viii). Marshall Berman's (1982) discussion of the double-edged experience of modernity as an opportunity for liberation, power and the transformation of self and world, but also as a phenomenon that can destroy who people are and all they hold dear, is also consistent with this interpretation of postmodernity. Taken together, all these critiques reveal the notion of 'postmodernity' to be a highly questionable one, and encourage the view that many contemporary social changes are best understood as the increased dominance of certain aspects of modernity over others, rather than as indicators of a radical break with modernity as such – a view expressed particularly well by Giddens.

For Giddens, Baudrillard's vision of a 'simulational world' is merely an 'aestheticised reflection' upon *modernity*, stimulated by chronic reflexivity (Giddens, 1990: 45–46). This analysis has the merit of drawing attention to the undeniably reflexive features of Baudrillard's 'reflections upon reflections', exemplified in his claim that television has become the world (Mellor and Shilling, 1994: 25; Baudrillard, 1983). It also precludes, however, the possibility that modernity could be transformed into something it has not been, essentially, in the past.

2. The debates over 'resacralisation' revolve essentially around three distinct arguments which can be summarised as follows: first, that secularisation did occur and is occurring still, despite (temporary) religious revivals (Wilson, 1976, 1982); second, that secularisation did occur but this process has now gone into reverse (Hammond, 1985; Turner, 1991); and third, secularisation was a sociological myth which never accounted adequately for the place and role of religion in contemporary life (Martin, 1966; Gill, 1989). The first of these positions is marked by a high degree of internal referentiality which allows all sorts of contradictory data to be used as evidence for secularisation: whether churches are empty or full they are signs of secularisation (Berger, 1990 [1967]), while the very popularity of 'New Religions' indicates modern persons' 'permanent condition of bereavement at the loss of community' which modernity inevitably fosters (Wilson, 1976: viii). This internal referentiality is increasingly hard to sustain in the light of available data concerning the religious attitudes and practices of modern Western persons, let alone with regard to the importance of religion globally

(Beckford, 1989, 1992). The second of these positions takes seriously the impact of modernity upon religion, particularly with regard to its marginalisation from public life, but uses Durkheimian notions of the centrality of the 'sacred' in social life to account for the appearance of new religious forms (Hammond, 1985). The third position rightly acknowledges the ideological dimension to secularisation theories produced by sociologists who were themselves sometimes fervently committed to the modern project. It fails to account satisfactorily, however, for the very real changes that have occurred in Western societies during the modern period with regard to the location, role and relative significance of religion for society. Warner's argument is a variation on this third position. While some writers have considered 'antisecularisation' or 'resacralisation' with regard to specific areas such as medicine where the changing experience of bodies is especially evident (McGuire, 1985), others have addressed the subject in a more general way (Hammond, 1985). Furthermore, some have explicitly associated resacralisation with the emergence of postmodernity (Berry and Wernick, 1992).

3. While such characteristics are interpreted as a sign of religion's decline by traditional secularisation theorists (Berger, 1990 [1967]; Bellah et al., 1985; Christiano, 1987; Tschannen, 1991), Warner notes that many sociologists have come to believe that such interpretations were developed to account for the European experience rather than the American one, and fail to appreciate that in the latter context there has never been one monolithic 'sacred canopy' providing a normative understanding of religion against which all other forms can be judged. In the USA, religion has always operated and thrived in an open market where no one form can take precedence over another (Warner, 1993; Hadden, 1987).

4. Michael Jindra (1994), for example, examines the emergence of *Star Trek* fandom as a religious phenomenon, examining how fans of the various TV series associated with *Star Trek* form communities marked by a 'canon' and a hierarchy, and experience persecution and ridicule from people who do not share such an intense commitment to the 'other-worldly' (i.e. space-focused rather than supernatural-focused) world of the TV shows.

5. The search for the sacred within these official institutions has even led commentators to the ritual powers of television (Dayan and Katz, 1988), a medium now most closely associated with the *collapse* of meaning (Featherstone, 1991).

6. One manifestation of this can be seen, nevertheless, in the seemingly growing number of far-right survivalist groups in the USA (Gibson, 1994).

7. This association continued for some time – an interesting example is provided by an early film portrayal of a train travelling towards a camera, a sight which prompted members of the audience to flee – and is often maintained within sectors of contemporary society (Falk, 1994).

7

CONCLUDING COMMENTS

The ambivalent bodies and divergent patterns of sociality considered in the previous chapter suggest an uneasy, and potentially volatile, cohabitation of two phenomena. On the one hand, there is a pervasive contractarian mentality incorporated within many modern institutions and forms of self-identity. On the other, there is the collective effervescence of new sacred, sensual solidarities. In reflecting further upon this uneasy relationship, our account of this Janus-faced form of embodiment can cast a fresh light upon the moral panics recurrent in much contemporary social and political discourse (Bellah et al., 1985, 1992; Bloom, 1988; Etzioni, 1993; Blankenhorn, 1995), and help explain why certain sociologists and social theorists have moved from being concerned with the issue of postmodernity to focusing on that of morality (Bauman, 1993; Meštrović, 1993; Stivers, 1996; Tester, 1997). This partial turn to morality runs counter to the dominant tendency in sociology to ignore questions of a moral nature (Archer, 1990: 113), but is nevertheless highly significant.

If social contracts seem fragile and precarious, if groups that understand themselves to be marginalised, oppressed or exploited are now, more than ever, *visibly* not prepared to recognise the established 'rules of the game' as valid, there are, perhaps, good reasons for this. The re-emergence of the sacred in effervescent forms of sociality signals the exhaustion of the moral basis for modern contractarian relationships. Debates about whether we are living in a modern or a postmodern society are giving way to more serious questions about the very possibility of a rational social order. The Protestant modern form of embodiment made such a social order imaginable. It did this by encouraging a highly cognitive, and rationalist, account of what it means to be a human being, and by seeking to replace the corporeal bonds of medieval Catholicism (volatile and violent though they sometimes were), with an idealised conception of human beings bound together by shared cognitive commitments. This form of embodiment, which 'sublimated' the effervescent character of sociality just as it sought to subjugate the dangerous potentialities of flesh, provided a moral basis for modernity which is steadily ebbing away across important tracts of social space. Based on an inherently fragile attempt to deny positive value to the desires, passions and sensations which are an inevitable part of embodied humanity, and an idealistic misconception about the nature of human sociality, this form has become progressively more unsustainable as its sacred referent has disappeared. Without it, contracts may have become increasingly important for many people, but they are also increasingly meaningless: contracts are no longer merely profane, which implies a relationship with the sacred, but are thoroughly banal, indicating their myopic self-referentiality.

Emile Durkheim's (1984 [1893]) analysis of what he refers to as the 'normal' development of modernity, in fact, makes the key point that sustainable contracts must have a moral basis. For contracts to be held as valid requires not only the force of law, but a basic equity concerning what is contracted. As he puts it, 'for the obligatory force of the contract to be entire, it is not sufficient for it to have been an object of express assent. It must also be fair, and it is not fair by the mere fact that it has been agreed verbally' (Durkheim, 1984 [1893]: 318). Without a common moral framework, grounded in a common form of embodiment, people cannot agree on what is 'fair' and contracts risk becoming redundant. As Durkheim argued, it is an error to believe all social relationships can be reduced to a contract.

However, Durkheim's (1984 [1893]) comments about the weakening of morality, or the 'collective conscience', with the 'abnormal' development of the division of labour might more accurately be applied to the general fate of modernity as a whole. Contestations arise that cannot be neutralised by institutional organisation, planning, or Enlightenment conceptions of rationality (Bhabha, 1994). Common, sacred sentiments can arise which do not necessarily bind individuals to society, but only to smaller, segmented groups. As Durkheim puts it, 'Subversive tendencies, lacking in future any countervailing force emerge more readily. Losing increasingly the transcendency that placed it, as it were, above human interests, the social organisation no longer has the same power to resist. Yet at the same time, it is more strongly under attack' (Durkheim, 1984 [1893]: 315).

Given his rather optimistic reading of the unifying capacities of sensual forms of sociality, Michel Maffesoli's (1996) work suggests that a breakdown in formal contracts is less significant than Durkheim understood it to be. In contrast to Maffesoli's analysis, however, we suggest that the gradual removal of collective effervescence from situations and symbols that bind together whole societies, and its concentration within sectional groups, manifests itself in the establishment of firm boundaries which create and consolidate conflictual differences (Collins, 1988; Shields, 1996). While Benedict Anderson (1991) talks about 'imagined communities', television, film and other media bombard us with numerous and varied imaginings of the breakdown of communities. In this respect, Meštrović (1994: 2) observes a scenario which is not confined to North America when he notes that 'the race riots that spread from Los Angeles to many other cities in the USA in April 1992 led many commentators to remark . . . that America suddenly seemed like the Balkans – that they could not believe that the US of A could be racked by ethnic conflict this late in its historical development'.

This is not to say that there ever was any golden age of contract in which people formulated agreements which were consensual and wholly inclusionary (Bauman, 1993; Pateman, 1988; Tester, 1992). There was not. Nevertheless, while the spread of print provided early modern Protestants separated by time and space with an unprecedented opportunity to cognitively imagine themselves as a 'community' bound by the Word of God, the rapid circulation of sensual imagery now provides people with unprecedented opportunities for seeing, tasting and touching the insufficiencies of contracts (Rodaway, 1994). These insufficiencies can be considered with regard to the heavily 'frontiered' character of advanced modern societies.

Frontier bodies

In *Purity and Danger* (1966) and *Natural Symbols* (1970), Mary Douglas portrayed the body as both a symbol and a metaphor for social cohesion, differentiation and conflict. During times of social crisis, when dominant identities and established bodies (those groups who have most power over the manipulation of this symbol) are threatened, Douglas argues that there is likely to be a more widespread concern with the maintenance and purity of bodily boundaries. In the light of her analysis, it is no accident that the body should have become an intensified object of concern at the same time that global processes are threatening to destabilise national boundaries (Featherstone, 1995a; Robertson, 1992). From political concerns to ensure the exclusion of 'alien bodies' from the Mexican borders of California and from the European Union, to academic attempts to purify and disembody intellectual discourse (Hunter, 1991; Rauch, 1993), the body has become a significant symbolic motif for our times.

In these conditions, social contracts become increasingly exclusionary. Groups of people who have experienced social or cultural marginalisation in the past may now be deemed full members of society at a formal level, but can still suffer discrimination resulting from those institutions, actions and symbols that continue to define them as corporeally polluted (Pateman, 1988; West, 1993: 269). This places historically marginalised groups in a highly ambivalent relationship with modernity. For example, Cornel West (1993) suggests that 'New World Africans are deeply modern in the sense of being exiles, banished from their native lands and forced to live as perennial "outsiders", finding a "home" only in a dynamic language and mobile music – never in a secure land, safe territory or welcome nation. The fundamental theme of new World African modernity is neither integration nor separation but rather migration and emigration.'

These understandings and sensations of exclusion and conflict are not confined to 'outsider' groups but seep through the 'armoured' bodies of the 'established' to create a sense of unease and even fear (Elias and Scotson, 1994 [1965]). In this respect, Sennett's (1994) analysis of the white middle class's fear of social engagement and its pursuit of safety and comfort is evident in, amongst other things, its promotion of the 'hard body', which is also a frontier body: a variant of the baroque modern habitus which prizes the appearance of power and control as one way of coping with the emotional and sensual. This hard body is no longer actually necessary in the world of high technology industry (Lingis, 1988), but it provides a corporeal trench into which the individual can retreat after engaging in chosen sensual activities and/or virtual technologies. The hard body may constitute a form of physical capital (Bourdieu, 1986), but it also acts as a physical and psychological frontier for armouring against other social groups. Having sealed themselves spatially, these people must seal their own flesh and seek to avoid body 'protests' against the deprivations of dieting (Chernin, 1983), and those maladies and diseases linked to the strictures of modern life (O'Neill, 1985; Turner, 1984).

As the paid work of the middle class does not generally involve intense physical labour but *cognitive* work (and cognitively directed emotion work), this allows the body to become a semi-autonomous zone in which the wills and desires of economically affluent persons can be exercised during their 'free time' (Ehrenreich, 1990: 233). This has had various manifestations. In the 1950s, for example, dieting became a middle-class preoccupation; in the 1970s this was transformed into the 'internal environmentalism' of health consciousness; and in the 1980s this was complemented by a developing obsession with 'fitness', where 'working out' became a 'balletic imitation of true work', a strenuous form of consumption which promised control, power and moral renewal symbolised by the 'hard body' (Ehrenreich, 1990: 233–234; see also Bourdieu, 1984).

Ehrenreich (1990: 236) also notes that the phenomenon of 'working out' reflects the middle class's desire for 'definition': in seeking a harder, more defined body, middle-class persons present 'a hard outline to the world', signifying their toughness and containment with regard to other social groups. The contemporary middle class's opposition to the delights of smoking, hard drinking and 'junk food' (which transcends health and fitness concerns to become a 'moral' issue) is thus a way of distinguishing itself from the lower classes (with whom such things become associated). This involves searching for distinction and differentiation by buying a Mercedes rather than a Ford, shopping at Bloomingdale's rather than K-Mart, dressing in natural rather than artificial fibres, and drinking expensive imported beers rather than cheaper domestic ones (Ehrenreich, 1990: 227–229). In each case, the middle-class preference for one activity or product over another is determined by their relative prestige, expensiveness and exclusivity. Once a middle-class taste filters down to other classes it tends to lose its original appeal and is replaced by something else (Bourdieu, 1984; Ehrenreich, 1990: 230); a cycle which is accelerated by the speed of change facilitated by body options.

This circulation and erosion of distinct bodies and practices, however, can result in considerable anxiety, producing a pressing need for reassurance and self validation (Gellner, 1993; Lasch, 1991 [1979]). Sensual experiences and emotions have here to be harnessed to a monitoring of the market and there is, in Marcuse's terms, always a danger of the body being dominated by a 'performance principle' which results in 'surplus repression' (Marcuse, 1962). There is no sacred 'loss of self' here, and no sensual satisfaction akin to Reich's implicit concern with an effervescent release of self in multidimensional relationships with other humans (Robinson, 1969).

As Bourdieu (1984) and Elias (1978 [1939], 1983) have noted, the search for distinction which can result in such outcomes has a long history. What is notable about the present period, however, is that these processes are becoming more extreme and more pervasive (Shilling, 1991). Ehrenreich (1990: 204) notes that differences in wealth and poverty in the cities of Los Angeles and New York have scandalised European visitors, but this pattern is also becoming evident in many European cities. As these extremes grow, the 'middle ground' gradually disappears and whole sections of the population find themselves struggling not to tumble towards the bottom. In this struggle, people are too busy ensuring that they get, and stay, on the right side of this class divide to concern themselves about broader symbolic unities. These pressures can manifest themselves in a fundamentalist opposition to forms of liberal education, for example, which threaten a localised world view of creationism and white supremacy (Robertson, 1992), but are evident even with regard to the practice of religion. There is evidence, for example, that many middle-class churches in America are having increasing trouble trying to get their members to reach out to disadvantaged others, while those who do reach out are often sceptical about the positive benefits of their efforts (Price and Wedam, 1995: 11–15). Ehrenreich (1990: 200) notes that 'It was possible, until the eighties, for a comfortable American to think of class as a form of cultural diversity, parallel to ethnicity or even "lifestyle"', but this is no longer possible. The different classes are now becoming so divergent in wealth, tastes and status that they are barely able to 'coexist in the same physical space' (Ehrenreich, 1990: 226).

Frontier cities

Ehrenreich's comments provide a basis on which to speculate about the relationship between 'frontier bodies' and some of those social forms which both contain and instrumentalise them. Frontier bodies are increasingly mapped out onto the patterns of cities, suburbs and towns in which people live; spaces which have themselves become heavily 'frontiered' social environments through which modern persons often have to find their way (Sibley, 1995; Small, 1994).

The vision of America as 'an endless frontier' has long referred to both geographic expansion and a belief in infinite material progress (Hayden, 1980: 24). Hutchison (1992) has suggested that from the nineteenth century to well into the twentieth, this vision was central to the dominant modern American identity and was supported by a strong modernist impulse within American Protestantism. The appearance of the baroque body and associated allegorical sensibilities, sensual solidarities and tribal fealties (wherein there is a resurgence of fleshy sensuality and a decline in the belief in universals and the possibility of social coherence), marks the problematisation of this identity.

Instead of stimulating a social contract mentality, the proliferation of information flows and diverse forms of sociality often operate within a frontier 'mentality'. This bodily orientation to the world no longer facilitates a modernist vision of expansion and progress, but promotes the construction of frontiers between different social groups. These frontiers are marked by the ordering powers of modernity, and promote a view of those who are resistant to this order as 'barbarians' (Bauman, 1995); a view which can be traced back to the ancient Greek treatment of alien others (Gouldner, 1965). The geographical spaces which mark the limits of civilised zones can change quickly, though, and are increasingly fragile (Sibley, 1995). Barbarians are always likely to be 'too close for comfort'; a situation which prompts repeated but precarious attempts to redraw lines of exclusion and to regain what Bell has referred to as 'insulating space' (Bell, 1973: 314; Stehr, 1994: 30). With the development of the baroque modern habitus, however, insulating spaces have to be everywhere; both outside and *inside* the body. As Clifford Geertz (1986: 112) puts it, 'foreignness does not start at the water's edge but at the skin's' (Robertson, 1992: 104).

These frontiers are evident in the changing relationships of particular social groups to the metropolis; changes marked by a decline in confidence and an increase in strategies of defensiveness and withdrawal which culminate in the construction of 'armoured villages' complete with security officers, guarded entrances, and video surveillance cameras (Hirsch, 1976). As Sennett (1994: 366) notes: 'The fears of touching which gave rise to the Venetian Ghetto have been strengthened in modern society as individuals create something like ghettos in their own bodily experience when confronted with diversity.' Castells (1989) refers to New York, one of the most 'informational cities' of them all, as a place of 'dreams and night-mares'. Referring us to the work of Fainstein et al. (1992) and Wilson (1991b), Webster supports this description: 'New York is at once the home of Wall Street and upmarket Manhattan and a city in which some 2,000 people are murdered annually and where the Bronx is synonymous with such acute deprivation that strangers can almost taste the fear when they unknowingly stray into its environs' (Webster, 1995: 204–205).

Given these observations, which are supported by other studies of 'global cities' such as Mike Davis's (1990) analysis of Los Angeles, it is not surprising if fears and unease 'seep through' the virtual communities of the affluent. As Webster (1995: 205) notes, the contrast between a '"metropolitan heaven" and an "inner city hell" is palpable'. People may indeed possess more flexibility and control over their bodies, but they exercise these choices in a wider environment increasingly bereft of these features. Virtual environments may provide for the cocooned and thoroughly artificial experience of freedom in a hostile city, while hard bodies provide a frontier of armouring when it becomes necessary to venture outside and cross city borders. Early modern Protestants were rarely 'at home' in their localised, earthly existence. However, while many of the contemporary urban middle classes may be comfortable in their homes they are, as Marx puts it, firmly alienated in this comfort (Marx, 1977 [1844]).

The gaze of the skyscraper

A characteristic feature of many American cities is the skyscraper, and this is an object which serves as a useful metaphor for the state of the contemporary metropolis. As Marin (1993) notes, skyscrapers exert a 'dominating gaze' over their environment; a gaze which signifies mastery of the surrounding geographical, historical and cultural features of a city. Building on this perspective, Price and Wedam (1995) have discussed the development of Chicago as a city, noting that the 'dominating gaze' of the city belonged to the Protestant middle classes who believed themselves to have a responsibility for the city as a whole. Although Chicago now has more skyscrapers than ever, the Protestant middle classes have lost their position of dominance over the city and dispersed to the suburbs, while it is no longer clear if there is one 'dominating gaze' in most cities any more. Even some of the multinational corporations trading in the information economy are locating to suburbs (Price and Wedam, 1995: 12).

The 'loss of leadership' and 'direction' to city life has become a common theme in recent studies. Bellah et al. (1992), for example, note that large numbers of Americans still live in the metropolis, and that city life has long been associated with dreams and aspirations of mobility and success. Nevertheless, many of these same people now idealise small-town rather than city life, and are drawn to cities largely for economic reasons. This 'decentring' of the city has been exacerbated by the construction of an extensive system of highways. Populations are now more easily able to live away from cities which become thoroughly economic and only marginally 'civic' centres (Bellah et al., 1992: 266–267). Financially secure people often move *through* cities, then, rather than identifying and attaching themselves to these places; accomplishing at most a sort of 'mobile togetherness' in which 'the logistics of speed' detach the body from the spaces through which it moves (Bauman, 1995; Sennett, 1994: 365).

This view of city development gives us but one perspective as it fails to acknowledge differences based on class and race. Far from being widespread, the view of Bellah and his colleagues is characteristically associated with the white middle class and, more latterly, with sections of the black bourgeoisie (West, 1993: 282). Lash and Urry (1994: 157) have noted, for example, that in the past Afro-Caribbeans in England and American blacks in the USA 'voluntarily migrated to white Protestant-dominated centres of industrial activity' to obtain work. However, sections of these peoples have now been left disproportionately in urban ghettos abandoned by both industry and white Protestants (Wilson, 1987, 1991a, 1991b).

These different trajectories are reflected in contemporary perceptions of city life. In a survey of Los Angeles, for example, white middle-class residents had fairly abstract images of the city, seeing different parts of the metropolitan area as linked together by the web of freeways. Working-class blacks and Chicanos, however, thought of the city in more localised terms, focusing on the neighbourhoods in which they lived and on those areas in the city perceived to be accessible to each group (Hummon, 1990: 19). The middle class's view of the city is not only more differentiated spatially, however, but a sense of fear of the dangers cities can hold is reflected in their lifestyle choices and where they locate their bodies. Herrnstein and Murray (1994: 104) note the flight of the 'cognitive elite' from the chaos of modern cities into affluent suburbs with better schools and lower crime rates. Lash and Urry (1994: 324) refer to this as a flight to 'tame zones'; 'areas of economic, political and cultural security, often with strong boundaries separating them off from the wild zones of disorganised capitalism' (Lash and Urry, 1994: 57; Wilson, 1991a, 1991b). The experience of the 'Diaspora' has superseded that of the 'melting pot' (Gilroy, 1993).

Middle-class whites with a positive view of city life tend to emphasise its diversity, its excitement and the opportunities it offers for self-development (Hummon, 1990: 77). On closer inspection, however, this celebration of diversity often serves to legitimise the opportunities cities offer for living amongst people with *similar* lifestyles or backgrounds, rather than for engaging with different types of people. As one of Hummon's (1990) urbanite respondents notes: 'Not everyone who lives here is sophisticated, but you can find enough of your own kind to feel comfortable no matter what your preferences are relative to music, jobs, travel, sex, whatever' (Hummon, 1990: 77–79). Thus, the tolerance, open-mindedness and liberal character of cities praised by urbanites may reflect a respect for individual choices but can also indicate indifference to the moral consequences of those choices. Herrnstein and Murray (1994: 104) note that when the 'cognitive elite' *does* remain in cities, it colonises particular areas and sends its children to private schools where they will be free of contact with other social groups. Transient contact with exotic 'others' may provide spectacles and diverse food for the sensorially hungry consumer, but the flux of living at the edge of the frontier must be counterbalanced by strategies for control (Said, 1978; Bhabha, 1994). The relevance of this point is all too easily illustrated with reference to the experience of those unable to purchase or manage such control. Recent levels of 'hate crimes' committed by skinheads in Britain, neo-Nazis in Germany, 'gay bashers' in the USA military, and anti-Semites in France reveal some of the costs attached to crossing frontiers or, more accurately, to being unable to prevent others crossing frontiers (Meštrović, 1994: 3).

In seeking control over their lives, many middle-class whites have become disillusioned with urban life and chosen to live in environments where they imagine they can organise their lives to a greater degree

(Hummon, 1990: 48). They may want the same thing as many city people –
to 'find enough of your own kind to feel comfortable' – but believe they
can find it elsewhere with their money. Many seek to find it in suburbs
(Baumgartner, 1988: 6). In this respect, while Simmel described the
metropolis as the ecological matrix of the money economy (Levine, 1985:
202; Simmel, 1955: 137), it might be appropriate to view the suburb as a
significant part of the ecological matrix of the information economy.

The moral expectations of 'baroque modernity'

It is worth looking briefly at Baumgartner's (1988) study of the 'moral
order' of the modern suburb, because this order can tell us a great deal
about some of the broader tensions within advanced modern societies.
Baumgartner's starting point is a recognition that late modern life is not
monolithic, but 'divided into numerous enclaves and subcultures defined by
occupations, social classes, ethnicities, lifestyles, organisational memberships, age groups and many other factors' (Baumgartner, 1988: 5). While
one can observe African-American, Mexican, Italian, Polish and Pakistani
'enclaves' in large American cities, it is also true that suburbs tend to have
homogeneous populations where people of particular social classes, and
races, can live amongst others like themselves. This homogeneity, and the
fact that suburbs are often largely residential centres for people who tend to
work in cities, means that suburban dwellers are relatively isolated from
strangers, an isolation which is not only a fact of social morphology but
also a 'moral expectation' (Baumgartner, 1988: 17, 103). This view is
reinforced by evidence that as highly paid jobs leave city centres, suburbanites show an increasing reluctance to even venture downtown (Price
and Wedam, 1995: 13). In the suburb studied by Baumgartner, racial
minorities were not only absent but were liable to be questioned by the
police should they find their way there for some reason, a situation
mirrored in the absence of the very poor (Hummon, 1990: 106). As
Baumgartner (1988: 103) notes, the suburb's residents live, for the most
part, in 'a world of their own'.

   This homogeneity does not imply strong bonds within the suburban
communities themselves, however, as suburbs characteristically contain few
public places. When suburbanites do make their way to the few public
locations which exist they do so in the privacy of their cars. Many middle-
class people are highly mobile, so that their networks of associates are
atomised and constantly shifting, allowing little time or opportunity for
strong social bonds to develop. Relatives usually live elsewhere and life
tends to be highly compartmentalised: relationships are often 'single-
stranded', social networks are not interconnected, and ties are scattered
through many different regions (Baumgartner, 1988: 91, 101–102).

   Baumgartner is concerned with how the suburban culture of weak social
ties encourages 'moral indifference'; in Bauman's (1993) terms, there is little
being for the other in this environment. This is manifest in the changing

relationship between suburbs and nearby cities. In Chicago, for example, the Episcopal Church can no longer control the financial contributions of suburban churches to the diocese, but must depend upon their voluntary contributions (Price and Wedam, 1993: 13). Within the suburb, the environment fosters restraint in the face of grievances and little willingness to engage in mutual aid, whether of a personal or, especially, of a monetary nature (Baumgartner, 1988: 133). The fluidity and transience of social relationships hinders social integration, and encourages an unwillingness to exercise social control over one another, resulting in a tolerance which is so extreme it can be called indifference. This indifference is also apparent within families, where relatives are free to defy or ignore each other's commands as they see fit. This positive evaluation of independence and the reluctance of most people to exercise any social control over others helps account for the relatively harmonious nature of suburbs: most suburbanites are keen to avoid conflict and the highly atomised and transient character of the suburb limits the potentiality for conflicts developing or being sustained (Baumgartner, 1988: 3, 65, 134).

Baumgartner's analysis of the endemic conflict avoidance characteristic of modern suburbs accords with Bloom's (1988: 228) view that there is in contemporary Western cultures a widespread apparent need to avoid all forms of conflict, which often amounts to a sense of disconnectedness from, and indifference to, the concerns of others: '"I can live without you" is the silent thought that steals into one's mind when such relations become painful' (Bloom, 1988: 349). Similarly, Lasch's (1991 [1979]) conception of the 'narcissistic personality' expresses an awareness of the refusal or inability of many modern persons to form deep or enduring relations with others. As Martin Amis (1995: 207) so aptly expresses it in his novel *The Information*, people are now encouraged to stop saying *hi* and to start saying *bye*. Individual contracts may provide a way to manage this form of life, but they encourage insensitivity and indifference (Bauman, 1995: 55–59).

Common to these viewpoints is a recognition of the overriding moral expectation of contemporary Western societies; the expectation that people will be left alone to live their lives as they want to. The banal associations of the middle classes, heavily dependent upon a cognitive control of the unpredictabilities of human corporeality, express the strongest form of this expectation but also manifest the inherent fragility of it: the 'wild zones' of modern cities expand and challenge them continually, just as bodies ultimately resist the demands of diets, exercise and discipline. What we mean by this is that sensual forms of association threaten to cross over from these wild zones (and one never really knows where these zones are, despite the apparent certainty of the television's association of them with inner city ghettos) and interfere with the controlled, ordered lives of the middle classes.

Drive-by shootings, gang conflicts and attacks on abortion clinics, for example, leave moral indifference behind and highlight instead a recovered and virulent sense of the sacred (Hertz, 1960; Girard, 1977 [1972]) which challenges the banal self-referentiality of the 'information economy'. These solidarities participate in a different moral order shaped not necessarily by cognitive control, but by the sensual impulses of effervescent bodies. Maffesoli's (1996: 42) celebration of the 'return of the irrational' as the appearance of 'warmth' beneath the 'moral chill' of modernity therefore looks rather idealistic. The return of the sacred is not merely the return to prominence of effervescent forms of sociality, but also the opportunity for new conflicts, dangers and fears.

Frontier worlds

In his magisterial study of civilising processes, Norbert Elias (1978 [1939], 1982 [1939]) argues that 'affect moderating' relations of interdependence at the intra-state level are much more advanced than their counterparts at the inter-state level. In this respect, while moral indifference to one's neighbours may lead to 'non-violent' neglect within a suburb or city, there is nothing morally indifferent about the conflict visited internationally by nation upon nation (Scheff, 1994). In his study of the Balkanisation of the West, for example, Stjepan Meštrović (1994) uses contemporary wars and conflicts to illustrate the ineffectiveness of rational dialogue and Enlightenment narratives, and the resurgence of a virulent, violent human sensuality (Bataille, 1992 [1973]). The turmoil in the Balkans, he argues, 'seems to have foreshadowed ominously the potential for widespread racism and ethnic conflict throughout the world, from China and Africa to Western Europe and the USA. By 1993, the cheerful confidence concerning a New World Order based on rationality and tolerance . . . turned into a cynical pessimism in relation to New World Disorder' (Meštrović, 1994: 3). The United Nations, instead of being seen as providing a successful impetus towards civilising processes, is judged to be a failure in relation to the modernist premise that bureaucracy and rationality can control nationalist passions (Meštrović, 1994: 10).

Interpretations of such disorder which remain within a restricted time-frame, however, lend themselves to forms of *fin de siècle* theorising which have shaped much postmodernism as well as liberal and conservative laments for the decline of community, and which continue a long tradition of painting doomsday scenarios, in different forms, near the end of each millennium (Bull, 1995). In order to understand the particular character of modern Western societies and their contemporary transformations, however, we must consider modern developments in a broader historical context than has often been the case, and be attentive to the stubborn persistence of the various embodied potentialities of humans. This is what we have sought to accomplish in this book. Instead of taking *fin de siècle* visions of apocalypse literally, then, the sense of violent consummation which appears in recent versions of these sociological 'Heart[s] of Darkness'

(Conrad, 1989 [1902]) may more productively be viewed as intimations of the human body's resilience to cognitive control and the enduring significance of sacred forms of sociality.

We may, or may not, be entering a period of decivilisation (Dunning et al., 1977; Mennell, 1990), but the modern Western world can no longer pretend that people can simply annex their fleshy sensuality to cognitive fantasies and stratagems, or that it is possible to ignore effervescent and socially consequential contacts with the sacred (Richman, 1995). Because this pretence has been central to the modern project thus far, abandoning it is already proving difficult and painful. Nor is this abandonment likely to prove unambiguously liberating. The emotions that emerge from social relationships and solidarities may enable people to 'keep warm together' in a world which too often appears out of control and morally bankrupt, but they can also prompt a passionate intensity, hatred and 'bloody revenge' (Scheff, 1994; Theweleit, 1987 [1977], 1989 [1978]). As Durkheim (1961 [1912]), Bataille (1986 [1957], 1992 [1973]) and Girard (1977 [1972]) understood, the world of the sacred is often violent, unpredictable and dangerous. If the modern project could continue to ignore the sensual human body, other than as a resource for commercial exploitation (Featherstone, 1991; Rodaway, 1994), it would continue its descent into banality. If it turns out that it cannot, then something approaching the volatility and passionate intensity which characterised medieval life may again impose itself upon large tracts of the Western world.

BIBLIOGRAPHY

Abbott, P. (1987) *Seeking Many Inventions: The Idea of Community in America*. Tennessee: University of Tennessee Press.

Abercrombie, N. (1986) 'Knowledge, order and human autonomy', in J.D. Hunter and S.C. Ainlay (eds), *Making Sense of Modern Times, Peter L. Berger and the Vision of Interpretive Sociology*. London: Routledge and Kegan Paul.

Abulafia, S. (1994) 'Bodies in the Jewish-Christian debate', in S. Kay and M. Rubin (eds), *Framing Medieval Bodies*. Manchester: Manchester University Press.

Adorno, T.W. (1967) *Prisms*. London: Neville Spearman.

Adorno, T.W. (1994) *Adorno: The Stars Down to Earth*, ed. and with an introduction by S. Crook. London: Routledge.

Agassiz, E. (1895) 'The diversity of origin of the human races', *Christian Examiner*. 49, 110–145.

Ahmed, A. (1992) *Postmodernism and Islam: Predicament and Promise*. London: Routledge.

Alexander, J.C. (ed.) (1988) *Durkheimian Sociology: Cultural Studies*. Cambridge: Cambridge University Press.

Alexandre, M. (1992) 'Early Christian women', in P.S. Pantel (ed.), *A History of Women in the West, Vol.1. From Ancient Goddesses to Christian Saints*. Cambridge, MA: The Belknap Press of Harvard University Press.

Althaus, P. (1986 [1966]) *The Theology of Martin Luther*. Philadelphia, PA.

Amis, M. (1995) *The Information*. New York: Harmony Books.

Anderson, B. (1991) *Imagined Communities. Reflections on the Origin and Spread of Nationalism*, revised edn. London: Verso.

Archer, M. (1988) *Culture and Agency*. Cambridge: Cambridge University Press.

Archer, M. (1990) 'Theory, culture and post-industrial society', in M. Featherstone (ed.), *Global Culture: Nationalism, Globalization and Modernity*. London: Sage.

Arendt, H. (1958) *The Human Condition*. Chicago: University of Chicago Press.

Ariès, P. (1974) *Western Attitudes toward Death from the Middle Ages to the Present*. Baltimore, MD: Johns Hopkins University Press.

Ariès, P. (1979 [1960]) *Centuries of Childhood*. Harmondsworth: Peregrine.

Ariès, P. (1981 [1977]) *The Hour of Our Death*. New York: Alfred A. Knopf.

Armstrong, D. (1983) *Political Economy of the Body: Medical Knowledge in Britain in the Twentieth Century*. Cambridge: Cambridge University Press.

Armstrong, D. (1987) 'Bodies of knowledge: Foucault and the problem of human anatomy', in G. Scambler (ed.), *Sociological Theory and Medical Sociology*. London: Tavistock.

Asad, T. (1983) 'Notes on body pain and truth in medieval Christian ritual', *Economy and Society*, 12 (3): 287–327.

Asad, T. (1988) 'On ritual and discipline in medieval Christian monasticism', *Economy and Society*, 16 (2): 159–203.

Askham, J. (1984) *Identity and Stability in Marriage*. Cambridge: Cambridge University Press.

Atlanta and Alexander (1989) 'Wild style: graffiti painting', in A. McRobbie (ed.), *Zoot Suits and Second Hand Dresses*. London: Macmillan.

Atyeo, D. (1979) *Blood and Guts. Violence in Sports*. New York: Paddington.

Aufderheide, P. (1986) 'Music videos: the look of the sound', in T. Gitlin (ed.), *Watching Television*, New York: Pantheon.

Bakhtin, M. (1984 [1965]) *Rabelais and His World*. Bloomington: Indiana University Press.

Ball, S. (ed.) (1990) *Foucault and Education: Disciplines and Knowledge*. London: Routledge.

Barnaby, F. (1986) *The Automated Battlefield*. London: Sidgwick and Jackson.

Barthes, R. (1977a) *Sade Fourier, Loyola*. London. Jonathan Cape.

Barthes, R. (1977b) 'The death of the author', in *Image–Music–Text*. Glasgow: Fontana.

Bataille, G. (1986 [1957]) *Eroticism*. New York: Marion Boyars.

Bataille, G. (1992 [1973]) *Theory of Religion*, trans. R. Hurley. New York: Zone Books.

Baudelaire, C. (1964 [1863]) *The Painter of Modern Life and Other Essays*. Oxford: Phaidon Press.

Baudrillard, J. (1983) *Simulations*. New York: Semiotext(e).

Baudrillard, J. (1993a) *Symbolic Exchange and Death*. London: Sage.

Baudrillard, J. (1993b) *The Transparency of Evil. Essays on Extreme Phenomena*. London: Verso.

Bauman, Z. (1989) *Modernity and the Holocaust*. Cambridge: Polity Press.

Bauman, Z. (1991) *Modernity and Ambivalence*. Cambridge: Polity Press.

Bauman, Z. (1992a) *Intimations of Postmodernity*. London: Routledge.

Bauman, Z. (1992b) *Mortality, Immortality and Other Life Strategies*. Cambridge: Polity Press.

Bauman, Z. (1993) *Postmodern Ethics*. Oxford: Blackwell.

Bauman, Z. (1995) *Life in Fragments. Essays in Postmodern Morality*. Oxford: Blackwell.

Baumgartner, M.O. (1988) *The Moral Order of a Suburb*. New York: Oxford University Press.

Bax, M. (1983) '"Us" Catholics and "them" Catholics in Dutch Brabant: the dialectics of a religious factional process', *Anthropological Quarterly*, 56 (4): 167–178.

Bax, M. (1987) 'Religious regimes and state formation: towards a research perspective', *Anthropology Quarterly*, 60 (1): 1–13.

Beauvoir, S. de (1972 [1949]) *The Second Sex*. Harmondsworth: Penguin.

Beck, U. (1992) *Risk Society: Towards a New Modernity*. London: Sage.

Beck, U. and Beck-Gernsheim, E. (1995 [1990]) *The Normal Chaos of Love*. Cambridge: Polity Press.

Beckford, J. (1989) *Religion and Advanced Industrial Society*. London: Hyman.

Beckford, J. (1992) 'Religion, modernity and postmodernity', in B.R. Wilson (ed.), *Religion: Contemporary Issues*. London: Belew.

Bell, C. (1992) *Ritual Theory, Ritual Practice*. Oxford: Oxford University Press.

Bell, D. (1973) *The Coming of Post-Industrial Society*. New York: Basic Books.

Bell, D. (1979) *The Cultural Contradictions of Capitalism*, 2nd edn. London: Heinemann.

Bell, D. (1980) *Sociological Journeys. Essays 1960–1980*. London: Heinemann.

Bell, S. (1993) 'Finding the male within and taking him cruising: drag king-for-a-day', in A. Kroker and M. Kroker (eds), *The Last Sex. Feminism and Outlaw Bodies*. London: Macmillan.

Bellah, R., Madsen, R., Sullivan, W.M., Swidler, A. and Tipton, S.M. (1985) *Habits of the Heart: Individualism and Commitment in American Life*. New York: Harper and Row.

Bellah, R., Madsen, R., Sullivan, W.M., Swidler, A. and Tipton, S.M. (1992) *The Good Society*. New York: Vintage.

Benedict, R. (1968 [1935]) *Patterns of Culture*. London: Routledge and Kegan Paul.

Benedikt, M. (1991) 'Cyberspace: some proposals', in M. Benedikt (ed.), *Cyberspace: First Steps*. London: MIT Press.

Benjamin, W. (1973) *Illuminations*, trans. H. Zone. London: Fontana.

Benn, S. and Peters, R. (1959) *Social Principles and the Democratic State*. London: Allen and Unwin.

Benton, J. (1977) 'Individualism and conformity in medieval western Europe', in A. Banini and S. Vryonis, Jr (eds), *Individualism and Conformity in Classical Islam*. Wiesbaden.

Benton, T. (1991) 'Biology and social science: why the return of the repressed should be given a (cautious) welcome', *Sociology*, 26 (1): 1–29.

Berger, J. (1972) *Ways of Seeing*. Harmondsworth: Penguin.

Berger, P. (1990 [1967]) *The Sacred Canopy. Elements of a Sociological Theory of Religion*. New York: Anchor Books.

Berger, P. and Kellner, H. (1964) 'Marriage and the construction of reality', *Diogenes*, 1–23.

Berman, M. (1981) *The Reenchantment of the World*. London: Routledge.
Berman, M. (1982) *All That Is Solid Melts into Air. The Experience of Modernity*. London: Verso.
Bernstein, B. (1971) 'On the classification and framing of educational knowledge', in M.F.D. Young (ed.), *Knowledge and Control*. London: Collier-Macmillan.
Bernstein, B. (1973) *Class Codes and Control. Vol. 2*. London: Routledge and Kegan Paul.
Bernstein, B. (1975) *Class Codes and Control. Vol. 3*. London: Routledge and Kegan Paul.
Berry, P. and Wernick, A. (eds) (1992) *Shadow of Spirit. Postmodernism and Religion*. London: Routledge.
Bhabha, H.K. (1994) *The Location of Culture*. London: Routledge.
Biezanek, A. (1964) *All Things New*. London.
Black, A. (1992) *Political Thought in Europe 1250–1450*. Cambridge: Cambridge University Press.
Blackstone, W. (1765) *Commentaries on the Laws of England*, in E. Kantorowitz (1957) *The King's Two Bodies. A Study in Mediaeval Political Theology*. Princeton, NJ: Princeton University Press.
Blankenhorn, D. (1995) *Fatherless America*. New York: Basic Books.
Bloch, M. (1965) *Feudal Society, Volume 1. The Growth of Ties of Dependence*. London: Routledge and Kegan Paul.
Bloom, A. (1988) *The Closing of the American Mind*. New York: Touchstone.
Bly, R. (1992) *Iron John. A Book about Men*. Sherborne: Element Books.
Bossy, J. (1985) *Christianity in the West 1400–1700*. Oxford: Oxford University Press.
Bottomley, F. (1979) *Attitudes to the Body in Western Christendom*. London: Lepus Books.
Bottomore, T. (1985) *Theories of Modern Capitalism*. London: Allen and Unwin.
Bouglé, C. (1926) *The Evolution of Values*, trans. Helen Sellars. New York: Henry Holt.
Bourdieu, P. (1977) *Outline of a Theory of Practice*. Cambridge: Cambridge University Press.
Bourdieu, P. (1984) *Distinction: A Social Critique of the Judgement of Taste*. London: Routledge and Kegan Paul.
Bourdieu, P. (1986) 'The forms of capital', in J. Richardson (ed.), *Handbook of Theory and Research for the Sociology of Education*. New York: Greenwood Press.
Bourdieu, P. and Wacquant, L.J.D. (1992) *An Invitation to Reflexive Sociology*. Chicago: University of Chicago Press.
Braudel, F. (1972) *The Mediterranean and the Mediterranean World in the Age of Philip II*, 2 vols, trans. Sian Reynolds. London: Fontana.
Braudel, F. (1973) *Capitalism and Material Life 1400–1800*. London: Weidenfeld and Nicolson.
Braudel, F. (1980) *On History*. London: Weidenfeld and Nicolson.
Braudel, F. (1984 [1979]) *Civilization and Capitalism 15th–18th Centuries. Vol. III The Perspective of the World*, trans. Sian Reynolds. London: Collins.
Brinkgreve, C. (1980) 'On modern relationships: the commandments of the new freedom', *Netherlands Journal of Sociology*, 18 (1): 47–56.
Brittan, A. (1979) *The Privatised World*. London: Routledge and Kegan Paul.
Broca, P. (1861) 'Sur le volume et la forme du cerveau suivant les individus et suivant les races', *Bulletin de la Société d'Anthropologie Paris*, 2, cited in S.J. Gould (1981) *The Mismeasure of Man*. Harmondsworth: Pelican.
Broca, P. (1862) 'Sur la capacité des crânes parisiens des diverses époques', *Bulletin de la Société d'Anthropologie Paris*, 3, cited in S.J. Gould (1981) *The Mismeasure of Man*. Harmondsworth: Pelican.
Brown, P. (1975) 'Society and the supernatural: a medieval change', *Daedalus*, 104 (2): 133–151.
Brown, P. (1976) *The Making of Late Antiquity*. Cambridge, MA: Harvard University Press.
Brown, P. (1981) *The Cult of the Saints: Its Rise and Function in Latin Christianity*. Chicago: University of Chicago Press.
Brown, P. (1982) *Society and the Holy in Late Antiquity*. London: Faber and Faber.
Brown, P. (1988) *The Body and Society*. London: Faber and Faber.

Brumberg, J.J. (1989) *Fasting Girls. The History of Anorexia Nervosa.* New York: Penguin Books

Bryant, J.M. (1994) 'Evidence and explanation in history and sociology: critical reflections on Goldthorpe's critique of historical sociology', *British Journal of Sociology*, 45 (1): 3–19.

Buci-Glucksmann, C. (1994) *Baroque Reason. The Aesthetics of Modernity.* London: Sage.

Bull, M. (ed.) (1995) *Apocalypse Theory and the Ends of the World.* Oxford: Blackwell.

Bulmer, M. (1989) 'The underclass, empowerment and public policy', in M. Bulmer, J. Lewis and D. Piachaud (eds), *The Goals of Social Policy.* London: Unwin Hyman.

Bunyan, J. (1768) *The Pilgrim's Progress.* London: Printed for J. Bunyan.

Burke, E. (1990) *A Philosophical Inquiry into the Origin of Our Ideas of the Sublime and Beautiful,* edited by A. Philips. Oxford: Oxford University Press.

Burke, P. (1983) *Popular Culture in Early Modern Europe.* London: Temple Smith.

Burke, P. (1987) *The Renaissance.* London: Macmillan.

Burkhardt, J. (1935 [1860]) *The Civilisation of the Renaissance in Italy.* New York.

Burkitt, I. (forthcoming) *Bodies of Thought: Social Relations, Activity and Embodiment.* London: Sage.

Burns, T. (1992) *Erving Goffman.* London: Routledge.

Burrows, R. (1995) 'Cyberpunk as social theory'. Paper presented at the BSA annual conference, 'Contested Cities', University of Leicester, April.

Burrus, V. (1994) 'Word and flesh: the bodies and sexuality of ascetic women in Christian antiquity', *Journal of Feminist Studies in Religion*, 10 (1): 27–51.

Butler, J. (1993) *Bodies That Matter.* London: Routledge.

Bynum, C.W. (1980) 'Did the twelfth century discover the individual?' *Journal of Ecclesiastical History*, 31 (1): 1–17.

Bynum, C.W. (1987) *Holy Feast and Holy Fast.The Religious Significance of Food to Medieval Women.* Berkeley: University of California Press.

Bynum, C.W. (1989) 'The female body and religious practice in the later middle ages', in M. Fehér, R. Naddaff and N. Tazi (eds), *Fragments for a History of the Human Body: Part One.* New York: Zone Books.

Bynum, C.W. (1991) *Fragmentation and Redemption: Essays on Gender and the Human Body in Medieval Religion.* New York: Zone Books.

Bynum, C.W. (1995) *The Resurrection of the Body in Western Christianity 200–1336.* New York: Columbia University Press.

Cameron, E. (1991) *The European Reformation.* Oxford: Oxford University Press.

Campbell, B. (1996) 'Gender, crime and community'. Paper presented at the 'Feminist Backlash Seminar Series', University of Southampton, February.

Campbell, C. (1987) *The Romantic Ethic and the Spirit of Modern Consumerism.* Oxford: Blackwell.

Campbell, T. (1981) *Seven Theories of Human Society.* Oxford: Clarendon Press.

Camporesi, P. (1988) *The Incorruptible Flesh: Bodily Mutilation and Mortification in Religion and Folklore.* Cambridge: Cambridge University Press.

Caplow, T., Bahr, H.M. and Chadwick, B.A. (1983) *All Faithful People: Change and Continuity in Middletown's Religion.* Minneapolis: University of Minnesota Press.

Carlen, P., Gleeson, D. and Wardhaugh, J. (1992) *Truancy. The Politics of Compulsory Schooling.* Buckingham: Open University Press.

Carroll, J. (1993) *Humanism: The Rebirth and Wreck of Western Culture.* London: Fontana.

Cascardi, A.J. (1992) *The Subject of Modernity.* Cambridge: Cambridge University Press.

Cashmore, E. (1994) *And Then There Was Television.* London: Routledge.

Cassirer, E. (1926) *Individuum und Kosmos in der Philosophie der Renaissance.* Leipzig: Teubner.

Castells, M. (1989) *The Informational City: Information Technology, Economic Restructuring and the Urban-Regional Process.* Oxford: Blackwell.

Cate, R. and Lloyd, S. (1992) *Courtship.* London: Sage.

Chadwick, O. (1990 [1964]) *The Reformation.* Harmondsworth: Penguin.

Chalmers, M. (1989) 'Heroin, the needle and the politics of the body', in A. McRobbie (ed.), *Zoot Suits and Second Hand Dresses*. London: Macmillan.

Charles, N. and Kerr, M. (1988) *Women, Food and Families*. Manchester: Manchester University Press.

Chartier, R. (ed.) (1989) *A History of Private Life. Vol. 3. Passions of the Renaissance*. Cambridge, MA: The Belknap Press of Harvard University Press.

Chateaubriand, F.A.R. (1856 [1802]) *Genius of Christianity*, trans. Charles I. White, cited in R. Nisbet (1993 [1966]) *The Sociological Tradition*. New Brunswick, NJ: Transaction Books.

Chatellier, L. (1989) *The Europe of the Devout: The Catholic Reformation and the Formation of a New Society*. Cambridge: Cambridge University Press and Editions de la Maison des Sciences de l'Homme.

Chernin, K. (1983) *Womansize. The Tyranny of Slenderness*. London: The Women's Press.

Chrisman, M.U. (1982) *Lay Culture, Learned Culture: Books and Social Change in Strasbourg, 1480–1599*. New Haven, CT: Yale University Press.

Christiano, K.J. (1987) *Religious Diversity and Social Change*. Cambridge: Cambridge University Press.

Clark, D. (ed.) (1991a) *Marriage, Domestic Life and Social Change*. London: Routledge.

Clark, K. (1960 [1956]) *The Nude. A Study of Ideal Art*. Harmondsworth: Pelican.

Clark, L. and Lange, L. (eds) (1979) *The Sexism of Social and Political Thought*. Toronto: University of Toronto Press.

Clark, N. (1995) 'Rear-view mirrorshades: the recursive generation of the cyberbody', *Body and Society*, 1 (3–4), 113–133.

Classen, C. (1993) *Worlds of Sense. Exploring the Senses in History and across Cultures*. London: Routledge.

Cohen, S. and Taylor, L. (1992) *Escape Attempts: The Theory and Practice of Resistance to Everyday Life*, 2nd edn. London: Routledge.

Cohn, N. (1975) *Europe's Inner Demons*. St Albans: Paladin.

Colas, D. (1991) 'Le moment Luthérien de la société civile', *Philosophie Politique*, 1: 41–54.

Collins, R. (1975) *Conflict Sociology*. New York: Academic Press.

Collins, R. (1988) 'The Durkheimian tradition in conflict sociology', in J.C. Alexander (ed.), *Durkheimian Sociology: Cultural Studies*. Cambridge: Cambridge University Press.

Congar, Y. (1972) *Yves Congar OP*. London: Sheed and Ward.

Connell, R.W. (1995) *Masculinities*. Cambridge: Polity Press.

Conrad, J. (1989 [1902]) *Heart of Darkness*. Harmondsworth: Penguin.

Constable, G. (1995) *Three Studies in Medieval Religion and Social Thought*. Cambridge: Cambridge University Press.

Coontz, S. and Henderson, P. (1986) 'Property forms, political power and female labour in the origin of class and state societies', in *Women's Work. Men's Property. The Origin of Gender and Class*. London: Verso.

Corbin, A. (1986) *The Foul and the Fragrant. Odor and the French Social Imagination*. Cambridge, MA: Harvard University Press.

Cornford, F.M. (1957) *From Religion to Philosophy*. New York: Harper.

Couliano, I.P. (1987) *Eros and Magic in the Renaissance*. Chicago: University of Chicago Press.

Crawford, R. (1987) 'Cultural influences on prevention and the emergence of a new health consciousness', in N. Weinstein (ed.), *Taking Care. Understanding and Encouraging Self Protective Behaviour*. Cambridge: Cambridge University Press.

Crook, S., Pakulski, J. and Waters, M. (1992) *Postmodernization: Change in Advanced Society*. London: Sage.

Crossley, N. (1994) *The Politics of Subjectivity: Between Foucault and Merleau-Ponty*. Aldershot: Avebury Press.

Crossley, N. (1995) 'Merleau-Ponty, the elusive body and carnal sociology', *Body and Society*, 1 (1): 43–63.

Csicsery-Ronay, I. (1991) 'Cyberpunk and neuromanticism', in L. McCaffery (ed.), *Storming the Reality Studio*. Durham, NC: Duke University Press.

Cupitt, D. (1992) 'Unsystematic ethics and politics', in P. Berry and A. Wernick (eds), *Shadow of Spirit. Postmodernism and Religion.* London: Routledge.

Darwin, C. (1955 [1896]) *The Expression of Emotions in Man and Animals.* New York: Philosophical Library.

David, M. (1993) *Parents, Gender and Education Reform.* Cambridge: Polity Press.

David-Menard, M. (1989 [1983]) *Hysteria from Freud to Lacan. Body and Language in Psychoanalysis.* Ithaca, NY: Cornell University Press.

Davies, J. (1993) 'From household to family to individualism', in J. Davies (ed.), *The Family: Is it Just Another Lifestyle Choice?* London: IEA Health and Welfare Unit.

Davis, C. (1994) *Religion and the Making of Society: Essays in Social Theology.* Cambridge: Cambridge University Press.

Davis, J.C. (1981) *Utopia and the Ideal Society: a Study of English Utopian Writing 1516–1700.* Cambridge: Cambridge University Press.

Davis, K. (1995) *Reshaping the Female Body. The Dilemma of Cosmetic Surgery.* London: Routledge.

Davis, M. (1990) *City of Quartz. Excavating the Future in Los Angeles.* New York: Vintage Books.

Dawkins, R. (1976) *The Selfish Gene.* London: Paladin.

Dayan, D. and Katz, E. (1988) 'Articulating consensus: the ritual and rhetoric of media events', in J.C. Alexander (ed.), *Durkheimian Sociology: Cultural Studies.* Cambridge: Cambridge University Press.

Deitch, J. (1995) 'Post human', in M. Featherstone and R. Burrows (eds), *Cyberpunk/Cyberspace/Cyberbodies.* London: Sage.

Delumeau, J. (1987) *Catholicism between Luther and Voltaire.* London: Burns and Oates.

Delumeau, J. (1990) *Sin and Fear. The Emergence of a Western Guilt Culture 13th–18th Centuries.* New York: St Martin's Press.

Denzin, N.K. (1987) *Interpretive Biography.* London: Sage.

Descartes, R. (1973) *The Philosophical Works of Descartes, Vol. I,* trans. E. Haldane and G.R.T. Ross. Cambridge: Cambridge University Press.

De Tocqueville, A. (1945 [1840]) *Democracy in America.* Vol. II. Ed. Philips Badley. New York: Alfred Knopf.

Dix, G. (1983 [1945]) *The Shape of the Liturgy.* New York: Seabury Press.

Dodds, E.R. (1951) *The Greeks and the Irrational.* Berkeley: University of California Press.

Douglas, A. (1977) *The Feminization of American Culture.* New York: Alfred. A. Knopf.

Douglas, J.W.B. (1967 [1964]) *The Home and the School. A Study of Ability and Attainment in the Primary School.* London: Panther.

Douglas, M. (1966) *Purity and Danger: An Analysis of Concepts of Pollution and Taboo.* London: Routledge and Kegan Paul.

Douglas, M. (1970) *Natural Symbols. Explorations in Cosmology.* London: The Cresset Press.

Douglas, M. (1972) 'Deciphering a meal', *Daedalus,* 101: 61–81.

Dronke, P. (1970) *Poetic Individuality in the Middle Ages.* Oxford: Oxford University Press.

Duby, G. (1977) *The Chivalrous Society.* Berkeley: University of California Press.

Duby, G. (1988) *A History of Private Life. Vol. 2. Revelations of the Medieval World.* Cambridge, MA: Harvard University Press.

Duffy, E. (1992) *The Stripping of the Altars: Traditional Religion in England c. 1400–c. 1580.* New Haven, CT: Yale University Press.

Dumont, L. (1982) 'The Christian origins of modern individualism', *Religion,* 12 (1): 1–28.

Dundes, A. (1980) *Interpreting Folklore.* Bloomington: Indiana University Press.

Dunn, J. (1969) *The Political Thought of John Locke: The Moral Vision of the American Founders and the Philosophy of Locke.* Cambridge: Cambridge University Press.

Dunn, J. (1984) *Locke.* Oxford: Oxford University Press.

Dunning, E., Murphy, P., Newburn, T. and Waddington, I. (1977) 'Violent disorders in twentieth century Britain', in G. Gaskell and R. Benweick (eds), *The Crowd in Contemporary Britain.* London: Sage.

Duncombe, J. and Marsden, D. (1993) 'Love and intimacy: the gender division of emotion work', *Sociology*, 27 (2): 221–241.

Dupont, F. (1989) 'The emperor – God's other body', in M. Fehér (ed.), *Fragments for a History of the Body. Part Three*. New York: Zone Books.

Duras, M. (1985) *The Lover*. London: Fontana.

Duras, M. (1986) *The Maladie of Death*. New York: Grove Press.

Durkheim, E. (1951 [1897]) *Suicide*. London: Routledge and Kegan Paul.

Durkheim, E. (1961 [1912]) *The Elementary Forms of the Religious Life*. London: Allen and Unwin.

Durkheim, E. (1973 [1914]) 'The dualism of human nature and its social conditions', in R.N. Bellah (ed.), *Emile Durkheim on Morality and Society*. Chicago: University of Chicago Press.

Durkheim, E. (1977 [1938]) *The Evolution of Educational Thought*, trans. Peter Collins. London: Routledge and Kegan Paul.

Durkheim, E. (1984 [1893]) *The Division of Labour in Society*. London: Macmillan.

Durkheim, E. and Mauss, M. (1975 [1902]) *Primitive Classification*, trans. R. Needham. Chicago: University of Chicago Press.

Durston, C. (1989) *The Family in the English Revolution*. Oxford: Blackwell.

Dyer, R. (1986) *Heavenly Bodies: Film Stars and Society*. New York: St Martin's Press.

Eade, J. and Sallnow, M.J. (eds) (1991) *Contesting the Sacred: the Anthropology of Christian Pilgrimage*. London: Routledge.

Ehrenreich, B. (1983) *The Hearts of Men: American Dreams and their Flight from Commitment*. London: Pluto.

Ehrenreich, B. (1990) *The Fear of Falling: The Inner Life of the Middle Class*. New York: Harper Perennial.

Eisenstadt, S.N. (1969) *The Protestant Ethic and Modernization*. New York: Basic Books.

Eisenstein, E.L. (1979) *The Printing Press in an Age of Social Change*, 2 vols. Cambridge: Cambridge University Press.

Elias, N. (1978 [1939]) *The History of Manners: The Civilizing Process, Volume 1*. New York: Pantheon Books.

Elias, N. (1982 [1939]) *State Formation and Civilization: The Civilizing Process, Volume 2*. Oxford: Blackwell.

Elias, N. (1983) *The Court Society*. Oxford: Blackwell.

Elias, N. (1985) *The Loneliness of the Dying*. Oxford: Blackwell.

Elias, N. (1987) 'The changing balance of power between the sexes – a process-sociological study: the example of the Ancient Roman state', *Theory, Culture and Society*, 4: 287–316.

Elias, N. (1988) 'Violence and civilization: the state monopoly of physical violence and its infringement', in J. Keane (ed.), *Civil Society and the State*. London: Verso.

Elias, N. (1991) *Symbol Emancipation*. London: Sage.

Elias, N. and Dunning, E. (1986) *Quest for Excitement. Sport and Leisure in the Civilising Process*. Oxford: Blackwell.

Elias, N. and Scotson, J. (1994 [1965]) *The Established and the Outsiders*. London: Sage.

Elton, G.R. (1963) *Renaissance and Reformation, 1300–1648*. Cambridge: Cambridge University Press.

Erben, M. (1993) 'The problem of other lives: social perspectives on written biography', *Sociology*, 27 (1): 15–25.

Erikson, E. (1950) *Childhood and Society*. New York: Norton.

Estes, C.P. (1992) *Women Who Run With The Wolves*. New York: Ballantine Books.

Etzioni, A. (1993) *The Spirit of Community*. London: Fontana Press.

Evans, J. (1990) 'Defining the subject. The rise and rise of the new PE', *British Journal of Sociology of Education*, 11 (2): 155–169.

Fainstein, S.F., Gordon, I. and Harloe, M. (eds) (1992) *Divided Cities: New York and London in the Contemporary World*. Oxford: Blackwell.

Falk, P. (1993) 'The representation of presence: outlining the anti-aesthetics of pornography', *Theory, Culture and Society*, 10 (2): 1–42.

Falk, P. (1994) *The Consuming Body*. London: Sage.

Falk, P. (1995) 'Written in the flesh', *Body and Society*, 1 (1): 95–105.

Fanon, F. (1970) *Black Skin, White Masks*. London: Paladin.

Featherstone, M. (1982) 'The body in consumer culture', *Theory, Culture and Society*, 1: 18–33.

Featherstone, M. (1991) *Consumer Culture and Postmodernism*. London: Sage.

Featherstone, M. (1995a) *Undoing Culture. Globalisation, Postmodernism and Identity*. London: Sage.

Featherstone, M. (1995b) 'Post-bodies, ageing and virtual reality', in M. Featherstone and A. Wernick (eds), *Images of Ageing*. London: Routledge.

Featherstone, M. and Burrows, R. (1995) 'Cultures of technological embodiment: an introduction', *Body and Society*, 1 (3–4): 1–20.

Featherstone, M. and Hepworth, M. (1991) 'The mask of ageing and the postmodern life course', in M. Featherstone, M. Hepworth and B. Turner (eds) (1991), *The Body: Social Process and Cultural Theory*. London: Sage.

Featherstone, M. and Turner, B.S. (1995) 'Body & society: an introduction', *Body and Society*, 1 (1): 1–12.

Featherstone, M. and Wernick, A. (eds) (1995) *Images of Ageing*. London: Routledge.

Featherstone, M., Hepworth, M. and Turner, B. (eds) (1991) *The Body: Social Process and Cultural Theory*. London: Sage.

Ferguson, H. (1992) *The Religious Transformation of Western Society*. London: Routledge.

Ferguson, W.K. (1948) *The Renaissance in Historical Thought: Five Centuries of Interpretation*. Boston.

Fields, K. (1995) 'Translator's introduction: Religion as an eminently social thing', in E. Durkheim (1995 [1912]) *The Elementary Forms of Religious Life*. New York: The Free Press.

Fife, R.H. (1957) *The Revolt of Martin Luther*. New York.

Finke, R. and Stark, R. (1986) 'Turning pews into people: estimating 19th century church membership', *Journal for the Scientific Study of Religion*, 25: 180–192.

Fiske, J. (1987) *Television Culture*. London: Routledge and Kegan Paul.

Fiske, J. (1991) 'Postmodernism and television', in J. Curran and M. Gurevitch (eds), *Mass Media and Society*. London: Edward Arnold.

Flandrin, J. (1979) *Families in Former Times: Kinship, Household and Sexuality*. Cambridge: Cambridge University Press.

Floud, R., Wachter, K. and Gregory, A. (1990) *Health, Height and History: Nutritional Status in the UK 1750–1980*. Cambridge: Cambridge University Press.

Foucault, M. (1979 [1975]) *Discipline and Punish: The Birth of the Prison*. Harmondsworth: Penguin.

Foucault, M. (1981 [1976]) *The History of Sexuality, Vol.1: An Introduction*. Harmondsworth: Penguin.

Foucault, M. (1988 [1984]) *The History of Sexuality. Vol. 3: The Care of the Self*. Harmondsworth: Penguin.

Frank, A. (1991a) *At the Will of the Body*. Boston: Houghton Mifflin.

Frank, A. (1991b) 'For a sociology of the body: an analytical review', in M. Featherstone, M. Hepworth and B.S. Turner (eds), *The Body: Social Process and Cultural Theory*. London: Sage.

Frank, A. (1995) 'As much as theory can say about bodies', *Body and Society*, 1 (1): 184–187.

Freud, S. (1961 [1930]) *Civilization and its Discontents*. New York: Norton.

Friedenthal, R. (1970) *Luther: His Life and Times*. New York: Harcourt, Brace, Jovanovich.

Fussell, S. (1991) *Muscle: Confessions of an Unlikely Body Builder*. New York: Poseidon Press.

Futuyama, D.J. (1986) *Evolutionary Biology*, 2nd edn. Sunderland, MA: Sinauer Associates.

Gallagher, C. (1987) 'The body versus the social body in the works of Thomas Malthus and Henry Mayhew', in C. Gallagher and T. Laqueur (eds), *The Making of the Modern Body. Sexuality and Society in the Nineteenth Century*. Berkeley: University of California Press.

Gallagher, C. and Laqueur, T. (eds) (1987) *The Making of the Modern Body. Sexuality and Society in the Nineteenth Century*. Berkeley: University of California Press.

Gardiner, M. (1992) *The Dialogics of Critique: M. Bakhtin and the Theory of Ideology*. London: Routledge.

Garfinkel, H. (1963) 'A conception of, and experiments with, "trust" as a condition of stable concerted actions', in O.J. Harvey (ed.), *Motivation and Social Interaction*. New York: Ronald Press.

Garland, D. (1991) *Punishment and Modern Society*. Oxford: Clarendon Press.

Geertz, C. (1973) *The Interpretation of Cultures*. New York: Basic Books.

Geertz, C. (1986) 'The uses of diversity', *Michigan Quarterly*, 25: 1.

Gehlen, A. (1956) *Urmensch und Spätkultur*. Bonn: Athenaum.

Gehlen, A. (1957) *Die Seele in technischen Zeitalter*. Hamburg: Rowhalt.

Gehlen, A. (1971) *Der Mensch: seine Natur and seine Stellung in der Welt*. Frankfurt: Athenaum.

Gellner, E. (1992) *Reason and Culture*. Oxford: Blackwell.

Gellner, E. (1993) *The Psychoanalytic Movement: The Cunning of Unreason*, 2nd edn. London: Fontana Press.

Giaccardi, C. (1995) 'Television advertising and the representation of social reality: a comparative study', *Theory, Culture and Society*, 12 (1): 109–131.

Gibson, J.W. (1994) *Warrior Dreams. Violence and Manhood in Post-Vietnam America*. New York: Hill and Wang.

Gibson, W. (1984) *Neuromancer*. London: HarperCollins.

Gibson, W. (1993) *Virtual Light*. London: HarperCollins.

Giddens, A. (1984) *The Constitution of Society*. Cambridge: Polity Press.

Giddens, A. (1985) *The Nation-State and Violence*. Cambridge: Polity Press.

Giddens, A. (1987) 'Structuralism, post-structuralism and the problem of culture', in A. Giddens and J. Turner (eds), *Social Theory Today*. Cambridge: Polity Press.

Giddens, A. (1990) *The Consequences of Modernity*. Cambridge: Polity Press.

Giddens, A. (1991) *Modernity and Self-Identity*. Cambridge: Polity Press.

Giddens, A. (1992) *The Transformation of Intimacy*. Cambridge: Polity Press.

Giddens, A. (1994) 'Living in a post traditional society', in U. Beck, A. Giddens and S. Lash (eds), *Reflexive Modernization. Politics, Tradition and Aesthetics in the Modern Social Order*. Cambridge: Polity Press.

Gill, C.B. (ed.) (1995) *Bataille. Writing the Sacred*. London: Routledge.

Gill, R. (1989) *Competing Convictions*. London: SCM Press.

Gilligan, C. (1982) *In a Different Voice: Psychological Theory and Women's Development*. Cambridge, MA: Harvard University Press.

Gilmore, D. (1990) *Manhood in the Making: Cultural Concepts of Masculinity*. New Haven, CT: Yale University Press.

Gilroy, P. (1993) *The Black Atlantic. Modernity and Double Consciousness*. London: Verso.

Girard, R. (1977 [1972]) *Violence and the Sacred*. Baltimore, MD: Johns Hopkins University Press.

Goddu, A. (1992) 'The failure of exorcism in the Middle Ages', in B.P. Levack (ed.), *Articles on Witchcraft, Magic and Demonology*. New York: Garland.

Goffman, E. (1961) *Asylums: Essays on the Social Situation of Mental Patients and Other Inmates*. New York: Anchor Books.

Goffman, E. (1963) *Behaviour in Public Places: Notes on the Social Organisation of Gatherings*. New York: Free Press.

Goffman, E. (1968) *Stigma: Notes on the Management of Spoiled Identity*. Harmondsworth: Penguin.

Goffman, E. (1969) *The Presentation of Self in Everyday Life*. Harmondsworth: Penguin.

Goffman, E. (1971) *Relations in Public: Microstudies of the Public Order*. London: Allen Lane.

Goffman, E. (1983) 'The interaction order', *American Sociological Review*, 48: 1–17.

Goldthorpe, J.H. (1991) 'The uses of history in sociology: reflections on some recent tendencies', *British Journal of Sociology*, 42 (2): 211–230.

Goldthorpe, J.H. (1994) 'The uses of history in sociology: a reply', *British Journal of Sociology*, 45 (1): 55–77.

Gombrich, E.H. (1989) *The Story of Art*, 15th edn. London: Phaidon.

Gordon, C. (ed.) (1980) *Michel Foucault. Power/Knowledge*. Brighton: Harvester Press.

Gossett, T.F. (1965) *Race: The History of an Idea in America*. New York: Schocken Books.

Goudsblom, J. (1987) 'The domestication of fire as a civilizing process', *Theory, Culture and Society*, 4: 457–476.

Goudsblom, J. (1989) 'Stijlen en beschavingen', *De Gids*, 152: 720–722. Cited in S. Mennell, 'The formation of we-images: a process theory', in C. Calhoun (ed.), *Social Theory and the Politics of Identity*. Oxford: Blackwell.

Gould, P. and White, R. (1986) *Mental Maps*. Boston, MA: Allen and Unwin.

Gould, S.J. (1984 [1981]) *The Mismeasure of Man*. Harmondsworth: Penguin.

Gouldner, A.W. (1965) *Enter Plato. Classical Greece and the Origins of Social Theory*. London: Routledge and Kegan Paul.

Gouldner, A.W. (1970) *The Coming Crisis of Western Sociology*. New York: Basic Books.

Gramsci, A. (1971) *Selections from Prison Notebooks*. London: Lawrence and Wishart.

Grant, M. (1971) *Gladiators*. London: Penguin.

Gray, J. (1992) *Men are from Mars, Women are from Venus*. New York: HarperCollins.

Green, H. (1986) *Fit for America: Health, Fitness, Sport and American Society*. New York: Pantheon.

Greyerz, K. von (1994) *Religion and Society in Early Modern Europe, 1500–1800*. London: Fierman Historical Institute.

Groethuysen, B. (1927) *Origines de l'espirit bourgeois en France. Vol. 1: L'Eglise et la bourgeoisie*. Paris.

Gurevich, A. (1985) *Categories of Medieval Culture*. London: Routledge and Kegan Paul.

Habermas, J. (1987) *The Philosophical Discourse of Modernity*. Boston, MA: Beacon Press.

Habermas, J. (1989) 'Modernity: an incomplete project', in H. Foster (ed.), *Postmodern Culture*. London: Pluto.

Hadden, J.K. (1987) 'Toward desacralizing secularization theory', *Social Forces*, 65: 587–611.

Haley, B. (1988) *The Healthy Body and Victorian Culture*. Cambridge, MA: Harvard University Press.

Hall, S. and Gieben, B. (eds) (1992) *Formations of Modernity*. Cambridge: Polity Press.

Hall, S. and Jefferson, T. (eds) (1976) *Resistance through Rituals. Youth Subcultures in Post-War Britain*. London: Hutchinson.

Haller, W. (1938) *The Rise of Puritanism*. New York: Columbia University Press.

Hamilton, B. (1986) *Religion in the Medieval West*. London: Edward Arnold.

Hamilton, P. (1992) 'The Enlightenment and the birth of social science', in S. Hall and B. Gieben (eds), *Formations of Modernity*. Cambridge: Polity Press.

Hammond, P. (ed.) (1985) *The Sacred in a Secular Age*. Berkeley: University of California Press.

Hanawalt, B. (1976) 'Violent death in fourteenth and early fifteenth century England', *Comparative Studies in Society and History*, 18 (3): 297–320.

Haraway, D. (1994 [1985]) 'A manifesto for cyborgs: science, technology and socialist feminism in the 1980s', in S. Seidman (ed.), *The Postmodern Turn. New Perspectives on Social Theory*. Cambridge: Cambridge University Press.

Harding, S. (1991) *Whose Science? Whose Knowledge? Thinking from Women's Lives*. Milton Keynes: Open University Press.

Hart, N. (1994) 'John Goldthorpe and the relics of sociology', *British Journal of Sociology*, 45 (1): 21–30.

Harvey, D. (1990) *The Condition of Postmodernity*. Oxford: Blackwell.

Hayden, T. (1980) *The American Future*. Boston.

Head, T. (1990) *Hagiography and the Cult of Saints*. Cambridge: Cambridge University Press.

Heidegger, M. (1977) *The Question concerning Technology and Other Essays*. New York: Harper and Row.

Heim, M. (1995) 'The design of virtual reality', *Body and Society*, 1 (3–4): 65–77.

Heimert, A. and Delbanco, A. (1985) *The Puritans in America. A Narrative Anthology.* Cambridge, MA: Harvard University Press.

Held, D. (1987) *Models of Democracy.* Cambridge: Polity Press.

Held, D. (1992) 'The development of the modern state', in S. Hall and B. Gieben (eds), *Formations of Modernity.* Cambridge: Polity Press.

Heller, A. (1990) *Can Modernity Survive?* Cambridge: Polity Press.

Hendry, L., Shucksmith, J., Love, J. and Glendinning, A. (1993) *Young People's Leisure and Lifestyles.* London: Routledge.

Herberg, W. (1960) *Protestant–Catholic–Jew: an Essay in American Religious Sociology.* New York: Doubleday.

Herdt, G. (1982) 'Fetish and fantasy in Sambia initiation', in G. Herdt (ed.) *Rituals of Manhood.* Berkeley: University of California Press.

Heritage, J. (1984) *Garfinkel and Ethnomethodology.* Cambridge: Cambridge University Press.

Hernnstein, R.J. and Murray, C. (1994) *The Bell Curve: Intelligence and Class Structure in American Life.* New York: Free Press.

Hertz, R. (1960) *Death and the Right Hand.* New York: Cohen and West.

Hester, M. (1992) *Lewd Women and Wicked Witches.* London: Routledge.

Hill, C. (1958) *Puritanism and Revolution. Studies in Interpretation of the English Revolution of the 17th Century.* London: Secker and Warburg.

Hill, C. (1966) *Society and Puritanism in Pre-Revolutionary England.* London: Secker and Warburg.

Hill, L. (1993) *Marguerite Duras: Apocalyptic Desires.* London: Routledge.

Hill, M. (1973) *A Sociology of Religion.* New York: Basic Books.

Hirsch, F. (1976) *Social Limits to Growth.* Cambridge, MA: Harvard University Press.

Hirst, P. and Woolley, P. (1982) *Social Relations and Human Attributes.* London: Tavistock.

Hobbes, T. (1957) *Leviathan,* ed. M. Oakeshott. Oxford: Oxford University Press.

Hobsbawm, E.J. (1964) *Labouring Men: Studies in the History of Labour.* London: Weidenfeld and Nicolson.

Hobsbawm, E. and Ranger, T. (1983) *The Invention of Tradition.* Cambridge: Cambridge University Press.

Hochschild, A. (1983) *The Managed Heart: Commercialization of Human Feeling.* Berkeley: University of California Press.

Hodge, B. and Tripp, D. (1986) *Children and Television.* Cambridge: Polity Press.

Holland, S. (1995) 'Descartes goes to Hollywood: mind, body and gender in contemporary cyborg cinema', *Body and Society,* 1 (3–4): 157–174.

Holmes, G. (1988) *The Oxford History of Medieval Europe.* Oxford: Oxford University Press.

Honneth, A. and Joas, H. (1988) *Social Action and Human Nature.* Cambridge: Cambridge University Press.

Howell, M.C. (1988) *Women, Production and Patriarchy in Late Medieval Cities.* Chicago: University of Chicago Press.

Howes, D. (ed.) (1991) *The Varieties of Sensory Experience: A Sourcebook in the Anthropology of the Senses.* Toronto: University of Toronto Press.

Huizinga, J. (1995 [1954]) *The Waning of the Middle Ages.* Garden City, NY: Doubleday.

Hummon, D.M. (1990) *Commonplaces: Community, Ideology and Identity in American Culture.* New York: State University of New York Press.

Hunt, L. (ed.) (1991) *Eroticism and the Body Politic.* Baltimore, MD: Johns Hopkins University Press.

Hunter, I. and Saunders, D. (1995) 'Walks of life: Mauss on the human gymnasium', *Body and Society,* 1 (2): 65–81.

Hunter, J.D. (1991) *Culture Wars. The Struggle to Define America.* New York: Basic Books.

Hutchison, W.R. (1992) *The Modernist Impulse in American Protestantism.* Durham, NC: Duke University Press.

Ignatieff, M. (1985) 'Is nothing sacred? The ethics of television', *Daedalus,* 114 (4): 57–78.

Iyengar, S. (1992) *Is Anyone Responsible? How Television Frames Political Issues.* Chicago: University of Chicago Press.

Jackson, S. (1981) 'Acedia, the sin and its relationship to sorrow and melancholy in medieval times', *The Bulletin of the History of Medicine*, 55: 172–186.

Jackson, B. (1993) 'Even sociologists fall in love: an exploration of the sociology of emotions', *Sociology*, 27 (2): 201–220.

James, A. (1990) 'The good, the bad and the delicious: the role of confectionery in British society', *Sociological Review*, 38 (4): 666–688.

Jameson, F. (1991) *Postmodernism or The Cultural Logic of Late Capitalism*. Durham, NC: Duke University Press.

Jary, D. and Jary, J. (1995) 'Transformation of Anthony Giddens – The continuing story of structuration theory', *Theory, Culture and Society*, 12: 141–160.

Jay, M. (1992) 'Scopic regimes of modernity', in S. Lash and J. Friedman (eds), *Modernity and Identity*. Oxford: Blackwell.

Jefferson, A. (1989) 'Bodymatters: self and other in Bakhtin, Sartre and Barthes', in K. Hirschkop and D. Sheperd (eds), *Bakhtin and Cultural Theory*. Manchester: Manchester University Press.

Jenks, C. (1995) 'The centrality of the eye in Western culture: an introduction', in C. Jenks (ed.), *Visual Culture*. London: Routledge.

Jensen, H.J. (1976) *The Muses' Concord: Literature, Music and the Visual Arts in the Baroque Age*. Bloomington: Indiana University Press.

Jindra, M. (1994) '*Star Trek* fandom as a religious phenomenon', *Sociology of Religion*, 55 (1): 27–51.

Johnson, C.L. and Johnson, F.A. (1980) 'Parenthood, marriage and careers: situational constraints and role strain', in F. Pepitone-Rockwell (ed.), *Dual-Career Couples*. Beverley Hills, CA: Sage.

Johnson, M. (1987) *The Body in the Mind: The Bodily Basis of Meaning, Imagination and Reason*. Chicago: University of Chicago Press.

Jones, S. (1994) *The Language of Genes*. London: Flamingo.

Jordan, T. (1995) 'Collective bodies: raving and the politics of Gilles Deleuze and Felix Guattari', *Body and Society*, 1 (1): 125–144.

Jordanova, L. (1989) *Sexual Visions. Images of Gender in Science and Medicine between the Eighteenth and Twentieth Centuries*. New York: Harvester Wheatsheaf.

Kane, P. (1996) 'There's method in the magic', *New Statesman*, 23 August pp. 24–27.

Kant, I. (1951 [1790]) *Critique of Judgement*, trans. J.H. Bernard. New York: Collier-Macmillan.

Kantorowicz, E. (1957) *The King's Two Bodies. A Study in Medieval Political Theology*. Princeton, NJ: Princeton University Press.

Katz, E. and Liebes, T. (1990) *The Export of Meaning*. London: Oxford University Press.

Kay, S. and Rubin, M. (1994) *Framing Medieval Bodies*. Manchester: Manchester University Press.

Kearney, R. (1995) 'Myths and scapegoats: The case of René Girard', *Theory, Culture and Society*, 12: 1–14.

Keen, M. (1984) *Chivalry*. New Haven, CT: Yale University Press.

Keller, S. (1977) 'The telephone in new (and old) communities', in Ithiel de Sola Pool (ed.), *The Social Impact of the Telephone*. Cambridge, MA: MIT Press.

Kelly, K. (1994) *Out of Control. The New Biology of Machines*. London: Fourth Estate.

Kempers, B. (1982) 'Die civilisatietheorie van Elias en civilisatie-processen in Italie, 1300–1550. Over de beschaafde strijd tussen generalisten en specialisten', *Amsterdams Sociologisch Tijdschrift*, 8 (4): 591–611, cited in S. Mennell (1989) *Norbert Elias*. Oxford: Blackwell.

Kierkegaard, S. (1944) *The Concept of Dread*. London: Macmillan.

Kilgour, M. (1990) *From Communion to Cannibalism*. Princeton, NJ: Princeton University Press.

Kilminster, R. (1994) '"The symbol theory" as a research programme'. Paper presented to 13th ISA World Congress of Sociology, Bielefeld, 18–23 July.

Kimbrell, K. (1993) *The Human Body Shop: The Engineering and Marketing of Life*. London: HarperCollins.

Klapisch-Zuber, M. (1990) 'Women and the family', in Jacques Le Goff (ed.), *The Medieval World*. London: Collins and Brown.

Koenigsberger, H.G. (1987) *Early Modern Europe 1500–1789*. London: Longman.

Koenigsberger, H.G., Mosse, G.L. and Bowler, G.Q. (1989) *Europe in the Sixteenth Century*. London: Longman.

Kracauer, S. (1993 [1940]) 'Photography', *Critical Inquiry*, 19 (3): 421–437.

Kroker, A. and Kroker, M. (1988) *Body Invaders: Sexuality and the Postmodern Condition*. Basingstoke: Macmillan.

Kroker, A. and Kroker, M. (eds) (1993) *The Last Sex. Feminism and Outlaw Bodies*. Basingstoke: Macmillan.

Kroker, A., Kroker, M. and Cook, D. (1989) *Panic Encyclopedia*. Basingstoke: Macmillan.

Kuhn, T. (1970) *The Structure of Scientific Revolutions*, 2nd edn. Chicago: University of Chicago Press.

Kumar, K. (1988) *The Rise of Modern Society: Aspects of the Social and Political Development of the West*. Oxford: Blackwell.

Kuzmics, H. (1988) 'The civilizing process', in J. Keane (ed.), *Civil Society and the State*. New York: Verso.

Lacan, J. (1975) *Encore: séminaire XX, 1972–3*. Paris: Seuil.

Ladurie, E. (1980 [1978]) *Montaillou. Cathars and Catholics in a French Village*. Harmondsworth: Penguin.

Lakoff, G. (1991) 'Metaphor and war: the metaphor system used to justify war in the Gulf', *Journal of Urban and Cultural Studies*, 2 (1): 59–72.

Landsberg, A. (1995) 'Prosthetic memory: *Total Recall* and *Blade Runner*', *Body and Society*, 1 (3–4): 175–189.

Laqueur, T. (1987) 'Orgasm, generation and the politics of reproductive biology', in C. Gallagher and T. Laqueur (eds), *The Making of the Modern Body. Sexuality and Society in the Nineteenth Century*. Berkeley: University of California Press.

Laqueur, T. (1992 [1990]) *Making Sex. Body and Gender from the Greeks to Freud*. Cambridge, MA: Harvard University Press.

Lasch, C (1991 [1979]) *The Culture of Narcissism: American Life in an Age of Diminishing Expectations*. New York: W.W. Norton.

Lash, S. and Friedman, J. (1992) 'Introduction: subjectivity and modernity's Other', in S. Lash and J. Friedman (eds), *Modernity and Identity*. Oxford: Blackwell.

Lash, S. and Urry, J. (1994) *Economies of Signs and Space*. London: Sage.

Latimer, H. (1974 [1549]) 'Sermon of the plowers', in M.H. Abrams (ed.), *The Norton Anthology of English Literature*, 3rd edn. New York: W.W. Norton.

Lawless, E.J. (1991) 'Rescripting their lives and narratives: spiritual life stories of pentecostal women preachers', *Journal of Feminist Studies in Religion*, 7 (1): 53–71.

Lawson, A. (1988) *Adultery. An Analysis of Love and Betrayal*. New York: Basic Books.

Le Bon, G. (1879) 'Recherches anatomiques et mathématiques sur les lois des variations du volume du cerveau et sur leurs relations avec l'intelligence', *Revue d'Anthropologies*, 2nd series, 2: 27–104, cited in S.J. Gould (1981) *The Mismeasure of Man*. Harmondsworth: Penguin.

Lechte, J. (1990) *Julia Kristeva*. London: Routledge.

Lefèbvre, H. (1956) *Blaise Pascal: l'homme et l'oeuvre*. Paris: Cahiers de Royaumont.

Lefèbvre, H. (1984) *Everyday Life in the Modern World*. New Brunswick, NJ: Transaction Books.

Le Gros Clark, W.E. (1970) *History of the Primates*. London: British Museum (Natural History).

Le Gros Clark, W.E. (1978) *Fossil Evidence for Human Evolution*, 3rd edn, ed. B. Campbell. Chicago: University of Chicago Press.

Lehmann, H. and Roth, G. (1990) *Weber's Protestant Ethic: Origins, Evidence, Contexts*. Oxford: Blackwell.

Lerner, G. (1993) *The Creation of Feminist Consciousness*. Oxford: Oxford University Press.

Levin, H. (1969) *The Myth of the Golden Age in the Renaissance*. Bloomington: Indiana University Press.

Levine, D. (ed.) (1971) *Georg Simmel. On Individuality and Social Forms*. Chicago: University of Chicago Press.

Levine, D. (1985) *The Flight from Ambiguity: Essays in Social and Cultural Theory*. Chicago: University of Chicago Press.

Levine, D. (1995) *Visions of the Sociological Tradition*. Chicago: University of Chicago Press.

Lévi-Strauss, C. (1981) *The Naked Man: Introduction to a Science of Mythology*, Vol. 4. New York: Harper and Row.

Lichtblau, K. (1995) 'Sociology and the diagnosis of the times, or: the reflexivity of modernity', *Theory, Culture and Society*, 12: 25–52.

Lindholm, C. (1990) *Charisma*. Oxford: Blackwell.

Ling, T. (1981) *Karl Marx and Religion*. London: Macmillan.

Lingis, A. (1988) 'Orchids and muscles', in D.F. Knell and D. Wood (eds), *Exceedingly Nietzsche*. London: Routledge.

Littel, F.H. (1958) *The Anabaptist View of the Church*. Boston.

Littler, C.R. (1985) 'Taylorism, Fordism and job design', in D. Knights, H. Willmott and D. Collinson (eds), *Job Redesign: Critical Perspectives on the Labour Process*. Aldershot: Gower.

Livingstone, F. B. (1969) 'Genetics, ecology and the origins of incest and exogamy', *Current Anthropology*, 10 (1).

Lohse, B. (1987) *Martin Luther. An Introduction to His Life and Work*. Edinburgh: Clark.

Lopes, D. (1993) 'A musica das imagens', *Sociedade e Estado*, 18 (1–2): 162–164.

Luckmann, T. (1967) *The Invisible Religion*. New York: Macmillan.

Lukes, S. (1973) *Emile Durkheim. His Life and Work: A Historical and Critical Study*. London: Allen Lane.

Luther, M. (1955 [1520]) 'The babylonian captivity of the Church', in J. Pelikan and H. Lehamnn (eds), *Luther's Works: Volume 36*. Philadelphia and St. Louis.

Lyman, S. (1990) 'Race, sex and servitude: images of blacks in American cinema', *International Journal of Politics, Culture and Society*, 4 (1): 49–77.

Lyotard, J-F. (1984) *The Postmodern Condition*. Manchester: Manchester University Press.

Lyotard, J-F. (1991) *The Inhuman. Reflections on Time*. Stanford, CA: Stanford University Press.

McGrath, A. (1993) *Reformation Thought*. Oxford: Blackwell.

McGuire, M. (1985) 'Religion and healing', in P. Hammond (ed.), *The Sacred in a Secular Age*. Berkeley: University of California Press.

MacIntyre, A. (1967) *Secularization and Moral Change*. London: Oxford University Press.

MacIntyre, A. (1981) *After Virtue*. Notre Dame, IN: University of Notre Dame Press.

MacKenny, R. (1993) *Sixteenth Century Europe: Expansion and Conflict*. London: Macmillan.

McLachlan, H. and Swales, J.K. (1980) 'Witchcraft and anti-feminism', *Scottish Journal of Sociology*, 4: 141–166.

McLuhan, M. (1962) *The Gutenberg Galaxy*. Toronto: University of Toronto Press.

McLuhan, M. (1964) *Understanding Media*. London: Routledge and Kegan Paul.

McManners, J. (1981) *Death and the Enlightenment. Changing Attitudes to Death among Christians and Unbelievers in Eighteenth-Century France*. Oxford: Clarendon Press.

Maffesoli, M. (1991) 'The ethic of aesthetics', *Theory, Culture and Society*, 8 (1): 7–20.

Maffesoli, M. (1993a) 'The social ambiance', *Current Sociology*, 41 (2): 7–16.

Maffesoli, M. (1993b) 'The imaginary and the sacred in Durkheim's sociology', *Current Sociology*, 41 (2): 59–68.

Maffesoli, M. (1996) *The Time of the Tribes. The Decline of Individualism in Mass Society*. London: Sage.

Manchester, W. (1992) *A World Lit Only by Fire. The Medieval Mind and the Renaissance. Portrait of an Age*. Boston: Little, Brown.

Mann, M. (1986) *The Sources of Social Power. Vol.1. A History of Power from the Beginning to AD 1760*. Cambridge: Cambridge University Press.

Mann, M. (1994) 'In praise of macro-sociology: a reply to Goldthorpe', *British Journal of Sociology*, 45 (1): 37–54.

Mannheim, K. (1991 [1936]) *Ideology and Utopia*. London: Routledge.

Mansfield, P. and Collard, J. (1988) *The Beginning of the Rest of Your Life*. London: Macmillan.

Maravall, J.A. (1986) *Culture of Baroque. Analysis of a Historical Structure*. London: Macmillan.

Marcuse, H. (1962) *Eros and Civilization: A Philosophical Inquiry into Freud*. New York: Random House.

Marcuse, H. (1972 [1964]) *One Dimensional Man*. London: Abacus.

Marin, L. (1993) 'Frontiers of utopia: past and present', *Critical Inquiry*, 19: 397–420.

Martin, D. (1966) 'Some utopian aspects of the concept of secularisation', *International Yearbook for the Sociology of Religion*, 2: 86–96.

Martin, D. (1980) *The Breaking of the Image: A Sociology of Christian Theory and Practice*. Oxford: Blackwell.

Martin, D. and Fine, G.A. (1991) 'Satanic cults, satanic play. Is "Dungeons and Dragons" a breeding ground for the devil?', in J.T. Richardson, J. Best and D.G. Bromley (eds), *The Satanism Scare*. New York: Aldine De Gruyter.

Martin, E. (1989 [1987]) *The Woman in the Body*. Milton Keynes: Open University Press.

Martin, J.R. (1977) *Baroque*. London: Allen Lane.

Marwick, A. (1988) *Beauty in History*. London: Thames and Hudson.

Marx, K. (1954 [1867]) *Capital Vol. 1*. London: Lawrence and Wishart.

Marx, K. (1977 [1844]) 'The holy family', in D. McLellan (ed.), *Karl Marx, Selected Writings*. Oxford: Blackwell.

Marx, K. and Engels, F. (1970 [1846]) *The German Ideology*. London: Lawrence and Wishart.

Mauss, M. (1973 [1934]) 'Techniques of the body', *Economy and Society*, 2: 70–88.

Mellor, P.A. (1991) 'Self and suffering: deconstruction and reflexive definition in Buddhism and Christianity', *Religious Studies*, 27: 49–63.

Mellor, P.A. (1993a) 'Reflexive traditions: Anthony Giddens, high modernity and the contours of contemporary religiosity', *Religious Studies*, 29: 111–127.

Mellor, P.A. (1993b) 'Death in high modernity: the contemporary presence and absence of death', in D. Clark (ed.), *Sociology of Death* (Sociological Review Monograph Series). Oxford: Blackwell.

Mellor, P.A. and Shilling, C. (1993) 'Modernity, self-identity and the sequestration of death', *Sociology*, 27 (3): 411–431.

Mellor, P.A. and Shilling, C. (1994) 'Reflexive modernity and the religious body', *Religion*, 24: 23–42.

Mennell, S. (1985) *All Manners of Food. Eating and Taste in England and France from the Middle Ages to the Present*. Oxford: Blackwell.

Mennell, S. (1987) 'On the civilising of appetite', *Theory, Culture and Society*, 4: 373–403.

Mennell, S. (1989) *Norbert Elias*. Oxford: Blackwell.

Mennell, S. (1990) 'Decivilising processes: theoretical significance and some lines of research', *International Sociology*, 5 (2): 205–223.

Mennell, S. (1994) 'The formation of we-images: a process theory', in C. Calhoun (ed.), *Social Theory and the Politics of Identity*. Oxford: Blackwell.

Mennell, S., Murcott, A. and Otterloo, A.H. van (1992) *The Sociology of Food and Eating: A Trend Report and Bibliography*. Working Paper 1/92, Department of Anthropology and Sociology, Monash University.

Merleau-Ponty, M. (1962) *The Phenomenology of Perception*. London: Routledge and Kegan Paul.

Merton, R.K. (1970) *Science, Technology and Society in Seventeenth Century England*. New York: Howard Fertig.

Meštrović, S.G. (1991) *The Coming Fin de Siècle: An Application of Durkheim's Sociology to Modernity and Postmodernity*. London: Routledge.

Meštrović, S.G. (1993) *The Barbarian Temperament. Toward a Postmodern Critical Theory.* London: Routledge.

Meštrović, S.G. (1994) *The Balkanization of the West. The Confluence of Postmodernity and Postcommunism.* London: Routledge.

Metz, C. (1982) *The Imaginary Signifier: Psychoanalysis and the Cinema.* Bloomington: Indiana University Press.

Meyrowitz, J. (1985) *No Sense of Place. The Impact of Electronic Media on Social Behaviour.* Oxford: Oxford University Press.

Michalski, S. (1993) *The Reformation and the Visual Arts: The Protestant Image Question in Western and Eastern Europe.* London: Routledge.

Midgley, M. (1979) *Beast and Man: The Roots of Human Nature.* London: Methuen.

Miles, M. (1992) *Carnal Knowing.* Tunbridge Wells, Kent: Burns and Oates.

Miller, J. (1994) *The Passion of Michel Foucault.* London: Flamingo.

Miller, S. (1983) *Special Interest Groups in American Politics.* New Brunswick, NJ: Transaction Books.

Moore, R.I. (1987) *The Formation of a Persecuting Society: Power and Deviance in Western Europe.* Cambridge: Cambridge University Press.

Morgan, D. (1991) 'Ideologies of marriage and family life', in D. Clark (ed.), *Marriage, Domestic Life and Social Change.* London: Routledge.

Morgan, D. and Scott, S. (1993) 'Afterward: constructing a research agenda', in S. Scott and D. Morgan (eds), *Body Matters. Essays on the Sociology of the Body.* London: Falmer Press.

Morgenthau, H. (1970) 'Reflections on the end of the republic', *New York Review of Books,* 15: 38–41.

Morris, C. (1972) *The Discovery of the Individual 1050–1200.* New York: Harper and Row.

Morris, C. (1980) 'Individualism in twelfth century religion. Some further reflections', *Journal of Ecclesiastical History,* 31 (2): 195–206.

Moser, W., Faria, R. and Coracini, M.J. (1993) 'Versoes do barroco: moderno e pos-moderno', *Sociedade e Estado,* 8 (1–2): 39–56.

Mouzelis, N. (1994) 'In defence of "grand" historical sociology', *British Journal of Sociology,* 45 (1): 31–36.

Mullett, M. (1984) *The Counter-Reformation and the Catholic Reformation in Early Modern Europe.* London: Methuen.

Myers, J. (1992) 'Nonmainstreaming body modification: genital piercing, branding, burning and cutting', *Journal of Contemporary Ethnography,* 21 (3): 267–306.

Nead, L. (1992) *The Female Nude. Art, Obscenity and Sexuality.* London: Routledge.

Nelson, J.T. (1992) *The Intimate Connection: Male Sexuality, Masculine Spirituality.* London: SPCK.

Nicod, M. (1980) 'Gastronomically speaking: food studied as a medium of communication', in M. Turner (ed.), *Nutrition and Lifestyles.* London: Applied Science Publishers.

Nietzsche, F. (1993 [1871]) *The Birth of Tragedy and the Genealogy of Morals.* Harmondsworth: Penguin.

Nilsson, M.P. (1949) *A History of Greek Religion.* Oxford: Oxford University Press.

Nisbet, R.A. (1993 [1966]) *The Sociological Tradition.* New Brunswick, NJ: Transaction Books.

Novack, M. (1991) 'Liquid architectures in cyberspace', in M. Benedikt (ed.), *Cyberspace: First Steps.* London: MIT Press.

O'Connor, P. (1992) *Friendships Between Women. A Critical Review.* New York: Harvester Wheatsheaf.

O'Connor, P. (1995) 'Understanding variation in marital sexual pleasure: an impossible task?', *Sociological Review,* 43 (2): 342–362.

O'Neill, J. (1985) *Five Bodies: the Human Shape of Modern Society.* Ithaca, NY: Cornell University Press.

O'Neill, J. (1989) *The Communicative Body.* Evanston: Northwestern University Press.

O'Neill, J. (1995) *The Poverty of Postmodernism.* London: Routledge.

Ong, W. (1971) *Rhetoric, Romance and Technology: Studies in the Interaction of Expression and Culture*. Ithaca, NY: Cornell University Press.

Ong, W. (1977) *Interfaces of the World: Studies in the Evolution of Consciousness and Culture*. Ithaca, NY: Cornell University Press.

Ong, W. (1982) *Orality and Literacy: the Technologizing of the World*. London: Methuen.

Orbach, S. (1986) *Hunger Strike: The Anorectic's Struggle as a Metaphor for Our Age*. London: Faber and Faber.

Osbourne, H. (1970) 'Baroque', in *The Oxford Companion to Art*. Oxford: Clarendon Press.

Ozment, S. (1993) *Protestants*. London: Fontana.

Packard, V. (1981 [1957]) *The Hidden Persuaders*. Harmondsworth: Penguin.

Pahl, R. (1995) *After Success. Fin de Siècle Anxiety and Identity*. Cambridge: Polity Press.

Pantel, P.S. (ed.) (1992) *A History of Women. From Ancient Goddesses to Christian Saints*. Cambridge, MA: Harvard University Press.

Parsons, T. (1960) *Structure and Process in Modern Societies*. Glencoe, IL: Free Press.

Parsons, T. (1967) 'Christianity and modern industrial society', in E. Tiryakian (ed.), *Sociological Theory, Values and Sociocultural Change*. New York: Harper.

Parsons, T. (1968 [1937]) *The Structure of Social Action*. New York: Free Press.

Parsons, T. (1969) *Politics and Social Structure*. New York: Free Press.

Pascal, B. (1962 [1670]) *Pascal's Pensées*. London: Harvill Press.

Pateman, C. (1988) *The Sexual Contract*. Cambridge: Polity Press.

Peacock, J.L. and Tyson Jr, R.W. (1989) *Pilgrims of Paradox: Calvinism and Experience among the Primitive Baptists of Blue Ridge*. Washington, DC: Smithsonian Press.

Pearson, G. (1987) *The New Heroin Users*. Oxford: Blackwell.

Pepitone-Rockwell, F. (ed.) (1980) *Dual Career Couples*. Beverley Hills: Sage.

Peters, E. (1980) *Heresy and Authority in Medieval Europe*. Cambridge: Cambridge University Press.

Peterson, R.A. (1994) 'Culture studies through the production perspective: progress and prospects', in D. Crane (ed.), *The Sociology of Culture*. Oxford: Blackwell.

Pfohl, S. (1993) 'Venus in microsoft: male mas(s)ochism and cybernetics', in A. Kroker and M. Kroker (eds), *The Last Sex: Feminism and Outlaw Bodies*. Basingstoke: Macmillan.

Pickering, W.S.F. (1984) *Durkheim's Sociology of Religion*. London: Routledge and Kegan Paul.

Poggi, G. (1978) *The Development of the Modern State*. London: Hutchinson.

Popkin, R. (1974) 'The philosophical basis of modern racism', in C. Walton and J. Anton (eds), *Philosophy and the Civilising Arts*. Athens, OH: Ohio University Press.

Porter, R. (1991) 'History of the body', in P. Burke (ed.), *New Perspectives on Historical Writing*. Cambridge: Polity Press.

Poster, M. (1995) 'Postmodern virtualities', *Body and Society*, 1 (3–4): 79–95.

Power, E. (1975) *Medieval Women*. Cambridge: Cambridge University Press.

Prestwich, M. (1985) *International Calvinism, 1541–1715*. Oxford: Clarendon Press.

Price, M. and Wedam, E. (1995) 'Class and social Christianity: community, faith and philanthropy in restructuring Chicago'. Paper presented at the Chicago Area Group for the Study of Religious Communities, University of Illinois at Chicago, April.

Rainwater, J. (1989) *Self-Therapy*. London: Crucible.

Rappaport, R. (1979) *Ecology, Meaning and Religion*. Richmond, CA: North Atlantic Books.

Rauch, J. (1993) *Kindly Inquisitors. The New Attacks on Free Thought*. Chicago: University of Chicago Press.

Rednour, S. (1993) 'Losing it', in A. Kroker and M. Kroker (eds), *The Last Sex. Feminism and Outlaw Bodies*. Basingstoke: Macmillan.

Reisman, D. (1950) *The Lonely Crowd: A Study of the Changing American Character*. New Haven, CT: Yale University Press.

Remenick, R. (1982) 'The sport of warriors on the wane: a case of cultural endurance in the face of social change', in W. Morgan (ed.), *Sport and the Humanities*. Knoxville, TN: University of Tennessee Press.

Rheingold, H. (1991) *Virtual Reality*. London: Mandarin.

Rheingold, H. (1994) *The Virtual Community: Finding Connection in a Computerized World*. London: Secker and Warburg.

Richardson, J.T., Best, J. and Bromley, D.G. (eds) (1991) *The Satanism Scare*. New York; Aldine De Gruyter.

Richardson, R. (1988) *Death, Dissection and the Destitute*. Harmondsworth: Penguin.

Richman, M. (1995) 'The sacred group. A Durkheimian perspective on the Collège de sociologie (1937–39)', in C. Bailey Gill (ed.), *Bataille. Writing the Sacred*. London: Routledge.

Ritzer, G. (1992) *The McDonaldization of Society*. London: Sage.

Robertson, R. (1992) *Globalisation*. London: Sage.

Robins, K. (1995) 'Cyberspace and the world we live in', *Body and Society*, 1 (3–4): 135–155.

Robinson, P.A. (1969) *The Sexual Radicals. Wilhelm Reich, Geza Roheim, Herbert Marcuse*. London: Temple Smith.

Rochberg-Halton, E. (1986) *Meaning and Modernity: Social Theory in the Pragmatic Attitude*. Chicago: University of Chicago Press.

Rodaway, P. (1994) *Sensuous Geographies: Body, Sense and Place*. London: Routledge.

Rodinson, M. (1988) *Europe and the Mystique of Islam*. London: I.B. Tauris.

Rogers, R.E. (1969) *Max Weber's Ideal Type Theory*. New York: Philosophical Library.

Rojek, C. (1995) *Decentring Leisure: Rethinking Leisure Theory*. London: Sage.

Rojek, C. and Turner, B.S. (1993) *Forget Baudrillard*. London: Routledge.

Roper, L. (1994) *Oedipus and the Devil. Witchcraft, Sexuality and Religion in Early Modern Europe*. London: Routledge.

Rorty, R. (1980) *Philosophy and the Mirror of Nature*. Oxford: Blackwell.

Rose, N. (1989) *Governing the Soul. The Shaping of the Private Self*. London: Routledge.

Rose, S. (1976) 'Scientific racism and ideology: the IQ racket from Galton to Jensen', in H. Rose and S. Rose (eds), *The Political Economy of Science*. London: Macmillan.

Rosen, G. (1992) 'Psychopathology in the social process', in B.P. Levack (ed.), *Articles on Witchcraft, Magic and Demonology*. New York: Garland.

Rosenberg, B.A. (1988) *Can These Bones Live? The Art of the American Folk Preacher*. Urbana: University of Illinois Press.

Rosenberg, C.E. (ed.) (1979) *Healing and History. Essays for George Rosen*. New York: Neal Watson Academic Publications.

Rovelstad, M. (1993) 'The Baroque library: 17th century vision', *Libri*, 43 (4): 289–308.

Rowntree, S. (1902) *Poverty: A Study of Town Life*. London: Macmillan.

Rucker, R, Sirius, R.U. and Queen, M. (eds) (1993) *Mondo 2000: A User's Guide to the New Edge*. London: Thames and Hudson.

Rudoksky, B. (1971) *The Unfashionable Human Body*. New York: Prentice-Hall.

Rueschemeyer, D. (1986) *Power and the Division of Labour*. Cambridge: Polity Press.

Rupp, G. (1969) *Patterns of Reformation*. London: Oxford University Press.

Russo, M. (1994) *The Female Grotesque: Risk, Excess and Modernity*. New York: Routledge.

Ruthven, M. (1989) *The Divine Supermarket*. London: Chatto and Windus.

Sachs, H. (1524) *The Argument of the Romanists against the Profiteering and Other Public Offenses of the Christian Community*. Nuremberg.

Said, E.W. (1978) *Orientalism. Western Conceptions of the Orient*. Harmondsworth: Penguin.

Sanders, C. (1989) *Customising the Body: The Art and Culture of Tattooing*. Philadelphia: Temple University Press.

Sartre, J-P. (1956) *Being and Nothingness: An Essay on Phenomenological Ontology*, trans. H. Barnes. New York: Philosophical Library.

Sassen, S. (1991) *The Global City. New York, London, Tokyo*. Princeton, NJ: Princeton University Press.

Sawday, J. (1995) *The Body Emblazoned*. Oxford: Blackwell.

Scarry, E. (1985) *The Body in Pain*. Oxford: Oxford University Press.

Scarry, E. (1994) *Resisting Representation*. Oxford: Oxford University Press.

Scheff, T.J. (1994) *Bloody Revenge. Emotions, Nationalism and War*. Boulder, CO: Westview Press.

Schiebinger, L. (1987) 'Skeletons in the closet: the first illustrations of the female skeleton in eighteenth century anatomy', in C. Gallagher and T. Laqueur (eds), *The Making of the Modern Body. Sexuality and Society in the Nineteenth Century*. Berkeley: University of California Press.

Schneemann, C. (1975) 'Cezanne she was a great painter', cited in L. Nead (1992) *The Female Nude. Art, Obscentiy and Sexuality*. London: Routledge.

Schulenburg, J. (1986) 'The heroics of virginity: brides of Christ and sacrificial mutilation', in M.B. Rose (ed.), *Women in the Middle Ages and the Renaissance: Literary and Historical Perspectives*. Syracuse, NY: Syracuse University Press.

Scribner, R.W. (1994) *For the Sake of Simple Folk: Popular Propaganda for the German Reformation*. Cambridge: Cambridge University Press.

Scribner, B., Porter, R. and Teich, M. (eds) (1994) *The Reformation in National Context*. Cambridge: Cambridge University Press.

Seidler, V.J. (1994) *Recovering the Self: Morality and Social Theory*. London: Routledge.

Sennett, R. (1992 [1974]) *The Fall of Public Man*. New York: W.W. Norton.

Sennett, R. (1994) *Flesh and Stone. The Body and the City in Western Civilisation*. London: Faber and Faber.

Shaffer, E.S. (1975) *Kubla Khan and the Fall of Jerusalem. The Mythological School in Biblical Criticism and Secular Literature 1770–1880*. Cambridge: Cambridge University Press.

Shields, R. (1996) 'Foreword: masses or tribes', in M. Maffesoli, *The Time of the Tribes. The Decline of Individualism in Mass Society*. London: Sage.

Shilling, C. (1991) 'Educating the body: physical capital and the production of social inequalities', *Sociology*, 25: 653–672.

Shilling, C. (1993a) *The Body and Social Theory*. London: Sage.

Shilling, C. (1993b) 'The body, class and social inequalities', in J. Evans (ed.), *Equality, Education and Physical Education*. London: Falmer Press.

Shilling, C. and Mellor, P.A. (1994) 'Embodiment, auto/biography and carnal knowing: the Protestant Reformation and modern self-identities', in 'Lives and Works' (special double issue of *Auto/Biography*) 3 (1) and 3 (2): 115–128.

Shilling, C. and Mellor, P.A. (1996) 'Embodiment, structuration theory and modernity: mind/body dualism and the repression of sensuality', *Body and Society*, 2 (4): 1–15.

Sibley, D. (1995) *Geographies of Exclusion. Society and Difference in the West*. London: Routledge.

Sica, A. (1988) *Weber, Irrationality and the Modern Social Order*. Berkeley: University of California Press.

Silk, M.S. and Stern, J.P. (1981) *Nietzsche on Tragedy*. Cambridge: Cambridge University Press.

Silverstone, R. (1994) *Television and Everyday Life*. London: Routledge.

Simmel, G. (1921 [1908]) 'Sociology of the senses: visual interaction', in R.E. Park and E. Burgess (eds), *Introduction to the Science of Sociology*. Chicago: University of Chicago Press.

Simmel, G. (1950) *The Sociology of Georg Simmel*, trans., ed. and with an introduction by Kurt Wolff. New York: Free Press.

Simmel, G. (1955) *Conflict and the Web of Group Applications*, trans. Kurt H. Wolff and Reinhard Bendix. Glencoe, IL: Free Press.

Simmel, G. (1968) *The Conflict in Modern Culture and Other Essays*, trans. Peter Etzkorn. New York: Teachers College Press.

Simmel, G. (1971 [1903]) 'The metropolis and mental life', in D. Levine (ed.), *Georg Simmel. On Individuality and Social Forms*. Chicago: University of Chicago Press.

Simmel, G. (1971 [1908a]) 'The stranger', in D. Levine (ed.), *Georg Simmel. On Individuality and Social Forms*. Chicago: University of Chicago Press.

Simmel, G. (1971 [1908b]) 'The poor', in D. Levine (ed.), *Georg Simmel. On Individuality and Social Forms*. Chicago: University of Chicago Press.

Simmel, G. (1971 [1908c]) 'Subjective culture', in D. Levine (ed.), *Georg Simmel. On Individuality and Social Forms*. Chicago: University of Chicago Press.

Simmel, G. (1971 [1910]) 'Sociability', in D. Levine (ed.), *Georg Simmel. On Individuality and Social Forms*. Chicago: University of Chicago Press.

Simmel, G. (1971 [1911]) 'The adventurer', in D. Levine (ed.), *Georg Simmel. On Individuality and Social Forms*. Chicago: University of Chicago Press.

Simmel, G. (1971 [1918]) 'The transcendent character of life', in D. Levine (ed.), *Georg Simmel. On Individuality and Social Forms*. Chicago: University of Chicago Press.

Simmel, G. (1990 [1978]) *The Philosophy of Money*, 2nd edn, ed. David Frisby. London: Routledge.

Sinkler, G. (1972) *The Racial Attitudes of American Presidents from Abraham Lincoln to Theodore Roosevelt*. New York: Doubleday Anchor.

Skinner, Q. (1978) *The Foundations of Modern Political Thought*. Cambridge: Cambridge University Press.

Slater, D. (1995) 'Photography and modern vision: the spectacle of "natural magic"', in Chris Jenks (ed.), *Visual Culture*. London: Routledge.

Small, S. (1994) *Racialised Barriers. The Black Experience in the United States and England in the 1980s*. London: Routledge.

Smelser, N. (1992) 'Culture: coherent or incoherent', in R. Munch and N.J. Smelser (eds), *Theory of Culture*. Berkeley: University of California Press.

Smith, A. (1950 [1776]) *An Inquiry into the Nature and Causes of the Wealth of Nations*. London: Methuen.

Smith, A. (1976 [1792]) *The Theory of Moral Sentiments*, eds D. Raphael and A. Macfie. Oxford: Clarendon Press.

Smith, D. (1991) *The Rise of Historical Sociology*. Cambridge: Polity Press.

Smith, J.Z. (1986) *Imagining Religion: from Babylon to Jonestown*. Chicago: University of Chicago Press.

Snell, B. (1948) *The Discovery of the Mind*. Oxford: Blackwell.

Sobchack, V. (1995) 'Beating the meat/surviving the text, or how to get out of this century alive', *Body and Society*, 1 (3–4): 205–214.

Sombart, W. (1967 [1913]) *Luxury and Capitalism*. Ann Arbor: University of Michigan Press.

Southern, R.W. (1962) *Western Views of Islam in the Middle Ages*. Cambridge, MA: Harvard University Press.

Southern, R.W. (1993 [1953]) *The Making of the Middle Ages*. London: Pimlico.

Sparks, R. (1992) *Television and the Drama of Crime*. Buckingham: Open University Press.

Spigel, L. (1992) *Make Room for TV: Television and the Family Ideal in Postwar America*. Chicago: University of Chicago Press.

Stark, R. and Finke, R. (1988) 'American religion in 1776: a statistical portrait', *Sociological Analysis*, 49: 39–51.

Starobinski, J. (1970) *Portrait de l'artiste en Saltimbanque*. Paris: Champs-Flammarion.

Stauffer, D.A. (1930) *English Biography before 1700*. Cambridge, MA: Harvard University Press.

Stehr, N. (1994) *Knowledge Societies*. London: Sage.

Stivers, R. (1994) *The Culture of Cynicism: American Morality in Decline*. Oxford: Blackwell.

Stivers, R. (1996) 'Toward a sociology of morality', *International Journal of Sociology and Social Policy*, 16 (1–2): 1–14.

Stone, A.R. (1991) 'Will the real body please stand up? Boundary stories about virtual cultures', in M. Benedikt (ed.), *Cyberspace: First Steps*. London: MIT Press.

Stone, L. (1977) *The Family, Sex and Marriage in England 1500–1914*. London: Weidenfeld and Nicolson.

Stone, L (1987) *The Past and the Present Revisited*. London: Routledge and Kegan Paul.

Stubbes, P. (1972) *The Anatomy of Abuses*. New York: Johnson Reprint Company.

Synnott, A. (1991) 'Puzzling over the senses: from Plato to Marx', in D. Howes (ed.), *The Varieties of Sensory Experience: A Sourcebook in the Anthropology of the Senses*. Toronto: University of Toronto Press.

Synnott, A. (1993) *The Body Social*. London: Routledge.

Tacussel, P. (1984) *L'attraction sociale*. Paris: Klincksieck.

Tannen, D. (1990) *You Just Don't Understand. Women and Men in Conversation.* New York: Ballantine Books.

Tawney, R. H. (1938 [1926]) *Religion and the Rise of Capitalism.* Harmondsworth: Penguin.

Taylor, C. (1978) *Hegel.* Cambridge: Cambridge University Press.

Taylor, C. (1985) *Philosophy and the Human Sciences.* Cambridge: Cambridge University Press.

Taylor, C. (1989) *Sources of the Self: The Making of Modern Identity.* Cambridge: Cambridge University Press.

Taylor, F. W. (1964) *Scientific Management.* New York: Harper.

Tester, K. (1992) *Civil Society.* London: Routledge.

Tester, K. (1995a) *The Inhuman Condition.* London: Routledge.

Tester, K. (1995b) 'Moral solidarity and the technological reproduction of images', *Media, Culture and Society*, 17: 469–482.

Tester, K. (1997) *Moral Culture.* London: Sage.

Theweleit, K. (1987 [1977]) *Male Fantasies. Vol. 1: Women, Floods, Bodies, History.* Cambridge: Polity Press.

Theweleit, K. (1989 [1978]) *Male Fantasies. Vol. 2: Male Bodies. Psychoanalysing the White Terror.* Minneapolis: University of Minnesota Press.

Thomas, K. (1973 [1971]) *Religion and the Decline of Magic.* Harmondsworth: Penguin.

Thompson, E.P. (1963) *The Making of the English Working Class.* Harmondsworth: Penguin.

Thompson, K. (1990) 'Religion: the British contribution', *British Journal of Sociology*, 41 (4): 531–535.

Tidrick, K. (1989 [1981]) *Heart Beguiling Araby. The English Romance with Arabia.* London: I.B. Tauris.

Tilly, C. (1975) 'Reflections on the history of European state-making', in C. Tilly (ed.), *The Formation of National States in Western Europe.* Princeton, NJ: Princeton University Press.

Tiryakian, E. (1974) *On the Margins of the Visible.* New York: Wiley.

Tiryakian, E. (1988) 'Durkheim, Mathiez and the French Revolution: the political context of a sociological classic', *Journal of Sociology*, 29: 373–396.

Tomas, D. (1991) 'Old rituals for new space', in M. Benedikt (ed.), *Cyberspace: First Steps.* London: MIT Press.

Tomas, D. (1995) 'Feedback and cybernetics: reimaging the body in the age of the cyborg', *Body and Society*, 1 (3–4): 21–43.

Tönnies, F. (1957 [1887]) *Community and Association.* Michigan: Michigan State University Press.

Touraine, A. (1995) *Critique of Modernity.* Oxford: Blackwell.

Trevor-Roper, H. (1969) *The European Witch-Craze.* Harmondsworth: Penguin.

Tschannen, O. (1991) 'The secularisation paradigm: a systematization', *Journal for the Scientific Study of Religion*, 30: 395–415.

Tseelon, E. (1995) *The Masque of Femininity. The Presentation of Woman in Everyday Life.* London: Sage.

Tudor, A. (1995) 'Unruly bodies, unquiet minds', *Body and Society*, 1 (1): 25–41.

Turner, B.S. (1982) 'The discourse of diet', *Theory, Culture and Society*, 1: 23–32.

Turner, B.S. (1984) *The Body and Society.* Oxford: Blackwell.

Turner, B.S. (1987) 'A note on nostalgia', *Theory, Culture and Society*, 4: 147–156.

Turner, B.S. (1991) *Religion and Social Theory*, 2nd edn. London: Sage.

Turner, B.S. (1992a) *Regulating Bodies: Essays in Medical Sociology.* London: Routledge.

Turner, B.S. (1992b) *Max Weber: From History to Modernity.* London: Routledge.

Turner, B.S. (1993) 'Outline of a theory of human rights', *Sociology*, 27 (3): 489–512.

Turner, B.S. (1994) 'Introduction', in C. Buci-Glucksmann, *Baroque Reason: The Aesthetics of Modernity.* London: Sage.

Turner, B.S. (1995) 'Introduction' in Christine Buci-Glucksman, *Baroque Reason.* London: Sage.

Turner, B.S. (1996) 'Introduction' in B.S. Turner (ed.), *The Blackwell Companion to Social Theory.* Oxford: Blackwell.

Ullman, W. (1975) *Medieval Political Thought*. Harmondsworth: Penguin.

Urry, J. (1990) 'The "consumption" of tourism', *Sociology*, 24: 23–35.

Vale, V. and Juno, A. (1989) *Re/Search No. 12. Modern Primitives*. San Francisco: Re/Search Publications.

Van Gennep, A. (1960) *The Rites of Passage*, trans. M. Vikedon and G. Coffee. Chicago: University of Chicago Press.

Van Reijen, W. (1992) 'Labyrinth and ruin: the return of the baroque in post-modernity', *Theory, Culture and Society*, 9 (4): 1–26.

Veblen, T. (1967 [1899]) *The Theory of the Leisure Class*. New York: Penguin Books.

Vierhaus, R. (1988) *Germany in the Age of Absolutism*. Cambridge: Cambridge University Press.

Virilio, P. (1994) *The Vision Machine*. Bloomington: Indiana University Press.

Von Balthasar, H.U. (1982) *The Glory of the Lord. A Theological Aesthetics. Vol. I. Seeing the Form*, trans. Erasmo Leiva-Merikakis. Edinburgh: T. & T. Clark.

Wacquant, L.J.D. (1995) 'Pugs at work: bodily capital and bodily labour among professional boxers', *Body and Society*, 1 (1): 65–93.

Walby, S. (1989) 'Theorizing patriarchy', *Sociology*, 23: 213–234.

Walker, D.P. (1981) *Unclean Spirits. Possession and Exorcism in France and England in the Late Sixteenth and Early Seventeenth Centuries*. London: Scholar Press.

Walter, T. (1991) 'Modern death: taboo or not taboo?', *Sociology*, 25: 293–310.

Walvin, J. (1982) 'Black caricature: the roots of racialism', in C. Husband (ed.), *'Race' in Britain*. London: Hutchinson.

Warner, M. (1978 [1976]) *Alone of All Her Sex: The Myth and Cult of the Virgin Mary*. New York: Knopf.

Warner, R.S. (1993) 'Work in progress toward a new paradigm for the sociological study of religion in the United States', *American Journal of Sociology*, 98 (5): 1044–1093.

Washburn, S.L. (1960) 'Tools and human evolution', *Scientific American*, September.

Washburn, S.L. (1978) 'Animal behaviour and social anthropology', in M. Gregory, A. Silvers and D. Sutch (eds), *Sociobiology and Human Nature*. San Francisco: Jossey Bass.

Watkins, S. and van de Walle, E. (1985) 'Nutrition, mortality, and population', in R. Rotberg and T. Rabb (eds), *Hunger and History*. Cambridge: Cambridge University Press.

Watt, I. (1957) *The Rise of the Novel. Studies in Defoe, Richardson and Fielding*. London: Chatto and Windus.

Weber, M. (1947) *The Theory of Social and Economic Organisation*, trans. A.M. Henderson and Talcott Parsons, ed. Talcott Parsons. Oxford: Oxford University Press.

Weber, M. (1948 [1919]) 'Science as a vocation', in H. Gerth and C.W. Mills (eds), *From Max Weber*. London: Routledge and Kegan Paul.

Weber, M. (1958) *The City*, trans. Don Martindale and Gertrude Neuwirth. Glencoe, IL: Free Press.

Weber, M. (1968 [1925]) *Economy and Society. Vol. 3*, ed. G. Roth and C. Wittich. New York: Bedminster.

Weber, M. (1991 [1904–5]) *The Protestant Ethic and the Spirit of Capitalism*. London: Counterpoint.

Webster, F. (1995) *Theories of the Information Society*. London: Routledge.

Weeks, J. (1991) 'Pretended family relationships', in D. Clark (ed.), *Marriage, Domestic Life and Social Change*. London: Routledge.

Weinstein, D. and Bell, R. (1982) *Saints and Society: The Two Worlds of Western Christendom, 1000–1700*. Chicago: University of Chicago Press.

Weisman, R. (1977) *Witchcraft in Seventeenth Century Massachusetts*. London University: Microfilms International.

Wendel, F. (1965) *Calvin: The Origins and Development of his Religious Thought*. London: Collins.

Wernick, A. (1991) *Promotional Culture: Advertising, Ideology and Symbolic Expression*. London: Sage.

West, C. (1993) *Keeping Faith. Philosophy and Race in America*. London: Routledge.

White, H. (1978) *Tropics of Discourse. Essays in Cultural Criticism*. Baltimore, MD: Johns Hopkins University Press.

Whittemore, R. (1988) *Pure Lives. The Early Biographers*. Baltimore, MD: Johns Hopkins University Press.

Wiley, J. (1995) 'No BODY is "doing it": cybersexuality as a postmodern narrative', *Body and Society*, 1 (1):145–162.

Williams, L. (1989) *Hardcore. Power, Pleasure and the 'Frenzy of the Visible'*. Berkeley: University of California Press.

Willis, P. (1977) *Learning to Labour*. Farnborough: Saxon House.

Wilson, B.R. (1976) *Contemporary Transformations in Religion*. London: Oxford University Press.

Wilson, B.R. (1982) *Religion in Sociological Perspective*. Oxford: Oxford University Press.

Wilson, E.O. (1978) *On Human Nature*. London: Tavistock.

Wilson, W.J. (1987) *The Truly Disadvantaged: The Inner City, the Underclass and Public Policy*. Chicago: University of Chicago Press.

Wilson, W.J. (1991a) 'Public policy research and "The Truly Disadvantaged"', in C. Jencks and P. Peterson (eds), *The Urban Underclass*. Washington, DC: Brookings Institution.

Wilson, W.J. (1991b) 'Studying inner-city social dislocation: the challenge of public agenda research', *American Sociological Research*, 56: 1–14.

Wilson, R.R. (1995) 'Cyber(body)parts: prosthetic consciousness', *Body and Society*, 1 (3–4): 239–259.

Winnick, M. and Winnick, C. (1979) *The Television Experience: What Children See*. Beverley Hills: Sage.

Winnicott, D.W. (1965) *The Maturational Processes and the Facilitating Environment*. London: Hogarth.

Winnicott, D.W. (1974) *Playing and Reality*. London: Hogarth.

Wittgenstein, L. (1953) *Philosophical Investigations*, ed. G.E.M. Anscombe and R. Rhees, trans. G.E.M. Anscombe. Oxford: Blackwell.

Wogan-Brown, J. (1994) 'Chaste bodies: frames and experiences', in S. Kay and M. Rubin (eds), *Framing Medieval Bodies*. Manchester: Manchester University Press.

Wolf, N. (1990) *The Beauty Myth*. London: Chatto and Windus.

Wouters, C. (1986) 'Formalisation and informalisation: changing tension balances in civilising process', *Theory, Culture and Society*, 3 (2): 1–18.

Wouters, C. (1987) 'Developments in the behavioural codes between the sexes: the formalisation of informalisation in the Netherlands 1930–85', *Theory, Culture and Society*, 4: 405–427.

Wright, A.D. (1982) *The Counter-Reformation: Catholic Europe and the Non-Christian World*. London: Weidenfeld and Nicolson.

Wuthnow, R. (1988) *The Restructuring of American Religion*. Princeton, NJ: Princeton University Press.

Wuthnow, R. (1989) *Communities of Discourse: Ideology and Social Structure in the Reformation*. Cambridge: Cambridge University Press.

Zaretsky, A. (1976) *Capitalism, the Family and Personal Life*. New York: Harper and Row.

Zijderveld, A. (1986) 'The challenges of modernity', in J.D. Hunter and S.C. Ainlay (eds), *Making Sense of Modern Times*. London: Routledge and Kegan Paul.

Zinn, M.B. and Eitsen, D.S. (1987) *Diversity in American Families*. New York: Harper and Row.

Zukin, S. (1988) *Loft Living*. London: Radius.

Zukin, S. (1990) 'Socio-spatial prototypes of a new organisation of consumption: the role of real cultural capital', *Sociology*, 24 (1): 37–56.

Zukin, S. (1992) 'Postmodern urban landscapes: mapping culture and power', in S. Lash and J. Friedman (eds), *Modernity and Identity*. Oxford: Blackwell.

INDEX

Note: names of people mentioned only once have been omitted